A JOURNEY DUE NORTH,

IN THE SUMMER OF 1856.

A
JOURNEY DUE NORTH;

BEING

NOTES OF A RESIDENCE IN RUSSIA.

BY

GEORGE AUGUSTUS SALA.

BOSTON:
TICKNOR AND FIELDS.
M DCCC LVIII.

RIVERSIDE, CAMBRIDGE:
PRINTED BY H. O. HOUGHTON AND COMPANY.

"Forasmuch as it is necessarie for alle those who minde to take in hande the travelle into farre and strange countreyes to endeavoure themselves, not only to understaunde the orders, commodities, and fruitfullnesse thereof, but also to apply them to the settynge forth of ye same, wherebye it may encourage others to ye like travaile; therefore have I thoughte goode to make a briefe rehearsalle of the order of this my travaile in Russia and Muscovia; because it was my chaunce to fall in with the northe-easte parts of Europe before I came to Muscovia, I will faithfullye exercise my knowledge therein."

> "*The Book of the great and mighty Emperor of Russia, and Duke of Muscovia, and of the dominions, orders, and commodities thereunto belonging: drawen by Richard Chancellour:* A.D. 1599."

"And whereas (he saith) I have before made mention how Muscovia was in our time discovered by Richard Chancellour, in his voyage toward Cathay, by the direction and information of M. Sebastian Cabota, who long before this had this secret in his minde, it is meete to telle that the same is largely and faithfully written in ye [illegible] by that learned yong manne Clement Adams scolemaster [illegible] as he received it at the mouth of the said Richa[illegible]

> "*The New Navigation* [illegible] *Muscovia by the Nort*[illegible] *d by Sir Hugh Wi*[illegible] *rd Chancello*[illegible]

CONTENTS.

A JOURNEY DUE NORTH.

I.

I BEGIN MY JOURNEY.

"I THANK Heaven," I said, when I came to Erquellines, on the Belgian frontier, "that I have done, for some time at least, with the deplorable everyday humdrum state of civilization in which I have been vegetating so long, and growing so rankly weedy. Not that I am about to forswear shaving, renounce pantaloons, or relinquish the use of a knife and fork at meal-times. I hope to wear clean linen for many successive days to come, and to keep myself *au courant* with the doings of London through the media of Galignani's Messenger and the Illustrated News, (thrice blessed be both those travellers' joys!) Nay, railways shall penetrate whither I am going, mixed pickles be sold wholesale and retail, and pale ale be attainable at a more or less exorbitant price. I am not bound for the Ethiopio-Christian empire of Prester John; I am not bound to sail for the island of Barataria; my passport is not made out for the kingdom of Utopia (would that it were); I cannot hope, in my journeyings, to see either the Yang-tse-Kiang, or the sources of the Nile, or the Mountains of the Moon. I am going, it is true, to t'other side of Jordan, which somewhat vague (and American) geographical definition may mean the other side of the Straits of Dover, or the Grecian Archipelago, or the Great Belt, or the Pacific Ocean. But, wherever I go, civilization will follow me. For I am of the streets, and streety—*eis ten polin* is my haven. Like the starling, I can't get out of cities; and now, that I have come sixteen hundred miles, it is but to another city—another tumour of streets and houses and jostling crowds; and from my windows I can see a post, and wires stretching from it, the extreme end of which I know to be in Lothbury, London.

I am not so wisely foolish to imagine or to declare that there is nothing new under the sun; only the particular ray of sunlight that illumines me in my state of life has fallen upon me so long, and dwells on me with such a persistent sameness, bright as it is, that I am dazed, and sun-sick; and, when I shut my eyes, have but one green star before me, which obstinately refuses to assume the kaleidoscopic changes I delight in. I must go away, I said. I must rub this rust of soul and body off. I must have a change of grass. I want strange dishes to disagree with me. I want to be scorched or frozen in another latitude. I want to learn another alphabet; to conjugate verbs in another fashion; to be happy or miserable from other circumstances than those that gladden or sorrow me now. If I could be hard up, for instance, on the Bridge of Sighs, or wistfully eyeing my last real at the Puerta del Sol; if I could be sued on a bill drawn in the Sanskrit character, or be threatened with arrest by a Mahometan hatti-sheriff's-officer; if I could incur perdition through not believing in the seven incarnations of Vishnu, instead of the thirty-nine Articles; if I could be importuned for copy by the editor of the Mofussilite, and not the Morning Meteor; if I could have the plague, or the vomito nero, or the plica polonica, instead of the English headache and blues, the change would be advantageous—salutary, I think. I am sure I should be much better off if I could change my own name, and forget my ownself for a time. But oh! civilization and Foreign Office passport system—George William Frederick Earl of Clarendon, Baron Hyde of Hindon, won't hear of that. I have made up my mind to change; I am determined, I said, to depart out of this kingdom; but the Earl and Baron insists on stamping, and numbering, and registering me (all for the small sum of seven and sixpence) before I go. George William Frederick pounces upon me as a British subject travelling abroad; asserts himself, his stars and garters, at great length, all over a sheet of blue foolscap paper, affectionately entreats all authorities, civil and military, to render me aid and assistance whenever I stand in need of them, (I should like to catch them doing any thing of the sort!) and sends me abroad with the royal arms, his own, and a five-shilling receipt stamp tacked to me, like a bird with a string tied to his leg.

I am bound on a stern, long, cruel, rigid journey, far, far away, to the extreme right-hand top corner of the map of Europe—but first Due North. And here I am at Erquellines on the frontier of the kingdom of Belgium; and this is why I thanked Heaven I was here. Not very far northward is Erquellines; and yet I felt as if I had passed the Rubicon, when a parti-coloured sentry-box, the counterfeit presentment of the peculiarly sheepish-looking Belgian lion sitting on his hind-legs, with the legend "Union is strength," (and, indeed, I think it would take a good many of these lions to make a strong one,) and a posse of custom-house officers—kindly, but pudding headed in appearance—told me that I was in the Royaume de Belgique.

I am, under ordinary travelling circumstances, exceedingly fond of the compact little kingdom of King Leopold. I look at it as a fat, sensible, easy-going, respectable, happy-go-lucky sort of country. Very many pleasant days and hours have its quaint, quiet cities, its roomy farm-houses, its picture galleries, and sleepy canal boats, its beer, and tobacco afforded me. I cannot join in the patriotic enthusiasm about '*les braves Belges,*' because I consider the Belgians—being a sensible people—to be the very reverse of valiant; neither can I sympathize much with the archæological public-spiritedness of those Belgian servants who are anxious to restore the Flemish language to its primeval richness and purity, and have published the romance of Reynard the Fox in the original Low Dutch. As I think it to be the most hideous dialect in Europe, I would rather they had let it be. And to say the truth, I am rather tired of hearing about the Duke of Alva, and of the Count of Egmont and Horn—though both worthy men in their way, doubtless—whose decollation and behaviour prior to and following that ceremony the Belgian painters have a mania for representing only second to our abhorred Finding-of-the-Body-of-Haroldophobia. And specially do I object to, and protest against, in Belgium, the Field of Waterloo and all appertaining thereto; the knavish livery-stable keepers in Brussels, who swindle you if you take a conveyance to the field; the beggars on the road; the magnified dustheap with the abashed poodle fumbling with a ball of worsted on the summit, and called the Mountain of the Lion; the disforested forest of Soignes; the indifferent outhouse called the farm of Hougomont, and the Voice from Waterloo, by the deceased Sergeant-Major Cotton. But I love Belgium, nevertheless—so did Julius Cæsar. Antwerp—though the multiplicity of Rubenses give me almost as much of a surfeit as a month's apprenticeship in a pastrycook's shop would do—Antwerp is my delight: I can wander for hours in that marvellous amalgam of the Alhambra, the Crystal Palace, and a Flemish mansion, the Exchange, and on the port I fancy myself in Cadiz, now in Venice, now in some old English seaport of the middle ages. Of Brussels it behoves me to speak briefly, and with reticence, for that charming, sparkling, lively, genial, warm-hearted little capital holds the very next place in my affections to Paris the beloved. Yet I stay only as many hours in Brussels, as, were I on another errand, I should stay days. Due North is my destination, so I go to Liege. I can't help gazing till I am satiated at the wondrous panorama that stretches out before me as we descend the four or five hundred feet gradient of descent that leads into the valley of the Meuse, and as the train slides down the precipitous almost fearful inclined plane I drink in all the marvels of the scene, enhanced as they are by the golden evening sunlight. I watch the domes and cupolas and quaint church spires, and even the factory chimneys, glorified into Oriental minarets by the delusive rays of the setting sun. Much should I like to alight at Liege, and seeking my inn take my rest there; but an inward voice tells me that I have no business in Liege, that still Due North is my irrevocable route, and so I let the train go on its rattling roaring route, and compose myself to sleep till it shall carry me at its gruff will and pleasure over the frontier of Prussia.

So; at last at Herbesthal, and beneath the sway of the Belgian lion's harmless tail no longer. I am testy and drowsy, and feel half inclined to resent, as a personal affront, the proceedings of a tall individual, cloaked, moustachioed, and helmeted, who appears Banshee-like at the carriage, pokes a lantern in my face, and, in the Teutonic tongue, demands my passport. I remember, however, with timely resignation, that I am going Due North, to the dominions of Ursa Major, the great Panjandrum of passports, and that I am as yet but a very young bear, indeed, with all my passport-troubles to come;

so I give the Baron Hyde of Hindon's letter of recommendation to the man in the helmet, and fall into an uneasy sleep again. I hope it may do him good!

Was it at Liege or Pepinstern on the Spa Road (how different from that other Spa-Road Station, I know, on the Greenwich Railway, where attic-windows blink at the locomotive as it rushes by, and endless perspectives of the ventilated brick lanes and fluttering clothes-lines tell of the ugly neighbourhood where outlying tanners dwell, and railway stokers live when they are at home; whereas this Spa Road is a delicious little gorge between purple underwooded hills, with gayly-painted cottages, and peasant-women in red petticoats, and little saints in sentry-boxes by the wayside, and along which I see ladies on horseback, and moustachioed cavaliers careering towards Spa, one of the most charming little watering-places in Europe); at which station was it, I wonder, that we changed the lumbering, roomy, drablined first-class carriages of the Nord, with their sheepskin rugs, and zinc hot-water boxes, for these spruce, glistening, coquettish carriages, so daintily furbished out with morocco leather, and plate-glass, and varnished mahogany—(when will English railway-travellers be emancipated from the villanous, flea-bitten pig-boxes, first, second, and third class, into which, after paying exorbitant fares they are thrust)—when was it that an imperceptible fluffiness, and albine tendency of hat, a shinyness of cap-peaks, an eccentricity of boot-tips, a braidiness of coats, a prevalence of embroidered travelling-pouches, a greenness of veils, a twinkling of spectacles, a blondness of beards, a gaudiness of umbrellas, and a gutturalness of accent, together with the bold and sudden repudiation of the doctrine that tobacco-smoking on railways is prohibited, and must only be furtively indulged in (the major part of the smoke finding its way up the coat-sleeve) with the reluctantly extorted consent of the young ladies who have nerves, and the pettish old gentlemen, and, above all, a wavering, mysterious, but potent smell, a drowsy compound of the odours of pomatum, sauerkraut, gas-meters, and stale tobacco-smoke, told me that I had crossed another frontier, and that I was in Germany?

The train being once more in motion in its way (south this time) towards Cologne, I perused my passport by the light of the carriage lamp, and saw where its virgin blueness had been sullied by the first patch of printing ink, scrawled writing and sand forming a visa. The Black Eagle of Prussia had been good enough to flap his wings for the first time on George William Frederick's talisman. He was good for a flight to Köln or Cologne; but he was dated from Aachen, which Aachen I have just left, and which,—bless me! where were my eyes and memory?—must have been Aix-la-Chapelle.

I consider it to have been an exceedingly lucky circumstance for the reader of this paper that I, the Digressor, did not arrive at the City of Cologne on the Rhine till half-past eleven o'clock at night; that it was pitch dark, and raining heavily; that entering a cab I caused myself to be driven "right away" over the bridge of boats to the Hotel Doopeepel, in the suburbs of Deutz; that, being dog-tired, I went immediately to bed, and that I left Cologne for Berlin by the first train at six A. M. the next morning. I consider this lucky for the reader, because if I had had any time to wander about the streets of Cologne, I should infallibly have launched into dissertations on the cathedral, the market-women, the aforesaid bridge of boats, the horrifying smells, the quaint houses, Jean Marie Farina, and—who knows!—the three kings and the eleven thousand virgins.

Under existing circumstances, all I at present have to say of the place is, that the landlord of the Grand Hotel Doopeepel, at Deutz, deserves a civic crown, or a large gold medal, or a sword of honour—at all events he ought to have his deserts; and I should like to have the task of giving him what he deserves, for the skill and ingenuity displayed in making my bill for a night's lodging, and some trifling refreshment, amount to five Prussian dollars, or fifteen shillings sterling. The best or the worst of it was, that I could not dispute any of the items. I had certainly had them all. Bed, wax lights, attendance, coffee, thimbleful of brandy, cigar, loaf of bread like a hardened muffin, couple of boiled eggs; but oh, in such infinitesimal quantities! As for the eggs, they might have been laid by a humming-bird. The demand of the bill was prodigious, the supply marvellously small, but I paid it admiringly, as one would pay to see a child with two heads, or a bearded lady.

There is a difference of opinion among travelling sages, as to whether a man ought under any circumstances to travel first-class by rail in Germany. The first-class carriages are luxurious—nay, even splendid vehicles, softly padded, lined with crimson velvet, and extensively decorated with silken fringes and curtains. On the other hand, the second-class carriages are also lined and padded, and are at least seventy-five per cent. more comfortable than our best English first-class carriages. Moreover, in the second-class, there are but two compartments to a seat for four persons, so that, if the carriage be not full, you may recline at full length on the cushions, which, in night-travelling, is very comfortable, and rejoices you much; but then the reverse to that medal is, that German second-class carriages are nearly invariably full to the window-sill. The Germans themselves repudiate the first-class stoutly, and it has passed into a Viator's proverb, that none but "princes, Englishmen, and fools, travel by the first-class." I have no particular affection for Englishmen abroad, but I like the company of princes, and you may often have worse travelling companions than fools; so I travel, when I can afford it, first class. There are other temptations thereto. The carriage is seldom more than half-full, if that, and you may change your place when you list, which, in a dragging journey of three hundred and fifty miles or so, is a privilege of no small moment; and you have plenty of side-room for your rugs, and your books, and your carpet-bags. Then, again, there are but six passengers to a carriage instead of eight; and again, besides the possible proximity of his effulgency the reigning Grand Duke of Gumpetpelskirchen-Herrenbonen, the Englîshman and the fool, you may have as a travelling companion a lady, young, pretty, tastefully dressed and adorably affable, as the triumphant majority of German ladies (bless them!) are; and this lady will smile at your mistakes in German, but without wounding your amour propre, and will teach you more of that hard-mouthed language—*vivâ voce*—in ten minutes than you would learn in a month from a grammar and vocabulary, or from university-professor Doctor Schinkelstrumpf's two-dollar lessons. And this lady (whom you long immediately to call "du," and fall on your knees in the carriage before) will ask you questions about the barbarous country you inhabit, and explain to you the use and meaning of common things, such as windmills, milestones, electric-telegraph posts, brick kilns, and the like, with a *naïveté* and simple-mindedness, deliriously delightful to contemplate; she will give you little meat-pies and sweet cakes to eat from her own amply-stored bags; she will even—if you are very agreeable and well-behaved—allow you to comfort yourself outwardly with a dash of eau-de-Cologne from a silver-mounted phial, and inwardly with a sip from a wicker-covered flask containing a liquid whose nature it is no business of yours to inquire; she will sing you little German *leider* in a silvery voice, and cut the leaves of your book with an imitation poniard;—and all this she will do with such an unaffected kindness and simple dignity that the traveller who would presume upon them, or be rude to her, must be a doubly-distilled brute and Pig, and only fit to travel in the last truck of an Eastern Counties fish-train, or to take care of the blind monkeys in the Zoological Gardens.

And all good spirits bless and multiply the fair ladies of Germany! They never object to smoking. There are certain carriages—"*fur Damen*"—into which the men creatures are not allowed to penetrate, and from which tobacco smoke is, as a rule, excluded, though it is difficult enough to banish the exhalations from the neighbouring carriages; but the ladies seldom (the nice ones never) patronize the carriages especially affected to their use. They just take railway pot-luck with the ruder sex; and as for smoking—cigar-smoking be it always understood—they like it; they delight in it; *elles en raffolent.* They know, sagacious creatures, that a traveller with a cigar in his mouth is twice a Man; that the fumes of the fragrant Havana loosen the tongue, and open the heart, and dispel awkwardness and diffidence; that he who wants to smoke, and is prevented from smoking, always feels aggrieved and oppressed, and is correspondingly sulky, disobliging, and morose. The only drawback to the society of the German lady in the railway carriage is this: that when she alights at a station, and in her handbell-toned voice bids you adieu and *bon voyage*—sometimes pronounced "*pon foyache*"—there are always waiting on the platform for her other ladies young and pretty as herself, or else moustachioed relations (I hope they *are* relations), who fall to kissing her, and pressing both her hands, till you fall into despair, and howl with rage in your crimson velvet prisoners' van. Then the train rolls away, and you feel that there is a nature-abhorred vacuum in the left-hand corner of your waistcoat, and that Fraulein von Name Unknown has taken your heart away with her, and is now, probably, hanging it over her chimney-piece as a trophy, as an Indian chief suspends the scalps of his enemies to the poles of his hunting-lodge.

On this present due-northern journey I must confess I did not lose my heart, for we were ladyless all the way; but the average first-class travelling companions I had. There was a Prince—so at least I conjectured the asthmatic old gentleman who left us at Düsseldorf to be; for who but a Prince could have possessed such a multiplicity of parti-coloured ribbons belonging to as many orders (a little soap and water would have done them a world of good) pinned on the breast of his brown surtout, so much fragrant snuff on his embroidered *jabot*, and such an impenetrably wise and aristocratic face? Yes, he must have been a Prince, with seventy-five quarterings at least on his 'scutcheon. Then there was an Englishman (besides your humble servant) and there was a Fool. Such a fool! *Insipiens serenissimus.* He was a Frenchman, fat, fair, *self-complacent*, and smiling, with some worsted-work embroidery on his head for a *couvrechet* like a kettle-holder pinned into a circular form. There were mediæval letters worked on it, and I tried hard to read "Polly put the kettle on," but could not. He was going to

Dresden, where he was to stay a week, and exhibited to us every ten minutes or so a letter of credit on a banker there, and asked us if we thought four thousand florins would be enough to last him during his sojourn. He was as profoundly, carelessly, gayly, contentedly ignorant of things which the merest travelling tyro is usually conversant with as a Frenchman could well be; but he knew all about the Boulevard des Italiens, and that was quite enough for him. He laughed and talked incessantly, but, like the jolly young waterman, it was about nothing at all. He could not smoke: it gave him a pain in his limbs, he said; but he liked much to witness the operation. Like most fools, he had a Fixed Idea; and this fixed idea happened to be a most excellent one—being no other than this, that the German beer was very good, (so it is, comparatively, after the Strasbourg and Biere de Mars abominations,) and that it was desirable to drink as much of it as could possibly be obtained. He alighted at every station, to drink a draught of creaming though mawkish beverage, and seemed deeply mortified when the train did not stop long enough for him to make a journey to the *buffet*, and half inclined to quarrel with me when I persuaded him to take a *petit verre* of cognac at Minden, as a corrective to the malt. But he was an hospitable and liberal simpleton, and when we declined ourselves to alight, he would come with a beaming countenance and a Tom-fool's joke to the carriage window, holding a great foaming glass tankard, with a pewter cover, of Bock Bier, or else a bottle of it to last to the next station. I am not ashamed to say that I drank his health several times between Düsseldorf and Hanover, and, what is more, wished him good health with all my heart.

The German railway *buffets* are capital places of "restoration;" true oases in the great desert of cuttings and embankments. The fare is plentiful, varied, and cheap—cheap, at least, if you received any thing like Christian money in change for the napoleons or five-frank pieces your money-changer gave for that blessed bank note signed "J. Fereaby," in the Palais Royal at Paris; but what intensity of disgustful reprobation can be sufficient to characterize the vile dross that is forced upon you, the debased fiddlers' money, that you are ashamed to put in your purse, and half inclined to fling out of the window; the poverty-stricken, clipped, measly, pockmarked, greasy, slimy *silbergroschen*, *neuegroschen*, *grosgroschen*, and *gudegroschen*, (the eulogistic adjectives silver, new, big, good, to these leprous testoons all breathe the bitterest satire.) A German refreshment room is a receptacle for all the lame, halt, and blind coins of the Zollverein, the monetary refuse of Prussia, Saxony, Bavaria, Austria, Hanover, Mecklenburg, and the infinite variety of smaller tinpot states; nay, you are very lucky if the waiters do not contrive to give you a sprinkling of Hamburg and Lubeck money, with a few Copenhagen sckillings, and Schleswig-Holstein marks. The rogues know that you have no time to question or dispute; they take care not to give you your change till the starting-bell rings; and by the time you have counted the abominable heap of marine-store money and have got over your first outbursts of passion, you are half-a-dozen miles away. As a climax or villany, the change they give you at one station is not current, or is said not to be so, at the next. Say, waiter at Bienenbuttel, is not this the case? And didst thou not contumeliously refuse my Prussian piece of ten groschen?

Why should it be that in England, the great market of the world, amply provisioned as it is, and with its unrivalled facilities of communication, refreshment rooms, not only on railways, but in theatres, gardens, and other places of amusement, should be so scantily and poorly furnished, and at such extortionate prices? Why should our hunger be mocked by those dried-up Dead Sea fruits, those cheesecakes that seem to contain nothing but sawdust, those sandwiches resembling thin planks of wood with a strata of dried glue between them, those three-weeks-old pork and veal pies, all over bumps full of delusive promise, but containing nothing but little cubes of tough gristle and antediluvian fat; those byegone buns with the hard, cracked varnish-like veneering; that hopeless cherry-brandy, with the one attenuated little cherry bobbing about in the vase like a shrivelled black buoy; that flatulent lemonade tasting of the cork and the wire, and of the carbonic acid gas, but of the lemon never; that bottled brown stout like so much bottled soapsuds; that scalding infusion of birch-broom miscalled tea; and that unsavoury compound of warm plate-washings facetiously christened soup? Why should English railway travellers be starved as well as smashed? Sir Frances Head tells us that they keep pigs at Wolverton, who, in course of time, are promoted into pork pies; but the promotion must surely go by seniority. Look, for comparison, at the French *buffets*, with the savoury soup always ready; the sparkling little *carafons* of wine, the convenient *cotelette*, the tempting slices of *pate-de-foie gras*, the crisp fresh loaves of bread, and all at really moderate prices. Look again at the German refreshment-rooms. That practical people (though they do indulge in smoking and metaphysics to such an extent) have a system of refreshment called "thumb restauration." This consists of the famous *butterbrod*, or compact little crust of bread and butter on which is laid ham, cold meat, poultry, game, dried salmon, or caviare! The first sight of that glistening black condiment startled me, and made me feel Due North more than ever.

Minden, Hanover, Brunswick, have been passed. The armorial white horse made his appearance at the second of these places on the coinage of the poor blind king, and on a flaring escutcheon in front of the railway terminus. At Brunswick there was a *fête* in honour of the twenty somethingeth of the anniversary of the accession of the reigning duke, which I suppose must be a source of great annual satisfaction to the sovereign in question, as well as to that other duke who doesn't reign but lives in Paris, paints his cheeks, wears the big diamonds, has an arsenal round his bedstead, and a mint of money underneath it, and is such a particular friend of the heaven-sent emperor Napoleon the Third. The terminus was plentifully decorated with evergreens and banners; there was a great deal of dust and music and beer-drinking going on, (the chief ingredients, with smoking, of a German *fête*,) and the platform was crowded with Brunswickers in holiday attire: beaux and belles in Teutonic-Parisian trim, and ruddy, straw-haired and straw-hatted country folk in resplendent gala-dresses. To give you a notion of the appearance of the more youthful female Brunswickers, I must recall to your remembrance the probable appearance of the little old woman, who, going to market, inadvertently fell asleep by the king's highway, and with whose garments such unwarrantable liberties were taken by a wretch by the name of Stout, a tinker by profession. The peasant girls of Brunswick look as the little old woman must have looked when she awoke from her nap; so brief are their skirts, and so apparently unrecognized among them is the use of the *supfusk* garments christened by our prudish female cousins on the other side of the Atlantic "pantalettes;" but they wear variegated hose with embroidered clocks, and their mothers have bidden them, as the song says, "bind their hair with bands of rosy hue, and tie up their sleeves with ribbons rare, and lace their boddice blue," and Lubin, happily, is not far away, but close at hand, and very pretty couples they make with their yellow hair tied in two ribboned tails behind. Mingling with the throng too, I see some soldiers I have been anxious, for many a long year, to be on visual terms with,—soldiers clad all in sable, with nodding black plumes, bugle ornaments to their uniforms, and death's-heads and cross-bones on their shakoes. These are the renowned Black Brunswickers; and I am strangely reminded, looking at them, of him that sate in the windowed niche of the high hall, alone, cheerless, brooding, thinking only of the bloody bier of his father, and of revenge: —of that valiant chieftain of the Black Brunswickers who left the Duchess of Richmond's ball to die at Quatre Bras.

I wish the Germans wouldn't call Brunswick Braunschweig; it destroys the illusion. I can't think of the illustrious house that has given a dynasty to the British throne as the house of Braunschweig. It is as cacaphonous in sound as would be the house of Physic-bottles, instead of the house of Medici, but our Teuton friends seem to have a genius for uglifying high-sounding names. They call Elsinore (Hamlet's Elsinore) Helsingborg; Vienna, Wien; Munich, München; Cologne, Köln, and the Crimea, Krim. Can there be any thing noble, proper to a famous battle-field where the bones of heroes lie whitening in the word Krim?

The Frenchman, who was a fool, left us at the Prussian fortress town of Magdebourg, where also the Englishman (who was any thing but a fool, a thorough man of the world, in fact, and of whom I intend you to hear further in the course of these travels) also bade me adieu at this station. Then I was left alone in my glory to ponder over the historical places I had been hurried through since six o'clock that morning; I thought of Düsseldorf, and

Overbeck the painter, of the battle of Minden, and the Duke of Cumberland and Lord George Sackville; of Hanover, George the First and his bad oysters; of Magdebourg and Baron Trenck, till I went to sleep, and waking found myself at Potsdam.

I found that I had another travelling companion here in the person of a magnificent Incarnation, all ringleted, oiled, scented, dress-coated, and watered-silk-faced, braided, frogged, ringed, jewelled, patent-leathered, amber-headed sticked, and straw-colored kid-gloved, who had travelled in the same train, from Cologne, but had been driven out of the adjoining carriage, he said by the execrable fumes of the German cigars, and now was good enough to tolerate me, owing to a mild and undeniably Havana cigar I lighted. This magnificent creature shone like a meteor in the narrow carriage. The lamp mirrored itself in his glistening equipment; his gloves and boots fitted so tightly, that you felt inclined to think that he had varnished his hands straw-color, and his feet black. There was not a crease in his fine linen, a speck of dust on his superfine Saxony sables, his waxed-moustachioes and glossy ringlets. I felt ashamed, embaled as I was in rugs and spatter-dashes, and a fur cap, and a courier's pouch, all dusty and travel-stained, when I contemplated this bandbox *voyageur*, so spruce and kempt, the only sign of whose being away from home, was a magnificent mantle lined with expensive furs, on the seat beside him, and who yet, he told me, had been travelling incessantly for six days. He talked with incessant volubility in the French and English tongues; the former seemed to be his native one; he knew everybody and everything I knew; he had started the journal from which I was accredited, and was the promoter of the club of which I was an unworthy member; and as to myself, he knew me intimately, so he said, though may I have six years' penal servitude with Lieutenant Austin late of Birmingham jail as Hulk Inspector if I had ever spoken to him before in my life; and a great many things and people I did not know. He seemed personally acquainted with every musical instrument and musician, from the piper that played before Moses to the Messrs. Distin and their Saxhorns. I began to fancy as he proceeded, that he must be that renowned and eccentric horn-player and mystificateur, who travels about Europe, Asia, Africa, America, Australia, and other parts of the world, accompanied by a white game-cock, and who was once mistaken for a magician by the Greeks of Syra through his marvellous feat of blowing soap-bubbles with tobacco-smoke inside them. I was in error, however. I learnt the wondrous creature's name before I reached Berlin; but although he refrained from binding me to secrecy, this is not the time nor place in which to reveal it.

Ten thirty P. M., a wild sweep through a sandy plain thinly starred with lights; then thickening masses of human habitations; then brighter coruscations of gas-lamps, and—Berlin. Here I am received with all the honours of war. Two grim guards with gleaming bayonets impress me, if they do not awe me, on the platform, as the carriage-door is flung open ; and a very tall and fierce police-officer in a helmet demands my passport. I observe that the continental governments always keep the policemen with the longest moustachioes, the largest bodies, and the most ferocious general aspect, at the frontier towns and railway termini. You always see the *élite* of the municipal force, the prize policemen, when you enter a foreign country, and those in power have a decided eye to effect. Behold me here, exactly half-way in my expedition Due North —which is not due north by-the-by, but rather northeast.

Behold me, come post-haste to Berlin, and half my journey due north accomplished. Now, when the northern end looms in sight, I find myself brought to a standstill. This is the twenty-seventh of April, and the flowers in England must be looking out their summer suits, yet here I am literally frozen up. It was my design, on quitting London, to proceed, viâ Berlin, to Stettin in Pomerania, and there to take the first steamer to St. Petersburg. Here is my fare, sixty-two dollars in greasy Prussian notes—like curl-papers smoothed out—here is my Foreign-Office passport, not *visé* yet for Russia, but which to-morrow will be ; here are my brains and my heart, bounding, yearning, for Muscovite impressions ; and there, at Stettin-on-the-Oder, is the Post-Dampfschiff *Preussischer-Adler* or Fast Mail-packet Prussian Eagle. What prevents the combination of these things carrying me right away to Cronstadt? What but my being frozen up? What but the ice in the Gulf of Finland?

In a murky office in Mark Lane, London, where I first made my inquiries into Muscovite matters, the clerks spoke hopefully of the northern navigation being perfectly free by the end of April. In Brussels, weather-wise men, bound Russia-wards, were quite sanguine as to the first day of May being first open water. But in Berlin, people began to shake their heads, and whisper ugly stories about the ice; and many advised me to take a run down to Leipzig and Dresden, and see the Saxon Switzerland; telling me significantly that I would have ample time to explore all central Germany before the northern waters were ruffled by the keel even of a cock-boat. There was a little band of Britons purposing for Petersburg at the table d'hôte of the Hotel de Russie, at Berlin, of whom I had the advantage to make one; and we fed ourselves from day to day (after dinner) with fallacious hopes of early steamers. A Roman citizen in a buff waistcoat, and extensively interested in tallow, (so at least it was whispered, though the Fumden Blad said merely Shortsix, Kaufmann aus England, and was silent as to his specialty,) was perfectly certain that a steamboat would start from Stockholm for Cronstadt on the fourth of May, and he expressed his determination to secure a passage by her; but as Sweden happens to be on the other side of the Baltic, and there was no bridge, and no water communication yet opened therewith, the Stockholm steamer was a thing to be looked at (in lithography, framed and glazed in the hall of the hotel) and longed for, rather than embarked in. We were all of us perpetually haunted by a sort of phantom steamer—a very flying Russian—commanded, I presume, by Captain Vanderdeckenovitch, whose departure some one had seen advertised in an unknown newspaper. This spectral craft was reported to have left Hull some time since—we all agreed that the passage-money out was nine guineas, inclusive of provisions of the very best quality, but exclusive of wines, liquors, and the steward's fee, and she was to call (after doubling the cape, I presume) at Kiel, Lubeck, Copenhagen, Konigsberg; Jerusalem, Madagascar, and North and South Amerikee, for aught I know. To find this ghostly bark, an impetuous Englishman—a north countryman with a head so fiery in hue that they might have put him on a post and made a lighthouse of him, and pendant whiskers like carriage rugs, started off by the midnight mail to Hamburg. He came back in three days and a towering rage, saying that there was ice even in the Elbe, and giving us to understand that the free cities of Hamburg, Lubeck, and Bremen, had concurred in laughing him to scorn at the bare mention of a steamer due north—yet awhile at least. By degrees a grim certainty broke upon us, and settled itself convincingly in our minds. To the complexion of the Preussischer-Adler we must come; and that Post-Dampfschiff would start from Stettin on Saturday, the seventeenth of May, at noon, and not one day or hour before.

I thought the three long weeks would never have come to an end. I might, had I been differently situated, have taken my fill of enjoyment in Berlin, and spent three pleasant weeks there. Unter den Linden, the Thier-Garten, Charlottenbourg, Potsdam, Krotts, the Tonhalle, Sans Souci, and Monbijou (pronounced *Zang Zouzy* and *Mongpichow*) are quite sufficient to make a man delectably comfortable on the spree: to say nothing of the art treasure-stored Museum, Rauch's statue of the Great Frederic, Kiss's Amazon, and the sumptuous Opera-haus, with Johanna Wagner in the Tanhaüser, and Marie Taglioni in Satanella. But they were all caviare to the million of Prussian blue devils which possessed me. I felt that I had no business in Berlin—that I had no right to applaud Fraulein Wagner—that I ought to reserve my kid-glove reverberations for Mademoiselle Bagdanoff: that every walk I took Unter den Linden was so many paces robbed from the Nevsky Perspective, and that every sight I took at the King of Prussia and the Princes of the House of Hohenzollern was a fraud on my liege literary masters, the Emperor of Russia and the scions of the house of Romanoff.

Conscience-stricken as I felt, though void of guilt, I had my consolations—few and spare, but grateful as Esmeralda's cup to the thirst-tortured Quasimodo. I heard the Oberon of Karl Maria von Weber performed with such a fervour and solemnity of sincerity, listened to with such rapt attention and reverent love—drunk up by a thousand greedy ears, bar by bar, note by note—from the first delicious horn-murmur in the overture to the last crash in the triumphant march, in the finale, that I began at last to fancy that I was in a Cathedral instead of a theatre, and half expected the congregation—I mean the people—to kneel when the bell rang for the fall of the curtain, and the brilliant lamps grew pale. An extra gleam of consolation was imparted to me, too, when I read in the *Schauspiel-zettel*, or play-bill, the printed avowal that the libretto of the opera had been into High Dutch rendered from the English of the Herr-Poem-Konstruktor J. R. Planché. Again; I saw the Faust of Wolfgang von Goethe—the Faust as a tragedy, in all its magnificent and majestic simplicity. I don't think I clearly comprehended fifty phrases of the dialogue; I could scarcely read the names of the dramatis personæ in the play-bill; and yet I would not have missed that performance for a pile of ducats; nor shall I ever forget the actor who played Mephistopheles. His name is a shadow to me now; the biting wit, the searching philosophy, the scathing satire in his speech were wellnigh Greek to me; but the hood, the gait, the gestures, the devil's grin, the vibrating voice, the red cock's feather, the long peaked shoes, the sardonically up-turned moustache, will never be erased from my mind, and will stand me in good stead for commentaries when (in the week of the three Thursdays, I suppose) I take heart of grace and sit down to study the giant of Weimar's masterpiece in the original. There was a pretty, blue-eyed, rosy-lipped Marguérite, whose hair had a golden sheen perfectly wondrous; and Faust would have been a senseless stock not to have fallen in love with her; but, alas! she was too fat, *and looked as if she ate too much;* and when she wept for Faust gave me far more the impression that she was crying because, like the ebony patriarch Tucker, familiarly hight Dan, she was too late for her supper. Still, I came away from Faust almost happy.

There might, perchance, at other times be a surly pleasure in the discovery that Berlin gloves are apparently unknown at Berlin—even as there are no French rolls in Paris—and that Berlin wool is very little sought after. There might have been some advantage gained to science by an attempt to analyze the peculiar smell of the capital of Prussia, which, to uninitiated noses, seems compounded of volatile essence of Cologne, (not the *eau*, but the streets thereof,) multiplied by sewer, plus cesspool, plus Grande Rue de Pera, plus Rue de la Tixeranderie after a shower of rain, plus port of Marseilles at any time, plus London eating-house, plus Vauxhall bone-boiling establishment, plus tallow factory, plus low lodging-house in Whitechapel, plus dissecting-rooms, plus the "gruel thick and slab" of Macbeth's witches when it began to cool.* There might have been a temporary relief in expatiating on the geological curiosities of Berlin, the foot-lacerating pavement, and the Sahara-like sandy plain in which the city is situate. There might have been a temporary excitement, disagreeable but salubrious, in losing, as I did, half my store of Prussian notes in a cab, and cooling my heels for three successive days at the Police Præsidium in frantically-fruitless

* It is doubtful whether this description, written nearly two years ago, would not now more aptly apply to Father Thames.

inquiries (in very scanty German) after my departed treasure—but there wasn't; no, not one atom. Though the Hôtel de Russie boasted as savoury a table-d'hôte as one would wish to find, likewise Rhine wine exhilarating to the palate and soothing to the soul, I began to loathe my food and drink. I longed for Russian caviare and Russian vodki. I came abroad to eat candles and drink train-oil—or, at least, the equivalent for that which is popularly supposed to form the favourite food of our late enemies—and not to feast on Bisque soup and *suprême de volaille.* Three weeks! they seemed an eternity.

The maestro whom I met at Potsdam, went back to Cologne cheerfully; he was not bound for the land of the Russ; and, having accomplished the object of his mission—which I imagine to have been the engagement of a few hundred fiddlers—departed in a droschky, his straw-coloured kids gleaming in the sunshine, and wishing me joy of my journey to St. Petersburg. Shall I ever get there, I wonder? The Englishman, who was a man of the world, didn't come back. He of the red head (Mr. Eddystone I christened him from his beacon-like hair) took rail for Königsberg, to see if there was anything in the steam-vessel line to be done there, and the buff waistcoat, who was commercially interested in tallow, boldly announced his determination not to stand it any longer, but to be off to St. Petersburg overland.

Overland! and why could not I also go overland? The railway, I reasoned, will take me as far as this same Königsberg, and proceeding thence by way of

Tilsit, Tauroggen, Mittau, Riga, and Lake Tschudi, I can reach the much-desired Petropolis. There is the *malle-poste*, or diligence; there is the extra-post; there is the private *kibitka*, which I can purchase, or hire, and horse at my own charges from stage to stage. The journey should properly occupy ABOUT six days. ABOUT! but a wary and bronzed queen's messenger, who converses with me (he ought to know something, for he is on the half-pay of the dragoons, is a lord's nephew and the cousin of a secretary of state, spent fifty thousand pounds before he was five-and-twenty, and is now ceaselessly wandering up and down on the face of the earth with a red dispatch-box, six hundred a-year, and his expenses paid)—the queen's messenger, bronzed and wary, shakes his head ominously. When the winter breaks up in Russia, he remarks, the roads break up too, and the travellers break down. He has often been overland himself, perforce, (where hasn't he been?) in winter; and he has such marrow-freezing stories to tell (all in a cool, jaunty, mess-room-softened-by-experience manner,) of incessant travelling by day and night, of roads made up of morasses, sand-hills, and deep gullies, of drunken drivers, of infamous post-houses, swarming with all the plagues of Egypt, naturalized Russian subjects; of atrociously extortionate Jew postmasters; of horses—rum ones to look at, and rummer, or worse ones, to go; of frequent stoppages for hours together; of an absolute dearth of anything wholesome to eat or drink, save bread and tea. He enlarges so much on the bruisings, bumpings, joltings, and dislocations to which the unfortunate victim of the nominally six, but more frequently twelve days' overland route is subject, that I bid the project avaunt like an ugly phantom, and, laying it in the Baltic Sea, determine to weather out the time as well as I can, till the seventeenth.

I can't stop any longer in Berlin, however, that is certain. So I drive out of the Oraneinberg Gate, and cast myself into a railway carriage, which, in its turn, casts me out at Stettin-on-the-Oder, eighty-four miles distant. And on the banks of that fearsome River Oder I pass May-day. In the Oder, too, I find the steamer in which, at some far remote period of my existence, I suppose I am to occupy a berth. I find the "Preussischer Adler;" but woe is me! she has taken to her bed in a graving-dock, and is a pitiable sight to see. There being something the matter with her boilers, they have dismasted her, leaving her nothing but clumsy stumps like wooden legs. They are scraping her all over, for some cutaneous disorder with which she is afflicted, I presume, and they are recoppering her bottom,—an operation which German shipwrights appear to me to perform with gum-arabic, Dutch metal, and a camel's-hair pencil. Altogether the "Prussian Eagle" looks such a woe-begone, moulting, tailless, broken-beaked bird, and so very unlike going to Cronstadt, that I flee from her in dismay; and boarding the "Geyser," which is trim, taut, and double-funnelled, steam swiftly through the Haf See to Swinemunde, and then across the East Sea to Copenhagen.

Plenty of time (*miserere me!*) to see all that is to be seen in the chief city of Denmark; to take the English company's railway to Roeskilde; to cross over to Malmoë in Sweden; to go back to Stettin—to the devil, I think, if this lasts much longer. There is a horrible persuasion forcing itself upon me now—that I live in Berlin: that my goal is there. Back to Berlin I go. Letters are waiting for me. People I didn't know from Adam a month ago, and don't care a *silbergroschen* for, offer to kiss me on both cheeks, and welcome me home. I suppose by this time I am a Prussian subject, and shall have to serve in the landwehr. Between that and blowing one's brains out there is not much difference.

I go back to Stettin, where I have a touch of the overland longing again (it is now the tenth of May), and a Jewish gentleman with an apple-green gabardine, lined with cat-skin, and a beard so ragged and torn, that I am led to surmise that he has himself despoiled the cats of their furry robes, and has suffered severely in the contest, is exceedingly anxious (he nosed me in the hotel lobby as an Englishman, within an hour of my arrival) that I should purchase a kibitka he has to sell. He only wants fifty thalers for it; it is a splendid kibitka, he says:—"*sehr hübsch, schrecklich! wunderschön*"—so I go to look at it; for I feel just in the sort of mood to buy a kibitka, or an elephant, a diving-bell, a mangle, an organ with an insane monkey to grind it, and throw myself into the Oder immediately afterwards. I look at the kibitka, which I am to horse from stage to stage, and I deserve to be horsed myself if I buy it, so lamentable an old shandrydan is it. I quarrel with the Jew in the cat-skins on the subject, who calls me lord, and sheds tears. Finding that I am determined not to throw away my thalers on his kibitka, he, with the elasticity in commercial transactions common to his nation, proposes that I should become the possessor of a splendid dressing-case with silver mountings; but on my remaining proof against this temptation, as well as against that of a stock of prime Hungarian tobacco, which is to be sold for a mere song, he changes blithely from seller to buyer, and generously offers to purchase at advantageous rates, and for ready money, any portion of my wardrobe I may consider superfluous. He is not in the least offended when I bid him go hang, in the English language, and walk away moodily—calling after me in cheerful accents (by the title of Well-born Great British Sir) that he has a fine English bull-pup to dispose of, dirt-cheap.

After this, I have another look at the "Preussischer Adler," which, by this time, has been turned, for coppering purposes, nearly keel upwards, and looks as if she had abandoned herself to despair, as I have. Walk the streets of Stettin I dare not, for I am pursued by the hideous spectre of Thomas Tilder aus Tyrol, of whom more anon. Yes, Thomas, in these pages shall you, like noxious bat on barn-door, be spread out with nails of type! And, as for Berlin, I am ashamed to show my face there again. The very clerks at the station seem to think it quite time for me to be in Russia; and I am afraid the head waiter at the Hôtel de Russie took it very ill that I came back last time. Yet I journey there, and back, and there again; and in one of my journeys to Berlin I have my passport made good for Russia. The process is a solemn and intricate one, and merits a few words of notice. There is plenty of time; they are hammering away at the Prussian Eagle's boilers yet. First, with great fear and trembling, I go to the hotel of the Russian embassy, which is a tremendous mansion, as big as a castle, under the Linden. I have borne the majority of Foreign Legations abroad with tolerable equanimity; but I am quite overcome here by the grandeur, and the double eagle over the gate, and the vastness of the court-yard, and the odour of a diplomatic dinner, which is being cooked (probably in stew-pans of gold from the Ural mountains); but I am especially awed by a house-porter, or Suisse, of gigantic stature, possibly the largest Suisse that ever human ambassador possessed. He is not exactly like a beadle, nor a drum-major, nor an archbishop, (he wears a gold-embroidered alb) nor a field-marshal, nor garter king-at-arms, nor my lord on May-day, but is something between all these functionaries in appearance. He has a long gilt-headed pole in his hand, much more like the "mast of some tall ammiral," than a Christian staff; and when I ask him the way to the passport-office, he magnanimously refrains from ejaculating anything about Fee-fo-Fum, or smelling the blood of an Englishman; and, instead of eating me up alive on the spot, or grinding my bones to make his bread, he tells me, in a deep bass voice, to enter the second door on the left through the court-yard, and mount two pair of stairs. Here, in but a seedy little bureau for so grand a mansion, I find a little round old gentleman in a grey flannel dressing-gown and a skull-cap, who looks more like my Uncle Toby than a Russian, offers me snuff from his box, (a present from the czar, perhaps,) and courteously desires to know what he can do for me. I explain my errand; upon which the little old gentleman shakes his head with Burleigh-like sagacity, as if granting a *visé* to a passport were no light matter, and, securing my papers, begs me to call again at three o'clock the following day. I call again at the appointed time, when it appears that the little old gentleman—or, at least, his diplomatic chiefs—have no orders, as yet, to admit English subjects into Russia; so there are telegraphic messages to be sent to Warsaw, where Count Gortschakoff is, and who most courteously telegraphs back, "By all means:"* and there are papers to be signed, and declarations to be made, and there is the deuce and all to pay. When all these formalities have been satisfactorily gone through, I begin to think it pretty nearly time for the passport to be ready, and ask for it; but the

* In that meritorious philo-Russian organ, the Nord, I saw, a few days since, an anecdote, apropos of telegraphic despatches, which, I think, will bear translation. Lord Granville, according to the Nord, had commissioned one Sir Acton to engage a house at Moscow for him. Sir Acton telegraphs to Lord Granville to know whether the terms demanded for the house will suit his lordship, whereupon Lord Granville telegraphs back, "Yes, my dear."

little old gentleman, shaking that head of his with much suavity, suggests to-morrow at a quarter to four. The chief secretary of legation, he says, is at Charlottenbourg, dining with the king, and without his signature the passport is not valid. I call again; but I suppose the secretary must be taking tea with some other member of the royal family, for no passport do I receive, and another appointment is made. This time I see my passport bodily, lying on a table, and by the amount of Russian hieroglyphics and double-eagle stamps covering every available blank space on its surface, it ought surely, to my mind, to be good from Revel to Tobolsk. But it is *noch nicht fertig*—not yet ready—the little old gentleman says. He speaks nothing but German—so, at least, he blandly declares; yet I notice that he pricks his ears up sharply, and that his eyes twinkle, when an irate Frenchman, whose errand is the same as mine (only he has been waiting ten days) denounces the Russians, in his native tongue, as a nation *de barbares.* I begin myself to get exceedingly cross, and impatient to know when I am to have the precious document; whereupon the little old gentleman looks at me curiously, as if he didn't quite understand what I meant, or perhaps as if I didn't quite understand his meaning.

"Where do you live in Berlin?" he asks, suddenly.

I tell him that I am stopping at the Hôtel de Russie, in which with a smile of five-hundred-diplomatist power, he makes me a bow, and tells me he will have the honour of bringing me the passport this present evening, at six o'clock. I ask if there is any charge for the *visé;* but, with another smile that would set a sphynx up in business on the spot, so inscrutable is it, he assures me that the *visé* is Gratis, gratis, and bows me out. I go home to dinner, and discourse to Mr. Erenreich on my passport tribulations.

"When he comes this evening," says this worthy landlord, "you had better give him a thaler at once. Otherwise you may perhaps find that he has left the passport at the Legation, and that it is impossible to obtain it before to-morrow."

The little old gentleman is punctual to his appointment, and I no sooner catch sight of him in the darkened *salle à manger*, than I hasten to slip the necessary note into his hand. He makes me a profusion of bows, and gives me my passport,—*gutt nach Russland* as he expresses it. "*Gutt nach Russland.*" When I spread the passport on the table, and recall the little old gentleman's words, I can't help feeling somewhat of a thrill. "*Gutt nach Russland*"—here are the double eagles, and the paragraphs scrawled in unknown characters, and my name (I presume) in such an etymological disguise that my wisest child, had I one, would despair of recognizing his own father in it. Yet the expenditure of three shillings has made me "good for Russia." But yesterday there was a gulf of blood and fire, and the thunder of a thousand guns between England and Russia! the Ultima Thule of St. Petersburg was as inaccessible to an Englishman as Mecca or Japan, and now, lo, a scrap of a stamped paper and a few pieces of gold will carry me through the narrow channel, that, ten months ago, the British government would have given millions to be able to float one gun-boat on.

"*Itsch chost von Daler*," says the commissionnaire with the umbrella. What he should want a Prussian dollar from me for, or why, indeed, he should exact any thing, passes my comprehension. He walked into my bedroom at the Drei Kronen this morning, at a dreadfully early hour, with his hat on, and his umbrella (a dull crimson in hue) under his arm. He bade me good morning in a cavalier manner, and informed me that he was the commissionnaire, to which I retorted that he might be the Pope, but that I wanted none of his company. The boots was packing my luggage, and he superintended the process with a serenely patronizing air, thinking possibly, that on the principle that "*l' œil du maître engraisse le cheval*," it is the eye of the commissionnaire that cords the trunks. Finding me indisposed for conversation (I had taken some genuine Russian caviare for breakfast with a view of acclimatizing myself early, and was dreadfully sick), he took himself and umbrella off to another apartment, and the boots expressed his opinion to me (in strict confidence) that he, the commissionnaire, was a *spitzbube*. This is all he has done for me, and now he has the conscience to come to me and tell me that his charges are "*chost von Daler*." He is authorized, it appears, by somebody who does not pay the thalers himself, to extort them from other people; and he points, with conscious pride, to some tarnished buttons on his waistcoat on which the Russian eagle is manifest.

Why do I give the commissionnaire the thaler he demands, and to which he has no sort of right? Why do I feel inclined to give two, three dollars, to invite him to partake of schnapps, to cast myself on his neck, and assure him that I love him as a brother? Why, because to-day is Saturday, the seventeenth of May, eleven o'clock in the forenoon, and I am standing on the deck—the quarter-deck, ye gods!—of the "Preussischer Adler," which good pyroscaphe has got her steam up to a maddening extent, and in another hour's time will leave the harbour of Stettin for Cronstadt..

New tail-feathers, new wing-feathers, new beak, new claws, has the "Preussischer Adler." A brave bird. There is nothing the matter with her boilers now, her masts are tapering, her decks snow-white, and I have no doubt that her copper glistens like burnished gold, and that the mermaids in the Baltic will be tempted to purloin little bits of the shining metal to deck their weedy tresses withal. A bran new flag of creamy tinge floats at her stern, and on it is depicted with smart plumage, and beak and claws of gold, an eagle of gigantic dimensions. And this is the last eagle with one head that I shall see on this side Jordan.

Every thing seems to be new on board. The saloon is gorgeous in crimson velvet, and mirrors, and mahogany and gold. There are the cleanest of sheets, the rosiest of counterpanes, the most coquettish of chintz curtains to the berths. All the crockery is new. All the knives and forks are new; and though I discover afterwards that they won't cut, they are delightfully shiny. There is a library of new books in a new rosewood case, and there is a new cabinet piano, tuned up to nautical-concert pitch, and whose keys when struck clang as sharply as the tongue of an American steamboat clerk. The stewards, of whom there are a goodly number, are all clad in glossy new uniforms of a fancy naval cut, and look like midshipmen at a Vauxhall masquerade. There is a spacious galley for cooking purposes, full of the brightest cooking utensils; a titillating odour issues therefrom, and there are four cooks, yea four, all in professional white. One has an imperial and gold watch-chain, one is flirting with the stewardess, (who is young, pretty, flounced, and wears her hair after the manner of the Empress Eugénie,) a third is smoking a paper cigarette, (quite the gentleman,) while the last, reclining in a grove of stewpans, is studying attentively a handsomely-bound book. What can it be? Newton's Principia, Victor Hugo's Contemplations, the Cuisinier Royal, or the Polite Letter-writer? "The Preussischer Adler," be it known, like her sister vessel the Vladimir, is an intensely-aristocratic boat. Both are commanded by officers respectively of the Prussian (!) and Russian (!!) navies. The fare by the Prussian Eagle is enormously high; nine guineas for a sixty hours' passage. On payment of this exorbitant honorarium she will carry such humble passengers as myself; but the ordinary travellers per "Preussischer Adler" are princes of the empire, grand-dukes, arch-electors, general-lieutenants, ambassadors, senators, councillors of state. And as for ladies—*tenez!*—the best edition of Almack's Revisited is to be found on board a Stettin steamboat. I start at the wrong end of the season to travel with the grandees, however. For this being the commencement of the navigation and of PEACE besides, the Russian aristocracy are all hurrying away from St. Petersburg as fast as ever they can obtain passports. The Vladimir, they tell me, has all her berths engaged up to the middle of July next, and the Prussian Eagle is in equal demand.

I should perhaps be more unexceptionably satisfied with the Adler's arrangements, if her crew would not persist in wearing moustaches and Hessian boots with the tassels cut off. It is not nautical. A boatswain, too, with stripes down his trousers, is to me an anomaly. I must dissent, too, from the system of stowing passengers' luggage per "Preussischer Adler." The manner of it appears to be this: a stalwart porter, balancing a heavy trunk on his shoulder, advances along the plank which leads from the wharf to the ship's side. He advances jauntily, as though he were not unaccustomed to dance *a coranto*. Arrived at the brink of the abyss, he stops, expectorates, bandies a joke in High Dutch with a compatriot who is mending his trousers in an adjacent barge, and bending slightly, pitches the trunk head foremost into the hold.

There is, I need scarcely say, a tremendous fuss and to-do with papers and policemen before we start, calling over names, verification or legitimation of passports, as it is called by the Russian consul, et cetera, et cetera; but I will say this, in honour of the "Preussischer Adler's" punctuality, that as the clock strikes noon we cast off from our moorings, and steam away through the narrow Oder. At Swinemunde I see the last of Prussia; henceforth I must be of Russia and Russian.

II.

I AM ABOARD THE PRUSSIAN EAGLE.

The feeling may be one of pure cockneyism, as puerile as when one sees a ship on the sea for the first time, but I cannot help it; I have a pleasure, almost infantine, when I remind myself that I am no longer performing a trite steamboat voyage on the Thames, the Seine, the Rhine, the Scheldt, or the Straits of Dover, but that I am in verity journeying on the bosom of the Baltic; that we have left the coast of Denmark far behind; that that low long strip of land yonder cingling the horizon is the Swedish island of Gothland, and that, by to-morrow at daybreak, we may expect to enter the Gulf of Finland.

Dear reader, if you are, as I hope, a lover of the story-books, would not your heart sing, and your soul be gladdened—would not you clap your hands for joy—ay, at fifty years of age, and in High Change, if you were to be told some fine morning that the story-books had come True, every one of them? That a livery-stable keeper's horse in Barbican had that morning put out the eye of a calender, son of a king, with a whisk of his tail; that Mr. Mitchell, of the Zoological Society, had just received a fine roc per Peninsular and Oriental Company's steamer; that there were excursions every day from the Waterloo station to the Valley of Diamonds; that Mr. Farrance of Spring Garden (supposing that eminent pastrycooking firm to have an individual entity) had been sentenced to death for making cream tarts without pepper, but had been respited on the discovery that he was the long-lost prince Moureddin Hassan; that several giants had been slain in Wales by Lieutenant-general Jack; that the Forty Thieves were to be tried at the next session of the Central Criminal Court; that a genii had issued from the smoke of a saucepan at Mr. Simpson's fish ordinary in Billingsgate; that the Prince of Wales had awakened a beautiful princess, who had been asleep, with all her household, in an enchanted palace in some woods and forests in the Home Park, Windsor; and that a dwarfish gentleman, by the name of Rumpelstiltskin, had lately had an audience of her most gracious Majesty, and boldly demanded the last of the royal babies as a reward for his services in cutting the Koh-i-noor diamond? Who would not forego a Guildhall banquet for the pleasure of a genuine Barmecide feast? who would not take an express train to Wantley, if he could be certain that the real original dragon, who swallowed up the churches, and the cows, and the people, was to be seen alive there? When I was a little lad, the maps were my story-books. The big marble-paper covered atlas, only to be thumbed on high days and holidays, had greater charms for me than even Fox's Martyrs or the Seven Champions. With this atlas and a paunchy volume with a piecrust cover (was it Brookes' or Maunder's Gazetteer?) what romances I wove! what poems I imagined! what castles in the air I built! what household words I made of foreign cities! what subtle knowledge I had of the three Arabias,—Arabia Petra, Arabia Deserta, and Arabia Felix! How I longed for the time when I should be big enough to go to Spain (shall I ever be big enough to make that journey, I wonder?)—what doughty projects I formed against the day when I should be enabled to travel on an elephant in Bengal, and a reindeer in Lapland, and a mule in the Pyrenees, and an ostrich in Kabylia, and a crocodile in Nubia, like Mr. Watertown! But my special story-book was that vast patch on the map of Europe marked Russia. In Europe, quotha! did not Russia stretch far, far into Asia, and farther still into America? I never was satiated with this part of the atlas. There was perpetual winter in Russia, of course. The only means of travelling was on a sledge across the snowy steppes. Packs of wolves invariably followed in pursuit, howling fearfully for prey. The traveller was always provided with a stock of live babies, whom he loved dearer than life itself, but whom he threw out, nevertheless, to the wolves, one by one, at half-mile distance or so. Then he threw out his lovely and attached wife (at her own earnest request, I need not say,) and then the wolves, intent on a third course, leaped into the sledge, and made an end of him. It used to puzzle me considerably as to how the horses escaped being eaten in the commencement, for the sledge always kept going at a tremendous rate; and I was always in a state of ludicrous uncertainty as to the steppes —what they were made of,—wood, or stone, or turf; whether children ever sat on them with babies in their arms; (but the wolves would never have allowed that, surely!) and how many steps there were to a flight. There was attraction enough to me, goodness knows, in the rest of the atlas; in boot-shaped Italy; in Africa, huge and yellow as a pumpkin, and like that esculent, little excavated; in the Red Sea; (why did they always colour it pea-green in the map?) but the vasty Russia with its appurtenances was my great storehouse of romance. The Baltic was a continual wonder to me. How could ships ever get into it when there were the Great and Little Belts, and the Kraken, and the Maelstrom, and the icebergs, and the polar bears to stop the way. Russia (on the map) was one vast and delightful region of mysteries, and adventures, and perilous expeditions; a glorious wonder-land of czars who lived in wooden houses disguised as shipwrights; of Cossacks continually careering on long-maned ponies, and with lances like Maypoles; of grisly bears, sweet-smelling leather, ducks, wolves, palaces of ice, forests, steppes, frozen lakes, caftans, long beards, Kremlins, and Ivan the Terribles. Never mind the knout; never mind the perpetual winter; never mind the passage of the Beresina,—I put Russia down in my juvenile itinerary as a place to be visited, coûte qui coûte, as soon as I was twenty-one. I remember, when I was about half that age, travelling on the top of an omnibus from Mile End to the Bank with a philosophic individual in a red plaid cloak. He told me he had lived ten years in Russia (Rooshia, he pronounced it,) and gave me to understand confidentially that the czar ruled his subjects with a rod of iron. I grieved when he departed, though his conversation was but common-place. I followed him half-way up Cornhill, gazing at the red plaid skirts of his cloak flapping in the breeze, and revering him as one who had had vast and wonderful experiences,—as a Sindbad the Sailor, multiplied by Marco Polo. Oh, for my twenty-first birthday, and my aunt's legacy, and hey for Russia!

The birthday and the legacy came and departed never to return again. I received sentence of imprisonment within three hundred miles of London, accompanied by hard labour for the term of my natural life; and though I was far from forgetting Russia—though a poor Silvio Pellico of a paper-stainer—I still cherished, in a secret corner of my heart, a wild plan of escaping from the Speilberg some day, and travelling to my heart's content. Russia faded by degrees into the complexion of a story-book, to be believed in, furtively, but against reason and against hope. And this dreamy, legendary state of feeling was not a little encouraged by the extraordinary paucity of fact, and the astonishing abundance of fiction to be found in all books I could obtain about Russia. Every traveller seemed to form a conception of the country and people more monstrous and unveracious than his predecessor; and I really think that, but for the war, and the Prisoners at Lewes, and the Times Correspondent, I should have ended by acceding to the persuasion that Russia was none other than the Empire of Cockaigne; and the Emperor Nicholas the legitimate successor of Prester John.

But, now, lo! the story-book has come true! This is real Russian writing on my passport; there are two live Russians playing *écarté* on the poop, and I am steaming merrily through the real Baltic. We may see the Mirage this evening, the chief mate says, hopefully. We may be among the Ice to-morrow, says weather-worn Captain Smith (not Captain Steffens, he is too prudent to allude to such matters, but another captain—a honorary navigator) ominously. Ice, Mirage, and the Gulf of Finland! Are not these better than a cold day in the Strand, or a steamboat collision in the Pool?

We are only thirty passengers for Cronstadt, and the "Preussischer Adler" has ample accommodation for above a hundred. It may not be out of place, however, to remark, that there is an infinitely stronger desire to get out of this favoured empire than to get into it. There have been, even, I am told, some Russians born and bred under the beneficent rule of the autocrat, who, having once escaped from the land of their birth, have been altogether so wanting in patriotic feeling as never to return to it; stedfastly disregarding the invitations—nay, commands—of their government despatches through their chanceries in foreign countries.

In Prussia and Denmark, and in my progress due north, generally, I had observed, when I happened to mention my intention of going to St. Petersburg, a peculiar curiosity to know the purport of my journey thither, quite distinct from official inquisitiveness. My interlocutor would usually ask "whether Monsieur sold?" and when I replied that I did not sell any thing, he would parry the question, and inquire "whether Monsieur bought?" Then on my repudiation of any mercantile calling whatsoever, my questioner would hint that music-masters and tutors were very handsomely paid in Russia. I devoted myself to the instruction, perhaps. No; I did not teach any thing; and, on this, my catechist after apparently satisfying himself from my modest appearance, that I was neither an ambassador nor a secretary of legation, would shrug up his shoulders and give a low whistle, and me a look which might, with extreme facility, be translated into, "*Que diable allez-vous faire dans cette galère?*" I have never been in New England; but, from the gauntlet of questions I had to run in Northern Europe, I believe myself qualified, when my time comes, to bear Connecticut with equanimity, and to confute the questionings of Massachusetts without difficulty.

We are thirty passengers, as I have said, and we

are commanded by Captain Steffens. Captain Steffens is red of face, blue of gills, black and shiny of hair, high of shirt-collar, and an officer of the royal Prussian navy. He will be Admiral Steffens, I doubt not, in the fulness of time, when the Prussian government has built a vessel large enough for him to hoist his flag in. About a quarter of an hour before we started, I had observed the red face and the high shirt-collar popping in and out—with Jack-in-the-box celerity—of a little state-room on the deck. I had previously been dull enough to take the first mate, who stood at the gangway, for the commander of the "Preussischer Adler," and to admire the tasteful variety of his uniform, composed as it was, of a monkey-jacket with gilt buttons, a sky-blue cap with a gold band, fawn-coloured trousers, and a tartan velvet waistcoat of a most distracting liveliness of pattern and colour. But it was only at the last moment that I was undeceived, and was made to confess how obtuse I had been; for then, the state-room door flying wide open, Captain Steffens was manifest with the thirty passengers' passports in one hand, and a tremendous telescope in the other, and arrayed besides in all the glory of a light-blue frock, a white waistcoat, an astonishing pair of epaulettes of gold bullion, ("swabs," I believe, they are termed in nautical parlance,) a shirt-frill extending at right angles from his manly breast, like a fan, and patent-leather boots. But why, Captain Steffens, why, did you suffer a navy cap with a gold-laced band to replace the traditional, the martial, the becoming cocked-hat? For with that telescope, that frill, those epaulettes, that rubicund visage, and that (missing) cocked-hat, Captain Steffens would have looked the very Fetch and counterfeit presentment of the immortal admiral who "came to hear on" the punishment of the faithless William Taylor by the "maiden fair and free," whom he had deserted, and which admiral not only "werry much applauded her for what she had done," but likewise appointed her to the responsible position of first lieutenant "of the gallant Thunderbomb."

But though unprovided with a cocked-hat, Captain Steffens turns out to be a most meritorious commander. He takes off his epaulettes after we have left Swinemunde, and subsides into shoulder-straps; but the long telescope never leaves him, and he seems to have an equal partiality for the thirty passports. He is always conning them over behind funnels, and in dim recesses of the forecastle; and he seems to have a special penchant for perusing mine, and muttering my name over to himself, as if there were something wrong about me, or the famous scrap of paper which has given me so much trouble. I step to him at last, and request to be permitted to enlighten him on any doubtful point he may descry. He assures me that all is right; but he confesses that passports are the bane of his existence. "Those people yonder," he whispers, motioning with his thumb towards where I supposed in the steamer's course is Cronstadt, "are the very deuce with passports, *lieber Herr.*" And he sits on the pile of passports all dinner-time; and, just before I go to bed, I discover him peeping over them with the chief mate, by the light of the binnacle-lamp, and I will be sworn he has got mine again, holding it up to the light.

Confound those passports! It appears to me that the traveller who has his passport most in accordance with the rule and regulation is subject to the most annoyance. At Stettin I had to go to the Russian consul's bureau to procure a certificate of legitimation to my passport before they would give me my ticket at the steam-packet office. The Muscovite functionary looked at my Foreign-Office document with infinite contempt, and informed me that, being an English one, it was by no means valid in Russia. When I explained to him that it had been *visé* by his own ambassador at Berlin, he disappeared with it, still looking very dubious, into an adjoining apartment, which, from sundry hangings and mouldings, and the flounces of a silk dress which I espied through the half-opened door, I conjecture to have been the boudoir of Madame la Consulesse. I suppose he showed the passport to his wife; and, enlightened, doubtless, by her superior judgment, he presently returned radiant, saying that the passport was *parfaitement en règle*, and that it was *charmant.* I can see him now, holding my passport at arm's length, and examining the Russian *visâ* through his eye-glass with an air half critical, half approving, as if it were some natural curiosity improved by cunning workmanship, and murmuring *charmant* meanwhile. He seemed so fond of it that it was quite a difficulty for him to give it me back again. He did so at last, together with the legitimation, which was an illegible scrawl on a scrap of paper like a pawnbroker's duplicate. I think his clerks must have known that my passport was in rule and charming, for they bestowed quite fraternal glances on me as I went out. To have a passport in regular order seems to be the only thing necessary to be thought great and wise and good in these parts; and, when a virtuous man dies, I wonder they don't engrave on his tombstone that he was a tender father, an attached husband, and that his passport was *parfaitement en règle*.

I wish that, instead of being thirty passengers, we were only twenty-nine; or, at all events, I devoutly wish that the thirtieth were any other than Captain Smith. He is a sea-captain; what right has he to be in another man's vessel? Where is his ship? He has no right even to the name of Smith—he ought to be Smit, or Schmidt, for he tells me that he was born at Dantzig; that it is only in the fourth generation that he can claim English descent. Indeed, he speaks English fluently enough, but with the accent of a Hottentot. When Captain Smith was an egg, he must indubitably have been selected by that eminent nautical poultry-fancier, Mother Carey, for chicken-hatching purposes, and a full-feathered bird of ill-omen he has grown up to be. He has had a spite against the "Preussischer Adler" from the outset; and I hear him grumbling to himself or the Baltic Sea—it does not much matter which, for he is always communing with one or the other—somewhat in this fashion: "Den dousand daler! twenty dousand daler! she gostet tinkering up dis time, and she not worth a tam; no, not one tam;" and so on. He has a camp-stool on which he sits over the engine hatchway, casting baleful glances at the cylinders, and grumbling about the number of dalers they have "gostet," and that they are "not worth a tam." I find him examining a courier's bag I have purchased at Berlin, and evidently summing up its value by the curt but expressive phrase I have ventured to quote. I discover him counting, watch in hand, the number of revolutions per minute of the engines, and muttering disparaging remarks to the steward. He takes a vast quantity of solitary drams from a private bottle, openly declaring that the ship's stores are to be measured by his invariable standard of worthlessness. Sometimes, in right of nautical freemasonry, he mounts the paddle-box bridge, and hovers over Captain Steffens (he is very tall) like an Old Man of the Sea, whispering grim counsel into that commander's ear, till Captain Steffens seems very much inclined to charge at him full butt with his long telescope, or to pitch him bodily into the Baltic. He haunts the deck at unholy hours, carrying a long pair of boots lined with sheepskin, which he incites the cook, with drams from his solitary bottle, to grease, and which he suspends, for seasoning, to forbidden ropes and stays. The subject on which he is especially eloquent is a certain ship—"Schibb" he calls it—laden with madapolams, and by him, at some remote period of time, commanded, and which went down off the island of Oësel, or Oosel, or Weasel, in the year eighteen hundred and forty-nine. He brings a tattered chart of his own on deck, (for the ship's charts, he confidentially remarks, are not worth his favourite monosyllable,) and shows me the exact spot where the ill-fated vessel came to grief. "Dere I lose my schibb, year 'vorty-nine," he says. "Dere; just vere my dumb is." (His dumb, or thumb, is a huge excrescence like a leech boiled down, and with a sable hat or nail-band.) "Dere de 'Schön Jungfrau' went down. Hans Schwieber was my mate, and de supercargo was a tam tief." This rider to Falconer's "Shipwreck," and an interminable narrative about a certain Stevedore of the port of Revel, who had the property of getting drunk on linseed-oil, are his two great conversational hobby-horses. It is very easy to see that he predicts a fate similar to that of the "Schön Jungfrau" for the "Preussischer Adler." Prussian sailors, according to him, are good for nothing. He wants to know where Captain Steffens passed his examination; and he denies the possibility of the vessel steering well, seeing that the Baltic is full of magnetic islands, which cause the needle to fly round to all parts of the compass at once. To aggravate his imperfections, he wears a tall hat, grossly sinning against all the rules of nautical etiquette; and he smokes the biggest and rankest of Hamburg cigars, one of which, like an ill-flavoured sausage, smoulders on the bench by his side all dinner-time. He evidently prefers the company of the second-cabin passengers, as a body, to ours; and audibly mutters that the first-class accommodation is not worth—I need not repeat what. Altogether, he is such a baleful, malignant, wet-blanket son of a gun, that I feel myself fast growing mutinous; and his sinister prophecies go on multiplying so rapidly, that I christen him Jonah, and am very much inclined to sign a round-robin, or to head a deputation of the passengers to Captain Steffens, praying that he may be cast into the sea. But where is the fish that would consent to keep such a terrible old bore for three days and nights in its belly?

As, when in a summer afternoon's nap you have been drowsily annoyed, some half-hour durant, by a big blue-bottle, and are suddenly awakened by the sharp agony of a hornet's sting full in the calf of your favourite leg, so, suddenly does the passive annoyance of Captain Smith's evil predictions cede to the active torture of Miss Wapps's persecution. Miss Wapps, English, travelling alone, and aged forty, has taken it into her fair head to entertain a violent dislike to me, and pursues me with quite a ferocity of antipathy. She is a lean and bony spinster, with a curiously blue-bronzed nose, and cheek-bones to match, and a remarkable mole on her chin with a solitary hair growing from it like One-Tree Hill at Greenwich. She has a profusion of little ringlets that twist and twine like the serpents of the Furies that had taken to drinking, and had been metamorphosed, as a punishment, into corkscrews. To see her perambulating the decks after they have been newly swabbed, holding up her drapery, and displaying a pair of baggy—well, I suppose there is no harm in the word—pantalettes, and with a great round flap hat surmounting all, she looks ludicrously like an overgrown school-girl. She is one of those terrible specimens of humanity who have a preconceived persuasion—a woman who has made up her mind about everything—arts, sciences, laws, learning, commerce, religion, Shakspeare, and the musical glasses—and nothing can shake, nothing convince, nothing mollify her. Her conclusions are ordinarily unfavourable. She stayed a few hours at the Drei Kronen at Stettin, where I had the advantage of her society, and she made up her mind at a very early stage of our acquaintance that I was an impostor, because I said I was going to St. Petersburg. "Many persons," she remarked, with intense acerbity, "talk of going to Russia, when they never go further than Gravesend. I am going to St. Petersburg to recover my property devastated by the late unchristian war." As this seemed a double-barrelled insinuation, implying not only my having stated the thing which was not, but also the unlikelihood of my possessing any property to be devastated or recovered, I began to feel sufficiently uncomfortable, and endeavoured to bring about a better state of feeling, by asking Miss Wapps if I might have the pleasure of helping her to some wine. She overwhelmed me at once with a carboy of vitriolic acid: she never took wine—never! And though she said no more, it was very easy to gather from Miss Wapps's tone and looks that in her eyes the person most likely to rob the Bank of England, go over to the Pope of Rome, and assassinate the Emperor of the French, would be the man who did take wine to his dinner. She flatly contradicted me, too, as to the amount of the fare (which I had just paid) from Stettin to Cronstadt. She had made up her mind that it was one hundred and fifty francs French money, and all the arguments in the world could not bring her to recognize the existence of such things as roubles or thalers. But where she was Samsonically strong against me was on the question of my nationality. As I happen to be rather swart of hue, and a tolerable linguist, she took it into her head at once that I was a foreigner, and addressed me as "Mossoo." In vain did I try to convince her that I was born and bred in London, within the sound of Bow-bells. To make the matter worse—it being necessary for me, during one of the endless passport formalities, to answer to my name, which is not very English in sound—it went conclusively to make out a case against me in the mind of Miss Wapps. She called me Mossoo again, but vengefully in sarcastic accents; and complained of the infamy of an honourable English gentlewoman being beset by Jesuits and spies.

On board, Miss Wapps does not abate one atom of her animosity. I have not the fatuity to believe that I am what is usually termed popular with the sex; but as I am, I hope, inoffensive and a good listener, I have been able to retain some desirable female acquaintances; but there is no conciliating Miss Wapps. She is enraged with me for not being sea-sick. She unmistakably gives me to understand that I am a puppy, because I wear the courier's bag slung by a strap over my shoulder; and when I meekly represent to her that it is very useful for carrying lucifer-matches, a comb, change, Bradshaw, cigars, eau-de-Cologne, a brandy-flask, and such small matters, she gives utterance to a peculiar kind of feminine grunt, something between that of an asthmatic pig and an elderly Wesleyan at a moving part of the sermon, but which to me plainly means that she hates me, and that she does not believe a word I say. She wants to know what the world is coming to, when men can puff their filthy tobacco under the noses of ladies accustomed to the best society? and when I plead that the deck is the place for smoking, and that all the other gentlemen passengers are doing as I do, she retorts, "More shame for them!" She alludes to the pretty stewardess by the appellation of "hussey," at which I feel vastly moved to strangle her; and she has an abominable air-cushion with a hole in it, which is always choking up hatchways, or tripping up one's legs, or tumbling over cabin-boys' heads like the Chinese cange. As a culmination of injury, she publicly accuses me at dinner of detaining the mustard designedly and of malice aforethought at my end of the table. I am covered with confusion, and endeavour to excuse myself; but she overpowers me with her voice, and Captain Steffens looks severely at me. I have an inward struggle after dinner, as to whether I shall give her a piece of my mind, and so shut her up for ever, or make her an offer of marriage; but I take a middle course, and subside into the French language, which she cannot speak, and in which, therefore, she cannot contradict me. After this, she makes common cause against me with Captain Smith (why didn't she go down in the "Schön Jungfrau?"); and as they walk the deck together I don't think I am in error in concluding that she is continuing to denounce me as a Jesuit and a spy, and that the captain has imparted to her his opinion that I am "not worth a tam!"

We have another lady passenger in the chief cabin; she is a French lady, and (she makes no disguise at all about the matter) an actress. She is going to Moscow for the coronation, when there are to be grand dramatic doings; but she is coming out thus early to stay with her mamma, also an actress, who has been fifteen years in St. Petersburg. "*Imaginez vous*," she says, "*dans ce trou!*" She is very pretty, very coquettish, very good-natured, very witty, and comically ignorant of the commonest things. Captain Steffens loves her like a father already, I can see. Even the grim Captain Smith regards her with the affection of a Dutch uncle. She dresses every morning for the deck, and every afternoon for dinner, with as much care as though she were still on her beloved Boulevard de Gand. Her hair is always smooth, her eyes always bright, her little foot always *bien chaussée*, her dress always in apple-pie order, her temper always lively, cheerful, amiable. She eats little wings of birds in a delightfully cat-like manner, and chirps, after a glass of champagne, in a manner ravishing to behold. She is all lithe movements, and silver laughter, and roguish sayings. *Enfin:* she is a Parisienne! What need I say more? She has a dozen of the gentlemen passengers at her feet as soon as she boards the "Preussischer Adler," but she bestows her arm for the voyage on Monsieur Alexandre, a fat Frenchman with a beard and a wide-awake hat; who is, I suspect, a traveller for some champagne house at Rheims. He follows her about like a corpulent poodle; he takes care of her baskets, shawls, and furs; he toils up ladders with camp-stools for her; he holds an umbrella over her to shield her from the sun; he cuts the leaves of books for her; he produces for her benefit private stores of chocolate and bon-bons; he sits next to her at dinner, and carves tit-bits for her; he pays for the champagne; he walks the deck with her by moonlight, shielding her from the midnight air with ample pelisses, and rolling his little eyes in his fat face. She is all smiles and amiability to him (as, indeed, to every one else); she allows him to sit at her feet; she gives him to snuff from her vinaigrette; she pats his broad back and calls him "*Mon bon gros;*" she is as familiar with him as if she had known him a quarter of a century; she orders him about like a dog or a black man; but is never cross, never pettish. She will probably give him the tips of her little fingers to kiss when she leaves him at Cronstadt; and, when some day perhaps she meets him by chance on the Nevskoi, she won't know him from Adam.

'Twas ever thus from childhood's hour—I mean, this is always my fate. Somebody else gets the pleasant travelling companions; I get the Miss Wappses. I never fall in love with a pretty girl, but I find she has a sweetheart already, or has been engaged for ten years to her cousin Charles in India, who is coming home by the next ship to marry her. Am I not as good as a wine-merchant's bagman? Never mind; let me console myself with the Russian.

The Russian is a gentleman whose two years' term of travel has expired, and who, not being able to obtain an extension of his leave of absence, and not very desirous of having his estates sequestered, which would be the penalty of disobedience, is returning, distressingly against his own inclination, to Russia, is an individual who looks young enough to be two or three and twenty, and old enough to be two or three and forty. How are you to tell in a gentleman whose hair, without a speck of gray, is always faultlessly brushed, oiled, perfumed, and arranged; whose moustache is lustrous, firm, and black; whose teeth are sound and white; whose face is perfectly smooth, and clear, and clean shaven; who is always perfectly easy, graceful, and self-possessed? The Russian speaks English and French—the first language as you and I, my dear Bob, speak it; the second as our friend, Monsieur Adolphe, from Paris, would speak his native tongue; by which I mean that the Russian speaks English like an Englishman, and French like a Frenchman, without hesitation, accent, or foreign idiom. He is versed in the literature of both countries, and talks of Sam Weller and Jerome Paturot with equal facility. I am, perhaps, not so well qualified to judge of his proficiency in Italian; but he seems to speak that tongue with at least the same degree of fluency as he converses in German, of which, according to Captain Steffens, he is a master. He laughs when I talk about the special and astounding gift that his countrymen seem to possess for the acquisition of languages. "Gift, my dear fellow," he says, "it is nothing of the kind. I certainly picked up Italian in six months, during a residence in the country; but I could speak French, English, and German long before I could speak Russian. *Nous autres gentilhommes Russes*, we have English nurses; we have French and Swiss governesses; we have German professors at college. As children and as adults we often pass days and weeks without hearing a word of Russian; and the language with which we have the slightest acquaintance is our own." The Russian and I soon grow to be great (travelling) friends. He talks, and seems to be well informed, on every body and every thing, and speaks about governments and dynasties in precisely the same tone of easy persiflage in which he discusses the Italian opera and the ballet. He tells me a great deal about the Greek church; but it is easy to see that matters ecclesiastical don't trouble "*nous autres gentilhommes Russes*" much. He has been in the army, like the vast majority of his order, and is learned in horses, dogs, and general sportsmanship; a branch of knowledge that clashes strangely with his *grassailléing* Parisian accent. He proposes *écarté* in an interval of chat; but finding that I am but a poor cardplayer, he shows me a few tricks on the cards sufficient to set a moderately ambitious wizard up in business on the spot, and contentedly relinquishes the pack for the pianoforte, on which he executes such brilliant voluntaries, that I can see the hard-favoured visage of Miss Wapps gazing down at us through the saloon skylight in discontented admiration—that decisive lady marvelling doubtless how such an accomplished Russian can condescend to waste his time and talents on such a trumpery mortal as I am. He shows me an album bound in green velvet, and with his cipher and coronet embroidered in rubies thereupon, and filled with drawings of his own execution. He rolls paper cigarettes with the dexterity of a Castilian caballero; and he has the most varied and exact statistical knowledge on all sorts of topics, political, social, agricultural, and literary, of any man I ever met with. And this is, believe me, as ordinary and every-day-to-be-found specimen of the Russian gentlemen as the unlettered, unlicked, uncouth, untravelled John Smith one meets at a Boulogne boarding-house is of an English esquire. My friend, the Russian, has his little peculiarities; without being in the slightest degree grave or sententious that facile mouth of his is never curved into a genuine smile; those dark-gray eyes of his never look you in the face; he seems never tired of drinking champagne, and never in the least flushed thereby; and finally and above all, I never hear him express an opinion that any human thing is right or wrong. If he have an opinion on any subject, and he converses on almost all topics, it is not on board the "Preussischer Adler," or to me, that he will impart it. With his handsome face and graceful carriage, and varied parts, this is the sort of man whom nine women out of ten would fall desperately in love with at first sight; yet he drops a witty anecdote or so about the sex, that makes me start and say, Heaven help the woman who ever falls in love with him!

It may have struck the reader, that beyond alluding to the bare fact of being on the Baltic, and in a fair way for Cronstadt, I have said little or nothing as yet concerning our actual voyage. In the first place, there is but little marine intelligence to be chronicled; for from Saturday at noon, when we started, to this present Monday evening, we have had uninterrupted fair weather and smooth water; and are gliding along as on a lake. And, in the second place, I generally avoid the subject of the sea as much as I can. I hate it. I have a dread for it, as Mrs. Hemans had. To me it is simply a Monster, cruel, capricious, remorseless, rapacious, insatiable, deceitful; sullenly unwilling to disgorge its treasures; mockingly refusing to give up its dead. But it must, and Shall, some day: the Sea. If any thing could reconcile me, however, to that baseless highway, it would be the days and nights we have had since Saturday. It is never dark, and the moon, beautiful as she is, is almost an intruder, so long does the sun lord it over the heavens, so short are his slumbers, (it is not far from the time and place where he rises at midnight,*) so gloriously strong and fresh does he come up to his work again in the

* At Tornea, in Sweden, on the twenty-first of June.

morning. And the white ships that glide on the tranquil sea, far far away towards the immensity of the horizon, are as auguries of peace and hope to me; and the very smoke from the boat's funnel that was black and choky at Stettin, is now, in the undying sun, all gorgeous in purple and orange as it rolls forth in clouds that wander rudderless through the empty sky, till the sea-birds meet them, and break them into fragments with their sharp-sected wings.

There is a very merry party forward, in the second cabin. Among them is a humorous character from the south of France, who is proceeding to Russia to superintend a sugar manufactory belonging to some Russian seigneur. He has been established by common consent chief wag and joke-master in ordinary to the Prussian Eagle. I hear shouts of laughter from where he holds his merry court long after I am snug in my berth; and the steward retails his latest witticisms to us at dinner, hot and hot, between the courses. He lives at free quarters, for his jests' sakes, in the way of wines, spirits, and cigars; and I don't think the steward can have the heart to take any money of him for fees or extras at the voyage's end. "*Qu'il est gai!*" says the French actress admiringly. As a wag he must, of course, have a butt: and he has fixed on a little, snuffy, old Frenchwoman, with a red cotton pocket-handkerchief tied round her head, who, with a large basket, a larger umbrella, and no other perceptible luggage, started up suddenly at Stettin. She has got a passport with Count Orloff's own signature appended to it, and does not seem to mind the Russians a bit. Who can she be? The Czar's fostermother, perhaps. The funny Frenchman (who never saw her before in his life) now calls her "*maman*," now assumes to be madly in love with her, to the infinite merriment of the other passengers; but she repulses his advances with the utmost good humour, and evidently considers him to be a wag of the first water. Many of this good fellow's jokes are of a slightly practical nature, and would, in phlegmatic English society, probably lead to his being kicked by somebody; but to me they are all amply redeemed by his imperturbable good humour, and his frank, hearty laughter. Besides, he won my heart in the very commencement by making a face behind Miss Wapps's back so supernaturally comic, so irresistibly ludicrous, that Grimaldi, had he known him, would have been jaundiced with envy. The great Captain Steffens favours this jovial blade, and unbends to him, they say, more than he has ever been known to do to mortal second-cabin passenger.

The ill-boding Captain Smith came to my berth last night, with a rattlesnake-like smile, to tell me we were off Hango Head, (a fit place for such a raven to herald,) and to refresh my memory about the ice; and here, sure enough, this Tuesday morning, we are in the very thick of floating masses of the frozen sea! Green, transparent, and assuming every kind of weird and fantastic shapes, they hem the "Preussischer Adler" round, cracking and groaning "like noises in a swound," as the Ancient Mariner heard them. Warm and balmy as the May air was ternight, it is now piercing cold; and I walk the deck a very moving bale of furs, which the courteous Russian has insisted on lending me. We are obliged to move with extreme caution and slowness, stopping altogether from time to time; but the ice gradually lessens, gradually disappears; the shores of the Gulf keep gradually becoming more distinct; and, on the Russian side, I can see white houses and the posts of the telegraph.

About noon on Tuesday, the twentieth of May, turning at the gangway to walk towards the steamer's head, I see a sight that does my eyes good. I have the advantage of being extremely short-sighted, and a view does not grow, but starts upon me. And now, all fresh and blue, and white, and sparkling and dancing in the sunlight, I see a scene that Mr. Stanfield might paint—a grove of masts, domes and steeples, and factory chimneys; a myriad of trim yachts and smaller craft, and, dotting the bright blue water like the Seven Castles of the Devil, with tier above tier of embrasures bristling with cannon, the granite forts of the impregnable Cronstadt. There is a big guard-ship behind us, and forts and guns on every side, and I feel that I am in for it.

"Lads, sharpen your cutlasses," was the signal of the Admiral who didn't breakfast in Cronstadt and dine in St. Petersburg. Let me put a fresh nib to my goosequill, and see what I can do, in my humble way, to make some little impression on those granite walls.

III.

I LAND AT CRONSTADT.

We had no sooner cast anchor in the harbour of Cronstadt, (it needed something to divert my attention, for I had been staring at the forts and their embrasures, especially at one circular one shelving from the top, like a Stilton cheese in tolerably advanced cut, till the whole sky swarmed before me, a vast plain of black dots,) than we were invaded by the Russians. If the naval forces of his imperial majesty Alexander the Second display half as much alacrity in boarding the enemies' ships in the next naval engagement as did this agile boarding-party of policemen and custom-house officers, no British captain need trouble himself to nail his colours to the mast. The best thing he can do is to strike them at once, or put them in his pocket, and so save time and bloodshed. On they came like cats, a most piratical-looking crew to be sure. There were big men with red moustaches, yellow moustaches, drab moustaches, grey moustaches, fawn-coloured moustaches, and white moustaches. Some had thrown themselves into whiskers with all the energy of their nature, and had produced some startling effects in that line. A pair of a light-buff colour, *poudré* with coal-dust (he had probably just concluded an official visit to some neighbouring engine-room,) were much admired. There were men with faces so sun-baked, that their eyes looked considerably lighter than their faces; there were others with visages so white and pasty that their little, black, Chinese eyes looked like currants in a suet-dumpling. And it was now, for the first time, that, with great interest and curiosity, I saw the famous Russian military greatcoat—that hideous *capote* of some coarse frieze of a convict-colour, half-grey, half-drab (the colour of inferior oatmeal, to be particular,) which is destined, I suppose, to occupy as large a place in history as the *redingote* guise of the first Napoleon. These greatcoats—buttoned straight down from the throat to the waist and from thence falling down to the heels in uncouth folds and gathered in behind with a buckle and strap of the same cloth—had red collars and cuffs, the former marked with letters in a fantastic alphabet, that looked as a Greek Lexicon might look after a supper of raw pork chops. The letters were not Greek, not Arabic, not Roman, and yet they had some of the characteristics of each abecedaire. These gentry were police officers; most of them wore a round flat cap with a red band; and if you desire further details, go to the next toyshop and purchase a Noah's ark, and among the male members (say Shem: Ham is too bright-looking) you will find the very counterpart of these Russian *polizeis*. One little creature, apparently about sixty years of age, almost a dwarf, almost hump-backed, and with a face so perforated with pockmarks that, had you permission to empty his skull of its contents, you might have used him for a cullender and strained maccaroni through him—but with a very big sword and a fierce pair of moustaches; this small Muscovite I named Japhet on the spot. He walked and fell (over my portmanteau, I am sorry to say) all in one piece; and, when he saluted his officer (which every one of the privates seemed to do twice in every three minutes,) and which salute consists in a doffing of the cap and a very low bow, he seemed to have a hinge in his spine, but nowhere else. There were men in authority amongst these policemen, mostly athletic, big-whiskered fellows, who looked as if they did the knocking-down part of the police business (shall I ever know better what these large-whiskered men do, I wonder?) These wore helmets with spikes on the top and the Double Eagle, in the brightest tin, in front. They must have been mighty warriors too, some of them; for many were decorated with medals and crosses, not of any very expensive materials, and suspended to ribbons of equivocal hue, owing to the dirt. On the broad breast of one brave I counted nine medals and crosses (I counted them twice, carefully, to be quite certain) strung all of a row on a straight piece of wire; and, with their tawdry scraps of ribbons, looking exceedingly like the particolored rags you see on a dyer's pole. Some had great stripes or galons of coppery-looking lace on their sleeves; and there was one officer who not only wore a helmet, but a green surtout laced with silver, the ornaments of which were inlaid with black dirt and grease in a novel and tasteful manner. The custom-house officers wore unpretending uniforms of shabby green, and copper buttons: and the majority of the subordinates, both *polizeis* and *douaniers*, had foul Belcher handkerchiefs twisted round their necks. There were two other trifling circumstances peculiar to these braves, which, in my quality of an observer, I may be allowed to mention. Number one is, that nearly all these men had no lobes to their ears.* Number two is, that from careful and minute peeping up their sleeves and down their collars, I am in a position to declare my belief that there was not one single shirt among the whole company. About the officer I cannot be so certain. I did not venture to approach near enough to him; but I had four hours' opportunity to examine the privates, (as you will shortly hear,) and what I have stated is the fact. A Hottentot private gentleman is not ordinarily considered to be a model of cleanliness. It is difficult in England to find dirtier subjects for inspection than the tramps in a low lodging-house; but for dirt surpassing ten thousand times anything I have ever yet seen, commend me to our boarding-party. They were, assuredly, the filthiest set of ragamuffins that ever kept step since Lieutenant-Colonel Falstaff's regiment was disbanded.

I am thus particular on a not very inviting subject, because the remarkable contrast between the hideous dirt of the soldiery on ordinary, and their scrupulous cleanliness on extraordinary occasions, is one of

* This is a physical peculiarity I have observed in scores of Russians—some of them in the highest classes of society.

the things that must strike the attention (and at least two of the senses) of every traveller in Russia. On parade, at a review, whenever he is to be inspected, a Russian soldier (and under that generic name I may fairly include policemen and douaniers in a country where even the postmen are military) is literally—outwardly at least—as clean as a new pin. But it would seem that it is only under the eye of his emperor or his general that the Muscovite warrior is expected to be clean; for, on every occasion but those I have named, he is the dirtiest, worst-smelling mortal to be found anywhere between Beachy Head and the Bay of Fundy. I am fearful, too, lest I should be thought exaggerating on the topic of shirts; but it is a fact that the Russians, as a people, do not yet understand the proper use of a linen or cotton under-garment. The moujiks, who wear shirts, are apparently in the same state of doubt as to how to wear them, as the Scottish Highlanders were on the subject of pantaloons after the sumptuary laws of seventeen hundred and forty-six. Poor Alister Macalister carried the breeches which the ruthless Sassenach government had forced on him, on the top of his walking-pole. Ivan Ivanovitch wears his shirt, when he is lucky enough to possess one, outside his trousers, after the manner of a surplice. The soldier thinks that the uniform greatcoat covers a multitude of sins, and wears no shirt at all. According to the accurate Baron de Haxthausen, the kit of every Russian soldier ought to contain three shirts; but theory is one thing, and practice another; and I can state, of my own personal experience, that I have played many games of billiards with Russian officers even, (you can't well avoid seeing up to your opponent's elbow at some stages of the game,) and that if they possessed shirts, they either kept them laid up in lavender at home, or wore them without sleeves.

The unsavoury boarders who had thus made the Preussischer Adler their prize, very speedily let us know that we were in a country where a man may not, by any means, do what he likes with his own. They guarded the gangway, they pervaded the wheel, and not only spoke to the man thereat, but rendered his further presence there quite unnecessary. They placed the funnel under strict surveillance, and they took possession of the whole of the baggage at one fell swoop, attaching to each package curious little leaden seals stuck on bits of string, and inscribed with mysterious hieroglyphs strongly resembling the Rabbinical cachets which the Hebrew butchers in Whitechapel Market append to their joints of meat. Then a tall douanier began wandering among the maze of chests, portmanteaus, and carpet-bags; marking here and there a package in abstruse and abstracted manner with a piece of chalk, as though he were working out mathematical problems. We were not allowed to carry the smallest modicum of luggage on our persons; and—as I had been incautious enough, just before our arrival in harbour, to detach my unlucky courier's bag from my side, and to hold it in my hand,—I was soon unpleasantly reminded of the stringency of the customs' regulations of the port of Cronstadt. The tall douanier pounced upon the harmless leather pouch quite gleefully, and instantaneously declaring (in chalk) on the virgin leather that the angle A. G. was equal to the angle G. B., added it to the heap of luggage which then encumbered the deck. There it lay, with the little French actress's swan-down boa, and I am happy to state, my old enemy—Miss Wapps's perforated air-cushion. But Miss Wapps made the steward the wretchedest man in Russia for about five minutes; so fiercely did she rate him on the sequestration of that chattel of hers.

There was a dead pause, a rather uncomfortable status quo about this time, everybody seemed to be waiting for the performances to begin, and the boarding-party looked, in their stiff, awkward immobility, like a band of "supers" waiting the arrival of the tyrant. Only the little creature who was nearly a hunchback was active; for the mathematical genius had gone to sleep, or was pretending to sleep on a sea-chest, with his head resting in his chalky hands. It seemed to be the province of this diminutive but lynx-eyed functionary to guard against the possibility of any contraband merchandise oozing out of the baggage after it had been sealed; and he went peering, and poking, and turning up bags and boxes with his grimy paws, sniffing sagaciously meanwhile, as if he could discover prohibited books and forged bank notes by scent. Captain Steffens had mysteriously disappeared; and the official with the silver-lace, inlaid with dirt, was nowhere to be found. About this time, also, it occurred to the crew—taking advantage of this forty-bars' rest—to send a deputation aft, consisting of a hairy mariner in a fur-cap, ear-rings, a piebald cow-skin waistcoat, a green shirt, worsted net tights and hessians, to solicit *trink-geld*, or drink-money. On the deputation ushering itself into my presence, with the view above stated, I informed it politely, and in the best German I could muster, that I had already paid an extravagant price for my passage, and that I would see the deputation fried before I gave it a groschen; and soon after this, the stewards, probably infected by some epidemic of extortion hovering in the atmosphere of Russia, began to make out fabulous bills against the passengers for bottles of champagne they had never dreamt of, and cups of coffee they had never consumed. And, as none of us had any Russian money, and every one was anxious to get rid of his Prussian thalers and silbergroschen, the deck was soon converted into an animated money-market, in which some of us lost our temper, and all of us about twenty per cent. on the money we changed.

There was a gentleman on board, of the Hebrew persuasion—a very different gentleman however from my genial friend from Posen, or from the merchant in cat-skins at Stettin—who had brought with him—of of all merchandise in the world!—a consignment of three hundred canary-birds. These little songsters had been built up into quite a castle of cages, open at all four sides; the hatches of the hold had been left open during the voyage; and it was very pretty and pastoral to hear them executing their silvery roulades in the beautiful May evening, and to see the Hebrew gentleman (he wore a white hat, a yellow waistcoat, a drab coat, light-gray trousers and buff slippers, and, with his somewhat jaundiced complexion, looked not unlike a canary-bird himself,) go down the ladder into the hold, to feed his choristers and converse with them in a cheerful and friendly manner. But he was in a pitiable state of tribulation; firstly, because he had learnt that the customs' duties on singing birds in Russia were enormous; and, secondly, because he had been told that Jews were not suffered to enter St. Petersburg.* He turned his coat-collar up, and pulled his hat over his eyes with a desperate effort to make himself look like a Christian; but he only succeeded in travestying, not in disguising, himself; for, whereas, he had looked a frank, open Jew, say, like Judas Maccabæus; he, now, with his cowering and furtive mien, looked unspeakably like Judas Iscariot. He was sorely annoyed, too, at the proceedings of one of the policemen, who, having probably never seen a canary bird before, and imagining it to be a species of wild beast of a diminutive size, was performing the

* I am not aware of the existence of any Oukase positively forbidding Jews to settle at St. Petersburg: but it is certain that there are no Jews in the Russian capital. In other parts of the empire a distinction is made between the Karaïm Jews, who abide by the law of the Old Testament, and the Rabbinical Jews, who hold by the Talmud. The former are tolerated and protected; but the latter are treated with great rigour, and are not permitted to settle in the towns.

feat of stirring it up with a long pole, by means of a tobacco pipe, poked between the wires of one of the cages, and was apparently much surprised that the little canary declined singing under that treatment. But, courage, my Hebrew friend! you have brought your birds to a fine market, even if you have to pay fifty per cent. *ad valorem* duty on them. For, be it known, a canary sells for twenty-five silver roubles in Russia—for nearly four pounds! and, as for a parrot, I have heard of one, and two hundred roubles being given for one, that could speak French.

The wag from the South of France had not been idle all this time. Who but he counterfeited (while he was not looking) the usage and bearing of the little semi-humpbacked policeman, and threw us into convulsions of laughter? Who but he pretended to be dreadfully frightened at the officer in the dirt-inlaid lace, running away from him, after the manner of Mr. Flexmore the clown, when he is told that the policeman is coming? Who but he addressed the very tallest douanier in the exact voice, and with the exact gesture of the immortal Punch (at which we went into fits, of course, and even the adamantine Miss Wapps condescended to smile), pouring forth a flood of gibberish, which he declared to be Russian. The douanier looked very ferocious, and I thought the wag would have been knouted and sent to Siberia; but he got over it somehow, and gave the customs' magnate a cigar, which that brave proceeded, with great gravity and deliberation, to chew, and they were soon the best friends in the world.

I was getting very tired of assuring myself of the shirtlessness of the boarders, whom I had now been inspecting for nearly three quarters of an hour, when Captain Steffens reappeared, this time without the telescope, but with the thirty passports as usual fluttering in the breeze, and a pile of other papers besides. He had mounted his epaulettes again, had Captain Steffens, and a stiffer shirt-collar than ever; and on his breast nearest his heart there shone a gold enamelled cross and a particoloured riband, proclaiming to us awe-stricken passengers and to the world in general, that Captain Steffens was a knight of one of the thousand and one Russian orders. It might have been a Prussian order, you may urge. No, no, my eyes were too sharp for that. Young as I was to Russia, I could tell already a hawk from a handsaw, and the august split crow of the autocrat from the jay-like black eaglet of Prussia. I think Captain Steffens's decoration was the fifteenth class of St. Michael the Moujik. The chief mate was also in full fig; and, though he could boast no decoration, he had a tremendous pin in his shirt, with a crimson bulb a-top like a brandy-ball. And Captain Steffens and his mate were both arrayed in this astounding costume evidently to do honour to and receive with respect two helmeted beings, highly laced, profusely decorated, and positively clean, who now boarded the steamer from a man-o'-war's gig alongside, and were with many bows ushered into the saloon.

Whether he had dropped cherublike from aloft, where he had been looking out for our lives, or risen like Venus from the salt-sea spray, or come with the two helmets in the gig—though I could almost make affidavit that he was not in it when it rowed alongside,—or boarded the Prussian Eagle in his own private wherry, or risen from the hold where he had lain concealed during the voyage, or been then and there incarnated from the atmospheric atoms; whether he came as a spirit but so would not depart, I am utterly incapable of judging; but this is certain, that at the cabin-door there suddenly appeared Mr. Edward Wright, comedian. I say Mr. Wright advisedly; because, although the apparition turned out to be a Russian to the back-bone, thigh-bone, and hip-bone, and though his name was very probably Somethingovitch or Off, he had Mr. Wright's voice, and Mr. Wright's face, together with the teeth, eye-glass, white ducks, and little patent tipped boots of that favourite actor. And he was not only Mr. Wright, but he was Mr. Wright in the character of Paul Pry—minus the costume, certainly, but with the eye-glass and the umbrella to the life. I am not certain whether he wore a white hat, but I know that he carried a little locked portfolio under one arm, that his eyes without the slightest suspicion of a squint were everywhere at once; that he grinned Mr. Wright as Paul Pry's grin incessantly; that he was always hoping he didn't intrude; and that he did intrude most confoundedly.

"Police?" I asked the Russian in a whisper.

My accomplished friend elevated and then depressed his eyebrows in token of acquiescence, and added "Orloff!"

"But Count Orloff is in Paris," I ventured to remark.

"I say Orloff when I speak of *ces gen là*," answered the Russian. "He is of the secret police—Section des Etrangers—counsellor of a college, if you know what that is? Gives capital dinners."

"Do you know him?"

"I know him!" repeated the Russian; and, for the first time during our acquaintance, I saw the expression of something like emotion in his face, and this expressed contemptuous indignation. "My dear sir, we do not know *ces gen là*, *nous autres*."

Mr. Wright was at home immediately. He shook hands with Captain Steffens as if he would have his hand off, clapped the first mate on the shoulder; who, for his part, I grieve to say, looked as if he would like to knock his head off; and addressed a few words in perfect English to the nearest passengers. Then he took the captain's arm quite amicably, and took the locked portfolio and the gleaming teeth (they were not Mr. Carker's teeth, but Mr. Wright's) and himself into the saloon. I was so fascinated at the sight of this smiling banshee, that I should have followed him into the cabin; but the wary *polizeis*, who had already turned everybody out of the saloon in the most summary, and not the most courteous manner, now formed a cordon across the entrance, and left us outside the paradise of the Prussian Eagle, like peris rather than passengers.

Captain Steffens, Mr. Wright, the two superior helmets, the thirty passports and the additional documents—which I conjecture to have been our lives and adventures from the earliest period to the present time, compiled by the Russian consul at Stettin, and the secretary of legation at Berlin, with notes by Captain Steffens, and a glossary by Mr. Wright —were closeted in the saloon from a quarter to one to a quarter to four, P. M., by which time (as the "Preussischer Adler" had fulfilled her contract in bringing us to Cronstadt, and would give us neither bite nor sup more) I was sick with hunger and kinder streaked with rage. What they did in the saloon during this intolerable delay, whether they painted miniatures of us through some concealed spyhole, or played upon the piano, or witnessed a private performance of Bombastes Furioso by Mr. Wright, or went to sleep, no man could tell. The wag from the South of France, who, notwithstanding the rigid surveillance, had managed to creep round to the wheel, came back with a report that the conclave were drinking champagne and smoking cigars. The story was not unlikely; but how was such an incorrigible joker to be believed? For three hours, then, there was nothing to be done but to satisfy myself that the *polizeis* were really shirtless, and to struggle with an insane desire to fly upon my portmanteau and open it, precisely because it was sealed up. The other passengers were moody, and my Russian friend was not nearly so fond of me as he was at sea. For, you must understand, my passport was good to Cronstadt; but once arrived there, there was another process of whitewashing to be gone through; and, to be intimate with a man whose papers might not be in rule, might compromise even *nous autres*.

The port of Cronstadt was very thronged and lively, and I feasted my eyes upon some huge English steamers from Hull and other northern English ports. It did me good to see the Union Jack; but where were the gunboats, Mr. Bull? Ah! where were the gunboats? Failing these, there were plenty of Russian gunboats—black, saucy, trim, diabolical, little crafts enough, which were steaming about as if in search of some stray infernal machine that might have been overlooked since the war-time. Far away through the grove of masts, I could descry the monarchs of the forest, the huge, half-masted hulks of the Russian line-of-battle ships. The stars and stripes of the great American republic were very much to the fore this Tuesday morning; and, as I found afterwards, the American element was what Americans would term almighty strong in Russia. There was nothing to be seen of Cronstadt, the town, but the spires of some churches, some thundering barracks, the dome of the museum, and forts, forts, forts. But Cronstadt the port was very gay with dancing skiffs, and swift men-o'-war boats with their white-clad crews, and little coteries of coquettish yachts. The sky was so bright, the water so blue, the flags so varied, the yachts so rakish and snowy-sailed, that I could have fancied myself for a moment in Kingstown harbour, on my way to Dublin, instead of St. Petersburg, but for the forts, forts, forts.

While I was viewing these things, and cursing

Mr. Wright, (was it for this that he won our hearts at the Adelphi for so many years, inveigling us out of so many half-price shillings, and insidiously concealing the fact of his connection with Count Orloff—now Prince Dolgorouki's secret police?) while I was smoking very nearly the last cigar that I was to smoke in the open air so near St. Petersburg, there had glided alongside and nestled under the shadow of our big paddle-boxes a tiny war-steamer, or pyroscaphe, with a St. Andrew or blue X cross on a white flag at her stern, and another little flag at her fore, compounded of different crosses and colors, and looking curiously like a Union Jack, though it wasn't one by any means. *Nigra fuit sed formosa ;* jet black was her hull, but she was comely-beautiful, a long lithe lizard carved in ebony, with an ivory streak on her back, (that was her deck,) and gliding almost noiselessly over the water. She looked not so much like a steamer as like the toy model of one seen through a powerful opera-glass; and her wheel and compass, and spider-web rigging, and shining brass bolts, and bees'-waxed blocks, would have looked far more in place in the toyman's window in Fleet Street, London, than in this grim Cronstadt. She had her little murder-popguns though—tapering little brass playthings, such as you may see by dozens in a basket, marked eightpence each, in the same toyshop window. This was a Russian-built boat, with Russian engines, engineers, and crew, and she seemed to say to me mockingly: "Ah! we have no war-steamers, haven't we? we are dependent upon England for our machinery, are we? Wait a bit!"

She was, in truth, as crack a piece of naval goods as I—not being a judge—could wish to see. She had a full crew of fine hardy fellows, spotlessly clean, and attired from head to foot in white duck. They were strapping, tawny, moustachioed men; mostly, I was told, Fins. Your true Russian is no sailor; though you may teach him to row, reef, and steer, as you may teach him to dance on the tight-rope. On the paddle-bridge there was an arm-chair, covered with crimson velvet, and in it, with his feet on a footstool, covered with the same material, sat the commander of the steamer. He was puffing a paper cigar; he was moustachioed and whiskered like a life-guardsman; he was epauletted and be-laced; he was crossed and medalled for his services at the siege of Belleisle, doubtless; he had spotless white trousers tightly strapped over his patent-leather boots; but he had not a pair of spurs, though I looked for them attentively; and those who state that such ornaments exist on the heels of Russian naval officers are calumniators. Instead of a sword, he wore a dirk at his side, with a gold and ivory hilt, very tasteful and shipshape; and, at the stern of the vessel there stood, motionless and rigid, a long man, with a drooping moustache like an artist's Sweetener, with a thoroughly Tartar face, and clad in the eternal coarse gray sack, who, they said, was a midshipman. He had a huge hour-glass before him, and two smaller quarter-hour glasses, which he turned with grave composure when the sand had run out.

On the deck of an adjacent lighter I could see,

for the first time, the genuine Russian national cos tume, on a score of stalwart, bearded men, clad in an almost brimless felt hat, (not unlike that patronized by the Connaught bog-trotters,) a sheepskin coat, with the skinny side out and the woolly side in, (Mr. Brian O'Lynn's favourite wear, and which he declared to be mighty convaniant,) baggy breeches, apparently of bedticking, and long, clumsy, thick-soled boots of leather, innocent of blacking, and worn outside the trousers. These poor devils had been lading a dutch galliot, and it being dinner-hour, I suppose had knocked off work, and were lying dead asleep in all sorts of wonderful positions. Prone to the deck on the stomach, with the hands and legs stretched out like so many turtle, seemed to be the favourite posture for repose. But one gentleman, lying on his back, presented himself to my view in a most marvellous state of foreshortening—leaving nothing visible to me but the soles of his boots, the convexity of his stomach, and the tip of his nose. By and by their time for turning to again came; and, when I saw the mate or foreman—or whatever else he was—of the gang, step among them with a long twisted ratan, like that of the jailer in the Bridewell scene of the Harlot's Progress, and remind them that it was time to go to work, by the gentle means of striking, kicking, and all but jumping on them, I received my first lesson, that I was in a country where flesh and blood are cheaper—much cheaper—than gentle Thomas Hood ever wotted of.

We had been in our floating prison with the

chance of being drowned, three hours in addition to the seventy-three we had consumed in coming from Stettin, when the door of the saloon was flung wide open, and a *polizei*, seemingly seized with insanity, began frantically vociferating "*Voyageur passport! Passport voyageur!*" at the very top of his voice; which cries he continued without intermission till he either ran down, like a clock, or was threatened by a discreet and scandalized corporal with the disciplinary application of the stick if he did not desist. Poor fellow! this was, very likely, all the French he knew, and he was proud of it! Taking this as a gentle hint that we were to enter the saloon for passport purposes, we all poured into that apartment *pêle mêle* like your honourable house to the bar of the Lords. And here we found several empty bottles and a strong smell of cigar-smoke, which rather bore out the wag's story of the champagne and cigars; and, sitting at a table, Mr. Wright, more toothy than ever, the captain, the helmets, and somebody else we little expected to see.

There were only twenty-nine passengers standing round the table. Do you understand now? The thirtieth passenger was one of the lot—one of *ces gens-là*—one of Count Orloff's merry men. So, at least, I conjecture, for he was the somebody else at the table, and he asked me, with all the coolness in the world—when my turn came, and as if he had never seen me before in his life—what my object in coming to Russia might be? I told him that I voyaged *pour mon plaisir*, at which reply he seemed but moderately satisfied, and made a neat note of it on a sprawling sheet of paper. I had noticed that he had been very taciturn, and, as I thought, deaf, during our passage—a white-faced hound!—but that he took to his victuals and drink very kindly; and this was his object for coming to Russia. Of course, a Russian government *employê* may travel for his pleasure, like other folks; especially on a probable salary of about forty pounds a year; and this pale functionary may have been returning from the baths of Spa or Wildbad; but it was very suspicious. I wonder how much he paid for his passage!

We did not get our passports back yet—oh no! but each traveller received a card on which was a big seal, in very coarse red wax, bearing the impress of the everlasting double eagle, and this was our passport from Cronstadt to Petersburg town. Very speedily and gladly we bade a long, long farewell to the "Preussischer Adler" and Captain Steffens; and, giving up our sealing-wax passports, stepped on board the pyroscaphe. She had her name in gilt capitals on her paddle-boxes; but I could not spell Russian then, and so remained ignorant on that subject. I ought not to omit stating that Mr. Wright—after telling us in a jaunty manner, that it was beautiful weather, beautiful weather, and that we had had a charming passage—disappeared. He did not remain in the saloon, and he did not come with us. Perhaps he returned aloft to resume his cherub duties, or floated away, or melted away, or sank away. At all events, he went right away somewhere, and I saw him no more.

During the three hours the pyroscaphe had been

lying alongside the "Preussischer Adler," there had been a long plank, neatly carpeted, sloping from the gangway of one vessel to that of the other. The sight of this plank, all ready for walking upon, and yet tabooed to mortal footsteps, had tantalized and riled us not a little. On the bulwark of the Adler there had been laid, at right angles to it but also sloping downwards, a long, heavyish beam of wood painted in alternate black and white streaks, which was to serve as a hand-rail for the ladies when they made the *descensus Averni.* The opposite extremity of this beam was held by a Russian man-of-war's man on the pyroscaphe's deck; a thick-set, mustachioed lout in white-duck cap, frock, and trousers. He held the beam in one hand, and supported his elbow with the other; and there and thus I declare he held it during three mortal hours. It would have been about as easy for him to stand on one leg during that period. I lost sight of him occasionally, as I paced to and fro on the deck; but, when I returned, he was always in the same position—stiff, motionless, impassible, with the beam in his right hand and his elbow in his left. I do not know what amount of stick would have fallen to this poor fellow's share if he had flinched or stumbled; but, when I tried to picture to myself an English, a French, or an American sailor in a similar position, I could not help admitting that Russia is a country where discipline is understood, not only in theory, but in practice.

The interior of the pyroscaphe did not belie her exterior. She was appointed throughout like an English nobleman's yacht. There was a tiny saloon with rosewood fixings, distemper paintings in gilt frames, damask hangings, held up by ormolu Cupids, and mirrors galore for the fair ladies to admire themselves in. The little French actress immediately converted one of them into the prettiest picture frame you would desire to see in or out of Russia; and, leaving Miss Wapps to inspect her blue-bronzed nose in another, I went on deck, where there were benches on bronzed legs and covered with crimson velvet, and camp-stools with seats worked in Berlin wool. I have been told that the officers of the Russian navy have a pretty talent in that *genre* of needlework. My Russian friend—who by this time had utterly forgotten (so it seemed) my existence—had found a friend of his in the person of the commander of the steamer, and the pair had retired to that officer's private cabin to drink champagne. Always champagne. I noticed that when they recognized each other at first, it was (oddly enough) in the French language that their salutations were interchanged.

We were yet in the Gulf of Finland, and the canal of the Neva was still far off, when Captain Smith—who, it will be remembered, had gone over to the enemy, or Wapps faction—came over to me with overtures of peace. He had somehow managed to save those boots of his out of the general confiscation wreck, and carried them now like buckets. He had his reasons for an armistice, the captain; for he remarked that we might be of great service to one another in the Custom-house. "You help me, and I'll help you," said Captain Smith.

This was all very fair and liberal, and on the live and let live principle, which I heartily admire; but, when the captain proffered a suggestion that I should help him by carrying the abhorred boots with the sheepskin linings, and proceeded to yoke me with them, milkman fashion, I resisted, and told him, like Gregory, that I'd not carry coals—nay, nor boots either. On this he went on another tack: and, conveying me to a secret place under the companion ladder, earnestly entreated me to conceal, on his behalf, underneath my waistcoat, a roll of very sleezy sky-blue merino, which he assured me was for a dress for his little daughter Gretchen, and which he had hitherto concealed in the mysterious boots. I must say that the sky-blue merino did not look very valuable: I don't think, in fact, that it was worth much more than a "tam;" and I did not relish the idea of becoming an amateur smuggler on other merchant's account. But what was I to do? The captain was a bore, but the father had a claim to my services. It was pleasant, besides, to think that the captain had a daughter at all—a bright-eyed little maid, with soft brown hair, perhaps; and I pictured her to myself in the sky-blue merino, sitting on the captain's knee, while that giant mariner told her stories of his voyages on the salt seas, and forbore in love from saying anything about the perilous ice and the magnetic islands; nay, glossed over his shipwreck off the Isle of Weasel, and made out the supercargo to be an angel of light rather than a "tam tief." So I smuggled Captain Smith's sky-blue merino through the Custom-house for him;

and if I had no sorer sin than that on my conscience I should go to bed with a light heart to-night.

In gratitude for this concession the captain prc posed a drink, to which I nothing loth—for I wa quite faint with the heat and delay—consented. Th refreshment-room was a little mahogany box below, with a cut-glass chandelier hanging from the ceiling, about half-a-dozen sizes too large for the apartment. There was a bar covered with marble, and a grave waiter in black, with a white neckcloth and white gloves: a waiter who looked as if, for private or political reasons, he was content to hand round schnapps, but that he could be an ambassador if he chose. There was a bar-keeper, whose stock of French was restricted to these three words, *Eau-de-vie*, *Moossoo*, and *Rouble-argent.* He made liberal use of these; and I remarked that, although it was such a handsome pyroscaphe with a chandelier and camp stools worked in Berlin wool, the bar-keeper took very good care to have the rouble-argent in his hand, before he delivered the Eau-de-vie to a Moossoo. Paying beforehand is the rule in Russia, and this is why the Russians are such bad paymasters. The little mahogany box is crammed with passengers, talking, laughing, and shaking hands with each other in pure good-nature, as men will do when they come to the end of a tedious journey. The wag from the south of France was in immense force, and incessantly ejaculated "Vodki! Vodki!" capering about with a glass of that liquor in his hand, and drinking and hobnobbing with everybody.

I tried a glass of vodki,* and immediately understood what genuine blue rain was. For this Vodki was bright blue, and it tasted—ugh! of what did it not taste? Bilge-water, vitriol, turpentine, copal-varnish, fire, and castor-oil! There was champagne, and there was Lafitte, too, to be had, Cognac, brantewein, schnapps, aniseed (of which the Russians are immoderately fond), and an infinity of butter-brods spread with caviare—no more, no more of that!—dried belouga, smoked salmon, cold veal, bacon, sardines, and tongue. I don't know the exact figures of the tariff of prices; but I know that there was never any change out of a silver rouble.

In this convivial little den, Captain Smith in his turn found a friend. This was no other than Petersen; and nothing would serve Captain Smith, but that I must be introduced to Petersen. "De agent vor de gompany that used do go do Helsingfors," he whispered. What company, and what the deuce had I to do with the gompany, or with Petersen? However, there was no help for it, and I was introduced. Petersen, daguerreotyped, would have passed very well for the likeness of Mr. Nobody; for his large head was joined to his long legs, with no perceptible torso, and with only a very narrow interval or belt of red plush waistcoat between. He had the face of a fox who was determined to be clean shaved or to die; and, indeed, there was not a hair left on his face, but he had gashed himself ter-

* Or Vodka, both terminations seem to be used indifferently.

ribly in the operation, and his copper skin was laced with his red oxide of lead blood. He had a hat so huge and so furry in nap, that he looked with it on like the Lord Mayor's sword-bearer, and he may indeed, have been the mysterious Sword-bearer's young man, of whom we heard so much during the sittings of the City Corporation Commission. When I was introduced to him as "Mister aus England," (which was all Captain Smith knew of my name), he opened his wide mouth, and stared at me with his fishy spherical eyes with such intensity, that I fancied that the sockets were popguns, and that he meant to shoot the aqueous globes against me. The open mouth, I think, really meant something, signifying that Petersen was hungry, and desired meat; for the Captain immediately afterwards whispered to me that we had better offer Petersen a beefsteak. Why any breakfast of mine should be offered to Petersen I know no more than why the celebrated Oozly bird should hide his head in the sand, and whistle through the nape of his neck; but I was stupefied, dazed with the vodki and the chandelier, the confusion of tongues, and Petersen's eyes and hat, and I nodded dully in consent. A beefsteak in Russia means meat and potatoes, and bread, cheese, a bottle of Moscow beer, and any pretty little tiny kickshaws in the way of pastry that may strike William Cook. Petersen, who had accepted the offer by lifting the sword-bearer's hat, began snapping up the food like a kingfisher; and as regards the payment, that we (Captain Smith being busily engaged somewhere else with his boots) turned out to be me, and amounted to a silver rouble. Three and threepence for Petersen! He was to give me some valuable information about hotels, and so forth, Petersen; but his mouth was too full for him to speak. He changed some money for me, however, and gave me, for my remaining thalers, a greasy Russian rouble note, and some battered copecks. I am inclined to think that Petersen benefited by this transaction considerably.

All at once there was a cry from the passengers above, of "Isaacs! Isaacs!" and, leaving Petersen still wolfing my beefsteak, I hastened on deck. We had entered long since the canal of the broad, shallow, false, shining, silvery Neva, in which the only navigable channel was marked out by flags. We had left on our right hand the palaces of Oranienbaum and Petergoff, and now we saw right ahead, flashing in the sun like the orb of a king, the burnished dome of the great cathedral of St. Izak. Then the vast workshops and ship-building yards of Mr. Baird; then immense tallow warehouses, (looking like forts again,) and then, starting up on every side, not by twos or threes, but by scores, and starting up as if by magic, the golden spires and domes of Petersburg!

I say starting up: it is the only word. Some half-dozen years ago I was silly enough to go up in a balloon, which, bursting at the altitude of a mile, sent its passengers down again. We fell over Fulham; and I shall never forget the agonizing distinctness with which houses, chimneys, churches seemed rushing up to us instead of we coming down to them. I specially remember Fulham church steeple, on which I expected every moment to be transfixed. Now, though the plane was horizontal, not vertical, the effect was exactly similar; and, as if from the bosom of the Neva, the churches and palaces started up.

We went, straight as an arrow from a Tartar's bow, into the very heart of the city. No suburbs, no streets gradually growing upon you, no buildings gradually increasing in density. We were there; alongside the English quay, in sight of the Custom-house and Exchange, within a stone's throw of the Winter Palace, hard by the colossal statue of Peter the Great, nearly opposite the senate and the Saint Synode, close to the ministry of war, within view of the Admiralty, and under the guns of the fortress, before you could say Jack Robinson.

The English quay? Could this be Russia? Palaces, villas, Corinthian columns, elegantly-dressed ladies with parasols and lapdogs, and children gazing at us from the quay, handsome equipages, curvetting cavaliers, and the notes of a military band floating on the air. Yes: this was Russia; and England was fifteen hundred real, and fifteen thousand moral, miles off.

The handsome granite quays and elegantly-dressed ladies were not for us to walk on or with just yet. A double line of police sentries extended from a little pavilion in which we landed to a low white-washed archway on the other side of the quay, from which a flight of stone steps led apparently into a range of cellars. Walking, tired and dusty, through this lane of stern policemen (Liberty and the ladies peeping at us over the shoulders of the *polizeis*,) I could not resist an odd feeling that I had come in the van from the house of detention at Cronstadt to the county gaol at Petersburg, and that I was down for three months, with hard labour; the last week solitary. Curiously enough, at balls, soirées, and suppers, at St. Petersburg, at Moscow, in town and country, I could never divest myself of that county-gaol feeling till I got my discharge at Cronstadt again, three months afterwards.

IV.

I PASS THE CUSTOM-HOUSE, AND TAKE MY FIRST RUSSIAN WALK.

SCHINDERHANNES, the renowned robber of the Rhine, once encountered, so the story goes, in a foraging expedition between Mayence and Frankfort, a caravan of a hundred and fifty Jews. It was a bitter January night: snow twelve inches deep on the ground, and Schinderhannes didn't like Jews. And so, in this manner, did he evilly entreat them. He did not slay them, nor skin them, nor extract their teeth, as did King John; but he compelled every man Moses of them to take off his boots or shoes. These he mixed, pell-mell, into a leathern salad, or boot-heap, and at daybreak, but not before, he permitted the poor frost-bitten rogues to find their *chaussures*, if they could. Setting aside the superhuman difficulty of picking out one's own particular boots among three hundred foot coverings, the subtle Schinderhannes had reckoned, with fiendish ingenuity, on the natural acquisitiveness of the Jewish race. Of course every Hebrew instinctively sought for the boots with the best soles and upper-leathers, and stoutly claimed them as his own; men who had never possessed any thing better than a pair of squashy pumps, down at heel, and bulging at the sides, vehemently declared themselves the rightful owners of brave jack-boots with triple rows of nails; and the real proprietors, showing themselves recalcitrant at this new application of the law of *meum* and *tuum*, the consequence was a frightful uproar and contention:—such a fighting and squabbling, such a shrieking and swearing in bad Hebrew and worse German, such a rending of gabardines and tearing of beards, and clawing of hooked noses, had never been in Jewry, since the days of Korah, Dathan, and Abiram. A friend of mine told me that he once saw the same experiment tried in a Parisian violon, or lock-up house, after a *bal masqué*. The incarcerated postilions du Longjumeau, titis, debardeurs, Robinson Crusoes, and forts de la halle becoming uproarious and kicking at the iron-stanchioned door, the sergents de ville entered the cell, and unbooted every living prisoner. And such a scene there was in the morning in the yard of the poste, before the masqueraders went to pay their respects to the Commissary of Police, that Monsieur Gavarni might describe it with his pencil, but not I, surely, with my pen!

I have related this little apologue to illustrate the characteristic, but unpleasant, proceedings of the Russian custom-house officers, when we had given up our keys, in one of the white-washed cellars on the basement of a building on the INGLISKAIA NABEREJENAIA, or English Quay, and when those officials proceeded to the examination of our luggage. Either they had read Mr. Leitch Ritchie's Life of Schinderhannes, or they had an intuitive perception of the *modus agendi* of the Robbers of the Rhine, or they had some masonic sympathy with the Parisian police agents; for such a turning up of boxes and turning out of their contents, and mixture of their severalties, pell-mell, higgledy-piggledy, helter-skelter, jerry-cum-tumble, butter upon bacon, topsy-turvy, muck, mess, and muddle, I never saw in my life. There was a villanous douanier, who held a bandbox under one arm, and seemed desirous of emulating the popular hattrick of Herr Döbler; for he kept up a continual cascade of gloves, collars, eau-de-Cologne bottles, combs, hair-brushes, guide-books, pincushions, and lace cuffs, till I turned to look for the accomplice who was supplying him with fresh bandboxes. Now, the custom-house officers of every nation I have yet travelled through, have a different manner of examining your luggage. Your crusty, phlegmatic Englishman turns over each article separately but carefully. Your stupid Belgian rummages your trunk, as if he were trying to catch a lizard; your courteous Frenchman either lightly and gracefully turns up your fine linen, as though he were making a lobster salad, or—much more frequently—if you tell him you have nothing to declare, and are polite to him, just peeps into one corner of your portmanteau, and says, *C'est assez!* Your sententious German ponders deeply over your trunk, pokes his fat forefinger into the bosom of your dress-shirts, and motions you to shut it again. But none of these peculiarities had the Russians. They had a way of their own. They twisted, they tousted, they turned over, they held writing-cases open, bottom upwards, and shook out the manuscript contents, like snow-flakes. They held up coats and shirts, and examined them like pawnbrokers. They fingered ladies' dresses like Jew clothesmen. They punched hats, and looked into their linings; passed Cashmere shawls from one to the other for inspection; opened letters, and tried to read their contents, (upside down,) drew silk stockings over their arms; held boots by the toes, and shook them; opened bottles, and closed them again with the wrong corks; left the impress of their dirty hands upon clean linen, and virgin writing-papers; crammed ladies' under-garments into gentlemen's carpet-bags, forced a boot-jack into the little French actress's reticule, dropped things under foot, trod on them, tore them, and laughed, spilt eau-de-Cologne, greased silk with pomatum, forced hinges, sprained locks, ruined springs, broke cigars, rumpled muslin, and raised a cloud of puff-powder and dentrifice.

And all this was done, perhaps not wantonly, perhaps only in ignorant savagery; but, with such a reckless want of the commonest care; with such a hideous vicarme of shouting, screaming, trampling, and plunging, that the only light I could view the scene in—besides the Schinderhannes one—was in the improbable event of Mr. and Mrs. KEELEY travelling through the country of the Patagonians, falling into a gigantic ambuscade, and having their theatrical wardrobe overhauled by those overgrown savages.

Yet I was given to understand that the search was by no means so strict as it had habitually been in former years. Special instructions had even been issued by the government, that travellers were to be subjected to as little annoyance and delay in passing through the custom-house as were possible. That some rigour of scrutiny is necessary, and must be expected, I am not going, for one moment, to deny: the great object of the search being to discover books prohibited by the censure, and Russian bank-notes —genuine or forged (for the importation or exportation of even good notes is illegal, and severely punished.) Touching the books, the Russian government is wise. *Il est dans son droit.* One volume of Mr. CARLYLE would do more harm to the existing state of things than millions of spurious paper roubles. Not but what the most jealous watchfulness is justifiable in the detection of forged notes, and the prevention of the real ones leaving the country, as models for forgery. The paper currency is enormous; there is nothing very peculiar about the paper of the note, and, though its chalcography is sufficiently complicated, and the dreadful pains and penalties denounced against the forgers, and the holders of forged notes, are repeated no less than three times in successively diminishing Russian characters on the back; the last repetition being literally microscopic; it is all plain sailing in printing and engraving, and there are few clever English or French engravers, who would have any difficulty in producing an exact copy of the "*Gossudaria Kredit Billiet*" of all the Russias. I have been told by government *employés*, and bankers' clerks, that they can detect a bad bank-note immediately and by the mere sense of touch; but I apprehend that the chief test of genuineness is in the state into which every note passes after it has been for any time in circulation; intolerable greasiness and raggedness. The mass of the people are so grossly ignorant, that the note might as well be printed in Sanscrit as in Russ for them: they cannot even decipher the figures, and it is only by the colour of the note that an Ischvostchik or a Moujik is able to tell you its value.

Among the hecatomb of luggage that had been brought from the deck of the pyroscaph into this cave of Trophonius, I had looked for some time vainly, for any thing belonging to me, one glimpse indeed I caught of my courier's bag, skimmering through the air like a bird, and then all resolved itself into anarchy, the confusion of tongues, and the worse confusion of wearing apparel again. My keys were of not much service, therefore, to the officer in charge of them; and it was of no use addressing myself to any of the douaniers or porters, for none of them spoke any thing but Russ. At length I caught sight of a certain big black trunk of mine groaning (to use a little freedom of illustration) under a pile of long narrow packing-cases (so long that they must have contained young trees, or stuffed giraffes,) addressed to his excellency and highness, &c., Prince Gortchakoff; and, being plastered all over with double eagle brands and seals, were, I suppose, inviolable to custom-house fingers. I pointed to the big black trunk; I looked steadily at the custodian of my keys, and I slipped Petersen's paper rouble (crumpled up very small) into his hand. The pink lid of his little gray eye trembled with the first wink I had seen in Russia; and, in another twinkling of that eye, my trunk was dragged from its captivity, and ready for examination. But there is a vicious key to that trunk which refuses to act till it has been shaken, punched, violently wrenched, and abusively spoken to; and while the officer, having exhausted the first, was applying the last mode of persuasion (in Russ) I availed myself of the opportunity to chink some of the serviceable Petersen's copeck pieces in my closed hand. The key having listened to reason, my friend, with whom I was now quite on conversational terms, made a great show of examining my trunk: that is to say, he dived into it (so to speak) head foremost, and came up to the surface with a false collar in his teeth; but it was all cry and no wool, and I might have had a complete democratic and socialist library and half a million in spurious paper money for aught he knew or cared. Then I gave him some more copecks, and said something to him in English, which I think he didn't understand; to which he responded with something in Russ, which I am perfectly certain I didn't understand; and then he chalked my box, and let me go free—to be taken into custody, however, immediately afterwards. He even recovered my courier's bag for me, which an irate douanier had converted into a weapon of offence, swinging it by a strap in the manner of the Protestant Flail to keep off over-impatient travellers. Such an olla podrida as there was inside that courier's bag, when I came to examine it next morning!

I need scarcely say that I had no Russian paper money with me, either in my luggage or on my person; and I must admit, to the honour of the Russian custom-house, that we were exempted from the irritating and degrading ceremony of a personal search. That system is, I believe, by this time, generally exploded on the continent—flourishing only in a rank and weedy manner in the half-contemptible, half-loathsome Dogane of Austrian Italy, and (now and then, when the officials are out of temper) at the highly important seaport of Dieppe in France. As for books, I had brought with me only a New Testament, a Shakspeare, and a Johnson's Dictionary. The first volume incurs no danger of confiscation in Russia. The Russians, to every creed and sect save Roman Catholicism and that branch of Judaism to which I have previously alluded, are as contemptuously tolerant as Mahometans. Russian translations of the Protestant version of the Bible are common; the volumes of the British and Foreign Bible Society are plentiful in St. Petersburg, and Russians of the better class are by no means reluctant to attend the worship of the Anglican Church, both in Moscow and Petersburg. But it is for the Romish communion that the Russians have the bitterest hatred, and for which all the energy of their persecution is reserved. Tolerated to some extent in the two capitals—as, where there are so many foreigners, it must necessarily be—it is uniformly regarded with distrust and abhorrence by the Greek Church; and I do believe that, in a stress of churches, an orthodox Russian would infinitely prefer performing his devotions before a pot-bellied fetish from Ashantee, than before the jewelled shrine of our Lady of Loretto.

I think, on the whole, I passed through the custom-house ordeal rather easily than otherwise. Far different was it with Miss Wapps, who, during the process of search, was a flesh sculptured monument of Giantess Despair, dovetailed with the three Furies blended into one. This uncomfortable woman had in her trunk—for what purpose it is impossible to surmise—the working model of a power-loom, or a steam-plough, or a threshing-machine, or something else equally mechanical and inconvenient; and the custom-house officer, who evidently didn't know what to make of it, had caught his finger in a cogged wheel, had broken one of his nails, and was storming in a towering rage at Miss Wapps, in Russ; while she, in a rage quite overpowering his in volume, was objurgating him in English, till a superior official charged at Miss Wapps, Cossack fashion, with a long pen, and conveyed her, clamouring, away.

Sundry red-bearded men, in crimson shirts and long white aprons, and with bare muscular arms, which would have been the making of them as artists' models in England, had been wrestling with each other and with me, both mentally and physically, for the honour of conveying my luggage to a droschky. But much more had to be done before I could be allowed to depart. All the passengers had to enter an appearance before a fat old gentleman in green, and bright buttons, who sat in a high desk, like a pulpit, while a lean, long man, his subordinate, sat at another desk below him, like the parson's clerk. This fat old gentleman, who spoke English, French, and German wheezily but fluently, was good enough to ask me a few questions I had heard before: as my age, my profession, whether I had ever been in Russia before, and what might be my object in coming to Russia now? He entered my answers in a vast leger, and then, to my great joy, delivered to me my beloved Foreign-office document, with the advice to get myself immatriculated without delay. Then I paid more copecks to a dirty soldier sitting at a table, who made "Muscovite, his mark," on my passport—for I do not believe he could write; then more copecks again to another policeman, who pasted something like a small pitch-plaster on my trunk; and then I struggled into a court-yard, where there was a crowd of droschkies; and, securing with immense difficulty two of these vehicles—one for myself and one for my luggage—was driven to the hotel where I had concluded to stop.

You have seen, in one of the panoramas that infest our lecture-halls, after painted miles of river, or desert, or mountain have been unrolled, to the tinkling of Madame Somebody on the piano, the canvas suddenly display the presentiment of a cheerful village, or a caravan of pilgrims, or an encampment of travellers, smoking and drinking under the green trees; then the animated picture is rolled away into limbo again, and the miles of mountain, or river, or desert, begin again.

So passed away the unsubstantial alliance of us thirty living travellers. We had walked, and talked, and eaten, and drunk together, and liked and disliked each other for three days and nights; and now we parted in the droschky-crowded yard, never to meet again. To revisit the same cities, perhaps inhabit the same streets, the same houses, to walk on the same side of the pavement, even to remember each other often, but to meet again no more. So will it be, perchance, with Greater things in the beginning of the End; and life-long alliances and friendships which we vainly call lasting, be reckoned merely as casual travelling companionships—made and broken in a moment in the long voyage that will last eternal years.

I am incorrigible. If you want a man to explore the interior of Australia, or to discover the North-west Passage, or the sources of the Niger, don't send me. I should come back with a sketch of Victoria Street, Sydney, or the journal of a residence in Cape Coast Castle, or notes of the peculiarities of the skipper of a Hull whaler. If ever I write a biography it will be the life of John Smith; and the great historical work which is to gild, I hope, the evening of my days, will be a Defence of Queen Elizabeth from the scandal unwarrantably cast upon her, or an Account of the death of Queen Anne. Lo! I have spent a summer in Russia; and I have nothing to tell you of the Altai mountains, the Kirghese tribes, Chinese Tartary, the Steppes, Kamschatka, or even the Czar's coronation. [I fled the country a fortnight before it took place.] I have learnt but two Russian cities, [it is true I know my lesson by heart,] St. Petersburg and Moscow; and my first-fruit of Petersburg is that withered apple the Nevskoï-Perspective. You know all about it already, of course. I can't help it.

In Brussels my first visit is always to the Manneken. On arriving in Paris I always hasten, as fast as my legs can carry me, to the Palais Royal; I think I have left a duty unaccomplished in London when I come to it after a long absence, if I delay an hour in walking down the central avenue of Covent Garden Market. These are *cari luoghi* to me, and to them I must go. I have not been twenty minutes established in Petersburg, before I feel that I am due on the Nevskoï; that the houses are waiting for me there; that the Nevskoïans are walking up and down, impatient for me to come and contemplate them. I make a mental apology for keeping the Nevskoï waiting, in order to indulge in a warm bath; after which I feel as if I had divested myself of about one of the twelve layers of dust that seem to have been accumulating on my epidermis since I left London. Then I reflect myself inwardly with my first Russian dinner; and, then, magnanimously disdaining the aid of a *valet de place*, or even of a droschky-driver; quite ignorant of Russ, and not knowing my right hand from my left in the way of Russian streets, I set boldly forth to find out the Nevskoï.

It is about seven in the evening. I walk, say three quarters of a mile, down the big street in which my hotel is situated. Then I find myself in a huge triangular place, of which the quays of the Neva form one side, with an obelisk in the midst. I touch my hat to a bearded man in big boots, and say "Nevskoï?" inquiringly. He takes off his hat, smiles, shows his teeth, makes a low bow, and speaks about a page of small pica in rapid Russ. I shake my head, say No bono, Johnny, (the only imbecile answer I can call up after the torrent of the unknown tongue,) and point to the right and to the left alternately, and with inquiring eyebrows. The bearded man points to the right—far away to the right, which I conjecture must be the other side of the river. "Na Prava," I think he says. I discover afterwards, that Na Pravo (the *o* pronounced as a French *a*) does mean to the right. To the right about I go, confidently.

I cross a handsome bridge of stone and wrought iron, on which stands a chapel, before whose shrine crowds of people of all classes are standing or kneeling, praying, and crossing themselves devoutly. When I am on the other side of the bridge, and standing in a locality I have already been introduced to—the English quay—I accost another man, also in beard and boots, and repeat my monosyllabic inquiry: Nevskoï. It ends, after a great deal more of the unknown tongue, by his pointing to the left. And to the left again I go, as bold as brass.

I pursue the line of the quay for perhaps half a mile, then, bearing to the left, I find myself in another place so vast, that I begin to pitch and roll morally like a crazy bark on this huge stone ocean. It is vast, solitary, with a frowning palace-bound coast, and the Nevskoï harbour of refuge nowhere to be seen. But a sail in sight appears in the shape of a soldier. A sulky sail he is, however; and, refusing to listen to my signal gun of distress, holds on his course without laying-to. I am fain, for fear of lying-to myself all the day in this granite Bay of Biscay, to grapple with a frail skiff in the person of a yellow-faced little girl, in printed cotton. Another monosyllabic inquiry, more unknown tongue (very shrill and lisping this time,) and ultimately a little yellow digit pointed to the northeast. Then I cross from where stands a colossal equestrian statue, spurring fiercely to the verge of an artificial rock and trampling a trailing serpent beneath his charger's feet, and on whose rocky pedestal there is the inscription " Petro Primo Catharina Secunda." I cross from the statue of Peter the Great some weary hundreds of yards over stone billows, (so wavy is the pavement,) to the northeast corner of that which I afterwards know to be the Admiralteeskaia Plochtchad, or great square of the Admiralty; but here, alas! there is a palace whose walls seem to have no cessation for another half mile, northeast. And there are no more sails in sight, save crawling droschkies, and I begin to have a sensation that my compass must be near the magnetic islands, when I unpreparedly turn a sharp angle, and find myself among a throng of people, and in the Nevskoï Prospekt.

It begins badly. It is not a wide street. It does not seem to be a long street. The shops don't look handsome; the pavement is execrable, and though people are plenty, there is no crowd. It is like a London street on a Sunday turned into a Parisian street just after an *émeute*. It ought to be lively at half-past seven in the evening in the month of May, in the very centre of an imperial city of six hundred thousand inhabitants. But it isn't lively. It is quite the contrary: it is deadly.

This is the place, then, I have been fretting and fuming to see: this is the Boulevard des Italiens of St. Petersburg. This the Nevskoï. As for the perspective, there is no perspective at all that I can see. It is more like Pimlico. There is a street in that royalty-shadowed suburb called Churton Street, in which the Cubit-Corinthian mansions at its head melt gradually into the squalid hovels of Rochester Row, Westminster, at its tail. The houses on the Nevskoï are big, but I expect them to make a bad end of it. Here is a palace; but not far off, I gloomily prophecy, must be Westminster, and the rat-catcher's daughter. And have I come all the way, not exactly from Westminster, but certainly from t'other side of the water, to see this? By this time I have walked about twenty-five yards.

I have not walked thirty-five yards, before my rashly-formed Nevskoï opinions begin to change. I have not walked fifty yards, before I discover that the Nevskoï is immensely wide and stupendously long, and magnificently paved. I have not walked a hundred yards, before I make up my mind that the Nevskoï-Perspective is the handsomest and the most remarkable street in the world.

There are forty perspectives, Mr. Bull, in this huge-bowelled city. I do not wish you to dislocate your jaw in endeavouring to pronounce the forty Muscovite names of these perspectives; so, contenting myself with delicately hinting that there is the Vossnessensk Prospekt, likewise those of Oboukhoff, Peterhoff, Ismaïloff, and Semenovskoï, I will leave you to imagine the rest, or familiarize yourself with them gradually, as they perspectively turn up in these my travels. But you are to remember, if you please, that the Nevskoï extends in one straight line from the great square of the Admiralty to the convent of Saint Alecksander-Nevskoï, a distance of two thousand sagenes, or four versts, or one French league, or three English miles! And you will please to think of that, Mr. Bull, or Master Brooke, and agree with me that the Nevskoï is something like a street. This astonishing thoroughfare, now one corridor of palaces and churches, and gorged with the outward and visible riches of nobles, and priests, and merchants, was, a century and a half ago, but a bridle-path through a dense forest leading from a river to a morass. The road was pierced in seventeen hundred and thirteen, and a few miserable wooden huts thrown together on its borders by the man who, under Heaven, seems to have made every mortal thing in Russia—Peter the Great. Now, you find on the Nevskoï the cathedral of Our Lady of Kasan, the Lutheran church of Saint Peter and Saint Paul, the great Catholic church of the Assumption, the Dutch church, the imperial palace of Anitchkoff, the splendid Alexksandra theatre, the Place Michel, with its green English square, its palace, and its theatre; the Strogonoff Palace, the Roumiantzoff Palace, the Galitzin Palace, the Belozelski Palace, the Branitzky Palace, the—the—for goodness' sake, go fetch a guide-book, and see how many hundred palaces more! On the Nevskoï are the façades of the curious semi-Asiatic bazaar, the Gostinnoï-Dvor, the imperial library, (O! British Museum quadrangles, glass roof, duplicate copies, five thousand pounds' worth of decoration, museum flea, and all, you are but a book-stall to it!) the Armenian church, the monuments of Souvorov, (our Suwarrow, and spelt in Russ thus: Cybopob,) of Barclay de Tolly. On to the Nevskoï débouch the aristocratic Morskaias, which, the Balchoi and the Mala, or Great and Little, are at once the Bond Streets and the Belgravias of Petersburg. On to the Nevskoï opens the Mala Millione, a short but courtly street terminated by a triumphal archway, monstrous and magnificent, surmounted by a car of Victory, with its eight horses abreast in bronze, and through which you may descry the red granite column of the Czar Alexksandra Pavlovitch (Napoleon's Alexander) and the immense Winter Palace. On to the Nevskoï yawns the long perspective of the Liteinaïa, the dashing street of the Cannouschina, or imperial stables, the palace and garden-lined avenue of the Sadovvaia, or Great Garden Street. And the Nevskoï is intersected by three Venice-like canals; by the canal of the Moïka, at the Polizeïsky-Most, or Police Bridge; by the Ekaterininskoï, at the Kasansky-Most, or Kasan Bridge; and by the Fontanka (Count Orloff's office—the office where ladies have been, like horses, "taken in to bait"—is on the Fontanka) at the Anitchkoff Bridge. At about five hundred sagenes from this bridge there is another canal, but not quite so handsome a one—the Ligoff. And at one extremity of this Nevskoï of wonders is a convent as big as an English market-town, and with three churches within its walls, while the other end finishes with the tapering golden spire of the Admiralty, (there are two Admiralties in this town-residence of the Titans,) which Admiralty has a church, a library, an arsenal, a museum, a dockyard, and a cadets' college under its roof, and such an unaccountable host of rooms, that I think every cabin-boy in the fleet must have a separate apartment there when he is on shore, and every boatswain's cat have a private storeroom for each and every one of its nine tails.

At the first blush, seven in the evening would not seem precisely the best chosen time for the minute examination of a street one had never seen before. In England or France, at this early spring-time, it would be sunset, almost twilight, blind man's holiday. And there is not a gas-lamp on the Nevskoï to illumine me in my researches. The posts are there: massive, profusely ornamented pillars of wrought-iron or bronze; but not a lamp for love or money. But you will understand the place when I tell you that it will be broad staring daylight on the Nevskoï till half-past eleven of the clock to-night; that after that time there will be a soft, still, dreamy, mysterious semi-twilight, such as sometimes veils the eyes of a woman you love, when you are sitting silent by her side, silent and happy, thinking of her, while she, with those inscrutable twilight orbs, is thinking of—God knows what, (perhaps of the somebody else by whose side she used to sit, and whom you would so dearly love to strangle, if it were all the same to her;) and then, at half-past one in the morning, comes the brazen staring morning light again. For from this May middle to the end of July, there will be no more night in St. Petersburg.

No night! why can't you cover up the sky then? why not roof in the Nevskoï—the whole bad city—with black crape? Why not force masks on all your slaves, or blind them? For, as true as heaven, there are things done here that God's sun should never shine upon. Cover up that palace. Cover up that house on the Fontanka. Cover up, for shame's sake, that police-yard, that Christians may not hear the women scream. Cover them up thick and threefold; for of a surety, if the light comes in, the truth will out, and Palace and Fontanka, house and Gaol-yard walls will come tumbling about your ears, insensate and accursed, and crush you.

At the Admiralty corner of the Nevskoï, I make my first cordial salutation to the fine arts in Russia. This long range of plate-glass windows appertains to an ingenious Italian, Signor Daziaro, whose handsome print-shop, with the elaborate Russian inscription on the frontage, has no doubt often pleased and puzzled you on the Boulevard des Capucines in Paris; and who has succursal fine-arts' establishments in Moscow, in Warsaw, and I believe also in Odessa, as well as this one in St. Petersburg. Daziaro is the Russian Ackermann's. For the newest portrait of the Czar, for the latest lithographs of the imperial family, for the last engraving after Sir Edwin Landseer, the last paysage by Ferogio, the last caricature (not political, be it well understood, but of a Lorette or *débardeur* tendency) of Gavarni or Gustave de Beaumont, you must go to Daziaro's. His windows, too, display the same curious thermometer of celebrity as those of our printsellers. A great man is disgraced, and sinks into oblivion. One day he dies, and then people suddenly remember him, (for about two days,) as he was before he wasn't. Presto! his portrait appears in Daziaro's window. Half-a-dozen copies of his portrait are sold during his two days' resuscitation; and then he is relegated to the portfolio again, and slumbers till his son wins a battle, or runs away with somebody else's wife, or is made a minister, or is sent to Siberia, or does something for people to remember and talk about (for about two days more,) what Monsieur his father was. When, failing the son's portrait, the astute Daziaro gives the respected progenitor another airing in the print-shop window; and so on till we ripe and rot, all of us. And thereby hangs a tale. Is this only Russian? Is it not so the whole world over? There was a thermometer of this sort in a print-shop at the corner of Great and Little Queen Streets, Lincoln's-Inn Fields, London, which I used to pass every morning; and the fresh portraits in the window were as good as the news of the day to me. The thermometer in Daziaro's is more apparent, more significant, and more frequently consulted; for this is a country where the news of the day is scarce; where, in an intolerable quantity of waste paper, there is about a copeck's worth of news; and where the real stirring daily intelligence is muttered in dark entries, and whispered behind hands in boudoirs, and glozed from lip to ear over tumblers of tea, and scribbled on blank leaves of pocket-books passed hastily from hand to hand, and then the blank leaves converted instantly into pipe-lights. As a general rule you can find out much easier what is most talked about by consulting Signor Daziaro's window, in preference to the Journal de St. Petersbourg.

Art, Daziaro *passim*, is in no want of patrons. The shop is thronged till ten o'clock in the evening (when all shops on the Nevskoï are closed). The stock of prints seems to comprise the very rarest and most expensive; and you may be sure that a liberal percentage has been added to the original price (however heavy) to meet the peculiar views of the Russian public. The Russian public—that which rides in carriages, and can buy beautiful prints, and has a soul to be saved—the only Russian public that exists of course, or is recognized on the Nevskoï; this genteel public does not like, and will not buy cheap things. Cheap things are low, common, vulgar, not fit for *nous autres.* Ivan Ivanovitch, the Moujik, buys cheap things. And so articles must not only be dear, but exorbitantly dear, or Andrei Andreivitch the merchant, who is rich but thrifty, would compete with *nous autres*, which would never do. Andrei will give a hundred roubles for his winter fur. This would be shocking to the genteel public; so crafty Frenchmen and Germans open shops on the Nevskoï, where a thousand silver roubles are charged and given for a fur pelisse, not much superior to the merchant's.

There are dozens of these "Pelz-Magasins," or furriers' shops, on the splendid Nevskoï, and even more splendid are their contents. In a country which even in the hotest summer may be described as the Polar Regions with the chill off—(imagine, if you like, a red-hot poker substituted for the icy pole itself)—and which for five, and sometimes six months in the year is a frigid hell, it may be easily conceived that furs, with us only the ornaments of the luxurious, are necessities of life. Ivan the Moujik does not wear a schooba or fur pelisse, but *pauvre diable* as he is, scrapes together eight or ten silver roubles wherewith to buy a touloupe, or coat of dressed sheepskin, whose woolly lining keeps him tolerably warm. But the humblest *employé* to Prince Dolgorouki, every one above the condition of a serf must have a schooba of some sort or other for winter. Some wear catskins, like my friend the Jew, who wanted me to buy the kibitka at Stettin. The Gostinnoï Dvor merchants wear pelisses of white wolfskin underneath their long cloth caftans. The fur of the squirrel, the Canada marmot, and the silver fox of Siberia, are in great request for the robes of burgesses' wives and *employés'* ladies. The common soldiers wear sheepskins under their gray capotes, the officers have cloaks lined with the fur of the bear or wolf. But *Nous Autres*—the Dvoryanin or Russian noble—the Seigneur, with his hundreds of serfs and hundreds of thousands of roubles—for him and for Madame la Princesse, his spouse, are reserved the sable pelisse, the schooba of almost priceless furs, thick, warm, and silky; a garment that is almost an inheritance, and which you spend almost an inheritance to acquire. One hundred and fifty pounds sterling—I have observed this—is the price of a first-class schooba on the Nevskoï. There are to be sure, certain murky warehouses in the Gostinnoï Dvor, where a Russian with a taste for bargaining and beating down (and that taste is innate to the Muscovite) may purchase a sable pelisse for a third of the money mentioned. In Germany, particularly at Leipsic, furs or *schoppen* are still cheaper; and one pelisse to each traveller passes through the custom-house duty free; yet the Russian aristocracy neglect this cheap mart, and hold by the Nevskoï Pelz-Magasins. We all remember what Hudibras says of the equality of pleasure between cheating and being cheated.

Next in importance to the furriers are the jewellers. Now I comprehend why the profession of a diamond-merchant is so important in Leipsic and Amsterdam, and where the chief market for diamonds is to be found. Every jeweller's window has an Alnaschar's basket of almost priceless gems displayed in it. Rings, bracelets, necklaces, carcans, vivières, ear-rings, stomachers, bouquets, fan-mounts, brooches, solitaires,—all blazing with diamonds so large that the stock of Howell and James, or Hunt and Roskell, would look but as peddlers' packs of penny trinkets beside them. No money in Russia! Put that figment out of your head as soon as ever you can: there is enough wealth in these Nevskoï shop-windows to carry on a big war for half-a-dozen years longer. They are not outwardly splendid though, these jewellers. No plate-glass, no Corinthian columns; no gas-jets with brilliant reflectors. There is an oriental dinginess and mystery about the exterior of the shops. The houses themselves in which the shops are situated have a private look, like the banker's or the doctor's or the lawyer's in an English country town magnified a thousand-fold; and the radiant stock is displayed in something like a gigantic parlour window, up a steep flight of steps. There is a miserable Moujik, in a crassy sheepskin, staring in at the diamonds, munching a cucumber meanwhile. This man-chattel is a slave, condemned to hopeless bondage, robbed, despised, kicked, beaten like a dog; and he gazes at Prince Legreeskoff's jewels with a calmly critical air. What right?—but, be quiet; if I come to right, what right have I to come to Muscovy grievance-hunting, when I have left a thousand grievances at home, crying to heaven for redress?

The tailors, whose name is that of ten legions, and who are very nearly all French and Germans, have no shops. They have magnificent suites of apartments on Nevskoï first-floors; and their charge for making a frock-coat is about eight guineas sterling, English. You understand now what sort of tailors they are. They are too proud, too high and mighty, to content themselves with the simple sartorial appellation, and have improved even upon our home-snobbery in that line; calling themselves not only Merchant Tailors, but *Kleider meisters* (Clothes masters); Undertakers for Military Habiliments (*Entrepreneurs d'habillemens militaires*); Confectioners of Seignorial Costume, and the like high-sounding titles. You are to remember that St. Petersburg is permanently garrisoned by the Imperial Guard, which is something like one hundred and fifteen thousand strong; that the epauletted mob of officers (whose pay is scarcely sufficient to defray the expenses of their boot-varnish) are, with very few exceptions, men of large fortune, and that the government does not find them in so much as a button towards their equipment. And as the uniforms are gorgeous in the extreme, and very easily spoilt, the Undertaker of Military Habiliments makes rather a good thing of it than otherwise in the capital of the Tsar.

Bootmakers abound—Germans, almost to a man—whose grim shops are fortalices of places, with stern jack-boots frowning at you through the windows. And shops and palaces, palaces and shops, succeed each other for mile after mile, till I am fairly worn out with magnificence, and, going home to bed, determine to take the Nevskoï-mixture as before, to-morrow.

V.

ISCHVOSTCHIK! THE DROSCHKY-DRIVER.

I am not quite certain, I must premise, as to the orthography of the Russian Cabby's name. It is a national characteristic of the Russians, never to give a direct answer to a question; and, although I have asked at least twenty times, of learned Russians how to spell the droschky-driver's appellation with correctness, the philologists were for the most part evasively dubious and readier to ask me questions about the head-dresses of the British Grenadiers, than to give me a succinct reply. Perhaps, they have not themselves yet made up their minds as to the proper position of the vowels and consonants in the word; for, though M. Karamsin is generally understood to have settled the Russian language some years since, considerable orthographical license yet prevails, and is, to some extent, tolerated. A sovereign, less conciliating than the Czar Alexander, would very soon set the matter right by an oukase; and woe to the Russian then, who didn't mind his P's and Q's! As it is, there seem to be as many ways of pronouncing the cabby's name, as the American prairie. I have heard him myself called indifferently Ischvostchik, istvosschik, issvostchik, and isvoschchik. When you hail him in the street, you are permitted to take another liberty with his title, and call out lustily iss'vosch!

The choice of a subject in the driver of a public conveyance, in any city, familiar as he must be to every traveller, is not very defensible on the score of novelty; but—as I should not have the slightest hesitation in taking a Piccadilly Hansom cabman as a type of character, and drawing him as best I could to the life, if I had a salutary purpose to serve —I shall make no more bones about sketching the ischvostchik, than if he were a new butterfly, or an inedited fern, or a Niam-Niam, or any other rare specimen entomological or zoological. And I have a plea, if needful, wherewith to claim benefit of clergy; this: that the ischvostchik is thoroughly, entirely, and to the back bone, in speech, dress, look, manners, and customs, Russian.

I was repeatedly told, while yet new to the Holy Land, that I must not take St. Petersburg as by any means a sample of a genuine Russian city. It was a French, a German, an English, a cosmopolitan town—what you will; but for real Russian customs and costumes, I must go to Moscow, to Novgorod, to Kasan, to Smolensk, to Kharkoff, or to Vladimir. Error. I do not think that in the whole world there exists a nation so thoroughly homogeneous as Russia. In our little scrap of an island, there are two-score dialects, at least, spoken; and a real north-countryman can scarcely make himself understood to a southerner; but here, if you will once bear in mind the two divisions of race into Great Russians, and Little Russians, you may go a thousand versts, without finding a vowel's difference in accentuation, or a hair's breadth alteration in a caftan, or a Kakoshnik. The outlying nationalities subject to the Double Eagle's sway—the Fins, the Laps, the German Russians, (Esthonians, Livonians, &c.,) the Poles, the Cossacks, and the Tartars, have of course their different languages and dresses; but they are not Russians: the Imperial Government recognizes their separate nationality in everything save taxing them, making soldiers of them, and beating them; but the vast mass of millions—the real Russians—are from province to province, from government to government, all alike. At the end of a week's journey, you will find the same villages, the same priests, the same policemen, the same Moujiks and Ischvostchiks, in appearance, dress, language, and habits, as at the commencement of your voyage. You who have crossed St. George's Channel to Dublin, or the Grampians to Edinburgh, will remember the striking contrast between the cabman you left in London, and the Irish car-driver who rattled you up Westmoreland Street, or the canny Jehu who conveyed you in a cab to your hotel in the Scottish metropolis. Take but a jaunt of half a dozen miles by rail out of London, and you will scarcely fail to remark the difference between Number nine hundred and nine from the Wellington Street stand, and the driver of the fly from the Queen's Arms, or the Terminus Hotel. They are quite different types of coachmanhood. But in Russia, the Ischvostchik who drives you from the Admiralty at St. Petersburg, to the Moscow railway station, is, to a hair of his beard, to a plait in his caftan, to a sneezing penultimate in his rapid Russ, the very counterpart, the own Corsican brother, of the Ischvostchik who drives you from the terminus to the Bridge of the Marshals in Holy Moscow, four hundred and fifty miles away. Stay: there is one difference in costume. The Petersburg Ischvostchik wears a peculiar low-crowned hat, with a broad brim turned up liberally at the sides; whereas, the Moscow cabby, more particularly, affects a Tom and Jerry hat with the brim pared closely off, and encircled by a ribbon and three or four buckles—a hat that has some remote resemblance to a genuine Connaught bogtrotter's head covering. *Du reste*, both styles of hat are common, and indifferently worn by the Moujiks all over Russia, only the low-crowned hat being covered with a silk nap, and in some cases with beaver, is the more expensive, and is, therefore, in more general use in Petersburg the luxurious. Don't believe those, therefore, who endeavour to persuade you of the non-Russianism of St. Petersburg. There is a great deal of eau-de-Cologne consumed there; the commerce in white kid gloves is enormous; and there is a thriving trade in wax candles, pineapple ices, patent leather boots, Clicquot's champagne, crinoline petticoats, artificial flowers, and other adjuncts to civilization. Grisi and Lablache sing at the Grand Opera; Mademoiselle Cerito dances there; French is habitually spoken in society; and invitations to balls and dinners are sent to you on enamelled cards, and in pink billets smelling of musk and millefleurs; but your distinguished Origin may come away from the Affghan ambassador's balls, or the Grand Opera, or the Princess Liagouschkoff's tableaux vivans, your head full of Casta Diva, the Valse à deux temps, and the delightful forwardness of Russian civilization; and your Origin will hail an Ischvostchik to convey you to your domicil; and right before you, almost touching you, astride on the splashboard, will sit a genuine rightdown child of Holy Russia, who is (it is no use mincing the matter) an ignorant, beastly, drunken, idolatrous savage, who is able to drive a horse, and to rob, and no more. Woe to those who wear the white kid gloves, and serenely allow the savage to go on in his dirt, in his drunkenness, in his most pitiable joss-worship (it is not religion), in his swinish ignorance, not only (it were vain to dwell upon that) of letters, but of things that the very dumb dogs and necessary cats in Christian households seem to know instinctively! Woe to the drinkers of champagne when the day shall come for these wretched creatures to grow raving mad instead of sillily maudlin on the vitriol brandy, whose monopoly brings in a yearly revenue of fifty millions of roubles (eight millions sterling) to the paternal government, and when the paternal stick shall avail no more as a panacea. I know nothing more striking in my Russian experience, than the sudden plunge from a hothouse of refinement to a cold bath of sheer barbarism. It is as if you left a presidential levée in the White House at Washington, and fell suddenly into an ambuscade of Red Indians. Your civilization, your evening dress, your carefully selected stock of pure Parisian French, avail you nothing with the Ischvostchik. He speaks nothing but Russ; he cannot read; he has nothing, nothing in common with you —closely shaven (as regards the cheeks and chin) and swathed in the tight sables of European etiquette, as you are—he in his flowing oriental caftan, and oriental beard, and more than oriental dirt.

It is possible, nay a thing of very common occurrence, for a foreigner to live half a dozen years in Russia, without mastering the Russian alphabet, or being called upon to say, "How do you do?" or "Good-night!" in Russ. Many of the highest Russian nobles are said indeed to speak their own language with anything but fluency and correctness. But, unless you want to go afoot in the streets, (which in any Russian town is about equivalent to making a pilgrimage to the Holy House at Loretto, with unboiled peas in your shoes,) it is absolutely necessary for you to acquire what I may call the Ischvostchik language, in order to let your conductor know your intended destination. The language is neither a very difficult, nor a very copious one. For all locomotive purposes it may be resumed into the following ten phrases.

1. Na prava—To the right.
2. Na leva—To the left.
3. Pouyiama—Straight on. Right a-head.
4. Stoï—Stop!
5. Pashol-Scorrei—Quick, go a-head.
6. Shivai—Faster.
7. Dam na Vodka—I'll stand something to drink above the fare.
8. Durak—Fool.
9. Sàbakoutchelovek—Son of a dog!
10. Tippian—You're drunk.

These phrases are spelt anyhow; the Ischvostchik language being a *Lingua non scripta*, and one that is studied orally, and not grammatically; but I have written them to be pronounced as in French; and, if any of my readers, intending to visit Russia, will take the trouble to commit this slender vocabulary to memory, they will find them to all droschky-driving intents and purposes sufficient for their excursions in any Russian town from Petersburg to Kasan.

There are some facetious Russians who supersede the verbal employment of the first four of these phrases by synonymous manual signs. Thus, being always seated outside, and immediately behind the driver, they substitute for "to the right," a sharp pull of the Ischvostchik's right ear. Instead of crying "to the left," they pull him by the sinister organ of hearing; a sound "bonneting" blow on the low-crowned hat, or indeed, a blow or a kick anywhere is considered as equivalent to a gentle reminder to drive faster; and, if you wish to pull up, what is easier than to grasp the Ischvostchik by the throat and twine your hand into his neckerchief, pulling him violently backwards, meanwhile, till he chokes or holds hard? It is not often, I confess, that this humorous system of speech without words is required, or, at least, practised in Petersburg or Moscow; but in the country, where *Nous Autres* are at home, these, and numerous other waggish modes of persuasive coercion, are in use for the benefit of the Ischvostchik. I remember a young Russian gentleman describing to me his overland kibitka journey from Moscow to Warsaw. He travelled with his mother and sister; it was in the depth of winter; and he described to me, in freezing accents, the horrors of his situation, compelled as he was to sit outside the kibitka by the side of the Ischvostchik, (or rather yemschik; for, when the droschky-driver drives post-horses he becomes a postilion, whether he bestride his cattle or the splash-board.) "Outside," I said, "was there no room inside the carriage?" "O, yes! plenty of room," was the naïve reply of this young gentleman; "but you see I had to sit on the box, because we had no servant with us, and there was nobody to beat the postilion." For the Russian driver on a Russian road, receives always as much, and frequently much more, stick than his cattle. (Ischvostchiks and Yemschiks are proverbially merciful to their beasts.) You have to beat him whether you fee him or not. Without the stick he will go to sleep, and will not incite his horses into any more rapid pace than that which is understood by a snail's gallop. It is a sad thing to be obliged to record; but it is a fact, that even as money makes the mare to go, so it is the stick that makes the Russian driver to drive; and, just as in the old days of Irish posting it used to be necessary for the near leader to be touched up on the flank with a red-hot poker before he would start, so the signal for departure to a kibitka driver is ordinarily a sounding thwack across the shoulders.

In the two great capitals, happily, words will serve as well as blows; and to the Petersburg or Moscow Ischvostchik the intimation of "Dam na vodka," or even "vodka," simply, will seldom fail in procuring an augmentation of speed. But I grieve to say that the epithets, "fool!" "you're drunk!" and especially the terrible adjuration "sabakoutchelovek!" "son of a dog!" are absolutely necessary in your converse with the Ischvostchik, particularly when the subject of fare comes to be discussed. Every Ischvostchik will cheat his own countrymen, and I need not say will stick it on to foreigners in the proportion of about two hundred and eighty-five per cent. He will not have the slightest hesitation in asking a rouble for a fifteen kopecks' course; and it is all over with you if you hesitate for a moment, or endeavour to reason out the matter (by nods, smiles, and shrugs) amicably. Pay him the proper fare, accompanying the payment by the emphatic "durak!" If this does not satisfy the Ischvostchik, utter the magical sabakoutchelovek in the most awful voice you can command, and walk away. If he presume to follow you, still demanding more money, I scarcely know what to advise you to do; but I know, and the Ischvostchik knows also, to his sorrow, what *Nous Autres* do under such circumstances. One thing, in charity and mercy, I entreat you not to do. Don't call in a police-soldier to settle the dispute. As sure as ever you have that functionary for an arbitrator, so sure are you to be mulcted of some more money, and so sure is the miserable Ischvostchik, whether right or wrong, whether he has received under or over fare, so sure is that slave of a slave either to have his nose flattened or a tooth or two knocked down his throat on the spot by the fist of the boutosnik, or police-soldier, or to be made to look in at the next convenient opportunity at the nearest police-station, or siège, and there to be scourged like a slave as he is, and like a dog as he ought not to be.

The way these wretched men are beaten, both openly and privately, is revolting and abominable. I have seen a gigantic police-soldier walk coolly down the Nevskoï, from the Pont de Police to the Kasan church, beating, cuffing across the face, pulling by the hair, and kicking every single one of the file of Ischvostchiks who, with their vehicles, line the kerb. To the right and left, sometimes on to the pavement, sometimes into the kennel and under their horses' feet, went the poor bearded brutes under the brawny fists of this ruffianly Goliath in a gray gaberdine. I saw him remount the Nevskoï to his standing-place, exactly repeating his pugilistic recreation—saw it from a balcony overhanging this same Nevskoï, where I was standing with ladies, and with officials in clanking spurs. We had a lap-dog, too, in the balcony, and in the saloon inside an Italian music-master was capering with his nimble fingers on a grand piano; while down below, the man in gray was felling the Ischvostchiks. What their offence had been—whether standing an inch too close to, or an inch too far from the pavement, I do not know; but I know that they were, and that I saw them, thus beaten; and I know that they took their hats off, and meekly wiped the blood from their mouths and noses; and gave way to not one word or gesture of resistance or remonstrance; but I know that, in the wake of that bad ship Graycoat, there were left such a trail of white vengeful faces, of such gleaming eyes, of such compressed lips, that were I Graycoat I would as soon pass through the nethermost pit, as down that line of outraged men, alone, at night, and without my police helmet and my police sword.

It is not pleasant, either, to know that every time your unfortunate driver happens to lock the wheel of a private carriage he is due at the police-station, there to consume the inevitable ration of stick; it is horribly unpleasant to sit, as I have often done, behind a fine stalwart bearded man—a Hercules of a fellow—and, when you see the tips of a series of scarlet and purple wheals appearing above the collar of his caftan and ending at the nape of his neck, to be convinced after much elaborate inductive reasoning, that there are some more wheals under his caftan—that his back and a police-corporal's stick have come to blows lately, and that the stick has had the best of it.

A droschky is a necessary of life in Russia; it is not much a subject for astonishment, therefore, that there should be above three thousand public droschkies alone in Saint Petersburg, and nearly two thousand in Moscow. Besides these, there are plenty of hack-calèches and broughams, and swarms of small private one-horse droschkies. Every *employé* of a decent grade in the Tchinn, every major of police, has his "one-horse chay." The great have their carriages with two, four, and six horses; and when you consider that it is contrary to St. Petersburgian etiquette for a gentleman to drive his own equipage; that the small merchant or tradesman even, rich enough to possess a droschky of his own, seldom condescends to take the ribbons himself; and lastly, that if not by positive law, at least by commonly recognized and strictly observed custom, no coachman whatsoever, save those who act as whips to foreign ambassadors, are allowed to depart from the old Russian costume, you may imagine how numerous the wearers of the low-crowned hat and caftans are in St. Petersburg.

Here is the portrait of the Ischvostchik in his habit as he lives. He is a brawny square-built fellow, with a broad bully-beef face, fair curly hair cropped round his head in the workhouse-basin fashion, blue eyes, and a bushy beard. I have seen some specimens of carroty whiskers, too, among the Ischvostchiks, that would do honour to the bar of England. His face is freckled and puckered into queer wrinkles, partly by constant exposure to wind and weather, torrid heat and iron frost; partly from the immoderate use of his beloved vapour-bath. The proverb tells us that there are more ways of killing a dog than hanging him—so there are more ways of bathing in Russia than the way that we occidental people usually bathe—the way leaning towards cleanliness, which is next to godliness. I cannot divest myself (from what I have seen) of the impression that the Russian *homme du peuple* is considerably dirtier after taking a bath than previous to that ablution. But I am launching into so vast and interesting a topic that I must be cautious, and must return to the Ischvostchik.

His hands and feet are of tremendous size; he is strong, active, agile; and his capacity for endurance of hardships is almost incredible. He wears invariably a long caftan or coat, tight in the waist and loose in the skirts, of dark blue or grass green cloth or serge, not by any means of coarse materials, and, if he be a well-to-do Ischvostchik, edged with two narrow rows of black velvet. This garment is neither single breasted nor double breasted—it is rather back breasted, the right lappel extending obliquely across the left breast to beneath the armpit. Under these arms, too, and again if his Ichvostchikship be prosperous, he has a row of sugar-loaf buttons, sometimes silvery, more frequently coppery, but never buttoning anything, and serving no earthly purpose that I am aware of. This caftan is in winter replaced by the touloupe, or sheepskin coat, to which I have previously alluded, and to which I give warning I shall have to call attention, many a time and oft, in the progress of these papers. Under the caftan or touloupe exists, perhaps, a shirt, (but that is not by any means to be assumed as an invariable fact,) and certainly, suspended by a ribbon, a little cross in brass, or a medal of St. Nicolaï, St. George, St. Serge, St. Alexander Nevsky, or some other equally revered and thoroughly Russian saint. "Few sorrows had she of her own—my hope, my joy, my Genévièvc," and few other garments of his own (though he has sorrows enough) has my Ischvostchik. A pair of baggy galligaskins, blue or pink striped, heavy bucket boots well greased, and he is nearly complete. Nay, let me not omit one little ornament wherewith he sacrifices to the Graces. This is his sash or girdle, which is twisted tightly round his waist. It always has been, in the beginning, dyed in the brightest and most staring hues; sometimes it has been of gold and silver brocade, and silk of scarlet and of blue; but it is most frequently, and when offered to the view of you, the fare, encircling the loins of the Ischvostchik, a rag—a mere discoloured rag, greasy, dirty, frayed, and crumpled. The Ischvostchik has a brass badge with the number of his vehicle, and an intolerable quantity of Sclavonic verbiage in relief; and this badge is placed on his back, so that you may study it, and make sure of your Ischvostchik, if you have a spite against him.

This is the Ischvostchik who, with his beard and blue coat, his boots and breeches, his once scarlet girdle, his brass badge in the wrong place; his diminutive hat (decorated sometimes with buckles, sometimes with artificial roses, sometimes with medallions of saints); his dirt, his wretchedness, his picturesqueness, and his utter brutishness; looks like the distempered recollection of a bluecoat boy, and the nightmare of a beef-eater, mingled with a delirium tremens' hallucination of the Guildhall Gog transformed into Japhet in the Noah's Ark.

VI.

THE DROSCHKY.

The Ischvostchik is not necessarily an adult. Though many of the class are men advanced in years, with beards quite snowy and venerable to look at, (terrible old rogues are these to cheat,) there are, on the other hand, numerous droschky-drivers who are lads—nay, mere children. It is desperately ludicrous to see a brat, some half-score years old, in full Ischvostchik accoutrement; for they will not bate an inch of the time-honoured costume; and adhere rigidly to the long caftan and the gaudy sash.

As large men's size appears to be the only pattern recognized for Ischvostchik boots and hats in Russia, the diminutive heads and spare little legs of these juvenile drivers are lost in a forest of felt and an abyss of boot-leather. I can recall now more than one of those little pale, weazened, frightened faces bonneted in a big hat, precisely like the man who is taking his wife's hand in that strange mirror picture of John Van Eyck's, in the National Gallery—the Alpha and Omega of art mechanism, as it seems to me; for if Van Eyck were the inventor of oil-painting, he has surely in this dawn-picture attained the highest degree of perfection in the nicety of manipulation to which that vehicle lends itself.

A plague on John Van Eyck, that he should make me unmindful of my Ischvostchik! I want an excuse, too, for returning to him, for I have something to say about the vehicle he gains his livelihood by driving—the Droschky. There is the same amount of despairing uncertainty prevalent concerning the orthography of this attelage—in plain English, a one-horse shay—as about its conductor. In half-a-dozen books and prints I find Droschky spelt in as many different ways: it appears as Droschka, Droski, Drotchki, Droskoï, and Drusschka; I am perfectly ignorant as to the proper method of writing the word; but I have elected Droschky as the most generally accepted, and I intend to abide by it.

The real Russian, or Moscow droschky, is simply a cloth-covered bench upon clumsy C springs on four wheels, with a little perch in front, which the driver bestrides. You, the passenger, may seat yourself astride, or sideways, on the bench. It may perhaps serve to give a more definite and pictorial idea of the droschky, if I describe it as a combination of elongated side-saddle, (such as are provided for the rising generation, and endured by long-suffering donkeys in the vicinity of the Spaniards Tavern at Hampstead,) and an Irish outside car. The abominable jolting, dirt, and discomfort of the whole crazy vehicle, forcibly recall, too, that Hibernian institution. There is a leathern paracrotte on either side, to prevent the mud from the wheels flying up into your face, and the bases of these paracrottes serve as steps to mount, and a slight protection in the way of footing against your tumbling out of the ramshackle concern into the mud: but the imbecility, or malevolence of the droschky-builder has added a tin, or pewter covering for this meagre flooring, and as your bones are being rattled over the Russian stones, your feet keep up an incessant and involuntary skating shuffle on this accursed pewter pavement. There is nothing to hold on by, save the driver, and a sort of saddle-pummel turned the wrong way, at the hinder end of the bench; the droschky rocks from side to side, threatening to tip over altogether at every moment. You mutter, you pray, you perspire; your hooked fingers seek little inequalities of the bench to grasp at, as Claude Frollo's tried to claw at the stone copings when he fell from the tower of Notre Dame; you are jolted, you are bumped, you are scarified; you are dislocated; and, all this while, your feet are keeping up the diabolical goose-step on the pewter beneath. Anathema, Maranatha! if there be a strong north wind blowing, (Boreas has his own way, even in the height of summer, in Petersburg,) and your hat be tempted to desert your head, and go out on the loose! There is such a human, or perhaps, fiendish perversity in hats, when they blow off—such a mean, malignant, cruel, and capricious persistence in rolling away, and baffling you—that I can scarcely refrain from shaking my fist at my vagrant head-covering while I am running after it, and swearing at it when I capture it; and punching its head well before I resettle it on my own. But what are you to do if your hat flies off in a droschky? You daren't jump out: sudden death lies that way. The driver will see you at Nishi-Novgorod before he will descend to recover it; although he has not the slightest shame in asking you to get down to pick up his whip. All you can do is to shut your eyes, tie a pocket-handkerchief over your head, and buy a new hat; which, by the way, will cost you, for a very ordinary one, ten silver roubles—a guinea and a half. As to stopping the droschky, getting down, and chasing the fugitive—that might be done in England; but not here. It seems almost as difficult to pull up a droschky as a railway train. The wheels would seem to be greased to such a terrific extent, that they run or jolt on of their own accord: and two hundred yards' notice is the least you can, in any conscience, give your Ischvostchik, if you want him to "stoi." Meantime, with that execrable north wind, where would your hat be? In the Neva, or half-way to the Lake of Ladoga.

When the Scythians (was it the Scythians, by the way?) were first made acquainted with horses, we read that their young men desirous of taking lessons in equitation were, to prevent accidents, bound to their mettlesome steeds with cords. I think it would be expedient, when a foreigner takes his first airing in a droschky, to tie him to the bench, or at least to nail his coat-tails thereto. The born Russians, curiously, seem to prefer these perilous vehicles to the more comfortable droschkies. They seldom avail themselves of the facility of bestriding the narrow bench, Colossus like, but sit jauntily sideways, tapping that deadly pewter with their boot-tips as confidently and securely as the Amazons who scour through the tan at the Hippodrome on bare-backed steeds. Ladies, even, frequently patronize these breakers on wheels. It is a sight to see their skirts spreading their white bosoms to the gale, like ships' canvas; a prettier sight to watch their dainty feet pit-a-patting on that pewter of peril I have before denounced. When a lady and gentleman mount one of these droschkies, and are, I presume, on tolerably brotherly and sisterly terms, it seems to be accepted as a piece of cosy etiquette for the lady to sit in the gentleman's lap.

While waiting at a house-door for a fare engaged therein, or at any other time that he is not absolutely compelled to be driving, the Ischvostchik has a habit of abandoning the splash-board, and reclining at full length on his back on the droschky bench, there to snore peacefully, oblivious of slavery, unmindful of the stick. To the full length of his trunk would be perhaps a more correct expression, for the bench is only long enough for his body down to the knees; and his big-booted legs dangle comfortably down among the wheels. He will sleep here, in the sun, in the rain, in weather hot and cold; and, were it not for casual passengers and the ever-pursuing police soldier, he would so sleep, I believe, till Doomsday. There is one inconvenience to the future occupant of the droschky in this; that, inasmuch as it is pleasant, in a hotel, to have your bed warmed, there are differences of opinion as to the comfort of having your seat warmed vicariously; especially when the animated warming-pan is a Russian and an Ischvostchik, and, and—well, the truth must out—ragged, dirty, greasy, and swarming with vermin.

I know that I am sinning grievously against good manners in barely hinting at the existence of such things; but I might as well attempt to write a book on Venice without mentioning the canals, as to chronicle Russian manners and customs without touching ever so delicately on the topic of the domestic animalculæ of the empire. There is a little animal friendly to man, and signifying, I have been given to understand, love, whose existence is very properly ignored in the select circles of refined England, but who is as familiar in good society at Petersburg as the lively flea is at Pera. It was my fortune, during a portion of my stay in Russia, to occupy an apartment in a very grand house on the

Nevskoï Perspective, nearly opposite the cathedral of Our Lady of Kasan. The house itself had an ecclesiastical title, being the Dom-Petripavloskoï, or house of St. Peter and St. Paul, and was an appanage of that wealthy church. We had a marble staircase to our house, imitation scagliola columns, and panels painted quite beautifully with Cupids and Venuses. A Russian lady of high rank occupied a suite of apartments on the same floor; and, late one night, when I was about retiring to rest, her well-born excellency (I used to call her the Queen of Sheba, she was so stately) condescended to order her body-servant to tap at my door, and tell me that the Barynia desired to speak with me. I accordingly had an interview with her at the door of her apartment, she being also about to retire for the night. She had something to show me, she said. Russian ladies always have something to show you—a bracelet, a caricature, a tame lizard, a musical box, a fly in amber, or some novelty of that description—but this was simply a remarkably handsome black velvet mantle, with two falls of rich black lace to it. I knew that it was new, and had come home only that afternoon from Madame Zoë Falcon's, the court modiste in the Mala Millionne; so, expecting that the countess, with the elegant caprice in which her distinguished position gave her a right to indulge, wished to have, even at two o'clock in the morning, the opinion of an Anglisky upon her mantle, I said, critically, that it was very pretty; whereupon, a taper finger was pointed to a particular spot on the mantle, and a silvery voice said, "*Re-*

gardez !" I did regarder, and, on my honour, I saw strolling leisurely over the black velvet, gravely, but confidently, majestic but unaffected, his white top-coat on, his hat on one side, his umbrella under his arm, (if I may be permitted to use such metaphorical expressions,) as fine a LOUSE as ever was seen in St. Giles's. I bowed and withdrew.

I must explain that I had previously expressed myself as somewhat skeptic to this lady respecting the animalcular phenomena of Russia; for I had been stopping in a German hotel at Wassily-Ostrow, where the bedrooms were scrupulously clean; and it must be also said that the lady in question, though a Russian subject, and married to an officer in the guards, had been born and educated in western Europe. Had she been a native Russian, little account would she have taken of such a true-born subject of the Czar at that late hour, I ween.

Although the violent and eccentric oscillations of a single-bodied droschky undoubtedly conduce to a frame of mind which is a sovereign cure for hypochondriasis, yet the drawbacks to its advantages (the last one especially) are so fearful, that I question whether it be worth while to undergo so much suffering as the transition from a state of chronic melancholy to one of raving madness. In the provinces, I am sorry to write it, it is ofttimes but Hobson's choice—this or none; but in St. Petersburg (and I suppose in coronation time at Moscow) there is no lack of double-bodied droschkies, in which you may ride without any very imminent danger of a dislocation of the arm, and a compound fracture of the thigh, or so, per verst. The form of the double-bodied droschky, though not very familiar to our Long Acre carriage architects, is well known in France. The inhabitants of the Rue du Jeu de Paume, at Versailles, must be well acquainted with it; for therein it was whilom (and is so still, I hope) the custom of the great French painter, Monsieur HORACE VERNET, to ride in a trim coquettish little droschky presented to him by the Czar Nicholas. In his latter days, his imperial friend did not like Horace quite so much; the impudent artist having been misguided enough to publish some letters which had the misfortune to be true, and not quite favourable to the imperial *régime*. This droschky was, it need scarcely be said, a gem of its kind—a model Attelage Russe. The horse—likewise a present from the emperor—was a superb coal-black *étalon* of the Ukraine; and to complete the turn-out, the driver was in genuine Ischvostchik costume—in hat, boots, and caftan complete. I want to see the double-bodied droschky in London, Ischvostchik and all. I am tired of tandems, dog-carts, mail-phaëtons, and hooded cabriolets, with tall horses and short tigers. What could there be more spicy down the road than a droschky, sparkling, shining, faultless to a nut, a rivet, as our matchless English coach-builders only know how to turn out an equipage; with a fast trotting mare in the shafts, and a driver with a bushy beard, a sky-blue caftan, shiny boots, and an Ischvostchik's hat? I think John Coachman would not object to growing a beard and wearing a caftan for a reasonable advance on his wages. I wonder if any of the stately English hidalgos I saw just before I left Russia—if any of those ethereally-born Secretaries of Legation, and unpaid *attachés*—will bring home a droschky from the land of the Russ, or, on their return, order one from Laurie or Houlditch. There are, perhaps, two slight obstacles to the naturalization of the droschky in England. In the first place, you couldn't have the Ischvostchik thrashed if he didn't drive well; in the next, the English gentleman is innately a driving animal. He likes to take the ribbons himself, while his groom sits beside with folded arms. In Russia, the case is precisely contrary. The Russian moujik is almost born a coachman; at all events, he begins to drive in his tenderest childhood. The Russian gentleman scarcely ever touches a pair of reins. The work is too hard; besides, is there not Ivan Ivanovitch to take the trouble off our hands? In St. Petersburg, it is entirely contrary to etiquette for a gentleman to be seen driving his own equipage; and I have no doubt that any gentleman so sinning would draw upon himself a reprimand from the emperor, or, at least, the evil eye of the police. This extraordinary government seems almost to be jealous of private equestrianism. In no capital in Europe do you see such a woful paucity of cavaliers as in St. Petersburg. I do not speak of the city proper, in which the execrable pavement is sufficient to ruin any horse's feet; but in the environs, where there are good roads, you seldom meet any persons in plain clothes on horseback. Either it is not *bon-ton* to ride in *mufti* (and, to be candid, there are very few gentlemen, save the members of the corps diplomatique, who ever appear out of uniform,) or to have a horse to one's self, and to ride it is considered in certain quarters an encroachment on the imperial prerogative of a cavalry force; or—and this I am led shrewdly to suspect is the real reason—the Russians are bad horsemen, and don't care about equitation when not upon compulsion. Be good enough to bear in mind that the Tartars and Cossacks, who live almost entirely on horseback, are not Russians. The Russian cavalry soldiers sit their horses in the clumsiest, painfullest manner you can conceive; and though they have the vastest riding schools, and the most awfully severe *manège* to be found anywhere, the Russian cavalry are notoriously inefficient as troopers; they are grenadiers on horseback, nothing more. They can do every thing, and more than western soldiers, in the way of manœuvring, curveting, and caracoling, of course—they MUST do it, or the omnipotent Stick will know the reason why; but, in actual warfare, it is astonishing how our friend the Cossack goes up to premium, and how the dragoon goes down to discount. The peasants of Little Russia make tolerably good troopers; which is difficult to understand, seeing that with them horses are scarce, and their principal experience in riding and driving is confined to oxen; but the Russian proper is almost as much a stranger to a horse's back as a man-o'-war's man is, though he, the Russian, has a natural genius for droschky-driving. And this I write after having seen a review of the Chevalier Guards, who, if size and magnificence of appointment are to be considered as a test of capacity, are the twelve hundred finest men upon the twelve hundred finest horses in the world.

Now and then—but it is a case of extreme rarity of occurrence—you see a *Gentilhomme Russe* driving (himself) a feeble imitation of an English dog-cart, in a leafy road on one of the pretty islands in the Neva. Every Russian, of whatever rank he may be—from the sun, moon, and starred general, to the filthy moujik; from the white-headed octogenarian to the sallow baby in the nurse's arms—every child of the Czar has a worn, pinched, dolorous, uneasy expression in his countenance, as if his boots hurt him, or as if he had a cankerworm somewhere, or a scarlet letter burnt into his breast, like the Rev. Mr. Dimsdale. They are not good to look at—Russian faces. People say that it is the climate, or the abuse of vapour baths, that gives them that unlovely look. But a bad climate won't prevent you from looking your neighbor in the face; two vapour baths per week won't pull down the corners of your mouth, and give you the physiognomy of a convict who would like to get into the chaplain's good graces. No. It is the Valley of the Shadow of Stick through which these men are continually passing, that casts this evil hang-dog cloud upon them. Well, imagine the *Gentilhomme Russe* in his dog-cart with four reins, no whip, and that rueful visage I have spoken of. By his side is a slave-servant, evidently shaved against his will, and who is of the same (hirsute) opinion still; for bristles are obstinately starting out of forbidden corners. He has a shabby blue cap with a faded gold lace band, and a livery that does not come within the wildest possibility of having been made for him. He tries mournfully to fold his arms, with those paws covered with dirty Berlin gloves, and he makes superhuman efforts not to fall asleep. Master and man are clearly in a wrong position. The horse (a first-rate one, with a flowing mane and tail) evidently despises the whole concern, and kicks his heels up at it. The dog-cart is badly built, the wheels are out of balance, and the paint is dingy. They never seem to wash Russian carriages; I have lived over a mews, and ought to know. This *Gentilhomme Russe* in the dog-cart is about as mournful a sight as is to be seen anywhere, even in Russia.

But, when the Russians are sensible enough to abandon imitation, and to stand or fall by their own native equipages, they can make a brave show. Of little, private, double-bodied droschkies, there are swarms; and in some of these you will see horses worth from seven to twelve hundred silver roubles each. Many a puny cornet in the guards, too, has his calèche lined with moiré-antique, and drawn by two splendid, black, Ukraine horses. I may observe that the horses never wear blinkers, and that, though full of mettle, they are very little addicted to shying. The harness is quite peculiar and Russian, consisting of a purple net of leather-work profusely spangled with small discs of silver. Only some of the court carriages are drawn by horses harnessed in the English manner. Pretty as their own caparisons are the Russians sigh for foreign fashions; and extravagant prices are given for a set of English harness. In the native harness there seem to be a good many unnecessary straps and tassels; but the backs of the horses are left almost entirely free, which has a very picturesque and wild horse of the prairie sort of effect. Coal black is the favourite hue; next, gray. With all horses, the sensible custom is observed of allowing the manes and tails to grow; and the consequence is, that the animals look about thrice as handsome and as noble (bless their honest hearts!) as the be-ratted, be-grayhounded steeds we see at home.

The coachman of the Princess Schiliapoff, (or any other princess you like to find a name for,) the conductor of those coal-black steeds, (the Schiliapoff has twenty-five hundred serfs, and half the Ogurzi Perspective belongs to her,) is own brother to the ragged, dirty Ischvostchik. Nor, though he is coachman to a princess, is his social position one whit better than that of Ivan Ivanovitch, sprawling on his back on the droschky bench. His caftan is made of superfine broadcloth, sometimes of velvet, slashed at the back and sides with embroidery, as if he had been knouted with a golden whip; his hat is of the shiniest nap, has a velvet band, a silver buckle, and is decorated with a bunch of rosy ribbons, a bouquet of artificial flowers, or a peacock's feather. He has a starched white neckcloth, buckskin gloves, rings in his ears; his hair is scrupulously cut, and his beard is bushy, well trimmed, oiled, and curled. He has a sash radiant with bright colours, and the top of a crimson silk shirt just asserts itself above his caftan.

It is probable that he sometimes gets meat to eat, and that he has decent sleeping accommodation in the stables, along with the horses. But he is a SLAVE, body and bones. The Princess Schiliapoff may sell him to-morrow if she have a mind. [To those who have an idea that Russian serfs cannot be sold away from the soil, I beg to recall Mr. Fox's recommendation to Napoleon Bonaparte on the assassination question, "Put all that nonsense out of your head."] The princess may send him to the police, and have him beaten like a sack if he take a wrong turning, or pull up at the wrong milliner's shop: the princess's majordomo may, and does, kick, cuff, and pull his hair, whenever he has a mind that way. The princess may, if he have offended her beyond the power of stick to atone for, send him as an exile to Siberia, or into the ranks of the army as a soldier. There are many noble families who pride themselves on having handsome men as coachmen; there are others, like Sir Roger de Coverley, who like to have old men to drive them. I have seen some of this latter category, quite patriarchs of the box, venerable, snowy-bearded old men, that might have sat for portraits of the Apostles in the Cartoons. It is pleasant, is it not, to be six feet high and as handsome as Dunois, and to be sold to pay a gambling debt? To be sixty years of age, and have a white head, and grandchildren, and to be scourged with birch rods like a schoolboy? And these good people are WHITE, Mrs. Harriet Beecher Stowe, — White, ma'am!

The Russian imperial court is a court; by which,

on the principle of coals being coals, I mean that the Czar has always in his train a vast number of grand dignitaries of the household, and *bonâ fide* courtiers, constantly attendant on and resident with him. These courtly personages, when they drive about in carriages, are permitted to have a footman on the box beside the coachman. This John Thomas, or Ivan Thomasovitch, to be strictly Russian, is unpowdered and unwhiskered. There is no medium in a serf's shaving here; he is either full-bearded or gaol-cropped. His shirt and indeed lower habiliments are doubtful, for he wears—over all, summer and winter—a huge cloak descending to his heels, of the very brightest scarlet,—a cloak with a deep cape and a high collar.* The edges of this garment are passemented with broad bands of gold embroidered with countless double eagles on black velvet, and these have such a weird and bat-like, not to say demoniac effect, that the Muscovite flunkey clad in this flaming garment, and with an immense cocked-hat stuck fore and aft on his semi-shaven head, bears a fantastic resemblance to an India-house beadle, of whom the holy inquisition has fallen foul, and who, shorn of his staff, but with his red cloak converted into a San Benito, is riding to an *auto da fé* in his

* The Russians are extravagantly fond of red. That a thing is red, implies with them that it is beautiful; indeed, they have but one word (*preknasse*) to express both redness and beauty. The favourite Russian flower is the rose; though, alas! that has far more frequently to be admired in paper or wax than in actual existence. A crimson petticoat is the holiday dress of a peasant girl: and to have a red shirt is one of the dearest objects of a moujik's ambition.

master's carriage. Some general officers have soldier-footmen, who sit in the rumble of the calèche in the military gray cloak and spiked helmet. The ambassadors have their chasseurs plumed, braided, and *couteau-de-chassed;* but, with these exceptions, the outward and visible sign of the flunkey is wanting in Petersburg. Yet everybody keeps a carriage who can afford it; and many do so who can't. I was very nearly having half a private droschky myself; the temptation was so great, the horses so good, the coachman so skilful, the difficulties of pedestrianism so great, the public conveyances so abominably bad. As I have remarked, the majority of carriage-keepers don't take footmen out with them. I have seen the great Prince Dolgorouki, the chief of the gendarmerie and secret police, the high and mighty wooden-stick in waiting at whose very name I tremble still, step out of one of those modest little broughams called "pill-boxes," open it, and close the door as if he knew not what a footman was, and walk up stairs to the second floor of a lodging-house, with his stars, his ribbons, his helmet, his sword, his spurs, unflunkeyed and unannounced. Fall not, however, into the obvious error of imagining that Ivan Thomasovitch the flunkey lacks in Russian households; within doors he swarms, multiplies himself orientally and indefinitely; but, out of doors, *Nous Autres* do without him.

Two words more, and I have done with the equipages of the great. Although there are probably no people on earth that attach so much importance to honorific distinctions, caste, costumes, and "sun, moon, and stars" decorations as the Russians; their carriage-panels are singularly free from the boastful imbecilities of that sham heraldry and harlequinading patchwork which some of us in the West throw like particoloured snuff into the eyes of the world to prove our high descent. And, goodness knows, the Russian nobility are barbarically well-born enough. They have plenty of heraldic kaleidoscope-work at home; but they keep it, like their servants, for grand occasions. For ordinary wear, a plain coronet on the panel, or—more frequently still—the simple initials of the occupant, are thought sufficient for a prince's carriage.

A last word. Since my return to Western Europe I have noticed that the dear and delightful sex who share our joys and double our woes—I mean, of course, the Ladies!—have adopted a new, marvellous, and most eccentric fashion in wearing-apparel. I allude to the cunning machines, of a balloon form, composed of crinoline, whalebone, and steel—called, I have heard—*sous jupes bouffantes*, and which I conjecture the fair creatures wear underneath their dresses to give them that swaying, staggering nether appearance, which is so much admired —by milliners—and which I can compare to nothing so closely as the Great Bell of Bow in a gale of wind, and far gone in the dropsy. What have the *sous jupes bouffantes* to do with the coachmen of the Russian boyards? you will ask. This. For a very swell coachman, there is nothing thought more elegant and distinguished than a most exaggerated bustle. The unhappy wretches are made to waspi-cate their waists with their sashes; and, all around in a hundred plaits, extend the skirts of their caftans. What species of under-garments they wear, or what mechanical means they adopt to inflate their skirts, I know not; but they have exactly the same Tombola appearance as our fashionable ladies. Isn't it charming, ladies? Only twenty years since, you borrowed a fashion from the Hottentot Venus, and now skirts are worn *à la Moujik Russe.*

There are some old Russian families who are yet sufficiently attached to ancient, pigtail observances, as to drive four horses to their carriages. The leaders are generally a long way ahead; there is a prevailing looseness in the way of traces; and the postilion, if any, sternly repudiates the bare idea of a jacket with a two-inch tail, and adheres to the orthodox caftan; a portion of whose skirts he tucks into his bucket-boots along with his galligaskins. Caftan and boots and breeches, breeches, boots, and caftan, bushy beard and low-crowned hat! Dear reader, how often shall I have to reiterate these words—how long will it be before you tire of them? There are sixty-five millions of people in this Valley of the Drybones; but they are all alike in their degree. The Russian people are printed, and there are thousands of impressions of gaudy officers struck in colours, gilt and tinselled like Mr. Parks's characters (those that cost three-and-sixpence); and there are millions of humble moujiks and ischvostchiks, roughly pulled and hastily daubed—only a penny plain and twopence coloured.

VII.

THE CZAR'S HIGHWAY.

"Let me," said somebody who knew what he was saying, "write the ballads of a people, and he may write their history who will." If the Czar of all the Russias would only allow me to make his roads for him, the great problem of the way out of barbarism in his empire could be solved by a child. There is no such civilizer as a good road. With even an imperfect highway disappear highwaymen, crawling beggars, dirty inns and extortionate charges, lazy habits, ignorance, and waste lands. Our shops, our horses' legs, our boots, our hearts, have all benefited by the introduction of Macadam; and the eighteen modern improvements mentioned by Sydney Smith can all be traced, directly or indirectly, to the time when it fortuitously occurred to the astute Scotchman (where are his Life and Times, in twenty volumes?) to strew our path with pulverized granite. I am convinced that our American cousins would be much less addicted to bowie-kniving, revolvering, expectorating, gin-slinging, and cow-hiding the members of their legislature, if they would only substitute trim, level, hedge-lined highways for the vile corduroy roads and railway tracks thrown slovenly anyhow, like the clothes of a drunken man, across prairies, morasses, half-cleared forests, and dried-up watercourses, by means of which they accomplish their thousand-mile trips in search of dollars. What a dreadful, though delightful place was Paris when I knew it first!—foul gutters rolling their mud-cataracts between rows of palaces; suburban roads alternating between dust-heaps and sloughs of despond; and boulevards so badly paved, that the out-patienced population were continually tearing them up to make barricades with. There have been no *émeutes* in Paris since boulevards were macadamized. Much of the Ribbonism, landlord-stalking from behind hedges, and Skibbereen starvation of Ireland, may be attributed to the baleful roads of bygone days, which were full of holes, known as curiosities, and on which the milestones were so capriciously distributed, that whereas every squire (of the right way of thinking) had one on each side of his park-gates, unpopular localities, and villages where tithe-proctors dwelt, were left without milestones altogether. Who was it that was chief of the staff to murderous Major-General Mismanagement in the Crimea? The hideous roads from Balaclava to the front. When the railway navvy took up the spade, the soldier's grave-digger laid his mattock down. What is it that impresses us mostly with the grandeur of the civilization of that stern, strong people who came to Britain with Cæsar, but the highways they made, whose foundations serve even now for our great thoroughfares, and which remain imperishable monuments of their wisdom and industry—the wonderful Roman roads. And flout nor scout me none for uttering truisms concerning roads in their relation to civilization; for Paris is rapidly surpassing our vaunted London City in excellence of pavement. New Street, Covent Garden, is in a bad way; the Victoria Road, Kensington, leaves much to be desired; and the Commissioners of Turnpike Trusts, all over the country, want looking after sharply. There is need for us to have sermons on the better care of the stones. If we don't keep a bright lookout for our pavements, we shall infallibly retrograde —decay—as a nation; and M. Ledru Rollin will rejoice. If we are unmindful of the Queen's highway, we shall inevitably come to clip the Queen's English, and break the Queen's peace, and to the dark ages. It behoves us especially to be watchful, for our protectors never forget to collect the Queen's taxes, roads or no roads.

The Czar's highway, which is literally his—for every thing in the empire, movable and immovable, animated and inanimated, is his own private and personal property *—is the worst highway that was ever seen.

The Czar's highway in his two metropolises, in his provinces and in his country towns, from north to south—from Karlsgammen, in Lapland, to Saratchikovskaïa, in Astrakhan—is the most abominable—

* I remember once asking a Russian gentleman (not, however, with the slightest expectation of receiving a direct answer) the amount of the Imperial Civil List. He scarcely seemed to understand my question at first; but he replied, eventually, that his Majesty "affected to himself" a certain gigantic sum (I forget how many million silver roubles, for I am boldly bankrupt in statistics); but "Que voulez-vouz," he added, "avec un Liste Civile? TOUT appartient au Czar, et il prend ce qu'il veut!"

I can't call it a corduroy road, or a kidney-potato road, or a sharp-shingle road—the most miserable sackcloth-and-ashes road that was ever invented to delight self-mortifying pilgrims, to break postilions' constitutions, horses' backs, and travellers' hearts. There is the iron road, as all men know, from Petersburg to Pawlosky, and also from the northern capital to Moscow. This last is kept in order by an American company, and is a road; but you understand that there can be railways and railways, and even out of rails and sleepers can Czarish men make iron roads to scourge, and make a difficult Avernus to us, withal. From Petersburg to Warsaw there is a *chaussée*, or road, which, by a fiction as beautiful and fantastic as a poem by Mr. Tennyson, is said to be macadamized. It is rather O'Adamized; there is a great deal more Irish gammon than Scotch granite about it; but it is perpetually being re-mended at the express command of the emperor. When he travels over it, the highway is, I dare say, tolerable; for the autocrat being naturally born to have the best of everything, his subjects have an extraordinary genius for supplying him with the very best, and the very best it is for the time being. When the Czar is coming, rotting rows of cabins change into smiling villages, bare poles into flowering shrubs, rags into velvet gowns, Polyphemus becomes Narcissus; blind men see, and lame men walk, so to speak. The Czar can turn anything except his satraps' hearts.

Of the provincial highways, and the vehicles that do roll upon them—kibitkas, telegas, and tarantasses, I shall have to speak hereafter. My object in this paper is to give some idea of the pavement of St. Petersburg, of which hitherto you have had but the glimpse of a notion in the words I have set down about ischvostchiks and concerning droschkies. I have come, by the way, on a new reading of the former multi-named individual. The correspondent of a Belgian newspaper calls him by the startling appellation of Ishwoschisky. I am not far from thinking that his real name must be Ishmael; for every man's (writing) hand is against him, and it is by no means uncommon for his hand to be against every man. There is a village in Carelia whose sons almost exclusively pursue the ischvostchik calling. There are a good many of them in St. Petersburg, where they have a high reputation as skilful drivers, and not quite so cheerful a renown for being all murderers. 'Gin an ischvostchik of this celebrated village meet with a drunken or a sleepy fare on a dark night, it is even betting that he will give the exact reading of the popular Scotch ditty, and make the fare into a "body" before he has long been coming through the ride.

Many persons endeavour to explain the badness of the St. Petersburg pavement by the severity of the climate, and the treacherous nature of the soil on which the city is built. The whole place is, it must be confessed, a double-damned Amsterdam; and it has often been with feelings akin to horror that I have peeped into a hole on the magnificent Nevskoï, when the workmen were mending the pavement—which they are incessantly occupied in doing in some part of the street during the summer months. At a distance of perhaps two feet from the granite slabs of the footpath, or the hexagonal wooden blocks of the roadway, you see the ominous rotting of wooden logs and piles on which the whole city is built, and at a dreadfully short distance from them you see the WATER—not so muddy, not so slimy, but the real water of the Neva. St. Petersburg has been robbed from the river. Its palaces float rather than stand. The Neva, like a haughty courtezan, bears the splendid sham upon her breast, like a scarlet letter, or the costly gift of a lover she hates. She revolted in eighteen hundred and twenty four, she revolted in 'thirty-nine, she revolted in 'forty-two, and tried to wash the splendid stigma away in floods of passionate tears. She will cast it away from her some day, utterly and for ever. The city is an untenable position now, like Naples. It must go some day by the board. Isaac's church and Winter Palace; Peter the Great's hut and Alexander's monolith will be no more heard of, and will return to the Mud, their father, and the Ooze, their mother.

In the Nevskoï Perspective and the two Morskaias, violent efforts have been made for years past, in order to procure something like a decent pavement. There is a broad foot-way on either side, composed of large slabs; but their uncertain foundation causes them now to settle one way, now on the other, now to present a series of the most extraordinary angular undulations. It is as though you were walking on the sloping roofs of houses, which had sunk into the boggy soil up to frieze and architrave; and this delusion is aggravated by the bornes, or corner-posts, set up to prevent carriages encroaching on the foot-pavement, which bornes, being little stumps of wood, just peering from the earth at every half-dozen yards, or so, look like the tops of lamp-posts. But the roof-scrambling effect is most impressive during the frequent occasions in the summer months, when the streets of St. Petersburg are illuminated. Most of the birthdays of the members of the Imperial family fall between May and August; and each scion of the illustrious house of Romanoff has an illumination to himself, by right of birth. You, who are yet fresh from the graphic and glowing description of the coronation illuminations at Moscow, by the man who fought the Battle of England in the Crimea, better and more bravely than the whole brilliant staff who have been decorated with the order of the Bath, and who would have gone there, for head-shaving purposes, long ago, if people had their due—doubtless, expect a very splendid account from me of illuminations at St. Petersburg. But it was my fortune to see Russia, not in its gala uniform, with its face washed, and all its orders on: but Russia in its shirt sleeves, (with its caftan off, leaving the vexed question of shirts or no shirts in abeyance, would perhaps be nearer the mark,) Russia at-home, and not expecting visitors till September—Russia just recovering its breath, raw, bruised, exhausted, torn, begrimed from a long and bloody conflict.

The best illuminations, then, that met my gaze,

were on the birth-night of the Empress-mother, and consisted of an indefinite quantity of earthen pots, filled with train-oil, or fat, and furnished with wicks of tow. These being set alight were placed in rows along the pavement, one to each little wooden post, or borne. It was the antediluvian French system of lampions, in fact, smelling abominally, smoking suffocatingly, but making a brave blaze notwithstanding, and, in the almost interminable perspective of streets and quays, producing a very curious and ghastly effect. At midnight you could walk a hundred yards on the Nevskoï, without finding a single soul abroad to look at the illuminations: at midnight it was broad daylight. The windows were all blind and headless; what distant droschkies there may have been, made not the thought of a noise on the wooden pavement; and these rows of blinking, flaring grease-pots resting on the earth, led you to fancy that you were walking on the roofs of a city of the dead, illuminated by corpse-candles. Take no lame devil with you, though, good student, when you walk these paving-stone house-tops. Bid him unroof, and what will it avail you? There are no genial kitchens beneath, no meat safes before whose wire-gauze outworks armies of rats sit down in silent, hopeless siege; no cellars sacred to cats and old wine; no dust-bins, where ravens have their savings-banks, and invest their little economies secretly. There is nothing beneath, but the cold, black ooze of the Neva, which refuses to divulge its secrets, even to devils—even to the worsest devil of all, the police. An eminently secretive river is the

Neva. Its lips are locked with the ice-key for five months. It tells no tales of the dead men that find their way into it somehow—even when the frost is sharpest, and the ice thickest. Swiftly it carries its ugly secrets—swiftly, securely, with its remorseless current, to a friend in whom it can confide, and with whom it has done business before—the Gulf of Finland. Only, once a-year, when the ice breaks up, the Neva is taken in the fact, and murder will out.

As for the gas-lamps on the Czar's highway, they puzzle a stranger in Russia terribly. There is every element of civilization in St. Petersburg, from Soyer's Relish to the magnetic telegraph; and, of course, the Nevskoï and the Morskaïas have their gas-lamps. They are handsome erections in bronze, real or sham, rich in mouldings and metallic foliage. On the quays, the lamp-posts assume a different form. They are great wooden obelisks, like sentry-boxes that have grown too tall, and run to seed, and they are *bariolè*, or smeared over in the most eccentric manner with alternate bars of black and white paint. In Western Europe, these inviting spaces would be very speedily covered with rainbow-hued placards relating to pills and plays and penny-newspapers; but I should like to see the bill-sticker bold enough to deface his Imperial Majesty's sentry-box lamp-posts, with his sheet of double-crown and his paste-brush! This is no place for the famous Paddy Clark, who, being charged before a magistrate at Bow Street, with the offence of defacing the august walls of Apsley House with a Reform placard, unblushingly avowed his guilt, and added that he would paste a bill on the Duke of Wellington's back, if he were paid for it. I am afraid that Mr. Clark would very soon be pasting bills beyond the Oural Mountains for the Siberian bears to read, if he were alive, and in Russia; or, that, if he escaped exile, he would swiftly discover that the Russian police have a way of posting bills on the backs of human houses very plain and legible to the view. They always print, too, in red ink. These black and white lamp-posts, common, by the way, all over Russia, and whose simple and elegant scheme of embellishment is extended to the verst-posts, the sentry-boxes, and the custom-house huts at the frontiers and town-barriers, are an emanation from the genius of the beneficent but insane autocrat, Paul the First; their peculiar decoration is due to the same imperial maniac, who issued oukases concerning shoe-strings, cocked-hats, and ladies' muffs, and whose useful career was prematurely cut short in a certain frowning palace at St. Petersburg, of which I shall have to tell by and by. When I see these variegated erections, I understand what the meaning is of the mysterious American striped pig. This must have been his colour.* It must in justice be admitted, that though Paul was a roaring madman,

* Did my reader ever notice the curious fancy that persons not quite right in their minds have for stripes and chequers, or at least for parallel lines? Martin van Butchell used to ride a striped pony. I saw a lunatic in Hanwell sit for hours counting and playing with the railings. Many insane persons are fascinated by a chess-board: and any one who has ever had a brain fever will remember the horrible attractions of a striped wall-paper.

there are other countries where the sentry-boxes, at least, are similarly smeared. I happened, lately, to traverse the whole breadth of the miserable kingdom of Hanover, coming from Hamburg; and for sixty miles the road-side walls, palings, and hedges, were painted in stripes of black and yellow—the national Hanoverian colours. I do not like thee, Hanover, thee, thy king, nor coinage. The Hanoverian postman, wear a costume seedily imitative of our General Post-Office *employés;* but the scarlet is dingy and the black cockade a most miserable mushroom. It made me mad to see the letter-boxes, and custom-house walls, and railway vans all flourished over with the royal initials G. R. exactly in the fat, florid characters we have seen too much of at home, and surmounted by a bad copy of the English crown. I thought we were well rid of the four Georges for good and all, and here was a fifth flourishing about to vex me. It may be that I looked at Hanover, its black and yellow posts, postmen, and king's initials, with somewhat of a jaundiced eye; for I had to stop at Hanover three hours in the dead of night, waiting for the express train from Berlin, which was behind time, as usual, and crawled into the station at last, like an express funeral. There is the worst beer at Hanover—the worst cold veal, the worst waiter——but let me go back to the lamp-posts of Petersburg.

Bronze on the Nevskoï; striped sentry-boxes on the quays; for second-rate streets, such as the Galernaia-Oulitza, or Great Galley Street, the Podialskeskaia, or Street of the Barbers, more economical lamp-posts are provided, being simply great gibbets of rough wood, to which oil-lamps are hung in chains. There are other streets more remote from the centre of civilization, or Nevskoï, which are obliged to be contented with ropes slung across from house to house, with an oil-lamp dangling in the middle (the old Reverbère plan) ; and there are a great many outlying streets which do without lamps all the year round. But oil, or gas, or neither, all the posts in Petersburg are lampless from the first of May to the first of August in every year. During those three months there is, meteorologically and officially, no night. It sometimes happens, as in this summer last past, that the days draw in much earlier than usual. Towards the end of last July, it was pitch dark at eight o'clock, P. M. The government of the Double Eagle, however, does not condescend to notice these aberrations on the part of the clerk of the weather. The government night, as duly stamped and registered, and sanctified by Imperial oukases, does not commence till nine P. M. on the first of August; and then, but not a day or hour before, the lamps are lighted. To me, the first sign of gas in the Nevskoï, after returning from a weary journey, was a beacon of hope and cheerfulness ; but the Russians welcome the gas back with dolorous faces and half-suppressed sighs. Gas is the precursor of the sleety, rainy, sopping autumn, with its fierce gusts of west wind; gas is the herald, the *avant-courier*, of the awful winter: of oven-like rooms, nose-biting outward temperature, frozen fish, frozen meat, frozen tears, frozen every thing. Some

Russians will tell you that the winter is the only time to enjoy St. Petersburg. Then there are balls, then Montagnes de Glace, then masquerades, then the Italian opera, then sleighing parties, then champaigne suppers. With warm rooms, and plenty of furs, who need mind the winter? But give a Russian a chance of leaving Russia, and see to whom he will give the preference,—to the meanest mountebank at a wooden theatre in Naples, or to Mademoiselle Bosio at the Balschoï-Theater here. The Russians have about the same liking for their winter as for their government. Both are very splendid; but it is uncommonly hard lines to bear either; and distance (the greater the better) lends wonderful enchantment to the view both of the frozen Neva and the frozen despotism.

A few of the great shops on the Nevskoï and the Morskaïas have an economical supply of gas-lamps, and there is a restaurant or two so lighted. Oil and camphene are, however, the rule, and both are extremely cheap; while, on the other hand, gas is—not so much from the scarcity of coal, but from the enormous expense of its transit—a very dear article of consumption. Some of the second-class shops have oil-lamps, with polished tin reflectors; but in the humbler underground chandlery shops, or lavkas, I have frequently found the only illumination to consist of a blazing pine torch, or a junk of well-tarred cable, stuck in a sconce. Rude, or altogether wanting in light, as these shops may be, there is always, even in the most miserable, a dainty lamp, frequently of silver, suspended by silver chains before the image of the joss, or saint.

In the year 'twenty-four, a French company, after an immense amount of petitioning, intriguing, and Tchinnovnik-bribing, obtained an authorization from the government to light the whole of St. Petersburg with gas. They dug conduits into which the water broke; they laid down pipes which the workmen stole; they went so far as to construct a gasometer on a very large scale behind the cathedral of Kasan. They had lighted some hundred yards of the Nevskoï with gas, when a tremendous fire took place at their premises, and the gasometer exploded, with great havoc of life and property. From 'twenty-four to 'thirty-nine, a period of fifteen years, not a syllable was heard about the formation of a new gas company. Public opinion, for once, was stronger than bribery; for the ignorant and superstitious populace persisted in declaring that the destruction of the gasometer was a judgment from Heaven to punish the *Fransouski-Labarki*, the French dogs, for erecting their new-fangled and heretical building in the vicinage of our Lady of Kasan's most holy temple. I don't think that Siberia and the knout, even, would have been very efficacious in making the moujiks work with a will at building new premises for the offending pipes and meters. Gas is heretical; but the Russians are slightly more tolerant of some other institutions that exist to this day just behind and all around the most holy Kasan church, whose immediate neighbourhood enjoys an extended reputation as being the most infamous with respect to morality in St. Petersburg. Strange that it should be the same in the shadow of Westminster's twin towers, in the shameful little dens about the Parvis Notre Dame at Paris, in the slums of St. Patrick's, Dublin.

The new gas company have not done much during the last sixteen years. In the suburbs there is scarcely any gas; and the gas itself is of very inferior quality, pale and flickering, and grudgingly dealt out. I need not say that the lamps are placed as high up as possible. The professional thieves would extinguish them else, or the Russians would steal the gas,—an act of dishonesty that, at first sight, seems impossible, but which, when you become better acquainted with my Sclavonic friends,—with the exquisite art by which they contrive to steal the teeth out of your head, and the flannel jacket off your body, without your being aware of the subtraction,—will appear quite facile and practicable. Gas in Russia! I little thought—writing the secrets of the Gas in this journal three years ago, and vainly thinking that I knew them—that I should ever see a Russian or a Russian gas lamp.

The huge open places, or Ploschads, like stony seas, into which the gaunt streets empty themselves, are uniformly paved with granitous stones, of which the shores of the Gulf of Finland furnish an inexhaustible supply. This pavement, if arranged with some slight regularity, would be in the early stage of progress towards tolerable walking space; but the foundations being utterly rotten, treacherous, and quicksandy, the unhappy paving-stones tumble about in a stodge of mud and sand; and the Ploschads are, consequently, almost incessantly under repair. This is especially the case in the month of April, at the time of the general thaw. Part of the pavement sinks down, and part is thrown up—the scoriæ of small mud volcanoes. Thousands of moujiks are immediately set to work, but to very little purpose. The ground does not begin to settle before May; and when I arrived in St. Petersburg, many of the streets were, for pedestrians, absolutely impassable. The immense parallel series of streets at Wassili-Ostrov—Linies, as they are called—and which are numbered from one to sixteen, as in America, were simply bogs, where you might drive, or wade, or stride through on stilts, but in which pedestrianism was a matter of hopeless impossibility. The government, or the municipality, or the police, or the Czar, had caused to be constructed along the centre of these Linies, gigantic causeways of wooden planking, each above a mile in length, perhaps, raised some two feet above the level of the mud, and along which the dreary processions of Petersburg pedestrians were enabled to pass. This was exceedingly commodious, as long as you merely wanted to walk for walking sake; but of course, wherever a perspective intersected the Linie, there was a break in the causeway, and then you saw before you, without the slightest compromise in the way of step, a yawning abyss of multi-coloured mud. Into this you are entitled either to leap, and disappear, like Edgar of Ravenswood, or to wallow in it *à la pig*, or to endeavour to clear it by a hop, step, and a jump. The best mode of proceeding, on the whole, is to hail a droschky or a moujik, and, like Lord Ullin, offer him, not a silver pound, but sundry copper copecks, to carry you across the muddy ferry; and this, again, may be obviated by your chartering an ischvostchik's vehicle in the first instance, and leaving the causeway to those who like leaping before they look.

The ground having become a little more solid, the pavement might naturally be expected to improve. So it does, on the Nevskoï; but, in the suburbs, the occupant of each house is expected to see to the proper state of repair of the pavement immediately before his dwelling. As the Russian householder is not precisely so much enamoured of his city and government as to make of his allotted space of street a sort of Tom Tidler's ground, with silver roubles and gold imperials, or to pave it with porphyry, Carrara marble, or even plain freestone, he ordinarily employs the cheapest and handiest materials that his economy or his convenience suggests. The result is a most astonishing paving-salad, in which flints, shards and pebbles, shingles, potsherds, brickbats, mortar, plaster, broken bottles, and pure dirt are all amalgamated. The mosaic is original, but trying to the temper—destructive to the boots, and agonizing to the corns.

On the Nevskoï, almost every variety of pavement has been successively tried; but with very indifferent success. From Macadam to India-rubber, each material has had its day. Asphalte was attempted, but failed miserably, cracking in winter and fairly melting in summer. Then longitudinal boards were laid down on the carriage-ways, in imitation of the plank roads in the suburbs of New York. Finally, M. Gourieff introduced the hexagonal wooden pave-

8

ment with which, in London, we are all acquainted. This, with continuous reparation, answers pretty well, taking into consideration that equality of surface seems utterly unattainable, that the knavish contractors supply blocks so rotten as to be worthless a few days after they are put down, and that the horses are continually slipping and frequently falling on the perilous highway. It is unpleasant, also, to be semi-asphyxiated each time you take your walks abroad, by the fumes of the infernal pitch-caldrons, round which the moujik workmen gather, like witches.

The long and splendid lines of quays (unrivalled in magnificence of material, construction, and perspective in the whole world) are paved with really noble blocks of Finland granite. It is as melancholy as irritating to see the foul weeds growing at the kerbs; to be obliged to mount to them (they are some fourteen inches above the level of the road) by a wretched monticule of mud or dust, like a vagrant's footway through a broken hedge; to mark how many of the enormous slabs are cracked right across; and how, at every six steps or so, a block has settled down below the level, so as to form the bed of a pool of foul water into which you splash.

Any one can comprehend, now, why every street in the Czar's gorgeous metropolis is a Via Dolorosa, and why there are so many thousand ischvostchiks in St. Petersburg. Looking-glass slipperiness in winter; unfordable mud in spring; simooms of dust in summer; lakes of sloppy horrors in autumn: these are the characteristics of the Czar's highway.

I know impossibilities cannot be accomplished; I know the horrible climate can't be mended; but I have hopes of the pavement yet. There is a certain portion of the Balchoï Morskaïa which has, for about ten yards, a perfectly irreproachable pavement. The legend runs that the Czar Nicholas, of imperishable memory, slipped and fell on his august back hereabouts some years ago, and that he signified his wish to the inhabitants of that part of the Morskaïa to have the pavement improved, or to know the reason why. It was improved with electric celerity, and it has been a model pavement ever since. I am not the Czar Nicholas, nor the Czar Alexander, nor a bridge and pavement engineer, nor a contractor for paving and lighting. I only point out the wrong, and leave it to others to suggest the remedy. But until the Czar's highway is improved, both *intra* and *extra muros*, so long will there be barbarism in the very heart of the Venice of the north. When Petersburg is well paved, then will the power of the stick decay, and the Tchinn no longer steal: but this is too much in the Nostradamus style of prophecy. When Russia has better roads, let us hope that there will be better people to travel on them, your humble servant included.

VIII.

GOSTINNOI-DVOR. THE GREAT BAZAAR.

In St. Petersburg, Moscow, Kasan, Odessa, Kieff, Wladimir, Smolensk, Novgorod, and Ekaterinoslaf —not only in these, but in every Russian government town whose proportions exceed those of a village— there is a Gostinnoï-dvor, (literally, Things Yard, *cour aux choses*,) or general bazaar, for the sale of merchandise and dry provisions. The conquered and treaty-acquired provinces—Polish, Swedish, German, and Turkish—have their markets and emporia; but the Gostinnoï-dvor is an institution thoroughly and purely Russian, and thoroughly Asiatic. It will be my province, in papers to come, to speak of the Gostinnoï-dvor at Moscow, in which the native and humble Russian element is more strongly pronounced, and which is a trifle more picturesque, and a great deal dirtier, than its sister establishment in Petropolis. To the Gostinnoï-dvor, then, of St. Petersburg, I devote this paper. It is vaster in size, and incomparably more magnificent in proportions and contents, than any of its provincial rivals; and to me it is much more interesting. It is here that you can watch in its fullest development that most marvellous mixture of super-civilization and ultra-barbarism; of dirt and perfumes; accomplished, heartless skepticism, and *naïve* though gross superstition; of prince and beggar; poodle and bear; prevailing tyrant and oppressed creature, which make St. Petersburg to me one magnificent, fantastic volume; a French translation of the Arabian Nights, bound in Russia, illustrated with Byzantine pictures, and compiled by slaves for the amusement of masters as luxurious as the old Persians, as astute and accomplished as the Greeks, as cruel as the Romans, as debauched as those who dwelt in the Destroyed Cities, and whom it is a sin to name.

In seventeen hundred and fifty, Russia being happy under the sway of the benign Czarine Elizabeth—the want of a central bazaar being sensibly felt in the swelling capital, and nothing existing of the kind but a tumble-down row of wooden barracks, as filthy as they were inconvenient, hastily run up by convicts and Swedish prisoners in the days of Petri-Velikè—an enormous edifice of timber was constructed on the banks of the Moïka, close to what was then called the Green Bridge, but is now known as the Polizeiskymost or Pont de Police. This was the first Gostinnoï-dvor in St. Petersburg. Five years later it incurred the fate of theatres in all parts of the world, and of every class of buildings in Russia,—that species of architectural measles known as a fire. It was burnt to the ground, together with a great portion of the quarter of the city in which it was situated; and its reërection, in stone, was soon after commenced on the spot where it now stands: on the left-hand side of the Nevskoï Perspective, and about a mile from the chapel-spire of the Admiralty. It forms an immense trapezoid, framed between four streets. Its two principal façades front the Nevskoï and the Sadovvaïa, or Great Garden Street, which last intersects the Perspective opposite the Imperial Library. The principal façade is one hundred and seventy-two sagenes long. There are three archines to a sagene, or eighty-four inches ; I think, therefore, that I am right, according to Cockeroffsky, in saying that there is a frontage of twelve hundered and four feet, or more than four hundred English yards, to the Gostinnoï-dvor. The reconstruction in stone did not extend very far. Funds came in too slowly ; or, more probably, were spent too quickly by those intrusted with them ; and, for a long time, the rest of the bazaar consisted of rows of barracks and booths in timber, which were all duly reconsumed by fire in seventeen hundred and eighty. The Gostinnoï-dvor was then taken in hand by the superb Catherine, who had a decided genius for solidity and durability in architecture ; and under her auspices, the great Things Yard assumed the form it now presents. Huge as it is, it only forms a part of that which the Russians call the Gorod or City of Bazaars ; for immediately adjoining it—inferior in splendour of structure, but emulous in stores of merchandise and vigour of traffic, are three other bazaars,—the Apraxine-dvor, the Stehoukine-dvor, and the Tolkoutchji-rinok, or Great Elbow-market, which last is the Rag Fair or Petticoat Lane of St. Petersburg : all the old clothes, and a great proportion of the stolen goods, of the capital being there bought and sold.

On the same side of the way as the Gostinnoï-dvor on the Nevskoï, and close to the commencements of its arcades, is the enormous edifice of the Douma, or Hôtel de Ville. This was originally built of wood, but has been gradually repaired and enlarged with stone, and has slowly petrified, as men's minds are apt to do in this marmorifying country. Its heart of oak is now as hard as the nether millstone; and stucco pilasters, and cornices in Crim-Tartar Corinthian, together with abundance of whitewash and badigeonnement, conceal its primitive log walls. This huge place (what public building in Petersburg is not huge?) is facetiously supposed to be the seat of the municipal corporation of St. Petersburg. There is a civil governor, or Lord Mayor, it is true, who is officially of considerably less account than the signification of an idiot's tale in the hands of M. le Général Ignatieff, the military Governor-General of St. Petersburg, without whose written authority no person can leave the capital. There is a president and six burgomasters, and a Council of Ten notable citizens; but all and every one of them—governors civil and governors military, burgomasters, and notables—are members of the celebrated and artistic corps of Marionnettes, of whose performances at Genoa and at the Adelaide Gallery most people must have heard, and who have a theatre on a very large scale indeed in Holy Russia. They are beautifully modelled, dressed with extreme richness, (especially as regards stars and crosses,) are wonderfully supple in the joints, and have the most astonishing internal mechanism for imitating the sounds of the human voice. The strings of these meritorious automata are pulled by a gentleman by the name of Dolgorouki, who succeeded that eminent performer, M. Orloff, as chief of the gendarmerie and High Police, and manager (under the rose) of sixty-five millions of Marionnettes. So perfectly is he master of the strings of his puppets, and so well is he acquainted with the departments behind the scenes of the Theatre Royal, Russia, that the ostensible lessee and manager, Alexander Nicolaïevitch, who inherited the property from his father, Nicolaïaleosandrovitch, (an enterprising manager, but too fond of heavy melodramas of the startling order,) is said to be rather afraid of his stage-manager. A. N. is a mild and beneficent middle-aged young man, whose dramatic predilections are supposed to lean towards light vaudevilles and burlettas, making all the characters happy at the fall of the curtain. He is not indisposed either, they say, to many free translations from the French and English; but the stage-manager of the Marionnettes won't hear of such a thing, and continues to keep the tightest of hands over his puppets. The most curious feature in all this is, that the stage-manager has himself a master whom he is compelled, no one knows why, to obey.

This master—a slow, cruel, treacherous, dishonest tyrant—is never seen, but dwells remote from mortal eyes, though not from their miserable ken, like the Grand Lama. His—her—its name is System. Liberal, nay, democratic stage-managers, have been known to assume the government of the sixty-five million dolls, and forthwith, in their blind obedience to system, to become intolerable oppressors, spies, and thieves. Things have gone wrong before now in the Theatre Royal; and several lessees have died of sore throat, of stomachache, of headache, and of compression of the œsophagus. But this abominable System has lived through all vicissitudes, and though immensely old, is as strong and wicked as ever.* The old hypocrite gives out occasionally that he is about to reform; but the only way to reform that hoary miscreant, is to strangle him at once, and outright. Your fingers are not unaccustomed to this work, most noble Boyards.

The only timber yet unshivered of the Douma, is the great watchtower, one hundred and fifty feet in

* A magnificent diamond *tabatière* full of snuff has recently been thrown into the eyes of Western Europe from the coronation throne at Moscow. The only real abolition of a grievance, in this much-belauded manifesto, is the removal of part of the tax on passports to native Russians, who, if they had families, were formerly obliged to pay something like four hundred pounds a-year to the government while travelling. The political amnesty is a cruel farce; not but that I believe the Emperor Alexander to be (though deficient in strength of mind) a sovereign of thorough liberal tendencies, and of extreme kindness of heart; but he dares not accomplish a tithe of the reforms he meditates. I was speaking one day to an intelligent Russian on this subject, (he was a republican and a socialist, but an accomplished gentleman,) who, so far from blaming the Czar for his meagre concessions to the spirit of the age, made a purely Russian excuse for him: "Que voulez-vous?" he said, "le Tsar lui-même a peur d'être rossé par la Police Secrète." The idea of the Autocrat of all the Russias being deterred from increased liberalism by bodily fear of the STICK is sufficiently extravagant; but there is, nevertheless, a great deal of truth in the locution.

height, which is entirely of sham marble, but real wood. There is a curious telegraphic apparatus of iron at the summit, and in this work the different fire-signals. They are in constant employment.

I can imagine no better way of conveying a palpable notion of things I have seen in this strange land, than to institute comparisons between things Russian, which my reader will never know, I hope, save through the medium of faithful travellers, and things familiar to us all in London and Paris. So. If you take one avenue of the glorious Palais Royal, say that where the goldsmith and jewellers' shops are, and with this combine the old colonnade of the Regent's Quadrant; if to this you add a dwarfed semblance of the Piazza in Covent Garden—especially as regards the coffee-stalls at early morning; if you throw in a dash of the Cloisters of Westminster Abbey—taking care to Byzantinize all the Gothic, but keeping all the chequered effects of chiaro-oscuro; if, still elaborating your work, you piece on a fragment of that musty little colonnade out of Lower Regent Street, which ought to belong to the Italian Opera House, but doesn't, and at whose corner Mr. Seguin's library used to be; if, as a final architectural effort, you finish off with a few yards of the dark entry in Canterbury Cathedral yard, and with as much as you like (there is not much) of that particularly grim, ghostly, and mildewed arcade at the Fields corner of Great Queen Street, Lincoln's Inn: if you make an architectural salmagundy of all these; spice with a flavour of the delightful up-and-down, under-the-basement, and over-the-tiles, streets of Chester; garnish with that portion of the peristyle of the Palace of the Institute in Paris, where the print-stalls are; and serve up hot with reminiscences of what old Exeter 'Change must have been like; you will have something of a skeleton notion of the outward appearance of the Gostinnoï-dvor. Further to educate the eye, I must relate, that round all the pillars there is a long Lowther Arcade broke loose, of toys and small ware; that the Palais-Royal-like shops are curiously dovetailed with bits of the Bezesteen at Constantinople; that amongst the diamonds and gold lace there is a strong tinge of Holywell Street: to plant the photograph well in the stereoscope, I must beg my reader to endeavour to imagine this London and Paris medley transplanted to Russia. There is a roaring street outside, along which the fierce-horsed and fierce driven droschkies fly; through the interstices of the arches, you see, first droschkies, then dust, then palaces, palaces, palaces, then a blue, blue sky; within a crowd of helmets, gray greatcoats, beards, boots, red shirts, sheepskins, sabres, long gray cloaks, pink bonnets, and black velvet mantles, little children in fancy bonnets; nurses in crimson satin, and pearl tiaras; and all this circulating in an atmosphere where the Burlington Arcade-like odour of pomatum and *bouquet à la reine* (for perfumes abound in the Gostinnoï-dvor) struggles with that of Russia leather, wax-candles, and that one powerful, searching, oleaginous smell, which is compounded of Heaven knows what, but which is the natural, and to the manor-born, smell of the sainted land. Mind, too, that the roofs are vaulted, and that no lamps, save sacred ones, are ever allowed to be here lighted; and that at about every interval of ten yards there is a frowning archway whose crown and spandrils are filled in with holy pictures, richly framed in gold and silver, and often more richly jewelled. For in this, the special home and house of call for commercial roguery, the arrangements for the admired Fetish-worship are on a very grand and liberal scale.

A lamp suspended before the picture of a saint is supposed to carry an indisputable policy of insurance with it in its sacred destination; but, votive lamps apart, not a light is allowed at any time, night or day, in the Gostinnoï-dvor. There are no cigar-shops, it need scarcely be said—nor magasins for the sale of lucifer-matches. The Russians have a peculiar horror of, and yet fondness for, lucifer-matches, or *spitchki*, as they are called. There is a popular notion among servants and peasants, that they are all contraband, (I never had the slightest difficulty in purchasing them openly,) and that their sale—except to nobles, of course—is prohibited by the government. There are so many things you may not do in Russia, that I should not have been the least surprised if this had really been the case. The Russian matches, I may add, are of the most infamous quality—one in about twenty igniting. I believe that it is considered rather *mauvais ton* than otherwise if you do not frictionize them on the wall to obtain a light. I had a Cossack servant on whom, on my departure from Russia, I bestowed a large box of wax-taper matches I had brought from

Berlin; and I verily believe that he was more gratified with the gift than with the few paper roubles I gave him in addition.

As soon as it is dusk the shops of the Gostinnoï-dvor are shut and the early-closing movement carried into practical operation by hundreds of merchants and shopmen. Within a very recent period, even, so intense was the dread of some fresh conflagration that no stove or fireplace, not so much as a brazier or chaufferette, was suffered to exist within the bazaar. The unfortunate shopkeepers wrapped themselves up as well as they could in pelisses of white wolfskin, (which in winter, forms still a distinctive item of their costume;) and by one ingenious spirit there was invented a peculiar casque or helmet of rabbit-skin, which had a fur visor buttoning over the nose something after the absurd manner of the convicts' caps at Pentonville prison. Some hundreds of cases of frost-bite having occurred, however, and a large proportion of the merchants' showing signs of a tendency to make up for the lack of outward heat by the administration of inward stimulants, the government stepped in just as the consumption of alcohol threatened to make spontaneous combustion imminent, and graciously allowed stoves in the Gostinnoï-dvor. These are only tolerated from the first of November to the first of the ensuing April, and are constructed on one uniform and ingenious pattern, the invention of General Amossoff. Thus remembering all these regulation stoves, that no wood has been used in the construction of the whole immense fabric—all being stone, brick, and iron, the very doors being lined with sheets of the last-named material; and recalling all the elaborate and severe police regulations for guarding the Gostinnoï-dvor against the devouring element, I should take it quite as a matter of course, were I to hear some fine morning that the pride of mercantile Petersburg had been burnt to the ground. Man has a way of proposing and Heaven of disposing, which slide in perfectly different grooves. Iron curtains for isolation, fireproof basements, and reservoirs on roofs, won't always save buildings from destruction, somehow; and though nothing can be more admirable than the precautions against fire adopted by the authorities, the merchants of the Gostinnoï-dvor have an ugly habit of cowering in their back shops, where you may frequently detect them in the very act of smoking pipes of Toukoft tobacco, up the sleeves of their wolf-skin touloupes, or poking charcoal embers into the eternal samovar or tea-urn. I have too much respect for the hagiology of the orthodox Greek Church to attribute any positive danger from fire to the thousand and one sacred grease-pots that swing, kindled from flimsy chains in every hole and corner; but, I know that were I agent for the Sun Fire Insurance, I would grant no policy, or, at all events, pay none, for a house in which there was a samovar. Once lighted, it is the best tea-urn in the world; the drawback is, that you run a great risk of burning the house down before you can warm your samovar properly.

The shops in the Gostinnoï-dvor are divided into lines or rows, as are the booths in John Bunyan's

Vanity Fair. There is Silkmercer's Row; opposite to which, on the other side of the street, are Feather-bed Row and Watchmakers' Row. Along the Nevskoï side extend Cloth-merchants' Row, Haberdashers' Row, and Portmanteau Row, intermingled with which are sundry stationers, booksellers, and hatters. The side of the trapezoid over against the Apraxine-dvor (which runs parallel to the Nevskoï) is principally occupied by coppersmiths and trunk-makers; the archways are devoted to the stalls of toy-merchants and dealers in holy images: while all the pillar-standings are occupied by petty chapmen and hucksters of articles as cheap as they are miscellaneous. It is this in-door and out-door selling that gives the Gostinnoï-dvor such a quaint resemblance to a Willis's Room Fancy Fair set up in the middle of White-chapel High Street. One side of the trapezoid I have left unmentioned, and that is the long arcade facing the Sadovvaïa, or Great Garden Street. This is almost exclusively taken up by the great Boot Row.

Every human being is supposed to be a little insane on some one subject. To the way of watches some men's madness lies; others are cracked about religion, government, vegetarianism, perpetual motion, economical chimney-sweeping, lead-mines, squaring the circle, or the one primeval language. Take your soberest, most business-like friend, and run carefully over his gamut, and you shall come on the note; sweep the lyre and you shall find one cracked chord. I knew a man once—the keenest at driving a bargain to be met with out of Mark Lane—who never went mad till two o'clock in the morning, and on one topic; and then he was as mad as a March hare. We think that we have such an excellent coinage; but how many a bright-looking shilling is only worth elevenpence halfpenny! We boast of our improved beehives; but how often the buzzing honey-makers forsake the hive, and house themselves in our bonnets! I have a Boswell (every writer to the lowliest has his Boswell) who professes to have read my printed works; and according to him I am mad on the subject of boots. He declares that my pen is as faithful to the boot-tree as the needle to the pole; and that, even as the late Lord Byron could not write half-a-dozen stanzas without alluding, in some shape or other, to his own lordship's personal attractions and hopeless misery, so I cannot get over fifty lines of printed matter without dragging in boots, directly or indirectly, as a topic for description or disquisition. It may be so. It is certain that I have a great affection for boots, and can ride a boot-jack as I would a hobby-horse. Often have I speculated philosophically upon old boots; oftener have I ardently desired the possession of new ones; and of the little man wants here below, nor wants long, I cannot call to mind anything I have an earnester ambition for than a great many pairs of new boots—good boots—nicely blacked, all of a row, and all paid for. I have mentioned, and admit this boot-weakness, because I feel my soul expand, and my ideas grow lucid as I approach the great Sapagi-Linie, or Boot Row of the Gostinnoï-dvor.

The Russians are essentially a booted people. The commonalty do not understand shoes at all; and when they have no boots, either go barefooted, or else thrust their extremities into atrocious canoes of plaited birch-bark. Next to a handsome kakoschnik or tiara headdress, the article of costume most coveted by a peasant-woman is a pair of full-sized men's boots. One of the prettiest young English ladies I ever knew used to wear Wellington boots, and had a way of tapping their polished sides with her parasol-handle that well-nigh drove me distracted; but let that pass—a booted Russian female is quite another sort of personage. In the streets of Petersburg the "sign of the leg" or a huge jack-boot with a tremendous spur, all painted the brightest scarlet, is to be found on legions of houses. The common soldiers wear mighty boots, as our native brigade, after Alma, knew full well; and if you make a morning call on a Russian gentleman, you will very probably find him giving audience to his bootmaker.

But the Boot Row of the Gostinnoï-dvor! Shops follow shops, whose loaded shelves display seemingly interminable rows of works addressed to the understanding, and bound in the best Russia leather. The air is thick and heavy—not exactly with the spicy perfumes of Araby the Blest—but with the odour of the birch-bark, used in the preparation of the leather. Only here can you understand how lamentably sterile we western nations are in the invention of boots. Wellingtons, top-boots, Bluchers, Oxonians, high-lows, and patent leather Albert slippers,—name these, and our boot catalogue is very nearly exhausted; for, though there are very many other names for boots, and cunning tradesmen have even done violence to the Latin and Greek languages, joining them in unholy alliance to produce monstrous appellations for new boots; the articles themselves have been but dreary repetitions of the old forms. What is the Claviculodidas-tokolon, but an attenuated Wellington? what is even the well-known and established Clarence but a genteel high-low?

But, in the Sapagi-Linie you shall find boots of a strange fashion, and peculiar to this strange people. There are the tall jack-boots, worn till within a few months since by the Czar's chevalier guards. They are so long, so stern, so rigid, so uncompromising that the big boots of our lifeguardsmen would look mere stocking-hose to them. They are rigid, creaseless, these boots: the eyes, methinks, of James the Second would have glistened with pleasure to see them; they seem the very boots that gracious tyrant would have put a criminal's legs into, and driven wedges between. They stand up bodily, boldly on the shelves, kicking the walls behind them with their long gilt spurs, trampling their wooden resting-place beneath their tall heels, pointing their toes menacingly at the curious stranger. As to polish, they are varnished rather than blacked, to such a degree of brilliancy, that the Great Unknown immortalized by Mr. Warren, might not only shave himself in them, but flick the minutest speck of dust out of the corner of his eye, by the aid of their mirrored surface. These boots are so tall, and strong, and hard, that I believe them to be musket-proof, bomb-proof, Jacobi-machine proof, as they say the forts of Cronstadt are. If it should ever happen that the chevalier guards went forth to battle, (how did all the correspondents in the Crimea make the mistake of imagining that the Russian guards as guards were sent to Sebastopol?) and that some of those stupendous cavaliers were laid low by hostile sabre or deadly bullet, those boots, I am sure, would never yield. The troopers might fall, but the boots would remain erect on the ensanguined field, like trees, scathed indeed, by lightning, and encumbered by the wreck of branches and foliage, but standing still, firm-rooted and defiant. But they will never have the good luck to see the tented field,—these boots,—even if there be a new war, and the chevaliers be sent to fight. The jack-boots have been abolished by the Czar Alexander, and trousers with stripes down the sides substituted for them. They only exist now in reality on the shelves of the Sapagi-Linie, and in the imagination of the artists of the illustrated newspapers. Those leal men are true to the jack-boot tradition. Each artist writes from Moscow home to his particular journal to assure his editor that his drawings are the only correct ones, and that he is the only correspondent to be depended upon; and each depicts costumes that never existed, or have fallen into desuetude long since. Wondrous publications are illustrated newspapers; I saw the other day, in a Great Pictorial Journal, some charming little views of St. Petersburg in eighteen hundred and fifty six, and lo! they are exact copies of some little views I have of St. Petersburg in eighteen hundred and thirty-seven. There is one of a bridge from St. Izaack's church to Wassily-Ostrow, that has been removed these ten years; but this is an age of go-aheadism, and it is not for me to complain. The jack-boots of the chevalier guards, however, I will no more admit than I will their presence in the Crimea: for wert thou not my friend and beloved, Arcadi-Andrievitch? count, possesser of serfs, honorary counsellor of the college, and cornet in the famous chevalier guards of the empress? Four languages didst thou speak, Arcadi-Andrievitch, baritone was thy voice, and of the school of Tamburini thy vocalization. Not much afraid of Leopold de Meyer, need'st thou have been on the piano-forte; expert decorator wert thou of ladies' albums; admirable worker of slippers in gold and silver thread; cunning handicraftsman in wax flowers, and dauntless breaker-in of untamed horses. In England, Arcadi-Andrievitch, thou wouldst have been a smock-faced schoolboy. In precocious Russia thou wert honorary counsellor, and had a college diploma, a droschki (haras), stud of brood mares, and a cornetcy in the Guards. There are hair-dressers in Russia who will force mustachios on little boy's lips (noble little boys), and they have them like early peas or hothouse pines; for everything is to be had for silver roubles, even virility. Arcadi-Andrievitch and I were great friends. He had been for some months expectant of his cornetcy, and longing to change his Lyceum cocked-hat, blue frock, and toasting-fork-like small sword, for the gorgeous equipments of a guardsman. He was becoming melancholy at the delay in receiving his commission; now, fancying that the Czar's aides-de-camp had sequestered his petition; now, that his Majesty himself had a spite against him, and was saying, "No! Arcadi-Andrievitch, you shall not have your cornetcy yet awhile;" now grumbling at the continual doses of paper roubles he was compelled to administer to the scribes at the War-office and the Etat Major. The Russians (the well-born ones) are such liars that I had begun to make small bets with myself that Arcadi-Andrievitch had been destined by his papa for the career of a Tchinovnik, or government clerk, and not for a guardsman at all; when the youth burst into my room one day, in a state of excitement so violent as to lead him to commit two grammatical errors in the course of half-an-hour's French conversation, and informed me, that at last he had received his commission. I saw it; the Imperial Prikaz or edict, furnished with a double eagle big enough to fly away with a baby. Arcadi-Andrievitch was a cornet. I am enabled to mention my Russian friends by name without incurring the slightest risk of compromising them, or betraying private friendship; for in Russia you do not call a friend Brownoff or Smithoffsky, but you address him by his Christian name, adding to it the Christian name of his father. Thus, Arcadi-Andrievitch, Arcadius the son of Andrew. You employ the same locution with a lady: always taking care to use her father's baptismal name. Thus, Alexandra-Fedrovna, Alexandra the daughter of Theodore.

To return to my Arcadi-Andrievitch. Though he

was but a little boy, he possessed, as I have remarked, a droschky; and in this vehicle, a very handsome one, with a fast trotter in the shafts, and a clever mare, *dressée à la vollée*, by the side, and driven by a flowing bearded moujik, his property, (who was like the prophet Jeremiah,) he took me home to see his uniforms. The young rogue had had them all ready for the last six weeks, and many a time, I'll be bound, he had tried them on and admired his little figure in the glass, late at night or early in the morning. Although this lad had a dimpled chin that never had felt the barber's shear, he had a very big house all to himself, on the Dvortsovaïa Nabéréjenaïa, or Palace Quay: a mansion perhaps as large as Lord John Russell's in Chesham Place, and a great deal handsomer. It was his house: his Dom; the land was his, and the horses in the stable were his, and the servants in the antechamber were his, to have and to hold under Heaven and the Czar. I forget how many thousand roubles, spending money, he had a year, this beardless young fellow. I saw his uniforms; the tunic of white cloth and silver; the cuirass of gold; the brilliant casque surmounted by a flowing white plume; the massive epaulettes, the long silver sash, together with a vast supplementary wardrobe of undress frocks and overalls, and the inevitable gray capote. "But where," I asked, "are the jack-boots I have so often admired in the Sapagi-Linie, and the military costume prints in Daziaro's window?" He sighed, and shook his head mournfully. The "Gossudar" (the lord) "has abolished the boots," he answered. "I used to dream of them. I had ordered four pairs—not in the Gostinnoï-dvor; for the bootmakers there are soukinsinoï (sons of female dogs)—but of my own sabakoutchelovek,—of a booter who is a German hound, and lives in the Resurrection Perspective. He brought them home on the very day that the boots were suppressed. He had the impudence to say that he could not foresee the intentions of the Imperial Government, and to request me to pay for them; upon which, I believe, Mitophan, my body servant, broke two of his teeth—accidentally, of course, in pushing him down stairs. He is an excellent bootmaker, and one whom I can conscientiously recommend to you, and has long since, I have no doubt, put on more than the price of my jack-boots and his broken teeth to my subsequent bills.—*Mais, que voulez-vous?*—Thus far Arcadi-Andrievitch; and this is how I came to know that the Chevalier Guards no longer wore jack-boots.

I wonder why they were swept away. Sometimes I fancy it was because their prestige, as boots, disappeared with the Czar Nicholas. Like that monarch, they were tall, stern, rigid, uncompromising; the cloth overalls were more suited to the conciliating rule of Alexander the Second. Nicholas, like Bombastes, hung his terrible boots to the branch of a tree, and defied those who dared displace them to meet him face to face. They were displaced, and he was met face to face, and the Czar Bombastes died in a rage, like a poisoned rat in a hole, in a certain vaulted chamber in the Winter Palace. I have seen the tears trickle down the cheeks of the Ischvostchiks passing the window of this chamber, when they have pointed upward, and told me that Uncle Nicolaï died there; and Nicholas indeed had millions to weep for him,—all save his kindred, and his courtiers, and those who had felt his wicked iron hand. There is a hot wind about the deathbeds of such sovereigns that dries up the eyes of those who dwell within palaces.

Far, far away have the jack-boots of the Empress's Guards led me from the Sapagi-Linie of the Gostinnoï-dvor, to which I must, for very shame, return. More boots, though. Here are the hessians worn by the dashing hussars of Grodno,—hessians quite of the Romeo Coates cut. Now, the jack-boot is straight and rigid in its lustrous leather all the way down, from mid-thigh to ankle; whereas to your smart hussar, there is allowed the latitude of some dozen creases or wrinkles in the boot about three inches above the instep, and made with studied carelessness. Then the body of the boot goes straight swelling up the calf. I doubt not but a wrinkle the more or the less on parade would bring a hussar of Grodno to grief. These hessians are bound round the tops with broad gold lace, and are completed by rich bullion tassels.

Surely it was a spindle-shanked generation that gave over wearing hessians; and a chuckle-headed generation that imbecilely persist in covering the handsomest part of the boot with hideous trousers. To have done with the Gostinnoï-dvor, you have here the slight, shapely boots of the militia officer,—light and yielding, and somewhat resembling the top-boots of an English jockey, but with the tops of scarlet leather in lieu of our sporting ochre; there are the boots worn by the Lesquians of the Imperial Escort, curious boots, shelving down at the tops like vertical coal-scuttles, and with quaint, concave soles, made to fit the coalscoop-like stirrups of those very wild horsemen; and, finally, there are the barbarically gorgeous boots—or rather, boot-hose—of the Circassians of the Guard,—long lustrous half-trews, of a sort of chain-mail of leather, the tops and feet of embroidered scarlet leather, with garters and anklets of silver fringe and beads, and with long, downward curved spurs of silver, chased and embossed.

The theme shall still be boots, for the Sapagi-Linie overflows with characteristic boots. Are not boots the most distinctive parts and parcels of the Russian costume? and am I not come from Wellington Street, Strand, London, to the Gostinnoï-dvor expressly to chronicle such matters? Am I not in possession of this, a Russian establishment, and is it not my task, like an honest broker's man, to take a faithful inventory of the sticks? Here are the long boots of Tamboff, reaching high up the thigh, and all of scarlet leather. These boots have a peculiar, and, to me, delightful odour, more of myrrh, frankincense, sandal-wood, benzoin, and other odoriferents, than of the ordinary birch-bark tanned leather. They will serve a double purpose. They are impervious to wet; and (if you don't mind having red legs, like a halberdier or a turkey-cock) are excellent things to splash through the mud in; for mud only stains them in a picturesque and having-seen-service sort of way; and if you hang them to dry in your chamber when you return, they will pervade the whole suite of apartments with a balmy, breezy scent of new dressing-case and pocket-book, combined with pot-pourri in a jar of vieux Sèvres, pastilles of Damascus, Stamboul tchibouk-sticks, and pink billet-doux from a countess. If you like those odours gently blended one with the other, you would revel in Tamboff boots. But perhaps you like the odour of roast meat better, and cannot abide the smell of any leather. There are as many men as many tastes as minds to them, we know. There are some that cannot abide a gaping pig; and I have heard of people who swooned at the sight of Shapsygar cheese, and became hysterical at the smell of garlic.

Who has not heard of the world-famous Kasan boots? Well; perhaps not quite world-famous—there are, to be sure, a good many things Russian, and deservedly celebrated there, which are quite unknown beyond the limits of the Empire. At all events, the boots of Kasan deserve to be famous all over the world; and I will do my best—though that may be but little—to make them known to civilized Europe. The Kasan boot supplies the long-sought-after and sighed-for desideratum of a slipper that will keep on—of a boot that the wearer may lounge and kick his legs about in, unmindful of the state of his stocking-heels (I do not allude to holes, though they will happen in the best regulated bachelor families, but to darns, which, though tidier, are equally distasteful to the sight,) or a boot-slipper, or slipper-boot, which can be pulled off and on with far greater ease than a glove; which cannot be trodden down at heel, and which will last through all sorts of usage a most delightfully unreasonable time. The Kasan boot is innately Tartar, and the famous Balsagi of the Turkish women—loose, hideous, but comfortable boots of yellow leather which they pull over their papouches when they go a bathing or a bazaaring—are evidently borrowed from the Kasan prototype. This, to be descriptive after having been (not unduly) eulogistic, is a short boot of the high-low pattern, usually of dark crimson leather (other colours can be had, but red is the favourite with the Russians.) There is a cushion-like heel, admirably yielding and elastic, and a sole apparently composed of tanned brown paper, so slight and soft is it, but which is quite tough enough and landworthy enough for any lounging purpose. It is lined with blue silk, whose only disadvantage is, that if you wear the Kasan boot, as most noble Russians do, (without stockings) the dye of the silk being rather imperfectly fixed, comes off on your flesh, and gives you the appearance of an ancient indigo-stained Briton. The shin and instep of the Kasan boot are made rich and rare by the most cunning and fantastic workmanship in silver-thread and beadwork, and mosaic and marqueterie, or buhl-work, or inlaying—call it what you will—of different-coloured leathers. There is a tinge of the Indian mocassin about it, a savour of the carpets of Ispahan, a touch of the dome of St. Mark's, Venice; but a pervading and preponderating flavour of this wild-beast-with-his-hide-painted-and-his-claws-gilt country. It isn't Turkish, it isn't Byzantine, it isn't Venetian, it isn't Moyenage Bohemian. Why or how should it be, indeed, seeing that it is a boot from Kasan in Russia? Yet it has, like the monstrous Gostinnoï-dvor, its most certain dim characteristics of all the first four mentioned nationalities, which all succumb, though, in the long run, to the pure barbaric Muscovite element, unchanged and unchangeable (for all thy violent veneering, Peter Veliké) from the days of Rurik and Boris-Goudonof, and the false Demitrius. Every rose has a thorn—every advantage its drawback; and the quaint, cosy, luxuriant boot of Kasan has one, in the shape of a very powerful and remarkably unpleasant odour, of which fried candle-grease and a wet day in Bermondsey would appear to be the chief components. Whether the men of Kasan have some secret or subtle grease wherewith to render the leather supple, and that the disagreeable odour is so inherent to and inseparable from it as the nasty taste from that precious among medicaments, castor-oil; or whether the Kasan boot smell is simply one of the nine hundred and twelve distinct Russian stenches, of whose naturalization in all the Russias, Euler, Malte-Brun, and other savans, scientific and geographical, have been unaccountably silent, is uncertain; but so it is. We must accept the Kasan boot as it is, and not repine at its powerful odour. Camphor will do much; philosophy more; acclimatization to Russian smells, most of all.

There is certainly no invention for morning lounging that can equal this delightful boot. Our common Western slipper is an inelegant, slipshod, dangling, prone-to-bursting-at-the-side imposition (that I had any chance of obtaining those beauteous silk-and-bead slippers thou hast been embroidering for the last two years, Oh, Juliana!) There is certainly something to be said in favour of the highly-arched Turkish papouche. It is very easy to take off; but then it is very difficult to keep on; though, for the purpose of correcting an impertinent domestic on the mouth, its sharp wooden heel is perhaps unrivalled. There are several men I should like to kick, too, with a papouche—its turned-up toe is at once contemptuous and pain-inflicting. I have heard it said that the very best slippers in the world are an old pair of boots, ventilated with corn-valves made with a razor; but the sage who gave utterance to that opinion, sensible as it is, would change his mind if I had bethought myself of bringing him home a pair of Kasan boots. I have but one pair, of which, at the risk of being thought selfish, I do not mean, under any circumstances, to deprive myself. I have but to thrust my foot out of bed in the morning, for the Kasan boot to come, as it were of its own volition, and nestle to my foot till it has coiled itself round it, rather than shod me. I may toast the soles of this boot of boots against the walls of my stove, (my feet being within them,) without the slightest danger of scorching my flesh or injuring the leather. I might strop a razor on my Kasan boot; in short, I might do as many things with it as with the dear old Leather Bottelle in the song; and when it is past its legitimate work it will serve to keep nails in, or tobacco, or such small wares.

The morning equipment of a Russian seigneur is never complete without Kasan boots. When you pay an early visit to one of these, you will find his distinguished Origin reclining on an ottoman, a very long Turkish chibouk, filled with the astute M. Fortuna's krepky tabaky between his lips, his aristocratic form enveloped either in a long Caucasian caftan of the finest sheepskin, or in a flowered Persian dressing-gown, a voluminous pair of charovars, or loose trousers of black velvet bound round his hips with a shawl of crape and gold tissue, while a pair of genuine Kasan boots (to follow out the approved three-volume novel formula) complete his costume. Stay—his Origin's head will be swathed in a silk pocket-handkerchief, which sometimes from its pattern, and sometimes from its uncleanliness, is not quite so picturesque. On a gueridon, or side-table, there will be a green velvet *porte-cigare*, a box of sweetmeats, a bottle of Bordeaux, a syphon of Selzer water, and a half-emptied tumbler of tea, looking very muddy and sticky in its glass prism. There will be a lap-dog in the room who has been taught to understand French, though a Cossack cur by four descents, and who, at the word of command, in that language, goes through the military exercise. There will be the lap-dog, Mouche, or Brio's, plate of macaroons and milk in the corner. There will be, very probably, a parrot, perhaps a monkey; but in default of these, certainly a musical box, or a guitar. Scattered round his Origin's feet, and on his ottoman, will be his Origin's morning light literature: Paul de Kock, Charles de Bernard, or Xavier de Montépin, their amusing and instructive works: [Gentlemen of the old school read Pigault, Lebrun, and Ducray-Duminil,] you never see any newspapers. His Origin does not care about boring himself with the Journal de St. Pétersbourg, or the Gazette de l'Académie; and as for the Times, Punch, the Charivari, they are not to be had, even for *Nous Autres* in Russia. You seldom see any Russian book, unless his excellency deigns to be a savant. What is the good of studying the literature of a language which *Nous Autres* never speak? There is a piano in a corner, with a good deal of tobacco-ash on the keys. There are some portraits of opera girls on the walls, and some more Paris Boulevard lithographs too silly to be vicious, though meant to be so. If my reader wants to see portraits of Our Lady, or of the Czar, he or she must go to Gavrilo-Ermovaïevitch, the merchant's house, or Sophron-Pavlytch, the moujik's cabin—not to the mansions of *Nous Autres*. There is about the chamber, either in costume, or accoûtrement, some slight but unmistakable sign of its owner not always wearing the Persian dressing-gown, the charovars, and the Kasan boots, but being compelled to wear a sword, a helmet, a gray greatcoat, and a stand-up collar; and there is, besides the parrot, the monkey, and the lap-dog, another living thing in some corner or other—in the shape of one of his Origin's serfs, who is pottering about making cigarettes, or puffing at a samovar, or polishing a watch-case, silently and slavishly as is his duty.

IX.

MERCHANTS AND MONEY-CHANGERS.

I HAVE heard boots spoken of (not in very polite society) by the name of Steppers. I am in a position, now, to trace the etymology of the expression. Steppers are derived, evidently, from the enormous Steppe boots which the merchants in the Sapagi-Linie have to sell. Do you know what mudlarks' boots are? I mean such as are worn by the sewer-rummagers of Paris, which boots cost a hundred francs a pair, and of which only three pairs are allowed by the municipality *per escouade*, or squad of mudlarks. Of such are the Steppe boots; only bigger, only thicker, only properer for carrying stores and sundries, besides legs, like Sir Hudibras's trunk-hose. I don't know if hippopotamus's hide be cheap in Russia, or rhinoceros's skin a drug in the market; but of one or other of this class of integuments the Steppe boots seem to be made. When they become old, the leather forms itself into horny scales and bony ridges; the thread they are sown with may turn into wire; the soles become impregnated with flinty particles, and calcined atoms of loamy soil, and so concrete, and more durable; but, as for wearing away on the outside, you never catch the Steppe boots doing that. They are not altogether exempt from decay, either, these Blunderborean boots; and, like Dead Sea apples, are frequently rotten within, while their exterior is stout and fair to look upon; for they are lined throughout (and an admirably warm and comfortable lining it makes) with sheepskin, dressed to a silky state of softness, and curried into little spherical tufts, like the wool on a blackamoor's head with whom the great difficulty of ages has been overcome, and who has been washed white. For ornament's sake, the sheepskin is superseded round the tops by bands of rabbit or miniver skin; and there is a complicated apparatus of straps, buckles, and strings, to keep the boots at due mid-thigh height. But there is a profligate insect called the moth,—a gay, fluttering, volatile, reckless scapegrace, always burning candles at both ends, and burning his own silly fingers in the long run, who has an irrepressible penchant for obtaining board and lodging gratis in the woolly recesses of the sheepskin lining. Here he lives with several other prodigals, his relatives, in the most riotous and wasteful fashion—living on the fat, or rather, the wool of the land, and most ungratefully devouring the very roof that covers him. He sneezes at camphor, and defies dusting; and he and his crew would very speedily devour every atom of your boot-linings, but for the agency of a very powerful and, to moth, deadly substance, called mahorka. Mahorka is the very strongest, coarsest, essential-oiliest tobacco imaginable. It smells—ye gods, how it smells! It smokes as though it were made of the ashes of the bottomless pit, mingled with the leaves of the upas-tree, seasoned with assafœtida and cocculus indicus. It is, altogether, about the sort of tobacco against which James the First might have written his Counterblast, and a pipe of which he might have offered the devil, as a digester to his proposed repast of a pig, and a poll of ling, with mustard. This mahorka (the only tobacco the common people care about smoking) is, by Pavel or Dmitrych, your servants, rubbed periodically into the lining of your boots, (and into your schooba, too, and whatever other articles of furriery you may happen to possess,) causing the silly moth to fly away—if, indeed, it leave him any wings to fly, or body to fly away with. It kills all insects, and it nearly kills you, if you incautiously approach too closely to a newly-mahorka'd boot. Pavel and Dmitrych, too, are provokingly addicted to dropping the abominable stuff about, and rubbing it into dress-coats and moire-antique waistcoats, not only irrevocably spoiling those garments, but producing the same sternutatory effects on your olfactory nerves, as though somebody had been burning a warming-pan full of cayenne pepper in your apartment. All things admitted, however, mahorka is a sovereign specific against moths.

Every social observance in Russia is *tranché*—peculiar to one of the two great classes: it is a noble's custom, or a moujik's custom, but is never common to both. Russian gentlemen, within doors, are incessant smokers; the common people use very little tobacco. You never see a moujik smoking a cigar, and very rarely even enjoying his pipe. In some of the low vodki shops I have seen a group of moujiks with one blackened pipe among them, with a shattered bowl and scarcely any stem, charged with this same mahorka. The pipe was passed from hand to hand, each smoker taking a solemn whiff, and giving a placid grunt, exactly as you may see a party of Irish bogtrotters doing in a Connemara shebeen. Down south in Russia—I mean in the governments of Koursk and Woronesch—there is a more Oriental fashion of smoking in vogue. Some mahorka, with more or less dirt, is put into a pipkin, in whose sides a few odd holes have been knocked; and the smokers crouch over it with hollow sticks, reeds, or tin tubes, each man to a hole, and puff away at the common bowl. It is not that the Russian peasant does not care for his pipe; but he has an uneasy consciousness that the luxurious narcotic is not for the likes of him. For him to fill the pipe of his lord and master, and roll the paper cigarettes; that should surely be sufficient. Havn't our British matrons somewhat similar feelings concerning their housemaids' ringlets?

This powerful mahorka is powerless against the Russian bug. That hateful brown-uniformed monster, who is voracious, blood-sucking, impudent, and evil-smelling enough to be a Russian functionary, and to have a grade in the Tchinn, laughs a horse-leech laugh at mahorka. He would smoke a pipe thereof without winking, I am convinced. I knew a lady in St. Petersburg whose sleeping apartment (hung with sky-blue silk, fluted, and forming one of a suite rented at two hundred roubles a month) was so infested with arch bugs, that she would have gone into a high fever for want of rest, if febrile symptoms had not been counteracted by faintness with loss of blood. She was a buxom woman originally, and grew paler and paler every day. She tried camphor; she tried vinegar; she tried turpentine; she tried a celebrated vermin annihilator powder, which had been given to her by my friend Nessim Bey, (otherwise Colonel Washington Lafayette Bowie, U. S.,) and which had been used with great success by that gallant condottiere while campaigning against the bugs—and the Russians—with Omer Pasha in Anatolia. But all was in vain. The brown vampires rioted on that fair flesh, and brought all their brothers, like American sight-seers. The lady was in despair, and applied, at last, to a venerable Russian friend, decorated with the cross of St. Stanislas, second class, high up in the ministry of imperial appanages, and who had resided for more than half a century in St. Petersburg.

"How can you kill bugs, general?" (of course he was a general) she asked.

"Madame," he answered, "I think it might be done with dogs and a double-barrelled gun!"

This, though hyperbolical, is really the *dernier mot* of the vermin philosophy. If you want to destroy bugs, you must either go to bed in plate-armour, and so, rolling about, squash them, or you must sit up patiently with a moderator-lamp, a cigar, and a glass of grog, and hunt them. You will be a mighty hunter before the morning. Don't be sanguine enough to imagine that you can kill the wretches with the mere finger and thumb. I have found a pair of snuffers serviceable in crushing their lives out. A brass wafer-stamp (if you have a strong arm and a sure aim) is not a bad thing to be down on them with; I have heard a noose, or lasso of packthread, to snare and strangle them unawares, spoken of favourably; but a hammer, and a ripping-chisel of the pattern used by the late Mr. Manning, are the best vermin annihilators! I think the Russian government ought to give a premium for every head of bugs brought to the chief police-office, as our Saxon kings used to do for wolves. Only I don't think the imperial revenue would quite suffice for the first week's premium—were it but the tenth part of a copeck per cent.

The subject of vermin always raises my ire, even when I fall across it accidentally. I have been so bitten! We can pardon a cripple for denouncing the vicious system of swaddling babies; and who could be angry with Titus Oates for declaiming against the iniquity of corporal punishment?

Unless I have made up my mind to take lodgings in the Boot Row of the Gostinnoï-dvor—which as there are no dwelling-rooms there, would be but a cold-ground lodging—it is very nearly time for me, I opine, to leave off glozing over boots, and go elsewhere. But I could write a quarto about them. Once more, however, like the thief at Tyburn, traversing the cart, often taking leave, because loth to depart, I must claim a fresh, though brief reprieve; for see! here are the children's boots; and you who love the little people must come with me, and gaze.

Such boot-vines!—such espaliers of shoes! such pendant clusters of the dearest, tottiest, nattiest, gaudiest, miniatures of grown-men's boots, all intended for young Russia! Field-Marshals' boots, Chevalier Guards' boots, steppe boots, courier boots, cossack boots, Lesquian boots, Kasan boots, but all fitted to the puddy feet of the civil and military functionaries of the empire of Lilliput. Long live the Czar Tomas Thumbovitch, second of the name! And all the boots are picturesque; for the Russians have a delightful custom of dressing their little children, either in the quaint old Muscovite costume, or in the dress of some tributary, or conquered, or mediatized nation. One of the *Nous Autres* adult, must wear, perforce, either some choking uniform, or else a suit from Jencens on the Nevskoï, and of the latest Parisian cut; but, as a little boy—from four to eight years old say, (for, after that, he becomes a cadet, and is duly choked in a military uniform, and bonneted with a military headdress,) he wears the charming costume of a little Pole, or a Circassian, or a Lesquian, or a Mongol, or a Kirghiz, or a Cossack of the Don, the Wolga, the Oural, the Ukraine, or the Taurida. Nothing prettier than to see these dumpy little Moscovs toddling along with their mammas, or their nurses, in the verdant alleys of the Summer Garden; huge, flattened-pumpkin shaped Cossack turban-caps, or Tartar tarbouches, or Volhynian Schliapas, or Armenian calpacks on their heads; their tiny bodies arrayed in costly little caftans, some of Persian silk stiff with embroidery, some of velvet, some of the soft Circassian camel and goat-hair fabrics, some of cloth of gold, or silver; with splendiferous little sashes, and jewelled cartouch-cases on their breasts, and sparkling yataghans, and three-hilted poniards (like Celtic dirks); and the multi-coloured little boots you see in the Gostinnoï-dvor, made of scarlet, yellow, sky-blue, black-topped-with-red, and sometimes white leather, which last, with a little pair of gilt spurs, are really delectable to look upon. As the children become older, these pretty dresses are thrown aside, and the boys become slaves, (thrice noble and slave-possessing though they be,) and are ticketted, and numbered, and registered, and drilled, and taught many languages, and not one honest or ennobling thing; for the greater glory of God, and our Lord the Czar. Would you quarrel with me for liking children in fancy dresses? In truth, I love to see them as fantastically-gayly dressed as silk, and velvet, and gay colours, and artistic taste can make them. Never mind the crosspatches who sneer about us in England, and say our children look like little Highland kilt-stalkers, and little ballet-girls. I would rather that, than that they should look like little Quakers, or little tailors, or little bankers, or little beneficed clergymen, or little donkeys, which last-named is the similitude assumed by the asinine jacket, trousers, frill, and round hat. Dress up the children like the characters in the story-books. They don't belong to our world yet; they are our living story-books in themselves, the only links we have between those glorious castles in the air and these grim banks, talking-shops, and union workhouses, on earth, here. I regret that the Russians do not oftener extend their picturesque choice of wardrobe to the little girls. Now and again, but very, very rarely, I have seen some infant Gossudarinia—some little lady of six or eight summers—dressed in the long, straight, wide-sleeved farthingale, the velvet and jewelled kakoschnik like the painted aureole of a Byzantine saint, the long lace veil, the broad girdle tied in an X knot at the stomacher, and the embroidered slippers with golden heels, which still form the *costume de cour* of the Russian ladies; but in too many instances the pernicious influence of Mesdames Zoë Falcon and Jessie Field, Marchandes des Modes, have been predominant; and the little girls are dressed after the execrable engravings in the fashion-books, in flimsy gauze and artificial flower bonnets, many-fringed mantelettes, many-flounced skirts, lace-edged pantalettes, open-work stockings, (pink silk, of course!) and bronzed-kid bottines. I mind the time when little girls at home used to be dressed prettily, quaintly, like little gipsies or little Swiss shepherdesses; but I shudder for the day now when, returning to England, I shall see small Venuses swaying down Regent Street with iron-hooped petticoats, and decapitated sugar-loaf-like Talmas, and bird-cage bonnets half off their little heads. Why not have the paniers—the real hoops—back, ladies, at once: the red-headed mules, patches, hair-powder, and all the rest of the Louis Quinze Wardour-Street shoppery, not forgetting the *petite soupers*, and the Abbés, and the Madelonnettes, and the Parc aux Cerfs? Be consistent. You borrow your hoops from the French ladies' great grandmothers—

are there no traditions of their morals to be imported, as good as new, in this year fifty-six?

To reform female costume is far beyond my powers. Much might be done, perhaps, by administering forty blows with a stick to every male worker in metals convicted of forging steel *sous-jupes*, and by sentencing every female constructor of a birdcage bonnet to learn by heart the names and addresses of all the petitioners against Sunday park bands. Still I am moved by a humble ambition to introduce a new little-boy costume into my native country. Very many of the Russian gentry dress their children in the exact costume (in miniature) of our old friend the Ischvostchik, and few dresses, certainly, could be so picturesque, so quaint, and so thoroughly Russian. There is a small nephew of mine somewhere on the southern English coast, and whom (supposing him to have surmounted that last jam-pot difficulty by this time) I intend, with his parents' permission, to dress in this identical Ischvostchik's costume. I see, in my mind's eye, that young Christian walking down the High Street, the pride of his papa and mamma, clad in a gala costume of Muscovite fashioning—a black velvet caftan with silver sugar-loaf buttons, and an edging of braid; a regular-built Ischvostchik's hat with a peacock's feather; baggy little breeches of the bed-ticking design; and little boots with scarlet tops! Bran new from the Gostinnoï-dvor have I the hats and boots. The custom-house officers of four nations have already examined and admired them, and—doubtless in their tenderness for little boys—have allowed them to pass duty free. There only remain the stern-faced men in the shabby coats at the Dover Douane, to turn my trunks into a Hampton Court maze, and I shall be able to bring those articles of apparel safely to the desired haven. Who knows but I may introduce a new fashion among the youth of this land; that the apothecary, the lawyer, nay, the great mayor's wife of Bevistown, may condescend eventually to array her offspring after the fashion I set! Lord Petersham had his coat, Count D'Orsay his hat, Blucher his boot, Hobson his choice, Howqua his mixture, Bradshaw his guide, Daffy his elixir, and Sir John Cutler his stockings,—why may not I aspire to day when in the cheap tailors' windows I may see a diminutive waxen figure arrayed in the Ischvostchik's costume I have imported and made popular?

Some of these little children's boots are quite marvels in the way of gold and silver embroidery. The Russians are nearly as skilful in this branch of industry as the Beguines of Flanders; and since the general confiscation of ecclesiastical property by Catherine the Second (who certainly adhered to the totoporcine principle in a right imperial manner,) there have been many convents in the interior of Russia which have been self-supporting, and have even acquired ample revenues, through the skill of the nuns and the orphan girls whom they receive as inmates, in embroidery. *Du reste*, Russians as a nation are adepts in elaborate handiwork—imitative only, be it well understood. You must set them to work by pattern, for of invention they are comparatively barren; but whether the thing to be imitated be a miniature by Isabey or an Aubusson carpet, a Limerick glove or a Napier's steam-engine, a Sèvres vase or a Grecian column, an Enfield rifle or a chronometer by Mr. John Bennett of Cheapside, they will turn you out a copy, so close, so faithfully followed in its minutest details, that you will have considerable difficulty in distinguishing the original from the duplicate. There is an immense leaven of the Chinese Tartar in the Tartar-Russian. The small eyes, the high cheek-bone, sallow complexions and nervous gesticulation, I will not insist upon; the similarities are so ethnologically obvious.* But there are many more points of resemblance between the Russians and the Chinese. Both people are habitually false and thievish, both are faithless in diplomacy, bragging in success, mendacious in defeat, cruel and despotic always. Both nations are jealous of, and loathe, yet imitate, the manners and customs of strangers; both have an exaggerated and idolatrous emperor-worship, and Joss-worship; both are passionately addicted to tea, fireworks, graven images, and the use of the stick as a penal remedy. Both have enormous armies on paper, and tremendous fleets in harbour, and forts impregnable (till they are taken, after which misadventure they turn up to have been nothing but mere blockhouses;) both nations are slaves to a fatiguing and silly etiquette; both are outwardly polite and inwardly barbarous; both are irreclaimably wedded to a fidgetty,

* It should be taken into consideration that of ethnology, as a science, I am totally ignorant.

elaborately-clumsy system of centralization—boards of punishments, boards of rewards, boards of dignities. Both, in organization, are intensely literary and academical, and in actuality, grossly ignorant. The Chinese have the mandarin class system; the Russians have the Tchinn with its fourteen grades—both bureaucratic pyramids, stupendous and rotten. The Chinese bamboo their wives; the Russians bamboo their wives ("And so do the English," I hear a critic say: but neither Russian nor Chinese incurs the risk of six months at the treadmill for so maltreating his spouse.) In both empires there is the same homogeneous nullity on the part of the common people—I mean forty millions or so feeding and fighting and being oppressed and beaten like ONE, without turning a hair in the scale of political power; and—here I bring my parallel triumphantly to a close—both nations possess a language which, though utterly and radically dissimilar, are both copious, both written in incomprehensible characters, both as arbitrary in orthography and pronunciation as their emperors are arbitrary in power, and both difficult, if not impossible, of perfect acquisition by western Europeans. I declare, as an honest traveler, holding up my hand in the court of criticism, and desirous of being tried by Lord Chief Justice Aristarchus and my country, that I never passed a week in Russia without thinking vividly of what I had read about the Celestial Empire; that it was impossible to read the list of nominations, promotions, preferments, and decorations in the Pekin—I beg pardon—I mean the St. Petersburg—Gazette, without thinking of the mandarins, and the peacocks' feathers, and the blue buttons, and the yellow girdles; that the frequent application of the stick was wonderfully like the rice-paper representations of the administration of the bamboo; that the "let it be so" at the end of an oukase of the Russian Czar, struck me as being own rhetorical brother to the "respect this" which terminates the yellow-poster proclamations of the Chinese emperor.

I must do the Russians the justice to admit that they do not attempt to tell the time of day by the cat's eyes; and that, though arrant boasters, they are not the miserable cowards the Chinese are. As a people, and collectively, the Russians are brave in the highest degree; but it is in their imitative skill that the Russians, while they excel, so strongly resemble their Mantchou Tartar cousins. They have, it is true, a sufficient consciousness of the fitness of things to avoid falling into the absurd errors to which the Chinese, from their slavish adherence to a given pattern, are liable. They do not, if a cracked but mended tea-cup be sent them as a model, send home an entire tea-service duly cracked and mended with little brass clamps; they do not make half-a-dozen pair of nankeen pantaloons, each with a black patch in the seat, because the originals had been so repaired; neither do they carefully scrape the nap off a new dress-coat at the seams, in faithful imitation of the threadbare model; but, whatever you choose to set before a Russian, from millinery to murder, from architecture to arsenic, that will he produce in duplicate with the most wonderful skill and fidelity. There is, to be sure, always something wanting in these wondrous Russian copies. In their pictures, their Corinthian columns, their Versailles fountains, their operas, their lace bonnets, there is an indefinable *soupçon* of candle-grease and bears' hides, and the North Pole, and the man with the bushy beard who had to work at these fine things for nothing—because he was a slave. Can you imagine a wedding trousseau, all daintily displayed—all satin, gauze, orange flowers, Brussels lace, and pink rosettes—which had been clumsily handled by some Boy Jones? Imagine the marks of thumbs and greasy sooty fingers dimly disfiguring the rich textures! That, to me, is Russian civilization.

X.

THE SLOBODA. A RUSSIAN VILLAGE.

THIS is the Sloboda, or village, say of Volnoï-Voloschtchok, and there are five hundred villages like it. Still you are to know that Volnoï-Voloschtchok is some twenty-imperial versts from the government town of Rjew, in the ·government of Twer, and as all men should know, about half-way to Mocow the Holy; the Staraï, or old town, as the Russians lovingly term it, and which holds the nearest place in their affections to Kieff the Holiest, which they call the mother of Russian cities. This, then, is the seigneural sloboda of Volnoï, (as we will conclude to call it, for shortness;) and you are now to hear all about it, and its lord and master.

I have come from Twer on the Volga, on what, in Bohemian euphuism, is known as the Grand Scud. This, though difficult of exact translation, may be accepted as implying a sort of purposeless journeying—a viatorial meandering—a pilgrimage to the shrine of our Lady of Haphazard—an expedition in which charts, compasses, and chronometers have been left behind as needless impediments, and in which any degree of latitude the traveller may happen to find himself in, is cheerfully accepted as an accomplished fact.

On the Grand Scud then, with a pocket-book passably well lined with oleaginous rouble notes, and a small wardrobe in a leathern bag, I have come with my friend, Alexis Hardshellovitch. You start at my fellow-traveller's patronymic, sounding, as it does, much more of a New York oyter-cellar than of a district in the government of Twer. Here is the meaning of Hardshellovitch. Alexis, though a noble Russian of innumerable descents, and of unmistakable Tartar lineage, though wearing (at St. Petersburg,) the rigorous helmet, sword, and choking suit; though one of the corps of imperial pages, and hoping to be a hussar of Grodno by this time next year, is in speech, habits, and manners, an unadulterated citizen of the smartest nation in the creation. For Alexis's father, the general, was for many years Russian Minister Plenipotentiary at Washington in the district of Hail Columbia! U. S.

While there, he very naturally fell in love with, and married, one of the beautiful young daughters of that land; and Alexis was the satisfactory result. After a hesitation of some seventy years standing, the general diplomatically made his mind up to die, and his family availed themselves of the circumstance to bury him. Madame the ex-Ambassadress remained in Washington, and his son, being destined for the Russian service, was sent to St. Petersburg to be educated. Fancy the young Anacharsis being sent from Athenian Academe to be educated among the Scythians; or imagine Mrs. Hobson Newcome, of Bryanstone Square, sending one of her dear children to be brought up among the Zulu Kaffirs! The unfortunate Alexis was addressed, with care, to two ancient aunts (on the Muscovite side,) in the Italianskaia Oulitsa at St. Petersburg. These ladies were of the old Russian way of thinking; spoke not a word of French; took gray snuff; drank mint brandy, and fed the young neophyte (accustomed to the luxurious fare of a diplomatic cuisne and Washington table d'hôtes) on Stchï (cabbage soup,) batwinja (cold fish soup,) pirogues (meat pies,) and kvass. He had been used to sit under the Reverend Dr. D. Slocum Whittler (Regenerated-Rowdy persuasion) in a neat whitewashed temple, where lyric aspirations to Zion were sung to the music of Moore's Melodies; he suddenly found himself in a land where millions of people bow down billions of times every day to trillions of sacred Saracens' heads. He was soon removed to the Ecole des Pages—that grand, gilt, gingerbread structure

(I do not call it so as in any way reflecting on its flimsiness, but because it is, outwardly, the exact colour of under-done gingerbread, profusely ornamented with gold-leaf,) in the Sadovvaïa, and which was formerly the palace of the Knights of St. John of Jerusalem. Here, he found French, German, and English professors; but though he has been four years a page, the poor lad has been in a continual state of bewilderment ever since he left America. He has scarcely, as yet, mastered the first flight of the Giant's Staircase of Russian lexicology; the Russian gift of tongues seems denied to him; his French smacks of German, and his German of French; and his English, which, miserable youth, is of all languages the one he delights most to speak, is getting into an ancient and fishy condition. He misses his grammatical tip, frequently. He has an extensive salad of languages in his head; but he has broken the vinegar-cruet, and mislaid the oil-flask, and can't find the hard-boiled eggs. All his sympathies are Anglo-Saxon. He likes roast meat, cricket, boating, and jovial conversation; and he is hand and foot a slave to the Dutch-doll-with-an-iron-mask discipline of the imperial pages, and the imperial court, and the imperial prisoners'-van and county-gaol system generally. He is fond of singing comic songs. He had better not be too funny in Russia; there is a hawk with a double head in the next room. He is (as far as he has sense enough to be) a republican in principle. The best thing he can do is to learn by heart, and keep repeating the Anglican litany, substituting Good Czar for Good Lord.

What a terrible state of things for an inoffensive and well-meaning young man! Not to know whether he is on his head or his heels, morally. To be neither flesh, nor fowl, nor good red herring, nationally. I wonder how many years it will take him to become entirely Russian: how long he will be before he will learn to dance, and perform the ceremony of the kou-tou—I mean the court bow—and leave off telling the truth, keeping the eighth commandment, and looking people straight in the face. Not very long, I am afraid. The Russian academical course of moral ethics is but a short curriculum; and, once, matriculated, you graduate rapidly. In no other country but Russia—not even in our own sunsetless empire, with its myriad tributaries—can you find such curious instances of denationalization. Alexis Hardshellovitch had a friend whose acquaintance I had also the honour of making, who was also in the *Corps des Pages*, and who came to samovarise, or take tea with us, one evening, in patent-leather boots and white kid gloves; and who talked so prettily about potichomanie and Mademoiselle Bagdanoff, the ballet-dancer, (all in the purest Parisian,) that I expected the next subjects of his conversation would be Shakspeare and the musical glasses. What do you imagine his name was? Genghis Khan! (pronounced Zinghis Khan.) He was of the creamiest Tartar extraction, and mincingly confessed that he was descended in a direct line from that conqueror. He was a great prince at home; but the Russians had mediatized him, and he was to be an officer in the Mussulman escort of the Czar. He had frequently partaken of roast horse in his boyhood, and knew where the best tap of mares' milk was, down Mongolian-Tartary way, I have no doubt; but I have seen him eat ices at Dominique's on the Nevskoï with much grace, and he was quite a lady's man.

Alexis Hardshellovitch does not feel his exceptional and abnormal position to any painful extent; inasmuch as, though one of the worthiest and most amiable fellows alive, he is a tremendous fool. He is a white Russian—not coming from White Russia, understand, but with white eyelashes, and fawn-coloured hair, and a suety complexion, and eyes that have not been warranted to wash, for they have run terribly, and the ground-colour has been quite boiled out of them. He has a glimmering, but not decided notion, of his want of brains himself. "I know I am ugly," he candidly says, "my dear good mother always told me so, and my father, who was *bel homme*, used to hit me cracks because I had such large ears. I must be ugly, because the Director of the Corps has never selected me to be sent to the palace as a page of the chamber. I should like to be a page of the chamber, for they wear chamarrures of gold bullion on their skirts behind; but they only pick out the handsome pages. They say I should give the Empress an attack of nerves with my ears. Yet I am a general and ambassador's son. I, Some—" He spits. "But I'm not a fool. No; I guess not. Prince Bouillabaissoff says I am a *bête;* but Genghis Khan tells me that I have the largest head of all the imperial pages. How can I be a fool with such a large head? Tell." The honest youth has, it must be admitted, an enormous nut. Though I love him for his goodness and simplicity, I am conscious always of an uneasy desire to take that head of his between my hands, as if it were indeed a nut, and of the cocoa species, and crack it against a stone wall, to see if there be any milk to be accounted for, inside.

I have been staying, in this broiling midsummer mad-dog weather, at the hospitable country mansion of Alexis Hardshellovitch's aunts; and we two have come on the Grand Scud in a respectable old calêche, supposed to have been purchased in France by the diplomatic general during the occupation of Paris by the allies in eighteen hundred and fifteen. It has been pieced and repaired by two generations of Russian coach-cobblers since; has been relined with some fancy stuff which I believe to have been, in the origin, window-curtains; the vehicle, probably, has not been painted since the Waterloo campaign, but the wheels are plentifully greased; we have an ample provision of breaks, and drags, and "skids;" we have three capital horses—one a little black Bitchok—lithe, limber, long-maned, and vicious, but an admirable galloper, and *dressée à la volée*, and we have a very paragon of a postilion or coachman, I scarcely know whether to call him Ischvostchik or Jemstchik, for now he sits on the box, and now he bestrides the splashboard, where the splinter-bar is his brother, and the traces make acquaintance with his boots. I say he is a paragon; for he can go a week without getting drunk, never falls asleep on the box, and however bad the roads may be, never lands the calêche in a deep hole. Inexhaustibly good-tempered and untiringly musical he is, of course; he would not be a Russian else. He belongs to Alexis—or rather, will do so at his majority; when that large-headed page will possess much land and many beeves—human beeves, I mean, with beards and boots, and baggy breeches. But I don't think that Alexis will administer much STICK to his slaves when he comes to his kingdom. He has a hard shell, but a soft heart.

It is lucky we have Petr' Petrovitch the paragon with us in our journey from Rjew, for we have long left the great Moscow Road, (I don't speak of the rail but of the *chaussée*) and have turned into an abominable *Sentier de Traverse*, a dreadful region, where marshes have had the black vomit, and spumed lumps of misshapen raven-like forest—black roots of trees—inky jungles, so to speak. Can you imagine any thing more horrible than a dwarf forest—for the trees are never tall hereabout—stems and branches hugger-muggering close together like conspirators weaving some diabolical plot, with here and there a gap of marsh pool between the groups of trees, as if some woodland criminals, frightened at their own turpitude, had despairingly drowned themselves, and ridded the earth of their black presence. Some corpses of these float on the surface of the marsh, but the summer time has been as merciful to them as the redbreasts were to the children in the wood, and has covered them with a green pall. There must be capital teal, and widgeon and snipe-shooting here in autumn—shooting enough to satisfy that insatiate sportsman, Mr. Ivan Tourguénieff; but, at present, the *genus homo* does not shoot. He is shot by red-dart, from the inexhaustible quiver of the sun. He does not hunt; he is hunted by rolling clouds of pungent dust, by disciplined squadrons of gnats, and by flying cohorts of blue-bottles and gadflies. The sun has baked the earth into angular clods, and our calêche and horses go hopping over the acclivities like a daddy-long-legs weak in the knee-joints over a home-baked crusty loaf. There is no cultivation in this part—no trees—no houses. I begin to grow as hotly thirsty as on that famous day when I drank out of the Pot, walking twenty miles, from Lancaster to Preston; but out of evil cometh good in Russian travelling. As you are perfectly certain, before starting, that you will not find any houses of entertainment on the road, except at stated distances; and that the refreshments provided there will probably be intolerable, no person in a sane mental condition either rides or drives a dozen miles in the country without taking with him a complete apparatus for inward restoration. We have a comfortable square box covered with tin, which unthinking persons might rashly assume to be a dressing-case, but which in reality contains a pint-and-a-half samovar; a store of fine charcoal thereunto belonging; a tchainik, or tea-pot of terra cotta, tea-cups, knives, forks, and tea-canister. If we were real Russians—hot as it is—we should incite Petr' Petrovitch to kindle a fire, heat the samovar, and set to tea-drinking with much gusto. As we have Anglo-Saxon notions, if not blood, we resort to that other compartment of the tin chest where the mighty case-bottle of cold brandy and water is—large, squab, flat, and fitting into the bottom of the box. Then, each lighting a *papiros*, we throw ourselves back in the calèche. Petr' Petrovitch has not been forgotten in the case-bottle line, and we bid our conductor to resume the grandest of Scuds. We have an indefinite idea that we shall come upon one of Prince Bouillabaissoff's villages in an hour or so. This, too, is about the time to tell you that Alexis, though an imperial page, is clad in a Jim Crow hat, a baker's jacket, nankeen pantaloons, and a Madras handkerchief loosely tied round his turn-down shirt collar. These are the vacations of the imperial pages—very long vacations they have—from May to August, and once in the country, Alexis may dress as he pleases; but in St. Petersburg, it would be as much as his large ears are worth to appear without the regulation choke outfit—the sword, casque, belt, and, to use an expression of Mumchance, "coat buttoned up to here." Friend of my youth! why canst thou not come with me from the Rents of Tattyboys to All the Russias? For here thou wouldst find, not one or two, but millions of men, all with their coats buttoned up to here.

I said ONE of Prince Bouillabaissoff's villages, for the prince is a proprietor on a large scale, and owns nearly a dozen, containing in all some twenty hundred douscha (souls) or serfs. But our Grand Scud principle is vindicated when we diverge from the marshes and the baked clods into the commencement of a smooth well-kept road, and learn from Petr' Petrovitch, whom we have hitherto foreborne interrogating, that we are approaching the village of M. de Katorichassoff.

The good Russian roads are oases between deserts. In the immediate vicinity of the seigneur's residence the roads are beautifully kept. No English park avenue could surpass them in neatness, regularity, smoothness,—nay, prettiness and cheerfulness. There are velvety platebandes of greensward by the roadside, and graceful poplars, and sometimes elms. But once out of the baron's domains, and even the outlying parts of his territory, the roads—high and bye—become the pitiable paths of travail and ways of tribulation, of which I have hinted in the Czar's Highway. There is a humorous fiction that the proprietors of the soil are bound to keep the public roads in order, and another legend—but more satirical than humorous—that the government pays a certain yearly sum for the well-keeping of the roads. Government money is an ignis fatuical and impalpable thing in Russia. You may pay, but you do not receive. As to the proprietors they will see the government barbacued before they will do any thing they are not absolutely compelled to do ; and the upshot of the matter is, that a problem something like the following is offered for solution. If two parties are bound to perform a contract of mutual service, and neither party performs it, which party has a right to complain ?

M. de Katorichassoff, however—or rather Herr Vandergutlers, his North German bourmister, or intendant, for the noble Barynn is no resident just now (Hombourg, roulette, and so forth)—would very soon know the reason why all the roads about the seigneurial village were not kept in apple-pie order. They say that in Tsarskoe-Selo palace gardens, near Petersburg, there is a corporal of invalids to run after every stray leaf that has fallen from a tree, and a police officer to take every unauthorized pebble on the gravel walks into custody. Without going so far as this, it is certain that there are plenty of peasants *mis à corvée*, that is, working three compulsory days' labour for the lord, to mend and trim the roads, clip the platebandes, and prune the trees; and the result is, ultimately, a charmingly umbrageous avenue through which we make our entrance into Volnoï-Voloshtchok.

Though M. de K. (you will excuse the rest of the name, I know) has only one village, he has determined to do every thing in it *en grand seigneur.* He has a church and a private police-station, and a common granary for corn; and, wonder of wonders! he has a wooden watchtower surmounted by a circular iron balcony, and with the customary apparatus of telegraphic signals in case of fire. As you can see the whole of the village of Volnoï—its one street, the château of the Barynn, and the mill of Mestrophan-Kouprianoritch—at one glance, standing on the level ground, and as there are no other buildings for ten miles round, the utility of a watchtower does not seem very obvious. Still, let us have discipline, or die. So there were watchmen, I suppose, at one time; but the balcony is tenantless now, and one of the yellow balls is in a position, according to the telegraphic code, denoting a raging conflagration somewhere. There is nothing on fire, that I know of, except the sun. Where is the watchman, too? There are plenty of vigorous old men with long white beards, who would enact to the life the part of that dreary old sentinel in Agamemnon the King, who, in default of fire, or water, or the enemy, or whatever else he is looking out for, prognosticates such dismal things about Clytemnestra's goings on and the state of Greece generally. Why didn't the terrible queen kill that old bore, same time she murdered her husband? He has been prosing from that watchtower going on three thousand years. There seems to be no necessity, either, for the watchtower to have any windows, but broken ones, or any door save four shameful old planks hanging by one wooden hinge, and for the hot sun to glare fiercely through crevices in the walls that have not been made by the wood shrinking, but by the absence of part or parcel of the walls themselves. Why empty balcony, why broken windows, why wooden hinges, why one hinge, why yawning walls? This: the lord is at Hombourg (—actress of the Folies Dramatiques—run of ill-luck on the red, and so forth,) and Herr Vandergutlers, his intendant's paramount business is to send him silver roubles. More silver roubles, and yet more! So those of his serfs who pay him a yearly rent, or obrok, have had that obrok considerably increased; and those who were *à corvée* have been compelled to go upon obrok; and everybody, man, woman, and child, patriarch and young girl, have been pinched, pressed, screwed, and squeezed, beaten, harassed, cozened, bullied, driven, and dragged by the North German intendant for more silver roubles—more silver roubles still—for M. de Katorichassoff, at Hombourg. There the man who deals the cards, and the woman who rouges her face, divide the Russian prince's roubles between them, (a simple seigneur here, he is Prince Katorichassoff at Hombourg;) and this is why, you can understand, that the fire-engine department has been somewhat neglected, and its operation suspended at Volnoï-Voloschtchok. As for the state of decay into which the building, though barely two years old, is falling, that is easily accounted for. The villagers are stealing it piecemeal. They have already stolen the lower part of the staircase, and thereby have been too clever for themselves, as they cannot get at the balcony, which, being of real iron, must make their mouths water. The hinges were originally made of wood, together with all the clamps, and rivets, and bolts employed in the lower part of the structure, through a knowledge of the fact patent and notorious, that iron anywhere within his reach is as much too much for the frail morality of a Russian peasant as of a South Sea native. He will steal the iron tires off wheels: he will (and has frequently) stolen the chains of suspension bridges. I don't think he would object to being loaded with chains, if he could steal and sell his fetters.

On domains like those of Prince Bouillabaissoff, the fire-engine and watch-tower organization is not a weak-minded caricature, but an imposing reality. And the importance of such a preventive establishment can with difficulty be exaggerated. Of course, his dwelling being of wood, and easily ignitable, the Russian is incredibly careless with combustibles. It is one large tinder-box. This is why fire-insurance companies do not flourish in Russia. It may certainly be asked what special reason the Russian has for adopting any precautions against conflagrations. Many reasons he certainly has not. He has about the same personal interest in his house as a pig might have in his stye. His breeder must give him four walls to live in, and a trough to eat his grains from,—but he may be driven to market any day,—he may be pork (and well-scored for the bakehouse) by next Wednesday week. Again, his house is not unlike a spider's web,—easily destroyed, easily reconstructed. The housemaid's broom, or the destroying element,—it is all the same; a little saliva to the one, and a few logs to the other, and the spider and the moujik are at work again. You don't ask a baby to mend his cradle. When it is past service papa goes out and buys him a new one. There is this paternal relation between the lord and the serf, (besides the obvious non-rod-sparing to avoid the child-spoiling one,) that the former is to a certain extent compelled to provide for the material wants of his big-bearded bantling. If Ivan's roof be burnt over his head, the lord must find him at least the materials for another habitation; if the harvests have fallen short, or an epizootis has decimated the country side, he must feed them. The serf tills the ground for his lord, but he must have seeds given him to sow with. The Russian peasant having absolutely no earthly future to look forward to, it is but reasonable that his proprietor should supply the exigent demands of the present moment. There is no absolute right of existence guaranteed; but the master's natural interest in the souls he possesses, having means sufficient to keep their bodies alive withal, obviously prompts him to keep them fed, and housed, and clothed. There are his lands; when they have done their three days' work for him, they may raise enough corn in the next three days' serivat to make their black bread with. There are his hemp, and flax, and wool,—their women can spin, themselves can weave such hodden gray as they require to cover their nakedness. There are his secular woods; they may cut pine-logs there to make their huts. As regards the rigid necessary,—the bare elements of food, covering, and shelter,—the nobility's serfs have decidedly the same advantage over the twenty millions or so of crown slaves (facetiously termed free peasants) as Mr. Legree's negroes have over the free-born British paupers of Buckinghamshire, or Gloucestershire, or—out with it—St. James's, Westminster, and St. George's, Hanover Square. In a crown village, in a time of scarcity, the sufferings of the free peasants are almost incredibly horrible. Then the wretched villagers, after having eaten their dogs, their cats, and the leather of their boots; after being seen scraping together handfuls of vermin to devour; after going out into the woods, and gnawing the bark off the trees; after swallowing clay and weeds to deceive their stomachs; after lying in wait, with agonized wistfulness, for one solitary traveller to whom they can lift their hands to beg alms; after having undergone all this, they go out from their famine-stricken houses into the open fields and waste places, and those that are sickening build a kind of tilt awning-hut with bent twigs covered with rags, over those that are sick, and they rot first and die afterwards. In famines such as these, the people turn black, like negroes; whole families go naked; and though, poor wretches, they would steal the nails from horses' shoes, the crank and staple from a gibbet, or the trepanning from a man's scull, they refrain wondrously from cannibalism, from mutual violence, and from any thing like organized depredations on the highway;—they fear the Czar and the police to the last gasp. Nor, do I conscientiously believe, if the richest shrines of the richest Sabors of all Petersburg, Moscow, Kieff, and Novgorod—heavy with gold and silver, and blazing with costly jewels—were to be set up in the midst of their breadless, kopeckless, village, would they abstract one jewelled knob from the crozier of a saint, one tinselled ray from the aureole of the Panagia. At last, when many have died, and many more are dying, a stifled wail, which has penetrated with much difficulty through the official cotton-stuffed ears of district police auditoria, district chambers of domains, military chiefs of governments, and imperial chancelleries, without number, comes soughing into the private cabinet of the Czar at the Winter Palace or Peterhoff. The Empress, good soul, sheds tears when she hears of the dreadful sufferings of the poor people so many hundred versts off. The imperial children, I have no doubt, wonder why, if the peasants have no bread to eat, they don't take to plum-cake; the emperor is affected, but goes to work; issues an oukase; certain sums from the imperial cassette are munificently affected to the relief of the most pressing necessities. Do you know, my reader, that long months elapse before the imperial alms reach their wretched objects? do you know that the imperial bounty is bandied—all in strict accordance with official formality, of the like of which I have heard something nearer home—from department to department—from hand to hand; and that to each set of greasy fingers, belonging to scoundrels in gold lace, and rogues with stars and crosses, and knaves of hereditary nobility, there sticks a certain percentage on the sum originally allocated? The Czar gives, and gives generously. The Tchinn lick, and mumble, and paw the precious dole, and when, at last, it reaches its rightful recipients, it is reduced to a hundredth of its size. Do you know one of the chief proverbs appertaining and peculiar to Russian serfdom?—it is this—"Heaven is too high, the Czar is too far off." To whom are the miserable creatures to cry? To Mumbo-Jumbovitch their priest, who is an ignorant and deboshed dolt, generally fuddled with kvass, who will tell them to kiss St. Nicholas's great toe? To the nearest police-mayor, who will give them fifty blows with a stick, if they are troublesome, and send them about their business? To the Czar, who is so far off, morally and physically? To Heaven? Such famines as these have been in crown villages, on the great chaussée road from Petersburg to Moscow. Such famines have been, to our shame be it said, in our own free, enlightened, and prosperous United Kingdom, within these dozen years. But I am not ashamed—no, pot-and-kettle philosophers, sympathizers with the oppressed Hindoo—no, mote-and-beam logicians full of condolence with the enslaved Irishman—I am not ashamed to talk of famines in Russia, because there have been famines in Skibbereen, and Orkney, and Shetland. The famine-stricken people may have been neglected, oppressed, wronged, by stupid and wicked rulers; but I am not ashamed—I am rather proud to remember the burst of sympathy elicited from the breasts of millions among us, at the first recital of the sufferings of their brethren,—the strenuous exertions made by citizens of every class and every creed to raise and send immediate succour to those who were in want. We commit great errors as a nation, but we repair them nobly; and I think we ought no more to wince at being reminded of our former backslidings, or refrain from denouncing and redressing wrongs wherever they exist, because, in the old time we have done wrongfully ourselves, than we ought to go in sackcloth, in ashes, because Richard the Third murdered his nephews, or abstain from the repression of cannibalism in New Zealand, because our Druidical ancestors burnt human beings alive in wicker cages.*

* The impressions hereabove set down respecting famine, and,

XI.

A COUNTRY HOUSE.

I WANT to say a word more about Ireland, not argumentatively, but as an illustration. I should have been dishonest in blinking Skibbereen; the more so, as in all the narratives I have heard of the social characteristics of these appalling visitations, I could not help being struck with their grim and minute similitude to some features of the Irish famine that came within my own knowledge at the time. Some of the coincidences were extraordinary. The patience of the people. Their swarthiness of hue from inanition. Their patience and meekness during unexampled agony; and, above all,

indeed, most of the information on the subject of the condition of the Russian peasantry which may hereafter be found in these pages, are derived, not from official documents, not even from the trustworthy pages of M. de Haxthausen, who though professedly favourable to the Russian government, and painting, as far as he can, *couleur de rose*, lets out some very ugly truths occasionally; but from repeated conversations I have held with Russian gentlemen, some high in office in ministerial departments, some men of scientific attainments, some university students, some military officers. All the facts I have rested my remarks upon have been told me with a calm, complacently-indifferent air, over tumblers of tea, and paper cigarettes, and usually accompanied by a remark of *c'est comme ça*. And I think I kept my eyes sufficiently wide open during my stay, and was pretty well able to judge when my interlocutors were lying, and when they were telling the truth.

their nakedness. To be naked and a-hungered would seem to be natural—the hungry man selling his clothes to buy bread; but these people, Irish and Russian, went naked when they had plenty of rags, unsalable, but warmth-containing. There seem to be certain extreme stages of human misery, in which a man can no longer abide his garments. I have a curious remembrance of being told by a relative, who was in the famine-stricken districts in eighteen forty-seven, that, once losing his way over a mountain, he entered a cabin to inquire the proper road, and there found seven people of both sexes, children and adults, crouching round an empty saucepan, and all as bare as robins! The eldest girl, who volunteered to show him the straight road, was modest as Irish girls are proud to be, and as she rose to escort him, clapped a wooden bowl over her shoulder, as if it had been the expansive cloak of the demon page whom we read of in the Percy Reliques.

I have been thinking of all these things and a great many more over tea and tobacco in the Starosta's house in M. de Katorichassoff's village. There Alexis and I are comfortably seated during the noontide heats. The Starosta's daughter would have washed our feet for us, as Penelope's handmaidens did for Ulysses, or Fergus MacIvor's duinhie wassals for Waverley, if we had had any inclination that way. Perhaps I had corns; perhaps Alexis, already becoming Russianized, had, like many of his patent leather-booted countrymen, no stockings on. It is certain that we did not avail ourselves of the footbath. The Starosta has informed us several times, and with as many profound bows, that his house no longer belongs to him, but that it, its contents, himself, his children and grandchildren, are ours, and at the absolute disposal of our excellencies. Excellencies! By the long-winded multisyllabic, but mellifluous epithets he has bestowed on Alexis he must have called him his majesty, his coruscation, his scintillation, his milky-way, by this time. The Russians are great proficients in low bows, and to *bien savoir tirer la révérence* is considered a superlative accomplishment. A distinguished Professor of Natural History attached to the University of Moscow—a great *savant* and a very taciturn man—once remarked to me gravely, that his brother Waldemar made the best bow of any boyard in the government of Simbersk, and added: "*Ce garçon là fera son chemin*"—and indeed this is a country where, by dint of continuous and assiduous bowing, you may make surprising way in fortune and dignity. If you will bow low enough you may be sure to rise high in the Tchinn; and if you don't mind grovelling a little on your stomach, and swallowing a little dust, there is no knowing to what imperial employment you may aspire. I think that Alexis has a secret admiration and envy of Genghis Khan, owing to the profoundly graceful bows that Tartar chieftain is so frequently making. I don't mind low bows. Perhaps if I knew an English duke I should be inclined to make him very low bows myself—at all events, I have compatriots who would; but it is inexpressibly painful and disgusting to a western traveller in Russia, when he happens to be on a visit at a gentleman's country house, to see stalwart bearded men positively falling down and worshipping some scrubby young seigneur. If a peasant has the slightest favour to ask of his lord—the promotion of his wife, for instance, from the scullery to the fine-linen laundry—he begins his suit by falling plump on his knees, and touching the earth with his forehead. Even in Petersburg where *Nous Autres* do not like to show the slave-owner's element more than they can help, I have seen a sprightly young seigneur keep a gray-haired servitor full ten minutes on his knees before him lighting his pipe—cheerfully calling him swinia and durac (pig and fool) meanwhile, and playfully chucking him under the chin with the toe of his Kasan boot.

We have refused the refreshment of vitchina, or dried pork, piroga, or meat pies, and ogourtzhoff, or salted cucumbers; but we have cheerfully accepted the offer of a samovar, which, huge, brazen, and battered, glowers in the midst of the table like the giant helmet in the Castle of Otranto. We have our own tea and cups in the tin chest, but the Starosta won't hear of our using either. He has tea—and capital tea it is—rather like tobacco in colour, and tasting slightly as if it had been kept in a canister in Mr. Atkinson the perfumer's shop; besides this, he has, not tumblers for us to drink our tea from, but some articles he has the greatest pride and joy in producing—porcelansky, he calls them, in a voice quavering with emotion, as he takes them out of the chest containing his valuables. The porcelansky consists of two very fair china tea-cups, one of them minus a handle, but the loss supplied with a neat curve of twisted iron wire, and both duly set in saucers. One saucer is indubitable china; it does not match the cup in size or pattern, certainly, but let that pass; the other is—the cover of one of those shallow earthenware pots in which preserved meats and anchovy paste are sold! I turn the familiar lid upside down, and there my eyes are gladdened with the sight of a coloured engraving burnt into the clay—the interior of Shakspeare's house at Stratford-upon-Avon! My thoughts immediately revert to Mr. Quain's oyster-shop in the Haymarket, London, and I burst out laughing, to the amazement and abashment of the Starosta, who, thinking I am ridiculing him for having placed his saucer with the handsome part underneath, hastens to explain to Alexis that the cup won't maintain its position unless the saucer is turned upside down, expressing his regret, as the picture, which he assumes to be a view of the Dvoretz Londoni-Gorod, or Palace of the City of London, is dolgo harasho (very handsome indeed). Alexis, it is needless to say, interprets all this; for my Russ is of the very weakest, as yet. Yet I cannot help a slight suspicion that my young friend's Moscov is not of the most powerful description, and that he makes very free translations of the Starosta's discourse for my benefit, and that like the dragoman in Eothen, he renders such a speech as "Your mightinesses are welcome; most blessed among hours is this, the hour of his coming," by "The old fellow is paying us a lot of compliments. We are welcome enough, that is certain." The Starosta never saw Alexis before, but he has known the calêche for years, and he knows that the lad's senior aunt is the Baronessa Bigwigitsin, and if the Russo-American chose to eat him out of house and home, the Starosta would bow lower than ever, so near-neighbourly is he, and such an unfeigned and disinterested attachment has he for the juvenile aristocracy. For, the Russian peasant, who is always burning a lamp before the shrine of his saint, astutely thinks that there is no harm in burning a candle to the other power, too: so he worships his seigneur, who is the very devil to him.

I have had two tumblers of tea; and by this time I have taken stock of the Starosta's house. It is the best in the village of Volnoï, and I should think the Starosta must have been a thrifty old gentleman, and must be by this time, pretty well to do in the world. I am sorry to hear from Alexis, however, that our venerable friend declares that he has not a copeck in the world, and that he and his family are "whistling in their fists" for hunger. "He is a liar," Alexis says, unaffectedly. "They are all liars." The Starosta's dwelling, though, does not offer many signs of penury or distress. Here is the inventory.

There is but one room on the ground-floor: a sufficiently vast apartment, of which the walls are of logs in all their native roundness, and the ceiling also of logs, but on which, to be quite genteel, some imperfect attempts at squaring have been made.

There is not a glimpse of white-washing, painting or paper-hanging to be seen. The great Russian painter and decorator, Dirtoff, has taken the chamber in hand, and has toned down walls, and ceiling, and flooring to one agreeable dingy gray. There is not much dust about; no great litter, where all is litter; not over-many cobwebs in the corners. The dirt is concrete. It is part of the party walls; and I think that a thoroughly good scrubbing would send the Starosta's house tumbling about his ears. There are two windows to the room; one is a show window—a large aperture, filled with a peculiar dull, gray, sheenless glass. The panes are so gently and uniformly darkened with dirt, that the window serves much more to prevent impertinent wayfarers from looking in, than to assist the inmates of the mansion in looking out. The second window is a much smaller casement, cut apparently at random high up in the wall, and close to the ceiling, and of no particular shape. Its panes are filled with something, but what that something may be I am unable to determine; not glass for a certainty, for the panes bulge inward, and some flap idly to and fro in the hot summer wind, which, like a restless dog, is wagging its tail in the sun outside;—rags, perhaps, paper it may be, dried fish-skins—a favourite preparation for glazing windows—very likely. Whatever it be, it produces a very unwholesome-looking semi-transparency; and big black spiders, tarrakans, and other ogglesome insects, crawl over its jaundiced field, like hideous ombres chinoises. One end of the apartment is partitioned off by a raw-wooden screen, some six feet in height; but whether that be the family bed-chamber or the family pigsty I am quite at a loss to say. The former hypothesis is scarcely tenable, inasmuch as beneath the image of the saint there is a sort of wooden pit, half above ground and half under it—half a sarcophagus and half a ditch—which from a mighty bolster—that gigantic sausage like sack of black leather must be a bolster, for I can see the oleaginous marks on it where heads have lain—and a counterpane *bariolé* in so many stripes and counterstripes of different colours that it looks like the union-jack, I conjecture to be the Starosta's family bed. His summer bed, of course; where his winter bed is we all know—it is there on the top of the long stove, where the heap of once white—now black with dirt and grease—sheepskins are. If I had any doubt about this wooden grave being a bed, it would be at once dispelled; first, by the sight of a leg covered with a dusty boot which suddenly surges into the air from beneath the waves of the particoloured counterpane like the mast of a wrecked vessel; and ultimately by a head dusty and dishevelled as to its hair, and bright crimson as to its face, which bobs up to the surface, glimmers for a moment, and then disappears—to continue the nautical simile—like the revolving pharos of the Kish Lightship. From a hiccup, too, and a grunt, I am further enabled to conjecture that there must be somebody in the bed; and from some suppressed whisperings, I am inclined to think that there are some small matters in the way of children down somewhere in the vast depths of this Russian Great

Bed of Ware. On the latter subject I am not enlightened; but on the former my mind is set at rest by the statement volunteered by the Starosta, that his eldest grandson Sophron is lying down there, "as drunk as oil"—whatever that state of intoxication may be. He went out this morning, it appears, to the Seignorial Kontova, or steward's office, with a little present to the Alemansky-Bourmister, or German Intendant of the Barynn, and on Gospodin Vandergutler's deigning to give Sophron some green wine, or vodki, Sophron deigned to drink thereof, till he found himself, or was found, in the aforesaid oily state of drunkenness. I should say myself, that Sophron is more what may be termed "dumb drunk;" for, on his grandfather seizing him by the hair of his head on one of its visits to the surface, and rating him in most abusive Russ, Sophron makes superhuman efforts to reply, but can get no further than an incoherent and inarticulate gabble; after which, leaving some of his hair behind like seaweed, he dives down to the bottom of the counterpane ocean—again to confer, I suppose, with his little brothers and sisters, or with Neptune, or the Nereides, or the Great Sea Serpent. "The ape and pig," says the vexed Starosta, "threw himself into the bed while I was at Mestrophan's mill. I could sober him in a moment with a bucket of water, but your excellencies will understand that I do not want to spoil the pastyel, (or bed,) which is of great civlation, (civilization,) and came from Moscow, where my eldest son Dmitri has been an Ischvostchik Macter for twenty years, paying one hundred and eighty silver roubles yearly to his lord and ours, the Barynn Vacil-Apollodorovitch, (M. de K.) and owning himself fourteen droschkies with the irhorses." Apparently fearing that he had let the cat somewhat out of the money-bag in alluding to the prosperous condition of his son Dmitri, the Starosta hastened to assure Alexis that the obrok (or yearly slave-rent) was a frightfully hard thing for a poor Christianin to pay, and that what with that and the police and the government dues, his poor Dmitri had nothing to feed or clothe his children with. "This is his son," he adds, pointing to the part of the counterpane where the oily drunkard had last foundered with all hands, and his cargo of green wine on board: "judge what we are able to do with such a cow's-nephew as this on our hands! However, if your excellencies will deign to pardon me, I will soon rid you of this Turk's-brother's presence." I don't know what Alexis answers to this harangue, but I hasten to assure the Starosta with much gesticulation, and many harostros and nitchevos, (all right and never mind,) that I have not the slightest objection to the drunken man in the bed, and, as he is quite dumb, that I rather liked his revolving lighthouse appearance than otherwise. The Starosta, however, apparently convinced that he or Sophron must be sinning against etiquette in some way or other, makes a last desperate plunge after that shipwrecked convivialist. He brings him to the shore after much puffing and blowing, and rolls or drags his long body across the floor and out at the front door, where, from some dull heavy sounds, and a terrific howling, I presume that he is correcting his grandson with a joint-stool, or a log of wood, or a crowbar, or a hatchet, or some switch-like trifle of that description. Then I hear the slush of the proposed bucket of water. The Starosta comes in, and reapologizes to Alexis; and when Sophron rejoins us, which he does in about ten minutes to fill the samovar, he is, though still very damp and somewhat tangled about the hair, and purply-streaked about the face, as grave, sober, and likely a young Russian as ever wore a red shirt and made beautiful bows.

I have spoken of the image of the saint. It is here that the Starosta's commercial secret oozes out. It is here that the paucity of copecks, and the sibilation in the fists for hunger becomes notorious as airy fabrications. Like every Russian peasant shopkeeper merchant—from the miserable moujik of a crown-village to the merchant of the first guild with his millions of roubles—Nicolai Iatchkoff, the Starosta's pride and pleasure is to have a joss in his house, as handsome as ever he can afford it to be. And a brave St. Nicholas he has. The picture itself is simply hideous—a paralytic saint with an enormous aureole, like a straw hat, sitting in a most uncomfortable attitude upon a series of cream-coloured clouds in regular tiers, like the wig of the Lord Mayor's coachman. It is painted, or rather daubed, in the most glaring and coarsest oil-colours; but the aureole above the saint's head is formed of metallic rays of a certain dull, yellow, Guinea-coast like appearance, that make me certain—though the Starosta would probably call St. Nicholas himself to witness that the contrary was the fact—that these rays are of pure gold. And there are some rings on St. Nicholas's fingers, and some stars on his alb and rochet, and a great bulb on his pastoral crook, that are green, and white, and crimson, and glisten very suspiciously. I have an idea that they are emeralds, and carbuncles, and seed-pearls, my friend Nicolai. I know the massive, chased, and embossed lamp that hangs, always kindled, before the image, to be silver; the picture itself is covered with a fair wide sheet of plate-glass; the whole is framed in rose-wood, carved and gilded in great profusion; and I should not at all wonder if the original cost of this image to the *soi-disant* impoverished Starosta had been five hundred silver roubles at the very least. St. Nicholas is one of the most popular and most considered of the Russian saints, and the late Czar probably owed no small portion of his immense influence to the fact of his bearing the same name as that saint of high renown. Touching St. Nicholas, there is a ludicrous tradition current among the Russian peasantry to the effect that he once had a theological dispute with Martin Luther, and that they agreed to settle it by a walking-match. It was to be so many hundred versts up a mountain, and neither party was to have any assistance beyond a stout walking-staff. For once the Protestant champion was victorious, for St. Nicholas was thoroughly blown before he had accomplished half the journey. The detested heretic came back triumphant, but with empty hands. "Where's your walking-stick, dog's son?" cried the good St. Nicholas. "Ant' please you, I ate it," answered his opponent. The wary Doctor Martin Luther had had a walking-stick constructed of good black-puddings twisted together, and had eaten as he walked—the creature comforts giving him such bodily strength that he had easily overcome his antagonist.

The large ground-floor apartment, as it may be called, though it is raised somewhat above the level of the soil, as you shall hear presently, is called the Balschoï-Isba, or Big Room; and sometimes, on the eternal *lucus a non lucendo*, however sombre it may be, the Beleeïa-Isba, or Chamber of Light. The space at the end, partitioned off like a churchwarden's pew, is considered as strictly private,—there is no admittance except on business. When I say private, I mean, of course, to persons of the peasant's own degree; the shaven-chins—by which title the hirsute moujiks sometimes designate those whose nobility, official standing, military employment, or foreign extraction, entitle them to go beardless—enter where they please, and do what they please, when they deign to enter a peasant's house. (And here a parenthesis respecting beards. One of the last items of advice volunteered to me by a very dear friend, just previous to leaving England for Russia, was to let my beard grow. I should find it so comfortable in travelling, he said. I had all the wish, though perhaps not the power, to effect this desirable consummation; but I very soon found, on my arrival at St. Petersburg, that if I wanted to be waited on with promptitude in hotels, spoken to with civility by police-officers, or received with politeness in society, I must go with a smoothly-shaven chin. Moustaches were generally patronized, whiskers tolerated; but a beard—the nasty moujiks wore beards! The only person moving in elevated Russian society, six months ago, who ventured to set the aristocratic squeamishness as to hairy chins at defiance, was the American minister, who was bearded like the pard. Then, in July, came out Lord Wodehouse, our ambassador, also wearing a beard of respectable dimensions; and the enormous influx of strangers into Moscow at the coronation fêtes, and the cosmopolitan variety of aristocratic beards wagged thereat, must by this time have familiarized the Russians with the sight of hairy chins unassociated with sheepskin coats and baggy breeches.)

Why "deign" to enter? you may ask. Why deign to do this or that? For I am conscious of having repeated the locution with considerable frequency. The fact is, that the Russian peasant does not say of his superior—and especially of his lord—that he eats, or drinks, or sleeps; but that he deigns to taste something; that he deigns to moisten his lips; that he deigns to take some repose. These words—he deigns—become at last so natural to the serf in speaking of his master, that it is anything but rare to hear from his mouth such phrases as these: "The Barynn deigned to have the measles. His excellency deigned to tumble down stairs. His lordship deigned to die." Isvolit Kapout! This, it seems to me, is the converse to the historical *tournure de phrase* of Lord Castlecomer's mamma when his lordship's tutor happened to break his leg, "which was so very inconvenient to my Lord Castlecomer." The miserable condition of the souls attached to the glebe is brought to your mind by a hundred slavish proverbs and expressions. Slavery is so well organized, and so saturates the social system, that the very dictionary is impregnated with slavish words. A people philologically servile, and whose proverbs exhale a spirit of dog-like obedience and hopeless resignation, and sometimes abject glorification of despotism, is indeed a rarity. The miserable Africans, debased as they have been by centuries of bondage, have no such popular sayings, if I remember rightly, as, " Cow-hide am good for niggers ;" " Woolly head and scored back always go together ; " " Sky too high up, Canada too far off." But among the Russian peasants, these are a few of the proverbs current and common : "A man who has been well beaten is worth two men who haven't been beaten." " Five hundred blows with a stick will make a good grenadier ; a thousand a dragoon ; and none at all a captain." " 'Tis only the lazy ones who don't beat us." Can anything be more horrible than this tacit, shoulder-shrugging, almost smirking acceptation of the stick as an accomplished fact,—of the Valley of the Shadow of Stick as a state of life into which it has pleased God to call them ! Again : " Heaven is too high : the Czar is too far off." This is simply Dante's *Lasciate ogni speranza* Russianized. Again : " All belongs to God and the Czar." " Though against thy heart, always be ready to do what thou art ordered to do." " One can be guilty without guilt." The last proverb, with the preceding one, imply an abnegation of the duties and responsibilities of manhood altogether. Its application justifies a serf in robbing and murdering at the command of his master; the serf is guilty, but the onus of guilt is on him who sets him on. There is one Russian proverb that breathes something like a feeble consciousness of the horrors of slavery, and the corresponding blessings of liberty. "The bird is well enough in a golden cage, but he is better on a green branch." There is another proverb I have heard, couched in a somewhat similar spirit: "The labourer works like a peasant, [a slave,] but he sits down to table like a lord." This is too politically and economically wise, I am afraid, to be genuine, and has probably been invented *ad hoc*, and placed in the mouth of the moujik by some anti-slavery philanthropists. In familiar conversation you will sometimes hear a Russian say: "Without cutting my head off, allow me to say," &c. This is a pleasant reminiscence of the formula anciently observed in commencing a petition to the Czar: "Do not order our heads to be cut off, O mighty Czar, for presuming to address you, but hear us!" The Russian equivalent to our verb "to petition" is "to strike the ground with one's forehead." And the "Yes, sir," of a tchelovik, or eating-house waiter, when you order a chop, is "Sluschett," (I hear and obey.) Will any man believe that this system of slavery, which would appear to be the growth of twenty centuries, which has its language, and proverbs, and folklore, is, in its authorized and consolidated form, barely two hundred and fifty years old? It only dates, legally, from the reign of Boris Godounoff. But I happened to speak of dictionaries. Oyez, oyez! let all men know that the imperial Catherine, second of that name, and of imperishable memory, positively issued, one day—perhaps in an access of capricious philanthropy, and after receiving a letter from D'Alembert—an oukase ordering the word Slave to be for ever and ever erased and expunged from the imperial dictionary. The philosophical firm of D'Alembert, Diderot, and Co., made a great deal of this at the time, and there have been some attempts to make more of it since. For my part, I must say that the imperial word suppression reminds me very much of the manner in which penitent (in Pentonville) housebreakers speak of their last burglary (accompanied by violence) as their culpable folly. And yet this wretched people seem as habituated and to the manner born to slavery, as if they had been serfs from the time when it was said to Ham, "A slave and a servant shalt thou be;" and as if there were really any truth in the grinning theory of the German traveller, that the Russian back was organized to receive blows, and that his nerves are less delicate than those of western nations.

The reader has been deigning, I am afraid, to wait a long time for the conclusion of the inventory of the Starosta's house at Volnoï; and I have been in truth an unconscionable time in possession. But the Starosta's house, though it is but a log hut, is full of pegs to hang thoughts upon; though I must now really leave the pegs, and give the walls a turn. There are thereupon some more works of art—secular ones—besides the ecclesiastical triumph of the blessed Saint Nicholas. In poorer cottages, (if the pretty, homely, ivy and honeysuckle smelling name of cottage can be applied to the dreary dull dens the Russians live in,) these lay pictures would probably be merely the ordinary Loubotchynia, vile daubs of the reigning Czar, or of Petr' Velikè, glaring on sheets of bark, or the coarsest paper. But the Starosta being rich, he has four notable engravings—real engravings, apparently executed in a very coarse *taille douce* upon white paper, brilliantly if not harmoniously coloured; framed, in what may be termed, cabbage rose-wood, so vividly red and shining is it, and duly glazed. There is, of course, the late Czar Nicholas—one of the portraits taken of him about twenty years since—when his admirers delighted in describing him as an Apollo with the bearing of Jupiter, and the strings of his lyre twisted into thunderbolts;—when he wore a tremendous cocked hat, shipped fore and aft. That eagle-crowned helmet on the imperial head—with which we became acquainted through the pleasant pages of Punch, was the invention of a French painter, or rather military draughtsman, of whom the Czar was so fond that he could scarcely be prevailed upon to allow him to leave Russia, much less withdraw his silver roubles from the bank—was not adopted till eighteen-forty-six or seven. There is, almost equally, of course, a portrait of another Czar—the White Czar—for whom, though he was their enemy, the Russian people have a singular and almost superstitious admiration. The Malakani, or little wise men of

Jalmboff, believed him, forty years since, to be the lion of the valley of Jehoshaphat, sent by Heaven to dethrone the false emperor, (the Malakani hold, like many others neither little nor wise, by the illegitimacy of the Romanoffs.) There are many thousands, if not millions, of the common Russians, who believe to this day that the secret of the reverses sustained by the holy Russian arms in the Crimea (the reverses themselves, believe me, are, notwithstanding the lies of the Invalide Russe, no secret at home, for thousands of crippled soldiers have gone home to their villages to tell how soundly they were licked in the valley of the Tchernaya,) that the secrets of the defeats of Alma, and Inkermann and Balaclava, and the Malakhoff, was in the presence among the French hosts of the famous White Czar, miraculously resuscitated, and reigning at this very time over the Ivansoutskïs in Paris-Gorod. One need not go so far as Volnoï-Volostchok to find a similar superstition. In the alpine departments of France there are plenty of peasants who believe that the astute gentleman who lives at the Tuileries (when he is at home, which is but seldom) is the self-same conqueror and king whose sweetest music was his horses' hoofs' notes as he galloped into conquered cities; who vanquished at Marengo, and was crowned at Notre Dame, and saw Moscow blaze before his eyes like a pine torch; and ran away from Waterloo, and died upon the rock; and did the work of forty centuries in but fifty-two years of the Pyramids' brick life.

The third picture, and the third whose presence

here is still a matter of course, (for the loyalty of the present must be satisfied as well as that of the past) is a portrait of the reigning Czar. His Alexandrian majesty is represented in the act of reviewing his doughty and faithful Preobajinski Guards. The emperor and his guard are drawn upon about the same size of relative grandeur as Garagantua and his courtiers in the illustrations to Rabelais, by the incomparable M. Gustave Doré. The emperor, according to the laws of Brook Taylor's Perspective, (which, not being in the forty-five volumes of the Russian code, must, consequently, be held utterly heretical, schismatic, and abominable,) is about twenty-five feet high. The Preobajinskis are about two relative inches in stature, horses and all. The emperor is charging very fiercely over their heads; he is waving a tremendous sword, and the plumes of his helmet are blowing to all the four points of the compass at once. His toes are manfully turned in, and his sinister thumb turned out, so that with his imperial head screwed a little obliquely, he looks not unlike Saint Nicholas in a field-marshal's uniform. Were the sword only a bâton, an ecclesiastical Punch would be nearer the mark. The gallant Preobajinskis—or rather their horses—are all standing manfully on their hind legs; and the patriotic artist—a Moscow man—has artfully depicted their mouths all wide open, so as to leave you no room for doubt that they are crying "Long live the Czar!" as with one throat. There is a brilliant *cortège* of princes and generals behind the Czar; and one of the grand-dukes—Constantine, I imagine—is holding an eye-glass like a transparent warming-pan, to his arch-ducal optic. I don't think that the Russian artist means to imply by this that his imperial highness is either short-sighted or affected; but an eye-glass or lorgnottsz, is held to be a great sign of "civlation" in Russia—almost as choice a specimen of the Persicos apparatus as a Moscow Madamsky, or French-milliner-made bonnet.

One word about the Preobajinski Guards before I finish with number three. I have read lately that they form a regiment of men with cocked-up noses, and that every soldier of a certain height and with a *nez retroussé* is sent into this corps. This is one of the stock stories with which the witty and wily Russians cram foreigners who go about with open ears and note-books; and they so cram them, I believe, with a mischievous view to the said foreigners afterwards printing these cock-and-bull stories, and so making themselves ridiculous, and their testimony unworthy of credit. There are some eighty thousand men in the Russian Guards up to the Preobajinski standard height; and I think I am giving an under estimate, when I say that forty thousand of them have cocked-up noses. It must be remembered that forty thousand Russian soldiers are as much alike as forty thousand peas, and that the cocked-up nose is the national nose. There is much truth, however, in the story, that great pains are taken in all the regiments of the Guards to match the men as much as possible in personal appearance by companies and battalions. Thus you will see the blue-eyed men filed together, the light-moustached men, the blue-bearded men, the small-footed men, and so on; but to send up all the tall men with cocked-up noses into the Preobajinski regiment would be very much like sending every Englishman who wears a white neckcloth to be waiter at the Bedford Hotel. Preobajinski means Transfiguration. The so-called Guards received their name from the Palace of Preobajinski, for whose defence they were first incorporated, and which was a favourite residence of Peter the Great.

With picture number four, I have done with this Volnoï Volotschok Louvre; or more properly National Gallery of Art, for the fourth tableau is eminently national. The scene depicted is one of the episodes of the late war, in which the Russians were so signally and uniformly victorious. Scene, a Russian church somewhere—very small and trim—a sort of holy front parlour filled with saints, and with striped curtains to the windows neatly festooned. *Dramatis personæ:* a band of terrible Turks, with huge turbans and baggy breeches—quite the March in Bluebeard Turks—the magnificent three-tailed bashaw Turks, not the sallow men with the tight coats and fezzes whom we are accustomed to. These ruthless Osmanlis have broken into the church, smashed the windows, pulled down the curtains, desecrated the altar, disfigured the saints, and massacred the pope or priest, who, in full canonicals, with a murderous sword sticking up perpendicularly from his collar-bone, lies with his head in a tall candlestick, and his feet towards the door. But the miscreant pork-repudiators have reckoned without their host. Behold the eleventh of the line—the Russian line—who have come to the rescue, and who turn the tables on the Turks in the most signal manner! Behold a whiskered Muscovite warrior, not dusting a Turk's jacket, but making eyelet holes in it with his good bayonet as the unbeliever tries to disfigure more saints. Behold another miserable Osmanli, his turban off, and his bare pate exposed, prostrate, and crying *peccavi;* suing for any infinitesimal fraction of quarter, while a zealous grenadier is rapidly sending him to perdition, by the favourite Russian process of dashing out his brains with the butt-end of his musket. Quarter, indeed! I marvel much where it was, when the Turks desecrated the church. Was it in the same part of Terra Incognita in which the English officer was beaten by a Russian market-woman for attempting to steal a goose, and in which fifteen Anglisky mariners and a captain rifled a moujik's house of a calf, a kakoshnik, and fifteen pewter spoons—both favourite subjects of delineation with the Russians? There are two little features of detail in this picture which I must mention, as they strike me as being very curious. Half-shattered on the floor of the church, there lies a large image of a black Virgin and Child—negro black, with thick lips. How came this, I wonder, into the Græco-Sclavonic archæology? And the rays from the lighted candles are made to resemble the aureoles or golden glories round the heads of the saints, and are ornamented with intricate geometrical engine-turnings. Any one who watches the outward religious practices of the Russians will be apt to consider them candle, if not fire worshippers; so intimately are devotion and candle-grease mingled in their visible worship; but be it as it may, the glory-headed candles strike me as being so purely Byzantine, that I cannot refrain from recommending them to the notice of the Pre-Raphaelite brotherhood. I should very much like to see Mr. Dante Rosetti's notion of a dark lantern in that state of ornamentation. Whether the Russians eat candles or not is still a moot point; but it is certain that vast numbers of the priests live upon candles. The subvention allowed them by the government is so miserably small, that, but from the revenue they derive from the sale of votive candles, many of them must inevitably starve.

Saving these four pictures, and the saint's image, which last is the precious jewel in the head of this toad-like place, there is no other evidence of attempts to sacrifice to the graces, in the Starosta's house. Every other article of furniture is of the commonest, coarsest, rudest, wigwamest description. The rotten door swings on leathern hinges, or strips of raw hide rather, like that of the watch-tower. There is a table formed of two long fir planks resting upon massive tressels. There is a scanty square of dirty leather on it, which I presume serves as tablecloth, and on which our samovar now rests. This tressel-table has a most hideous resemblance to the high bench platform you see in a parish deadhouse; and I am horrified by the coincidence, when Alexis tells me that when a man dies in these parts his corpse is laid on the table to be howled over, and that to say that "Ivan is on the table" is synonymous, in popular parlance, with saying that Ivan is dead. I want to be off from the Starosta's house immediately after this; but, Alexis (who is the laziest young cub between here and Npookhopersk) won't hear of it, and says that the horses haven't had half enough rest yet; so I continue my inventory. All round the Balschoï-Isba there runs a low wide bench, contrived a double debt to pay; for the surplus members of the family, for whom there is no room in the family-vault bed, lounge on the bench by day, and sleep on it by night. I wish I knew what there was in the churchwarden's pew behind the partition. More beds? Alexis thinks not. The Starosta's riches, perhaps. Will Alexis ask? Alexis asks, or says that he does, and listens to a voluble explanation on the part of the Starosta, with a desperate attempt at an expression of wisdom in his large face; but, when I ask him for a translation, he says it doesn't matter; and I have a worse opinion of his Russ than ever.

Alexis is sitting in a malformed Chinese puzzle on a large scale of timber, once painted green, and which was once, to the Starosta's great pride, a garden chair belonging to the absentee, M. de Katorichassoff. I, with my usual selfishness and disregard for the feelings of others, (I have the best teacup, too,) have usurped an old, long, low, dormeuse fauteuil of gray Utrecht velvet, (the dearly-beloved furniture covering of the Russians—Vlourssky, they call it, *par excellence*,) which, from age and maltreatment, resembles in its black and tawny bundlings nothing half so much as the skin of an incorrigible old Tom, who has had rather a bad night of it on the tiles. Still, if the old chair had four legs instead of three, it would be a very comfortable old chair. There are no other chairs, no other seats, save the bench, and that offered—if it be not too sacred a thing to sit down upon—by that vast chest of wood painted black, in the corner.

This chest has a formidable iron hasp, and a padlock almost as big as a knocker, and is further braced with iron bands. It is also screwed to the floor, I have no doubt. It is the sort of chest that Sinbad the sailor might have taken with him on his voyages, or that the piratical merman in Washington Irving's delightful Knickerbockeriana might have floated away on in the storm. It is a chest that I should like to fill with dollars, and sprawl at full length upon till death came for change for a three-score-and-ten pound note. It is such a chest as might have served for the *pièce de resistance* in the Misletoe-bough tragedy—if this were a baron's hall instead of a Russian moujik's hut, and if a Russian baron's retainers were ever blithe and gay, or kept Christmas holiday.

I suppose that in this chest the Starosta keeps his discharge from the army—he served fifty years since, and was at the Borodino—which he cannot read, but whose big black eagle he is never tired of admiring. Likewise, the Sonnik, or Russian Interpreter of Dreams, coarsely printed at Kief on grey paper, and illustrated with glaring daubs, whose letterpress is likewise Chaldee to him, but which he causes one of his son's wives who can read (she was a lady's maid once) to spell over to him occasionally. The interpretations do not stand him in very valuable stead, certainly, for he has generally forgotten the dreams themselves before he has vicarious recourse to the dream-book. Laid up within the recesses of this monstrous chest, not in lavender, but in a blue cotton pocket-handkerchief well impregnated with mahorka, is the Starosta's blue cloth caftan of state—a robe only worn on the most solemn and jubilatory occasions, such as one of the angel's visits (so few and far between are they) of the lord of the manor to his lands, or the great ecclesiastical fêtes of the egg-eating Easter, and the peppermint brandy-moistened Assumption. This caftan is an ample robe, possibly of genuine indigo-dyed English broadcloth, which would be worth at Leeds or Bradford, its birthplace, perhaps fifty shillings; but for which the Starosta has paid at the fair of Wishnoï-Woloschtchok (which you are not, by any means, to confound with my Volnoï) as much as one hundred roubles in paper assignations, or twenty-five in silver—a matter of four pounds English. There are real silver buttons to it, and it is lined with silk, and encircled by the gold and silver embroidered girdle which, carefully wrapped in tissue-paper, lies beside it; it is a very swellish and dashing garment. His Starostaship's ordinary or work-a-day costume is a long loose coat of coarse gray frieze—very Irish in texture, though not in fashion; and a bell-crowned hat—we have not yet seen it on his head, though—decidedly Irish, both in material and make. The sash is of gaudy colours, but of the coarsest cotton fabric: purchased at the Gostinnoï-dvor of Tver, most likely, and manufactured in the sham Manchester mill of some seigneur anxious to increase his revenues by cotton lordism. Was there ever such a land of contradictions as this Muscovy? Our heaven-born aristocracy, or at least their great majority, think trade and manufactures derogatory to the pearls and velvet of their coronets. It is a standing joke with us that we have one peer of the realm who has so far forgotten his dignity as to be a coal-merchant, and another who is a tinman. Yet the Russian aristocracy, incomparably the proudest in the world, do not think it a slur on their dignity to work cotton-factories, soap-boiling establishments, beetroot sugar-bakeries, candle manufactories, tanneries, paper-staining and floorcloth works, and iron-foundries. Imagine "Norfolk, Westminster, and Co., bone-boilers, Vauxhall, London!"

In this trunk of suppositions the wealthy Starosta has—sing it, oh choir of Westminster Abbey!—three shirts of three different colours; the red, white, and blue; but he wears them not. No; wary old man! He keeps them against the day when Sophron, the oily drunkard shall be married, or some one or other of his numerous grandchildren shall enter into the wedded state. There is, actually and politically, a considerable infusion of communism in the rival institutions of this incoherent nightmare country; and, as regards garments, the doctrines of Messrs. Proudhon and Robert Owen are astonishingly prevalent among the common people. The fable of the two friends who had but one coat, hat, and addenda between them is realized here. Sons wear their father's shirts, and grandsires their grandson's hats. The socialism as regards boots is wonderful. The peasant lasses wear the peasant lads' boots habitually (not as a task allotted to a subjugated sex, of wearing the new boots easy for the men-folk to walk in, but turn and turn about. If Vacil be at home, Tatiana goes to the fields in Vacil's upper leathers, and *vice versâ*.) Very frequently there are but two pair of boots to a very numerous family, and great economy is necessarily observed in wearing them. You may often see, even in the suburbs of Petersburg and Moscow, gangs of peasant girls and young men returning from the day's work, the comeliest and strongest wearing their family boots, the others shod either with the ordinary lapti, or bark-basket shoes, or going altogether barefoot. If it be rainy weather, the much-prized family boots are carried slung crosswise over the shoulders. No Vacil or Tatiana dare, for his or her life, run the risk of injuring the paternal slippers by contact with mud or water. The result, on the return to the paternal hovel, would be such a fearful application of leather—not boot leather, but of a thinner and more flexible description, and not to the feet, as would cause Vacil to howl, and Tatiana to cry her not very handsome eyes out. A bran new pair of boots are to a Russian a prize of infinite value. I have seen a Moujik, or an Ischvostchik, who has been able to treat himself to such a luxury, for the first time in two years, perhaps, lying on a bench, or—and this is just as likely—on the ground, with his new booted legs raised high above his head against a wall, contemplating their newness, toughness, and thickness, and inhaling their villanous odour with the half-drowsy, half-delirious mansuetude of an opium-eater of the Theriarki-Tcharchi, over his fifth pipe.

The Starosta must have a fur robe, too, in this chest; as well as those filthy sheepskins which lie on the top of the stove. It must be a foxskin schouba; or, perhaps, a brown-bearskin, originally the property, of a very grisly customer of that ilk, shot in a Carelian forest, by one of his sons while on a hunting excursion with his noble Barynn, and which he, having been miserably hugged, clawed, and mangled in the ursine strife, was graciously allowed to keep. And, finally, in this chest of chests, there is a leathern bag full of copper copecks, and odd pieces of the strangest and most ancient coins the Starosta has been able, in the course of a long lifetime, to collect. The Russians, high and low, have a curious and decided turn for numismatics. There is scarcely a gentleman of any pretensions to taste, who does not possess something like a cabinet of rare and antique coins and medals; and I have seen in some merchant's leather-bag collections, such weird, barbaric, dark age moneys and tokens, as would make the eyes of the curators of our museums to twinkle, and their mouths to water.

This is the house of the Starosta. After all, I might have given a very lucid idea of a Russian peasant's house, by repeating a succinct description given me by a certain young Russian, soon after my arrival in St. Petersburg. "A moujik's house," he said, "is dark, and made of wood; the floor is gray; the walls are gray, and the roof is gray; you can cut the smell of oily fish and cabbage-soup with a hatchet, and at night you can hear the bugs bark." (*Vous entendrez aboyer les punaises.*)

XII.

RUSSIANS AT HOME.

THIS is the order of afternoon—June the month, and two hours past meridian the time. Do you never please yourself in striving to imagine what people are doing thousands of miles away at such and such an exact moment? It must be merry this golden June season in gay Sherwood. Bold Robin Hood has thrown his crossbow by, and feels quite honest, though somewhat a-dry, and is gone to drain a flagon of the best, in the leafiest glade of the wood with that Friar, who is always thirsty. Will Scarlett is determined that his nose shall vie in hue with his name, and is toasting jolly June in the sunshine with Allen-a-Dale, who has got his rebec in fine tune, and carols to it till the birds grow jealous, and think him a very over-rated performer. Midge the Miller is indubitably singing with the best of them, for Midge, though the careful Percy has somehow overlooked the inference, was evidently a Cheshire man, and resided on the banks of the River Dee, where who so jolly as he? As for Little John, at most times rather a saturnine and vindictive outlaw, inciting the dishonest but peaceable Robin to cut off the heads of bishops and pitch them into their graves, in addition to rifling them of their mitres and pastoral rings—Little John is laughing very heartily, in his own misanthropical manner, to think that it is June, and fine weather, and that it will soon be the height of the season for pilgrimages to the wealthy shrines; and Maid Marian—what should or could she be doing in her bower, but weaving many-coloured chaplets and garlands, and singing songs about summer and the roses in June?

So all is merry this June day in my imaginary Sherwood, and in many other real and tangible localities and living hearts my fancy could paint at this moment, far, far away. This is a merry time, I am sure, for some scores of gauzy bonnets with pretty faces behind them; for hampers with many bottles containing something else besides salad mixture; for steamboat decks, for pic-nic turfs, for Kenilworth and Netley ruins, for the bow-window at the Trafalgar, for eight hours at the seaside, for excursion vans, for Sunday-school festivals with their many flags and monstrous tea-drinkings; for the man with the trombone, and the gipsies at Norwood and the Saint Sebastianzed artillery man at chalky Rosherville; for the solemn chestnut trees and timid deer of Bushey, and the pert pagoda and shaven lawns of Cremorne; for many thousand happy men and women and children, who are disporting themselves in God's good summer season. I cannot linger further on the delights which mirth can give; but I sum them all up in a presumed Sherwood, and the assumption that it is very merry there. But, I am compelled to confess mournfully, also, that the genuine merriment I can recall is on the wrong side of fifteen hundred miles away, and that it is the very reverse of merry in the month of June in the village of Volnoï Voloschtchok.

Merry! Imagine the merriment of a Cagot village in Bearn in the middle of the Middle Ages; imagine the joviality of the Diamond in Derry, before Kirke's ships broke through the Boom. Imagine the conviviality of a select party of Jews beleaguered in the castle of York, with the king's surgeon dentists, to the number of some thousands, outside. Imagine the enjoyment of a Rabelais bound to board and lodge with a John Calvin. I think any of these réunions would surpass, in outside gayety at least, the cheerfulness of a Russian Sloboda, and of the Russians at home therein. Alexis Hardshellovitch and I emerge from the Starosta's house, and wander up and down the longitudinal gap between the houses, which may, by an extreme stretch of courtesy, be called the main street. I may here mention that the street, regarded as a thoroughfare, is as yet imperfectly understood in Russia. The monstrous perspectives of St. Petersburg have few imitations in the provinces. There are even traces remaining in modern Moscow of the circular streets of the WEND villages; some of which yet remain in the Altmark, and in the province of Luneborg in Germany, and are common in the purely Sclavonic parts of Russia. The houses are jostled one against the other in a circle, more or less regular, and there is but one opening for ingress or egress. The cause of this peculiar form of construction is doubtless to be traced to the old Ishmaelitish times, when every village's hand was against its neighbour. In many of the Russian governments there are still villages consisting of a single street, closed at one extremity, resembling what in western cities is termed a blind alley. I feel a density of dulness and mental melancholy settling on me in such a place; the houses begin to look like cellular vans; the few trees like gibbets; the birds—the human ones I mean—like gaol-birds; the whole place seems plague-stricken, or panic-stricken, or famine-stricken, or all three at once.

As for "Life," social acceptation of the term, there is not a pinch of it in the whole gray snuff-box of a hamlet. I am not difficult to please as to villages. I don't expect to find green lanes, trim hedges, ivy-grown churches, smiling cottages, rosy children, ponds with ducks, and cows, and sheep, looking as though they had been washed and spruced up for the especial benefit of Mr. SIDNEY COOPER, R. A., who had sent word he was coming. I don't expect these things, as a matter of course, anywhere but in an English village. I have seen some of the dullest, dreariest, ugliest villages under the sun in France and Germany and Belgium. The clean village of Brock is not so clean as it is, and much more hideous than it might be; and I am given to understand that an American "Shaker" village is calculated, for gloominess in aspect and deficiency in the picturesque, to "whop all creation" quite hollow. Still I am inclined to think that a village peopled by primitive Puritans, who had espoused the deceased wives' sisters' husbands' wives of Mormon elders, and had afterwards been converted to the Shaker way of thinking, must be a community of roaring prodigals compared to the inhabitants of Volnoï.

Beyond the watchtower, there is not one building to give individuality to the village, or any sign of communal organization. The Starosta's house is two or three sizes larger than its fellows; the only other hut that may be called a public building is the granary, which is a barn of considerable size; but houses and barns are all alike—all littered at one farrow by one inexorable gray, dull, dingy, timber-bristled sow. The very poorest moujik's house is the diminished counterpart of the reputedly wealthy Starosta's dwelling. There is nowhere any sign of the humblest decoration, the feeblest attempt at porch or summer-house building, or parasitical shrub-training, or painting, or whitewashing, or even paling-pitching. There is not a bench before a door; but it must be admitted that over each doorway there is a rough fir board, on which is branded rather than painted, in red and white, the rudest resemblance of a bucket, a hatchet, a saw, a ladder, a coil of ropes, and similar implements. These Egypto-Cherokee implements mean that the dwellers in the doorways, are respectively bucket-men, hatchet-men, saw-men, and so forth; add that, in case of fire, they are bound to provide those implements, and to do suit and service with them to their Barynn towards the extinction of the conflagration. If I want to see cottage porches and trailing plants, Alexis tells me I must go to Ekaterinoslaf, some hundreds of versts off, or to the (said to be) smiling villages in the governments of Koursk and Woronesch. If I want to see peasants' dwellings otherwise than in the interminable gray garb, I must visit the Slobodas of wealthy and puissant seigneurs—the Orloffs, Demidoffs, and Tchérémetieffs, where the houses are painted in all the colours of the rainbow; where the Starosta's house has a garden before and a garden behind; and where there is positively a church whose timbered sides are painted without, and plastered within, and whose dome and cupolas are daubed the brightest blue, and bespangled with stars in burnished copper. Not this for Volnoï. Here all is gray; yet it is far from the sort of place where Beranger's Merry little gray fat man would elect to take up his abode. Road, and palings, and scant herbage, and stones, and houses are all of the exact tint of modellers' clay. One longs not for the darling green of English scenery, for that is hopeless and unattainable, but for even the yellow smeared houses of eastern towns, or the staring white of French villages. There is but one variation in hue,—far up above where the sun dwells; and there it is indeed a hot and copper sky, and the sun at noon is bloody. But the great master of light and shade disdains to throw Volnoï into *chiaro-oscuro*. He will parch and wither, and blaze up its surface with a uniformly-spread blast of burning marl; but he will give it no dark corners, no chequered lights—no Rembrandt groves of rich brown—no Ostade diamond touches of pearly brilliancy.

There is so deep rooted a want of confidence in the quicksand-like soil of Russia on the part of the dwellers in towns, as well as those who abide in the country, that the foundations of the houses reach far above the earth. In St. Petersburg, indeed, the basement of every house is vaulted, like the bullion offices at the Bank of England. But in villages such as this, precautions have been taken to prevent the poor timber house being blown away, or tumbling to pieces, or falling head over heels, or sinking right through the rotten earth, and coming out at the antipodes. By a species of compromise between the dog-kennel, the hen-roost, and the pigeon-cote styles of architecture, the houses are themselves perched upon blocks of granite, a material common enough in this country, and admirably suited to the sculpture of monoliths to great men, were there any great men in it to raise monoliths to. *En attendant*, they raise statues to the rascals. There is naturally between the planks of the ground-floor, and the ague-steeped, malaria-emitting marshy ground beneath, a space some fourteen inches in height, and this space is a hothouse for foul weeds, a glory-hole for nameless filth and rubbish, and a perpetually fresh field and pasture new for saurian reptiles and elephantine vermin. The houses forming the oulitza, or street, are not contiguous. They are detached villa residences, with irregular intervals, offering prospects of gray dust-heaps and copper sky. But with not so much as a clothes-pole which a Jonah could sit under with the hope that he might be overshadowed by a gourd in the morning.

No shops. Shops are a feature of village life not yet understood in a Russian sloboda. Even in government towns of some pretensions—even in the Gorods—where there are two or three churches to every hundred inhabitants—shops for the sale of the commonest necessaries of life are wofully scanty in number. There are some houses (in the towns) where bread is sold; and in the meanest villages there is the usual and inevitable quota of government dram-shops; but for every other article of merchandise,—whether you desire to purchase it wholesale or retail,—you must go, as in a Turkish town in Asia Minor, or in a Hindostanee cantonment, to the bazaar, which is in a Gostinnoï-dvor on the smallest, seediest, rag-shoppish scale, but called by the same high-sounding name, and which is as much the centre of sale and barter transactions, as though it were either one of the stately edifices in which the buyers and sellers of St. Petersburg the heathen, and Moscow the holy, spend or gain their millions of roubles. There is no Gostinnoï-dvor, of course, in such petty villegiaturas as Volnoï, and the happy villagers effect their little marketings in this wise. The major proportion of the poor food they eat, they produce themselves. The coarse grain they and their cattle fodder on is either garnered in their own bins behind their own hovels, or is drawn, under certain restrictions, and in stated rations—(in times of scarcity)—from the common granary. Though small their village home, the Imperial Government, in its wisdom and mercy, and bent on comforting its people, has thrown the ill-boding shadow of its eagle wings over a noisome shebeen of a vodki-larka, or grog-shop, where, on high days and holidays, the children of the Czar may drink themselves as drunk as soot, without fear of punishment; and where, on non-red letter days, they get drunk with no permission at all—and are duly sobered by the stick afterwards. For raiment, the women weave some coarse fabric for common wear, and spin some sailcloth-like linen; as for calicoes and holiday garments, the Starosta and the Bourmister are good enough to make that little matter right for the people between them. They clothe the naked, for a consideration, and in their beneficence take payment in the smallest instalments for the goods supplied; but woe to the moujik or the baba who is behindhand in his or her little payments to those inexorable tallymen.

For, the chief prop or basis of the municipal authority is, of course, the Holy Stick; whose glorious, pious, and immortal memory will, no doubt, be drunk by Russian tories of the old school, and with nine times nine, a century hence. As I intend hereafter to speak of the H. S. in its institutional point of view, and to show that, like the tchinn, it has a pyramidal and mutually cohering and supporting formation; I have only to hint, in this place, that the happy villagers get an intolerable amount of it, both from the Bourmister and the Starosta. The Bourmister is the great judge—Minos, Rhadamanthus, and Æacus combined—under the Pluto of this Tartarus, the absent M. de Katerichassoff. The Bourmister has power to order his adjoint the Starosta, for all his long beard and venerable aspect, to undergo the discipline of the stick; he has the power to order the Starosta's great-grandmother to be flogged, were it possible for that old lady to be alive. The young men of the village, the young maidens thereof, the children, and the idiots, and the sick people, can all at the word of command from the north German intendant, be lashed like hounds; or, at his pleasure, he can send them—thirty miles' distance, if he chooses—to a police station, with a little note to the nadziratelle or polizie-kapitan; which note is at once honoured by that functionary, who takes care that, as far as there is any virtue in the battogues or split-canes, the person entitled to receive the amount of toco for which the bill is good, shall have no cause to complain of the police rate of discount. Discount! the generous nadziratelle will oft-times give the moujik an odd dozen for luck.

The Bourmister's authority, then, is almost as awful and irresponsible as that of the captain of a man-of-war thirty years ago, (the nearest approach to the Grand Seigneur I can think of,) and he can order the gratings to be rigged, and the hands to be turned up for punishment, whenever things are not going shipshape, or he is out of temper. The Starosta more closely resembles the boatswain. He has no special authority, under the articles of war, to beat, but he does most consumedly. The Bourmister can cause any slave man or woman to be stripped, tied up, and flogged; but he does it officially, and with a grim mocking semblance of executing justice. The Starosta kicks, cudgels, punches, and slaps—not officially, but officiously. The one state of things resembles the punishment inflicted by Dr. Broomback, the schoolmaster,—the other, the thrashing administered by the fourth-form boy to his fag. But there is not much to choose between the two inflictions, as far as the amount of pain suffered. The dorsal muscles are as easily contused by the bully-boy's hockey-stick as by the schoolmaster's cane; and a whip, as long as it is a whip, will hurt whether it be wielded by a police-corporal, or by a brutal peasant.

Among a people so constantly beaten as are the Russians, it would naturally be expected that whenever the beaten had the power, they would become themselves the beaters, and that their wives and children, their cattle and domestic animals would lead a terrible time of it. This is not the case. Haxthausen, with an apologetic shrug for the abominations of the stick *régime*, says, "Tout le monde donne des coups en Russie," and goes on to say that, the father beats his son, the husband his wife, the mother her daughter, the child his playfellow, and so forth. I am thoroughly disinclined to believe this. From all I have seen of the common people, they appear to treat each other with kindness and forbearance. A father may occasionally pitch into his drunken son; but the Russians at home are far removed from being systematically violent and cruel. There is this one grand protection to the married ladies, that the Russian husband when drunk, is, instead of a tiger, the most innocent of ba-a lambs. It never by any chance occurs to him to jump upon the wife of his bosom, or to knock her teeth down her throat, or to kneel on her chest, or to chastise her with a poker. When most drunk he is most affectionate. We have all of us heard the stock Russian story, stating it to be the custom for a Russian bride to present her future lord and master with a whip on the wedding-day, and to be afterwards known to express discontent if her husband was lax in the exercise of the thong on her marital shoulders. Such an event, I have good reason to believe, is as common in Russia as is the sale of a wife in Smithfield, and with a halter round her neck, among us in England. Yet Muscovite husbands will lie quite as long under the imputation of wife-whipping as the English husbands do under the stigma of wife-selling, and as unjustly. In this case the saddle is placed on exactly the wrong horse. A Russian peasant has really no objection to sell his wife; and for a *schtoff* or demi-John of vodki will part with his Tatiana or Ekaterina cheerfully. The Englishman will not barter away his moiety, but he keeps her, and bruises her. To their horses and cattle the Russians are singularly merciful, preferring far more to drive them by kind words than by blows. In general, too, the women seem to treat the babies and little children with all desirable kindness and affection; the only exceptional case I can recall was narrated to me by a Russian gentleman, who told me that in some villages of the government of Tchernigoff there was a perfect epidemic among the women (only) for beating their children; and that they were in the habit of treating them with such ferocious brutality, that the severest punishments had to be applied to the unnatural parents, and in many cases the children had to be separated from them. I must state, to whichever point of the argument it may tend, that my informant was himself a slave-owner; and I am the more bound to make the statement, because I have frequently heard similar stories of the almost inexpressible cruelties of slave-mothers to their children, from slave-owners from the southern states of America. It is a curious circumstance, although quite foreign to the analogy sought to be here conveyed, that the village of L'Estague, near Marseilles, which was originally colonized in the old Roman times, bears at this day a precisely identical disreputation for the cruelty of the mothers towards the children.

The picture of a Russian village and Russians at home, without a portrait of the institution which serves the Muscovite moujik for inglenook, cooking-range, summer siesta-place, winter bed, wardrobe, gossiping-place, and almost sole comfort and alleviator of misery—the Peetch, or stove—would be an imposture. I want the limner's and wood-engraver's aid here, desperately; but, failing that, I must go to my old trade of paper-staining, and word-stencilling, and do my best to draw the peetch with movable types and printer's ink.

The Russian aristocratic stove, white, sculptured, monumental, gigantic, is like the sepulchre of some great man in an abbey, which has been newly restored and beautified. The Russian popular—I dare not for my ears' sake say democratic—stove is, without, wondrously like an English parish church with a flat roof. And the model is not on so very small a scale either; for I have seen stoves in Russian houses, which, as a Shetland pony is to a Barclay and Perkins' Entire horse, might be compared in magnitude to that smallest of parish churches—St. Lawrence's in the Isle of Wight. The stove, like the church, has a square tower, on whose turret pigeons coo; a choir and aisles, a porch and vestry. It is a blind church, having no windows; but it has plenty of doors, and it has vaults beneath its basement, where unsightly bodies do lie. The stove stands sometimes boldly in the middle of the principal apartment, as a church should do in the centre of its parish; sometimes it is relegated against one of the walls, three parts of whose entire side it occupies. The stove has a smoke-pipe, through which the fumes of the incandescent fuel pass (but not necessarily) into a chimney, and out of a chimney-pot. But anywhere out of the house is thought quite sufficient, and the chimney-pot may be up-stairs or down-stairs, or in my lady's chamber, so long as the smoke has a partial outlet somewhere. I say partial, for smoke has odd ways of curling up and permeating through old nooks and corners, and pervading the house generally. It comes up through chinks of the floor in little spirals; it frays in umbrella-like gusts from the roof-tree; it meets you at the door, and looks out of the window; so that you can seldom divest yourself of the suspicion that there must be something smouldering somewhere which will blaze out shortly—which there frequently is, and does. Now for the peetch in its entirety. Keep the ecclesiastical image strongly in your mind; for here is the high square tower, and there the long-bodied choir and aisles. But you are to remember that the peetch is composed of two separate parts of separate nationalities. The long body is simply the old Russian stove—a hot sarcophagus—a brick coffin with fire matter within, like that of a dead man who burns before his time. This simple brick vault full of combustion, dates from the earliest period of authentic Muscovite research. It is the very same stove that was used in the days of Rurik, and the Patriarch Nikon, and Fedor-Borissovitch. It is the very same stove, that the most savage of savage tribes would almost intuitively construct,—a hole dug in the ground, a framework of branches, the food and fuel placed upon it, and the whole covered in with a roof of boughs and clay plastered over it. Not that boughs, or branches, or wet clay, enter into the architecture of the actual Russian stove; but the principle is the same. And I am not covertly insisting on the barbarism of the Russian people because their stove is so simple. What is our famous and boasted Register Stove, or Rippon and Burton's improved grate, but a hole in the wall, with a fire-receiver uniting the capacities of an elliptical St. Lawrence's gridiron and a distorted birdcage? What is the French fireplace but a yawning cavern, with logs on dogs, in the most primitive style of adjustment? What is the French poele, or stove, but a column of St. Simeon Stylites, with a pedestal rather too hot for the feet of the saint, and an iron tail curling the wrong way? What is the Belgian stove, which advances so impertinently into the very middle of your chamber, but a lady's work-table in cast-iron, and with bandy legs? What is the German stove but a species of hot-pump, insufferably conceited and arrogant—turning up its white porcelain nose in a corner of the room, and burning timber living, I may so call it, at the rate of two Prussian dollars a day? There is, indeed, a stove I love; a fireplace, which combines mental improvement and instruction with the advantages of physical warmth and light. This is the fireplace whose sides are lined with the old Dutch tiles. In glorious blue and white, there were on these tiles depicted good and moving histories. Joseph was sold to his brethren on these tiles; Ananias came to a bad end, together with his wife Sapphira, for saying the thing that was not; the Good Samaritan left a cerulean twopence at a smoke-dried inn; and jolly Squire Boaz met Ruth a-gleaning, and at once inspired a Hebrew poet to write the most charming pastoral in the world, and inspired an Irish copyist to compose the libretto of the opera of "Rosina." There are no fire-places with Dutch tiles now. I have been in Holland; and, in their rooms, they have register stoves, and Simeon Stylites' columns. I can forgive almost that Dutch-built King of England who threw our Art back half a century—I mean William the Third—who spoilt the Tower of London, introduced the cat-o'-nine-tails into the English navy, would never go to the theatre, and wouldn't let his gentle wife have any green peas, for the one and simple fact that it was in his reign that fireplaces with Dutch tile-linings became common in England. From these fire-places, with their white and blue Scripture stories, little Philip Doddridge and little Sam Wesley learnt, at their mother's knees, lessons of truth and love and mercy. There are no Doddridges and Wesleys to expound to us now. Doddridge is a dean with two thousand a year, busily occupied in editing Confucius and defending bad smells; and Wesley is a clown who sings a sacred Tippetywitchet in a music-hall where people are killed. Least of all I am entitled to accuse the Russians of uncivilization in their stone building, seeing that their method of keeping the burning game alive is nearly identical with the process adopted by the shepherds on the melancholy downs of Hampshire and Sussex. The Corydon with the crook, and with the ragged smock-frock and the eight shillings a week, takes Monsieur Hedgehog, covers him up with clay—how Russian! sticks him in a hole in the ground, which he fills up with fire, and then covers that up with clay and turf again; and capital eating—hot, succulent, and gravy-yielding, is this same Signor Hedgehog, when you dig him out of the clay again. Such a hedgehog dinner with a shepherd on a lonely down, a wise dog sitting about two yards off, now sniffing the hot regale, and sententiously anticipatory of bones and fragments, now wriggling that sapient nozzle of his in the ambient air as if his scent were seven-league reaching, and he could smell out mutton misbehaving itself miles off, now casting a watchful back-handed eye—I mean, by the misnomer, when the optic is cast back by a half-upwards, half-sideways jerk of the head—upon the silly sheep—silly enough to eat their perpetual salad without asking for Doctor Kitchener's mixture; silly enough to be made into continual chops without remembering that there is many a ram who is more than a match for a man. Such a noontide meal—a gray sky above, and a neutral tint in the perspective, discreet silence during the repast, monosyllabic conversation and a short pipe afterwards—is a most philosophical and instructive entertainment. The edge is rather taken off the Aristotelian aspect of the encounter when the shepherd, like the needy knife-grinder, asks you for sixpence for a pot of beer, to drink your honour's health in.

On the long body of the stove, the Russian peasant dozes in summer, and sleeps without disguise in winter. When his miserable life is over they lay him out—that is, they pull his legs, and try to uncrisp his fingers, and tie his jaw up with a stocking, and put a copeck on each eyelid, and press a painted image to his senseless lip, and place an iron trencher, with bread and salt on it, on his breast, and don't wash him—on the stove; if there happens to be a scarcity of tables in the mansion. On the top of the stove the mother makes her elder children hold down her younger children to be beaten—it is almost as convenient for that purpose as the bench in the yard of a police-gaol; on the top of the stove, Ivan Ivanovitch and Dmitri Djorjevitch lean on their elbows with beakers of quass, and saucers full of salted cucumbers between, disputing over knavish bargains, making abstruse calculations upon their inky-nailed fingers with much quickness, taking the name of their Lord in vain to prove the verity of assertions to which Barabbas is one party and Judas the other; and ultimately interchanging dirty rags of rouble notes, with grins and shrugs, and spittings and crossings. I have previously had occasion to remark that the only test exercised by the uneducated Russians, as regards the value of a bank-note, is in its colour. The fifty rouble note is gray; the twenty-five rouble note is violet; the ten ditto, red; the five ditto, blue; the three ditto, green; lastly, the one rouble note is a yellowish brown. You frequently hear a moujik say, "I earned a blue yesterday;" "he has stolen a red;" "he lost a brown," &c. A monetary dispute between two Russians frequently concludes by the disputants embracing and mutually treating each other to liquor: in such a case, you may be perfectly certain that both parties—A and B—have made a good thing of it; but that some third party, not present,—say C—has been most awfully robbed, swindled, and cozened in the transaction. On the flat roof of the stove, finally, the Russian peasant is supposed to pass the only happy period of his life—that of his dozing slumbers. And it is positively—I have heard it from all sorts of differently actuated informants, hundreds of times—a standard and deeply rooted impression or superstition with the moujik, call it which you will, that while he is in dreamland, he really walks and talks, and eats and drinks, and loves, and is free, and enjoys himself; and that his waking life—the life in which he is kicked, and pinched, and flogged, and not paid—is only an ugly nightmare, which God in his mercy will dispel some day.

Rashly have I said that the top of the stove is the only place (saving the vodki shop; that exception is always to be assumed) where the Russian peasant can enjoy himself. At the bottom of the peetch, likewise, can he enjoy the *dulce desipere in loco*. For, as between the floor of the outer house itself and our mother earth there is an open basement, or glory hole, so between the bottom of the stove and the flooring there is also a longitudinal cavity; some fourteen inches high, perhaps, and some five feet and a half long; the depth, of course, corresponding to that of the peetch, which is ordinarily about forty inches wide at the top. Within this cavity, on ordinary days, odd matters are thrust—immondices of every description, broomsticks, buckets, and coils of rope. It is the sort of cavity where ravens might establish a joint-stock bank for savings, and rob each other, as directors and shareholders, dreadfully. I have passed over the standing armies of vermin, who—if it be not inconsistent to say so—lie there armed *cap-à-pie*. But once a week, Ivan Ivanovitch, the moujik, having divested himself of every article of clothing, crawls into this longitudinal cavity, and there lies till he is half-suffocated. On emerging from this oven, the Baba Tatiana, his wife, douses him with pails of hot water, till he is half-drowned. He speedily reënters into his clothes, which have been neatly baking in the front part of the stove, to kill the vermin; and this is the Russian bath. If the fortunate moujik be a starosta, or at all removed from the usual abject poverty, he will have, in lieu of this, a sort of hot-brick kennel built in his backyard, by the side of his pigstye and his dung and dust heap; and this, with a small antechamber for dousing purposes, forms his vapour-bath. The hole under the stove, however, and the hot-water pail afterwards, with a bucket of nice cold water occasionally, are the most popular components of a Ruski banyi, or Russian bath. Baking wearing apparel, in order to divest it of its animated lining, was, I was inclined to think before I visited Russia, a device confined to our English gaols and houses of correction. The first intimation I had of the practice being to the manner born in Muscovy, was apropos of a tea-party. The lady of the house where I was fortunate enough to receive that pleasant hospitality, had sent her little boy out for some tea-cakes; and as the Russian high-priced flour is the best in the world, and the Esthonian and Livonian bakers, who almost monopolize the baking trade in St. Petersburg, are most cunning in their art, the substitutes for Sally Lunns are delicious. The little boy came back betimes with a bag of tea-cakes, and a very pale and frightened face, and being questioned, said that he had wandered, through curiosity, into the bakehouse, and that there was a man's head in the oven. He was sure it was a head, he reiterated, because he wore a hat. Whereupon a Russian gentleman who was present burst out into loud laughter, and deigned to explain to us that, among us *gens du peuple* it was a common custom to send a hat to the baker's when the little animals signifying love, who boarded and lodged within it, became too troublesome. I know that the horrible story spoilt my appetite for Sally Lunns that evening, and my tea too, though it was of the very best—from Poudachoff's, and cost eight roubles a pound.

Now for a word concerning the square church-tower. This is called the Poêle Hollandaise or Amsterdam stove, and was brought from the land of dykes and dams by the all-observant Peter the Great. Breast high in this Amsterdam stove, is the ordinary continental cooking apparatus, with circular cavities for the saucepans and bainmari pans, should he happen to possess any. Underneath, at about six inches height from the ground, is the range of family vaults; a longitudinal tunnel extending the entire length of the stove, and heating the whole fabric. This is filled, every other day or so, with logs of timber, chopped to about the size of an English constable's police baton. The apertures of the stove are left open until this fuel attains a thoroughly red heat, and no more gas can be emitted; all is then carefully closed up. The stove is, in fact, nothing but a brick brazier of charcoal; but I am almost willing to believe, as the Russians proudly boast, that they have some peculiar art and secret in the construction of stoves; for I have never heard of any cases of asphyxia through their use. The samovar, too, which is apparently a most deadly piece of copper-smithery, is usually found to be innoxious; though I cannot help thinking that either a Russian stove or a Russian tea-urn would very soon make cold meat of a small tea-party in Western Europe. When the fuel is out in the long tunnel, and pending a fresh supply, then is the time for the thrifty Baba, or moujik's housewife, to bake the rye-bread. She is quite ignorant of the use and appliance of the domestic spatula, or baker's peel. She pokes the bread in with a broomstick, and fishes it out with a long instrument, which, for a long time, I considered to be a mere agricultural stimulant to hay, to wit, a pitchfork, but which I was afterwards told was specially devoted to the removal of the bread from this primitive oven.

An old Russian peasant-man who almost dotes, and a drunken varlet floundering on a bed, are all that we have seen yet human in Volnoï. Sophron and the Starosta shall now give place to the wives, the children, and the young maidens of the Sloboda; yet, when I come to tackle them, my ambition to possess pictorial talent sensibly diminishes—so little rosiness, so little beauty, so few smiles have claims upon my palette among the youngest women and girls.

It is to be understood, that I have long since given up, and no more insist on, that long and fondly-preserved Annual tradition of the beauty of peasant girls, the merry ways of peasant children, the prettiness of villages, the picturesqueness of peasant costume. I have buried the fallacious tradition along with other illusions. I give up pifferari, the Saltarella, purple vines, the rayed petticoats, and miniature tablecloth head-dresses of Italian Contadine, the harvesters of Leopold Robert, the brigands of Pinelli, the high-laced caps and shining sabots of little Normande paysannes, the pretty Welsh girl with a man's hat, the skirt of her gown drawn through the pocket-holes, and a goat following at her heels; the lustrous eyes and henna-tipped fingers of Turkish women, the pretty bare feet and long dark hair of the maids of Connaught, the buy-a-broom quaintness of the yellow-haired Alsaciennes, the ribboned boddices, straw hats, and chintz skirts of our own comely peasant girls in merry England. I know how melancholy are the habitations and ways of poverty. I know that Blankanese flower-girls, Contadine, Normande paysannes, Turkish houris, Connaught maidens, barefooted and beauteous, are conventional artificialities, made to order, exhibited, ticketed, and appraised, for the benefit of artists' studios, aristocratic families who like Norman wet-nurses, writers of oriental poems, the frequenters of the Alster Bassin promenade at Hamburg, and the artists who illustrate the wild Irish novels.

So, prepared for the prosaic, I am not disappointed at as great a paucity of the beautiful as of the picturesque among Russian peasant women. But, as in the homeliest, plainest villages in the west, I have seen and delighted in some rough gayety, and an unpretending neatness and a ruddy comeliness, that to me compensated for any absent amount of Annualism in feature, form, or attire, I cannot avoid feeling as though I had swallowed the contents of a belt of Number-four shot—so heavy am I—when I consider the women and children here. The negro slave will laugh, and jest, and show all his white teeth, before half the wounds from his last cutting-up are healed; but the Russian peasant, male or female, is—when sober—always mournful, dejected, doleful. All the songs he sings are monotonous complaints, drawling, pining, and despairing. You have heard how the Swiss soldiers used to weep and die sometimes for homesickness at the notes of the Ranz des Vaches. The Muscovite moujik has a perpetual home-sickness upon him; but it is a sickness, not for, but of his home. He is sick of his life and of himself. When drunk, only, the Russian peasant lights up into a feeble corpse-candle sort of gayety; but it is temporary and transient, and he sobers himself in sackcloth and ashes.

Home is not as a home held by in any class in Russia. It very rarely happens that moujiks who from serfs have become merchants of the second guild, and amassed large fortunes, ever think in their declining days of retiring to the village which has given them birth, or even of making bequests beneficial to their native place at their death. Soldiers too, when discharged after their time of service has expired, scarcely ever return to their village. They prefer becoming servants and Dvorniks in the large towns. "Eh! and what would you have them do?" a vivacious Russian gentleman, with whom I had been conversing on the subject, asked me. They are no longer serfs, and are of no use to their seigneur. They are no longer young, and are no longer wanted for the conscription. What would you have them do in this village of yours? What indeed? Governmentally-inclined philosophers say that the Russians are so patriotic that home is home to them, "be it ever so homely," throughout the whole extent of the empire, and that they are as much at home in the steppes of the Ukraine as in the morasses of Lake Lodoga. I am of opinion myself, that the homely feeling does not exist at all among the Russian people. Russian military officers have told me that an epidemic melancholia sometimes breaks out among young recruits which is broadly qualified as a *Mal du Pays;* but I think it might be far better described as a *Mal de Position.* The position of a recruit for the first six months of his apprenticeship is, perhaps, the most intolerable and infernal noviciate which a human being can well suffer—a combination of the situation of the young bear with all his troubles to come, the monkey upon that well-known allowance of many kicks and few halfpence, the hedgehog with his prickles inwards, instead of outwards, and the anti-slavery preacher whose suit of tar and feathers is just beginning to peel off. When, however, the recruit has swallowed sufficient stick, he very soon gets over his *Mal du Pays.* Rationally envisaging the question of home-loving in nationalities, the Great Britons

(English, Irish, and Scotch), though the greatest travellers and longest residents abroad, are the people most remarkable for a steadfast love for their home, and a steadfast determination to return to it at some time or another. After them must be ranked the French, who always preserve an affectionate reverence for their *pays;* but for all the sentimental Vaterland and Suce-Heimweg songs of the Germans, the hundreds of German tailors, bootmakers, and watchmakers, one finds in every European capital, seem to get on very well—at least, up to threescore and ten, or thereabouts—without looking forward to a return home. Your Dane or Swede, so long as he remains in his own land, is very fond of it; but, once persuaded to quit it, he thoroughly naturalizes himself in the country which he has adopted, and forgets all about Denmark and Sweden. As to the Americans, they never have any homes. They locate; and as gladly locate at Spitzbergen as at Hartford, Connecticut. The Poles, perhaps, are really attached to home; but the Czar is in possession; and we know that the most home-loving Briton would be loth to go back to his little house in Camberwell if he was aware of an abhorrent broker's man sitting in the front parlour.

There is a Baba, a peasant girl, who is sitting listlessly on a rough-hewn bench at the door of one of the homogeneous hovels. She is not quite unoccupied, for she has the head of a gawky girl of ten on her knee, and is—well, I need not describe the universal pastime with which uncleanly nations fill up their leisure time.

The Baba is of middle size; a strong, well-hung, likely wench enough. Her face and arms are burnt to a most disagreeable tawny, tan brown: the colour of the pigskin of a second-hand saddle that has been hanging for months—exposed to every weather—outside a broker's shop in Vinegar Yard, Drury Lane, London, is, perhaps, the closest image I can give of her face's hue. Nay; there is a wood, or rather preparation of wood, used by upholsterers—not rosewood, ebony, mahogany, walnut, oak, but a fictitiously browned, ligneous substance, called Pembroke. I have seen it, at sales, go in the guise of a round table for one pound nine. I mind it in catalogues: pembroke chest of drawers—pembroke work-table. I know its unwholesome colour, and dully, blinking sheen, which no beeswax, no household-stuff, no wash-leather can raise to a generous polish. Pembroke is the Russian peasant complexion. The forehead low and receding. The roots of the hair of a dirty straw-colour, (growing in alarmingly close proximity to the eyebrows, as if they were originally the "same concern," and the low forehead a bone of contention which had grown up between them and dissolved the partnership.) Set very close together, in this brown face, are two eyes—respectable as to size—and light-blue in colour, which, as the orbs themselves are quite lustreless and void of speculation, has a very weird—not to say horrifying—effect. The nose broad, thick, unshapely, as if the os-nasi had been suddenly covered up with a lump of clay, but that no refinements of moulding, no hesitating compromises between the Roman, the pug, and the snub had been gone through. It is as though Nature had done some million of these noses by contract, and they had been clapped indiscriminately on as many million moujik faces. Not to grow Slawkenbergian on the subject of noses, I may conclude, nasally, by remarking that the nostrils are wide apart—quite circular—and seemingly punched, rather than perforated, with a violent contempt of reference to the requirements of symmetry of position. The mouth is not bad,—lips red enough—teeth remarkably sound and white—and the entire features would be pleasant, but that the mouth-corners are drawn down, and that the under lip is pendulous—not sensuously, but senselessly. The chin has a curious triangular dimple in the centre; for all the organs of hearing visible, the Baba might be as earless—she is certainly as unabashed—as Defoe; the neck is the unmitigated bull pattern: short, clumsy, thick-set, and not, I am afraid, very graceful in a young female; the shoulders broad and rounded (that back is well accustomed to carrying burdens, and prodigious burdens the Russian women do carry sometimes); the feet are large, long, and flat, the hands not very large, but terribly corrugated as to their visible venous economy. How could it be otherwise, when every species of manual labour (they build log-houses, though I have not seen them lay bricks) except horse-driving, is shared with the ruder sex by women? The Babas of a Russian village have their specially feminine employments, it is true. They may spin flax; they may weave; they may cook; they may wash linen;

but it is at the sole will and pleasure of the seigneur or the bourmister, if they are in *Corvée* to him, to set them tasks of sawing wood, or plastering walls, or dragging trucks, or whatever else may suit his seignoral or bourmistral caprice. If the Baba, or her husband, or father, or whoever else owns her labour —for an independent spinster, an unprotected Russian female is, save in the upper classes, not to be found—is at obrok, instead of corvée, the employments he may give to his Baba may be even more miscellaneous. I have seen women in Russia occupied in the most incongruous manner; standing on ladders, whitewashing, sweeping streets, hammering at pots and kettles, like tinkers; driving pigs; and, in the Gostinnoï-dvors, selling second-hand goods by auction?

I have alluded to the Baba's feet. The Russian nobility are as sensitive as the late Lord Byron as to the aristocratic presages to be drawn from a small hand and foot. I have frequently heard in Russian society that genteel dictum common in England, that no person can be well-born unless water will flow beneath the arch of his instep without wetting it. I believe that in the short reign of his late Majesty Richard, third of that name, similar notions began to be entertained in polite society with reference to humps.

The Baba's dress is not pretty. To do her justice, though, there cannot be the slightest doubt as to her possession of—well, not a shirt—that is a masculine garment, but a ——, but it is unpardonable to mention in English what every English lady will name in the French language without a shadow of hesitation—well: a white cotton or very coarse linen under-garment. And this ordinarily innermost garment is very liberally displayed; for the gown-sleeves are very scanty—mere shoulder-straps, in fact: and the real sleeves are those of the under-garment, to name which, is to run in peril of deportation to that Cayenne of conversaziones—Coventry. There is an equally generous display of body linen, more or less dazzlingly white in front,—the garment forming an ample gorget from the neck to the waist, the bust of the gown being cut square, of the antique form, with which you are familiar in the portraits of Anne Boleyn, but very much lower. In aristocratic Russian society the ladies have their necks and shoulders as *décolletées* as the best modern milliner among us could desire; and in aristocratic Russian theatres the ballerine are as scantily draped as at home here; but, among the *gens du peuple*, remnants of oriental jealousy and seclusion of women are very perceptible, and the forms are studiously concealed. But for an eccentricity of attire, I am about to point out, high boots, long skirts, and high necks are productive of a most exemplary shapelessness and repudiation of any Venus-like toilettes, as arranged by those eminent modistes, the Mademoiselles Graces.

This trifling eccentricity consists in the Russian peasant women having a most bewildering custom of wearing a very tight waist at mid-neck, and a very full bust at the waist. Their corsage presents the aspect of the section of a very ripe, full pear, resting on its base. Beneath the clavicles all is as flat as a pancake; where we expect to profit by the triumphs of tight-lacing as productive or a genteel and wasp-like waist, we find this astonishing protuberance. The waist is upside down. How they manage to accomplish this astonishing feat; whether they lacteally nourish dumb-bells or babies made of pig-lead; whether it be physical malformation, or some cunning sub-camicial strapping and bandaging; whether it be the effect of one or of all these, I am not aware; but there is that effect in the Baba—baffling, puzzling, and to me as irritating as though the girl wore a shoe on her head, or broad-brimmed hats on her feet. (There is, by the way, really a shoe-shaped coiffure prevalent among the peasant girls of Tarjok and Twer. They do not wear the kakoschnik, but in lieu of that picturesque head-dress they assume a tall conical structure of paste-board, covered, according to their means, with coloured stuff, silk or velvet, and ornamented with ribbons, spangles, bits of coloured glass, and small coins. The apex of the sugar-loaf cap leans forward curvilineally, and then is again turned up at the extreme peak, somewhat in the manner of a Turkish slipper or papousch. This when, as is frequently the case, it has a streaming veil behind, bears a quaint resemblance to the old peaked head-dresses we see in Strutt.) Why am I now irritated because this Russian slave-woman chooses to go into a feeble-minded course of ridiculous deformity? She is not one whit more absurd, or more deformed, than the high-born ladies in the West, with the hair so scragged off their sheep's heads, with the watch-glass waists, with the men's coats and tails and big buttons, with the concave pancakes for hats; with the eleven balloon-skirts one above another, one I presume, of wood, one of block-tin, one of steel, one of whalebone, one (I know) of the horse, another (may be) of the cat; a seventh, perchance, of the nether-millstone. Now I think of it, I am more, much more, irritated at the Guys, who go about civilized streets,—the Guys who ought to be beautitiful women. I cry out loudly against the fashions at noon-day. I clench my fist on the public pavement. I dare say the police have noticed me. I feel inclined to pull off my shoes, like George Fox, the roaring Quaker, and walk through the streets of Lichfield, or London, or Paris, crying, Woe! to the wicked city.

On her head, the Baba wears a very old, foul, dingy, frayed, and sleezy yellow shawl, tied carelessly under her head, in a knot like a prize-fighter's fist; one peak of which shawl falls over her head, on to her back, like the peak of the cagoule of a black penitent. It is a very ugly, dirty, head-covering: with a tartan pattern it would be first-cousin to the snood of a Highland shepherdess, and it is even more closely related, in general arrangement, to the unsightly head-shawl worn by the factory-girls of Blackpool and Oldham. But, this is only her every-day head-dress. For Sundays and feast-days she has the kakoschnik, than which no prettier or gracefuller coiffure could be found, after the jewelled turban of the Turkish Sultana has been admitted as the pearl of pearls, and light of the harem of beauty and grace.

The kakoschnik is a shallow shako, (that worn by our artillerymen twenty years since, but not exceeding, here, four inches in depth, may be taken as a sufficiently accurate model,) shelving from front to back, concave as to summit, and terminated at the back with a short, fan-like veil of white lace. The kakoschnik is worn quite at the back of the head; the parting of the hair, as far as where our tortoise-shell comb uprises in the back-hair, being left uncovered. In wet weather, this kakoschnik is but an inefficient protection for the head; but the Baba disdains, when once she has assumed the national head-dress, to cover it with the inelegant shawl-cowl. In a dripping shower she will, at most, pull the skirt of her gown over her head. The substructure of the kakoschnik is buckram—more frequently pasteboard. It is covered with the richest and brightest-coloured material the Baba can afford to buy. It is decorated with trinkets, spangles, silver copeck pieces, (now prohibited,) gold-lace: nay, according to her degree in the peasant hierarchy, seed-pearls, and, in extreme cases of wealth, real precious stones. The Russian women have to the full as great a penchant for decorating their persons with gold and silver coins as have the maids of Athens and the khanums of Turkey for twining sequins and piastres in their hair. A few years ago there was quite a mania in society for wearing bracelets and necklaces formed of new silver five-copeck pieces, strung together. These are about the size of our silver pennies—somewhat thicker, not broader in diameter, (a copeck is worth about five-eighths of a halfpenny,) and being beautifully coined, are delightful little ornaments. But the government sternly prohibited such a defacing of the current coin of the empire, and plainly hinted at the possible eventualities of the Pleiti or whip and Siberia, in the case of recalcitrant coin-tamperers.

The Russian girl who possesses a jewelled kakoschnik must, of course, have the rest of her costume to match, in richness and elegance. Some travellers —Mr. Leozon le Duc, and M. Hommaire de Hell among the number—declare that they have been in Russian villages on great feast-days, the Pentecost, for example, where the maidens were promenading in kirtles of cloth of gold, tunics of satin and silver brocade; white silk-stockings; kakoschniks blazing with real gold and jewelry; red morocco shoes; lace veils of application-work falling to the heels; heavy bracelets of gold and silver; pearl necklaces; diamond ear-rings; long tresses of hair interlaced with ribbons and artificial flowers. Nothing richer or more picturesque than this could well be imagined; but I am afraid that Annualism is marvellously prevalent in the description. Novaïa Ladoga, I think, is mentioned as one of the villages where this splendacious costume is to be seen. That there is a Lake of Ladoga, I know; and a village by the name of Novaïa Ladoga is probable; but I am apprehensive that the way to that village on gala days is difficult, and dangerous, and doubtful; that the only way to go to it is "straight down the crooked lane, and all round the square ;" and that the Pentecost time, when the village maidens walk about in cloth of gold, red morocco shoes, and diamond earrings, will be in the year of Beranger's millennium.

XIII.

HEYDE'S.

The widow Heyde is dead, and Zaccharaï reigns in her stead; but Heyde's is still: even as Tom and Joe's coffee-houses in London are still so called, though Tom and Joe have been sleeping the sleep of the just these hundred years, and Jack and Jerry may be the tapsters now, in their place. So Heyde, being dead, is Heyde still. *Le roi est mort! vive le roi!*

That beefsteak and trimmings with which on board the little pyroscaphe that brought me to this Vampire Venice—this Arabian Nightmare—this the reality of Coleridge's distempered, opium-begotten Xanadu; (for here of a surety lives, or lived, the Kubla Khan who decreed the stately pleasure dome, and possessed the caverns measureless to man, through which ran that river down to the sunless sea;)—that beefsteak and trimmings, rouble-costing, with which coming to Xanadu—I mean St. Petersburg—I was incautious enough to feed the wide-mouthed Petersen, did not turn out wholly unproductive to me. The quality of that beefsteak and etceteras was not strained. It may, or it may not have fallen like the gentle dew from heaven on Petersen: but it undeniably blessed him that gave and him that received it. Petersen's stomach was filled, his wide mouth satisfied; so he was blessed: the gratitude of repletion, (I have seen a tiger in a menagerie wink like the most beneficent of charity-dinner stewards after a more than ordinarily succulent shin-bone,) the beatitude of fulness led him to bestow on me a small, ragged, and dirty scrap of paper, on which was scrawled in German, and in—something I thought at first to be the mere caligraphic midsummer madness of Petersen, but which I afterwards discovered to be his best Russ—these words, "Heyde's—Cadetten-linie, Wassily-Ostrow—young Mr. Trobbener's recommendation at J. Petersen." Who the mysterious young Mr. Trobbener was, I never was able to discover. Did Petersen recommend him, or he Petersen? Were Petersen and Trobbener the same personages? Was Petersen himself young Mr. Petersen, or old Mr. Petersen? Was he of any age, or for all time, or for none? Be it as it may, through the medium of this paper, I too was blessed; for though on the first impulse I was inclined to scorn Heyde's and to put Petersen down as an unmitigated tout, it turned out that by an accident—by a mere fluke of shiftlessness of purpose—I did not go to the Hôtel Napoléon, or the Hôtel Coulon, or the Hôtel Klee, or to the Hôtel des Princes, or to Mrs. Spink's, or to the Misses Benson's, or to any of the ordinary hotels or boarding houses where ordinary and sensible travellers usually turn up on their first arrival in Petropolis. Carrying out the apparent decision in the superior courts that I am never to do any thing like anybody else, I managed to lose all my fellow-travellers in the yard of the temporary custom-house on the English quay, (I hasten to observe for the benefit of the critics who are waiting round the corner for me with big sticks, that the custom-house is at the southern extremity of Wassily-Ostrow, and that the cellars where we were searched were but a species of luggage chapel-of-ease to the greater Douane.) Then, going very vaguely down unto Droschky, I fell at last among Heyde, luggage and all. A very excellent find; a nugget of treasure-trove it was to me; for I declare that with the exception of the fortress of Cronstadt, (the congeries of forts, yards, workshops, guardships, and gunboats, I mean,) which is one eye-blinding instance of apple-pie order and new-pin cleanliness, the Hôtel Heyde is the only perfectly clean place—bar none: nor palaces, nor churches, nor princess's châlets in the Islands—with which, in the Russian Empire, this traveller is acquainted. The Hôtel Heyde smelt certainly of soap and soup; but both were nice smells and not too powerful. It was reported that one bug had been bold enough to cross the Neva from the Winter Palace to Heyde's some years previously; but, whether he was paddled across the river in a gondola, or driven across the Novi-Most, or New Bridge, in a droschky, was never known. He came to Heyde's, but broke his heart the first night in a miserable attempt to make an impression on the skin of the traveller for a German toy-merchant, just arrived from the fair of Nishi-Novgorod, (where there are bugs that bite like sharks, who have been under articles to crocodiles.) A housemaid nosed him in the lobby next morning; but he saved himself from the disgrace of public squashing by suicide, and they show his skin in the bar to this day.

To be a little serious, Heyde's was from top to bottom scrupulously and delightfully clean. I have no interest in proclaiming its merits to the world. I have paid my bill. I am never going there again. I don't know Heyde—I mean Zacharaï—personally; for it was with Barnabay Brothers, his representatives, that I always transacted business. Still, I can conscientiously recommend to all future purposing Russian travellers, the Hôtel Heyde, as being clean and comfortable. It is dear, and noisy, and out of the way; but that is neither here nor there. If I had a few of Heyde's cards with me, I would distribute them as shamelessly as any hotel tout on Calais Pier; and my opinion of Petersen now is, that he is not merely a wide-mouthed and carnivorous wolf-cub, in a beaver porringer—like the city sword-bearer, who goes about the world seeking eleemosynary beefsteaks and trimmings—but that he is a philanthropist, who, disgusted at the narrow mindedness and heart-sterility of the company that used to go to Helsingfors, has proposed to himself as a mission the perpetual pyroscaphal parcurrence of the Neva from Petersburg to Cronstadt and back again, and the ceaseless distribution of unclean scraps of paper telling in Teuton and in Sclavonic of Heyde's, and young Mr. Trobbener, and himself, simply because he is a philanthropist, and that Heyde's is clean, and he, Petersen, has stayed there, and knows it.

I came to Heyde's—though but one man—in two droschkies, like that strange animal one of which came over in two ships. In this wise. I don't mean to imply, literally, that I had one droschky for my body, and another for my legs, *à la Américaine;* though I was quite fatigued enough to have rendered that means of conveyance, had it been in accordance with the proprieties of Petersburg, or even with possibility, delightful. But this was not to be. My having two droschkies was necessitated by there being none but the little Moscow side saddles on wheels disengaged, which hold indeed two passengers; but, in the way of luggage, will not accommodate so much as a carpet-bag in addition to the human load. How ever my luggage was loaded, or managed to be kept on the little rickety bench with the little wild beast with the long mane and tail in it, and the large wild man in the caftan, the beard, and the boots, bestriding where the splash-board ought to have been, but wasn't—I have not the slightest idea. However, with a bump, some jolts, and some screams, my luggage was heaped on one droschky, and I on another; then everybody had some copecks given them—including an official in Hessian boots who suddenly appeared from a back door in the yard (I really conjectured it to be the dust-hole) who demanded seventy-five, in French, haughtily, who received them very unthankfully, and who, saying something to another official, dressed in gray, (he had five copecks,) which I suppose was Open Sesame! disappeared majestically into the dust-hole again. Open Sesame! let us out into a dusty street; for I and the droschky-drivers and the travellers had all been prisoned within the custom-house's moated grange till this, and it had pleased the man in the dust-hole to let us out.

The phaethon droschkies, the double-bodied droschkies, the calêche droschkies, had all driven away hotelwards through the dust—I did hope that Miss Wapps might be well bitten that same night; and I was alone with the droschkies, the dust, and the Petersen's bit of paper. There was dust on either side, and dust beneath, and dust behind us, and dust before, and nothing more, save the occasional vision of the luggage-droschky a-head, which was bumping up and down and in and out of the pulverous cloud in a most extraordinary manner. I now first became acquainted with the fact, that as soon as a Russian Ischvostchik gets on a tolerably long road-way, he gives his horse his head, and throwing up his own legs, yells with delight, and is —till he is compelled to heave-to by the menacing halberd of a Boutotsnik—supremely happy. We were in the Perspective of something or other—the Dusty-Bobboff Perspective I was inclined to call it at the time—and the driver, anticipating with joy a quiet mile or so of furious driving, suddenly gave the vicious little brute he was driving his head, following it with the usual performances of leg-elevating, arm-flourishing, and yelling. I decidedly thought that Ischvostchik had gone mad. The horse being given his head, took in addition his four shoes, his hocks, his tail, and every thing that was his, and made good use of them, scrambling, tearing, pawing along, and I almost was led to think yelling as well as his maniacal driver. What was I to do? What could I do, but catch hold of the Ischvostchik, at last, quite frantically by the shoulders, and entreat him to stop. For a wonder, he understood me, as I thought intuitively; but, as I afterwards found, from my hurried Stop! stop! being very like to the short, sharp Russian stoï! stoï!

I have heard gentlemen who ride to hounds talk of the remarkably fine burst they have had after that carrion with the bushy tail some November morning. I have read the terribly grotesque epic of Miss Kielmansegge and her golden leg; Bürger has told me in Lenore how fast the dead ride; I have seen some Derbies, Oaks, and Doncasters; I have travelled by some express trains; I have seen Mr. Turner's picture of Hail, rain, steam, and speed; and now, if for hail you will substitute dust, and for rain hot wind, and for steam a wild horse, and increase the speed as many times tenfold as you like, you will have a picture of me in the droschky, and the droschky itself flying through the dusty Perspectives of Petersburg.

Over a bridge I know, where there was a shrine-chapel, open at the four sides, where people were worshipping. Then dust. Then along a quay. More dust. And then the seemingly interminable flight along Perspectives. And at last, Heyde's.

A building, apparently about a third of the size

of the Bank of England, with the Corinthian pilasters beaten flat, with a hugeous blue signboard somewhat akin to that dear old Barclay and Perkins one in the England I may never see again; on this signboard Heyde's, with some of the unknown tongue beneath. Beyond, over the way, and some miles on either side, houses considerably bigger than Heyde's, all painted either in white or more glaring yellow, and with some red but more green roofs.* And, save our party, not a living soul to be seen. A defection of one took place immediately from our band, small as it was, the luggage Ischvostchik, feeling, no doubt, athirst—how thirsty was I!—incontinently diving down some stone steps into a semi-cellar that yawned beneath Heyde's parlour windows. Such half-cellars—not level with the pavement, and not an honest area depth beneath it—are common in the grandest streets of Petropolis. The meanest little shops crawl at the feet of gigantic buildings, like Lazarus lying in his rags before Dives's door. The cellar in which my Ischvostchik had disappeared was, I was not slow in concluding, a Vodki shop: first, from the strong spirituous

* Comparison, even with the diminution of a third, to the vastness of the Bank of England is of course a little extravagant; but I wished to give the reader a notion, there and then, of the astonishing size of even private houses in St. Petersburg. The great imperial rule is carried out even in architecture as in government. *Aut Cæsar, aut Ivan Ivanavitch*, who is considerably less than a nullity. In Russian houses there are but two classes—hovels and palaces. I know one lodging-house in St. Petersburg, close to the Moscow Railway Terminus, which has more than two thousand inmates.

odour which exuded therefrom; next, from the unmistakable sign of a bunch of grapes rudely carved in wood, and profusely gilt, suspended over the doorway. And have I not a right to call this a remarkable people, who keep grog-shops, and sell meat-pies, in the basement of their palaces? I was about to collar the second Ischvostchik to prevent his fleeing too; but he, good fellow, wished to see me comfortably into Heyde's, or was, perhaps, anxious about the fare, and he remained. He was so anxious about this fare that he demanded it at once with passionate entreaties and gesticulations, crying out, when I gave him to understand by signs that he would be paid when I was inside, "Nietts Geyde! Nietts Geyde! Sitchas!" Why should he have objected to be paid by Heyde, or at Heydes, or Geydes, as he called it? Wearied at last with manual language, I asked him how much he and his brother Jehu thought themselves entitled to; whereupon he held up such a hand—the hand in a baronet's scutcheon was nothing to it for bigness, boldness, and beefiness—and cried out, "Roubliy cerebram! Roubliy cerebram!" counting one, two, three fingers; from which I gathered that he wanted three roubles—nine and sixpence—for a twenty minutes' drive. But I did not pay him; for, with the exception of one English sixpence, one Irish harp halfpenny, one Danish Rigsbank schilling, and some very small deer in the way of copecks and silbergroschen, I had no money.

I have been keeping the reader a most unconscionable time at Heyde's Hotel door; but I am certain that I was kept there a most unconscionable time myself. The Ischvostchik who didn't go to the Vodki shop, and who had so great an objection to being paid by Geyde, hung himself—that is about the word—not for suicidal but for tintinnabulatory purposes, to a great bell that projected from the doorjamb like a gibbet, or a wholesale grocer's crane. He swung about, tugging at this bell till I could hear it booming through the house like a Chinese gong, but nobody answered it. There was a great balcony on the first floor, with a Marquise verandah above it, and in this balcony a very stout gentleman smoking a cigarette. I shouted out an inquiry to him in French and German, as to whether there was anybody in the house, but he merely smiled, wagged his fat head, and didn't answer me. He was either very deaf or very rude. Nobody came, while before me glared the great closed door of Heyde's which was painted a rich maroon colour, and had a couple of great knob bell-handles, like the trunnions of brass cannon. Nobody came. It was now nearly six o'clock, but the sun was blazing away with noontide vigour, and seemingly caring no more than my friend Captain Smith for any curfews that might toll the knell of parting day. And the infernal dust, with no visible motive influence, came trooping down the street in rolling caravans of brown, hot, stifling clouds. And the Ischvostchik kept swinging at the demoniac bell, which kept booming, and nobody came; and I began to think of crying aloud, this is not Petropolis or Petersburg of Russia, but the city of Dis, and Francesca of Rimini passed by in that last cloud caravan, and yonder bell-swinger is not an Ischvostchik, but P. Virgilius Maro, inducting me, Dante Alighieri, into the mysteries of the Inferno. Would that I had Dante's stool to sit upon—to say nothing of the genius of that Florentine!

A bearded party in a red shirt (his beard was red too) eventually put in an appearance through the tardy opening of the maroon-coloured door. He exchanged a few compliments or abusive epithets—they may have been one, they may have been the other—with the Ischvostchik; then, closing the door again, he disappeared and left me to desolation.

How long we might have continued dwellers at the threshold at Heyde's inhospitable door is exceedingly uncertain—perhaps till the cows came home, perhaps till I went mad—but, just as I began to speculate on one or other of those eventualities, it suddenly occurred to my Ischvostchik to call out in a tone of triumph, "Geyde na Dom," which I conjectured to be a sort of Muscovite pæan for Heyde being to the fore. And, following out the discovery he had announced with such Eureka-like elocution, the droschky-driver did no more nor less than turn one of the brass-cannon-trunnion-like door-handles and walk me into Heyde's hall. It was the old story of Mahomet and the Mountain. Heyde would not come to us, so we were obliged to go to Heyde's—which, by the way, we might perhaps have done a quarter of an hour previously. But I never was the right man in the right place yet, nor did the right thing. The second or luggage Ischvostchik—he who had been so prompt in disappearing into the vodki-shop, and who had now returned smelling very strongly of that abominable black-sheep of the not-at-any-time-over-reputable Alcohol family—evidently thought very little of my strength of purpose in obtaining admittance into an hotel. He, with a contemptuous leer on his face, (which, round and flat, and straightly touched for line and feature, was not unlike the mystic dial that crowns the more mystic columns in the inner sheet of the Times newspaper,) seemed to taunt me with my inability to get into Heyde's; to imply, moreover, that he knew well enough how to effect an entrance, because he hated me as an Anglisky, and hated the other Ischvostchik, his brother, for being his brother, simply.

The sun had been brightly glaring outside; the hall of Heyde's was painted above and on either side a cool green; and the transition from the brazen desert outside to these leafy shades was pleasant as unexpected. It would have been much pleasanter, though, had we found any one living soul to welcome us; but nobody came.

At the extremity of the hall there commenced a very dark stone staircase, beneath which there was a recess, most uncomfortably like a grave with a bed in it. My eyes had been very much tried by the glare without and the green within, and my knowledge of external objects was blurred, not to say rendered null and void, by sundry elaborate geometrical patterns of fantastical design and parti-coloured hue swimming about in the verdant darkness. So I was not able to aver with any degree of distinctness whether there were anybody or not on the bed in the recess that looked like a grave. Not so with the Ischvostchik; he with cat-like agility dived into the recess, and, after many struggles, brought into the greenness the man with the red shirt who had whilom opened the front door, and shut it again in our faces. Him he shook and objurgated in much violent Russ; at last he seemed to make the red-shirted door-shutter comprehend for what reason a very tired traveller should arrive at an hotel in St. Petersburg in two droschkies—himself in one, his luggage in another. He cried out "Portier, portier!" and darting down a dark corridor, presently returned with a little old man, in faded European costume—very snuffy, stupid, semi-idiotic, as it seemed to me. I could not at all make out to what nation, if any, he had in the origin belonged; but I managed to hammer a few words of German into him, to the effect that I was very tired and dusty and hungry, and that I required a bed, food, a bath, and the payment of the droschky. I don't think he clearly understood a tithe of my discourse, but on the retina of his mind there gradually, I imagine, became impressed the image of a traveller who wanted to spend his money at Heyde's, and ultimately fee him, the porter, with silver roubles. So he rang a HAND-BELL, which brought down one of the brothers Barnabay who manage Heyde's for Zacharaï the Mythic; and this brother Barnabay, (it was the stout brother,) understood me, the droschkies, the difficulty, everything. Would I, dear lord, as I was, show him my passport? This was before Barnabay quite understood anything. I showed him my passport. He was so delighted with it as to keep it, buttoning it up in a stout coat-pocket, but assuring me that it was *Ganz recht—ganz recht!* and immediately became as fond of me as though he had known me from infancy, or as though I had been his other brother, and a Barnabay. He had my rugs, my courier's bag, my spare caps and writing-case off my arms and shoulders instantaneously. That famous hand-bell was tinkled again, and two more red-shirted slaves of the bell appearing, a room was ordered to be prepared and a bath to be heated for me. I had scarcely opened my mouth to tell him that I had no more Russian money, and that he must pay the droschky, when he had paid both. And now I, on my part, understood why the Ischvostchiks had wished me to pay them, and cried, "*Nietts Geyde! Nietts Geyde!*" for, from their pitching my luggage viciously into the hall, from their pouring out a strain of half-whining, half-threatening remonstrances, and from Barnabay being evidently on the point, at one stage of the proceedings, to apply the punishment, not of the stick, but of the square-toed boot upon them, it is anything but doubtful that *Geyde* (represented by Zacharaï's representative Barnabay brother) was hard upon the Ischvostchiks, and gave them no more—perhaps a little less—than their fare. I am of opinion, too, that Geyde's or Heyde's was a little hard upon me, too, subsequently, in the bill relative to that same cab fare; but surely somebody must be cheated, as a Russian shop-keeper once naïvely remarked to me,) and who so fit to be cheated as an Inostranez —a stranger—and, what is much worse, an Anglisky?

Leaving the Ischvostchiks to lament, or curse, or pray for us in the hall, (I don't know which it was, but they made a terrible noise over it,) the nimble Barnabay skips before me up the great stone staircase, which grows much lighter as we ascend, and which I begin to notice now (being somewhat recovered from the glare and the greenness,) is of that new-pin like degree of cleanliness I have before hinted at. Then we push aside a glass door, and enter a vast chamber, half-American bar, half-Parisian café in appearance; for, at a long counter customers are liquoring, or painting—or drinking drams, tell the unslanged truth; and at little marble tables, customers are smoking and drinking demi-tasses: but wholly Russia, for all that; for I can see, towering through the tobacco-clouds, a giant stove, all carvings and sculpture, like Sir Cloudesly Shovell's monument in Westminster Abbey. Then another glass-door; then another corridor; then the door of apartment Number Eighteen; then another hand-bell is tinkled, and a real Russian chambermaid appears to open the bedroom door, and a real German waiter —for there is no promotion from the ranks at Heyde's; and the red-chemised slaves of the bell are kept in their proper places—asks me, in first-rate North German, what I will have for dinner.

The first sight of apartment Number Eighteen startles me, and I confess not very favourably. If that little recess beneath the staircase on the basement were like a grave; Number Eighteen is horribly like a family vault. It is of tremendous size—very dark—and the bed, which is covered with snowy white drapery, is very long, narrow, uncurtained, and a very short distance removed from the floor; and has the closest and most unpleasant family resemblance to the tomb of a Knight Templar. If, in addition to this, I write that this long white bed is all alone, by itself, in the middle of the vault—I mean the bedchamber—that the inevitable stove seems even higher, bigger, and whiter that Sir Claudesly Shovell's monument in the *café;* that the chest of drawers is dreadfully like a brick sarcophagus; that there are some massive, gloomy shelves, on which there are no coffins as yet, but which I fancy must have been designed to receive those last of snuff-boxes, which are to titillate the nose of humanity; that the windows, though very numerous, are very small; that the folding-doors of a great mahogany wardrobe yawn tombfully, as though they were the portals of the inner chamber of death; that there is one corner cupboard which I can almost make oath and swear, is the identical corner cupboard reserved by the especial NEMESIS for years —the corner cupboard where the skeleton is—when I have given this hurried inventory of the furniture of Number Eighteen, it is a work of supererogation to relate that, being a nervous man, I shake my head when Barnabay Brother tells me the terms—two roubles a day, exclusive of attendance—and that I ask midly whether I cannot have a smaller, lighter, cheaper apartment. But I cannot have anything smaller, cheaper, lighter, Zimmer. All else is full, engaged up to the eyes, three deep, till to-morrow fortnight, till the Greek calends. I can go over to the Napoléon, to the Coulon, to the Deymouth, to the Klee, to the Princes, but I shall find everything (not that this poor house, dear lord, would wish to lose your distinguished, and, of consideration, patronage!) as full as the tomb of the Eleven Thousand Virgins at Cologne. This "funerals performed" allusion jars upon my nerves again, as having unpleasant reference to the family vault view of things in general. But, as I find I can't well obtain any other accommodation; as I opine I can turn out and engage cheaper apartments in a private house to-morrow; as the vault, though a vault, looks a remarkably clean mausoleum, and does not by any means give me the impression that it is haunted even by the ghost of a flea,—such as poor dear William Blake, the supernaturalist painter, saw what time he witnessed a fairy's funeral in a garden by moonlight—I accede to the terms, and am swiftly at home at Heyde's.

I say at home—and swiftly; because no sooner have I accepted to sit at Heyde's, at fourteen silver roubles a week, than I become in Barnabay's mind, no longer a wandering traveller, higgling and haggling for accommodation—but "Nummer achtsehn,"—Number Eighteen, duly housed and recognized; my passport in Heyde's pocket (you will observe that I use the terms Heyde's, Barnabay, Zacharaï, somewhat indifferently; but is it not all one with regard to nomenclature, when all is Heyde's?) my name on Heyde's house-slate, my name, in far more enduring characters already, in Heyde's leger: for, has he not paid the Ischvostchiks, and is not that the commencement of a goodly score?

At home at Heyde's, I have to repeat; for perhaps, while the Brother Barnabay is chalking me up as Number Eighteen, one red-shirted slave of the bell has devoided me of almost every particle of apparel, and has, by some astonishing feat of gymnastic ability, got on to some adjacent housetop, where I can see him, and hear him brushing them, and hissing meanwhile in approval, ostler fashion. Another vassal is preparing an adjacent bath-room, which (always remember that we are in a German hotel) is on the ordinary hot-water principle, and not the stewpan, combined with chemical distillery, finished off by Busbeian discipline and buckets-of-cold-water, Russian vapour-bath. Serf number three, the twin brother of the two others, has uncorded my luggage, and is now tugging away at my boots, with so good-humoured a grin on his willing bearded countenance that I am far more inclined to slap him on the shoulder than to remember that my feet are swollen, and that he has nearly dislocated my ankle. You find among the poor slave Russians—I can scarcely say the poorest, lowest, most degraded, when all are degraded, and low, and poor; all figures of Zero, to swell the millions of roubles their masters possess, and make those Units wealthy and powerful—the kindest faces, the most willing, obliging, grateful dispositions in the world. To qualify that old Billingsgate locution, which, coarse as it is, is exactly applicable here, "Barring that a Russian moujik is a liar and a thief, no one can say that black is the white of his eye." He is kind; he is grateful; he is affectionate; not quarrelsome when drunk; untiringly industrious; (when on his own account, he will idle the lord's time away, and who can wonder?) ordinarily frugal; and as astonishingly self-denying as an Irish peasant when he has a purpose to serve. His vices are the vices of barbarism; and here comes the difficulty in his treatment to those who are even most disposed to treat him kindly. I declare of my own knowledge that it is impossible to live in Russia, among the Russians, without feeling that the serfs—from domestic servants to farm labourers, from ladies' waiting-maids to village babas—laugh at what we should call kindness, and despise a master who does not act on the principle of a word and a blow. It is impossible to avoid becoming to a certain degree hardened and brutalized by the constant spectacle of unrestrained tyranny on the one hand, and by the impossibility of resistance on the other. Every one beats, and kicks, and cuffs, and calls his inferiors opprobrious epithets; would it be surprising that, through mere habit, the most ardent lover of freedom fell into some of the despotic ways of those he lived amongst? I am glad to say that I lived too short a time in the Russian Rome for it to be seldom if ever necessary to me to do as the Romans do; yet I have often been conscious and ashamed of a temptation to administer the argument of Mr. Grantley Berkeley—the punch on the head—for what would in England have been considered, if an offence at all, one only to be visited by a word of reproof; I have often been conscious, and more ashamed, of speaking to droschky-drivers, and waiters, and Ivan generally, in a manner that, employed towards a cabby or a coally in England would have infallibly brought on the punching of my head, if not the knocking down of my body altogether.

Of Heyde's more anon; whether the family vault bedroom did or did not contain ghosts, and who the fat man was who was smoking the cigarette in the balcony, and answered not when I spoke to him.

XIV.

MY BED AND BOARD.

A great writer has somewhere told a story of a man about town—Crockey Doyle, was, I think, his name—who became very popular in society through the talent he possessed for making apologies. He would give offence purposely, and be in the wrong advisedly, in order to be able to make, afterwards, the most charming retractations in the world. No one could be long angry with a man who apologized so gracefully; so he became popular accordingly, was asked out to dinner frequently; and was eventually, I dare say, popped into a snug berth in the Tare and Tret Office.

I have not the easy eloquence of Crockey Doyle.

I am not popular. My most frequent Amphytrions are Humphrey, Duke of Glo'ster, or the head of the great oriental house of Barmecide and Company. And no one, I am sure, would ever dream of giving me a place. Yet I am for ever making apologies. Like the gambler's servant, who was "always tying his shoe;" like Wych Street, which is always vehicle-obstructed; like a friend of mine, who, whenever I meet him, is always going to his tea, and never, seemingly accomplishes that repast; I am always apologizing either for the things I have done, or for the things I ought to and have not done. I have apologized in England, and in France, and in Germany; here I am again, a self-accusing clown apologizing in St. Petersburg of Russia; and I have little doubt that if I live I shall be apologizing in Pekin, or New Orleans, or the Island of Key West.

My apologies in the present instance are due to my readers, firstly, for having loitered and lingered outside the door of Heyde's, and for having described every thing concerning that hotel save the hotel itself. Secondly, for having placed the words Hand-Bell in the large capitals without offering the slightest explanation as to why that diminutive tintinnabulum should be so suddenly promoted in the typographical scale.

Touching the first, though you might have put me down merely as a bore—telling you of things that did not interest you, or desirous of spinning a lengthened yarn out of one poor thread—or as a simpleton, nervous and ashamed, who lingers long in the vestibule of a mansion in which there is a feast prepared, and he invited thereto, and takes his goloshes off and on, instead of going up stairs boldly, and making his bow to the hostess ;—though this may have been your conviction, I had, in truth, a deep-laid and subtle design to impress you with a notion of what an opposite a Russian is to an English or a continental hotel, and how fundamentally Oriental are the habits and manners of the people I am cast among. The Russian hotel is, in fact, nothing more than a Smyrniote or Damascene caravanserai—vast, lonely, unclean, thickly peopled, yet apparently deserted,—the same caravanserai, into whose roomy courtyard you bring your camels, your asses, and your bales of silks, and drugs, and pipes, and Persian carpets; in whose upper chambers you may have equivalents for pilaff and rice,—may go to bed afterwards armed, for fear of thieves, and for want of them fight with vermin. Heyde's—tell it to all nations—is clean; and Heyde's, internally, is German; but its exterior arrangements have been Russianized against the Heydian will; and its inferior *valetaille* are all Muscovite; hence the difficulty of entrance; hence the listlessness of the outer domestics; hence the necessity of the HAND-BELL I am about to apologize for presently, and which is nothing more than a substitute for the hand-clapping which, in the East, brings the cafegi with the coffee and chibouks, and in the Arabian Night's Entertainments, the forty thousand black slaves with the jars of jewels on their heads.

In the worst town's worst inn, I will not say closest to the mere territorial Russian frontier, but in

German Russia—say in Riga or Mittau—there is, instantly on the arrival of the modestest bachelor traveller, with the compactest of valises, a tremendous hurry-scurrying to and fro of porters, boots, (*hausknechts*, the Germans call them,) chambermaids, waiters, and even landlords. The carillon of a great bell summons all these hotel myrmidons from the vasty deep of the billiard-room and the corridors as soon as your cab-wheels are heard in the courtyard. The landlord advances with the stereotyped grin, and the traditional hand-rubbing peculiar but common to all hotel landlords, from mine host of the Garter in England to mine host of the Hôtel de Londres at Riga. The hausknecht shoulders your luggage, and disappears with it before you say whether you mean to stop at the hotel or not; the portier (pronounced porteer; tremendous men are German porteers—Titans with gold aiguillettes on their shoulders, and selling on their own private account cigars the choicest, for those who like them,) the portier pays your cab, asks your name, and says there are no letters for you as yet, (he has never seen you before in his life,) but he rather thinks there will be, next post. The waiter, or waiters, skimmer about undecidedly, but ready for every thing, from an order for champagne to an order for a sheet of letter-paper; the chambermaid immediately converts herself into a Mont Blanc of towels and a hot spring of Iceland, in the way of cans of boiling water; the very white-vested and night-capped cook peeps through the grated window of his kitchen—a prisoner in no respect connected with Chillon—and beams on you a greasy ray of assurance, that though your dinner may be dear and dirty, it shall be hot and oleaginous. Finally, the landlord, with the grin and the rubbed hands, conducts you in a mincing canter up many staircases, and through many corridors; and you are unpassported, unbooted, undressed, and in bed, in about the same manner I have described in the last chapter. Now, all of this takes place inside Heyde's, but not one atom on the exterior thereof. You may come in a droschky, or one of the flaming Nevskoï omnibuses—licensed to carry other passengers besides human ones—or in a hearse, or in the Lord Mayor's coach, supposing the transportation of that vehicle to be possible; but not the slightest attention will be paid to you, till you get in. You might as well be that Mr. Ferguson who was told, that although other matters might be arranged on an amicable footing, he could not lodge there (wherever "there" was) on any consideration. Inside Heyde's there is pleasant gnashing of teeth over a good German dinner; outside Heyde's there is wailing at the apparent impossibility of getting any dinner at all.

But I am inside Heyde's now, and have my bed and board there. I stay at Heyde's a month and mark its ways, and note them with the informer's pen. To have done with the apologies, I hope I have explained that outer delay on the Heydian frontier satisfactorily; to have done with the handbell let me tell you that unless you have your own servant with you (and to have a servant I should counsel every traveller in Russia who possesses the means; and if he possess them not, what the deuce is the good of his travelling in Russia at all? you have not the slightest chance of having any attention paid to your wishes as regards refreshment, or any thing else unless you tinkle a hand-bell. The Russians understand wire-bells no more than they do chimes; they must have the immediate and discordant jingle. It is no good calling "Waiter!" "Garçon!" "Tchelovek!" or "Kellner!"—without the bell. Tchelovek, or as the case may be, calls "Sitchass!" (directly) but cometh not; but, ring your hand-bell (Kolokol) and he is at your beck and call instantaneously. He hears and obeys. He will bring you any thing. He will stand on his head if you gratify him with copecks sufficient.

Very good to me are my bed and board at Heyde's. Cheerful when I wish it. Lonely when I so desire it. Let us have the lonely object first.

I have bought at an Italian artists' colourman's on the Nevskoï, *un pinceau de Rafaelle*,—a box of water-colours,—Newman, Soho Square; how strange the Prince of Wales's plumes and "Ich dien" on the cakes look here, in Muscovy!—at a price for which I could have purchased a handsome dressing-case and fittings, in London and Paris. When I am tired of the noise and turmoil of the buffet (for I am alone in Russia, as yet, and have very few acquaintances and no friends) I retire into the family vault, and make sketches of the strange things and people I have seen in the streets. They are very much in the penny-valentine manner of art—pre-Adamite, rather than pre-Rafaellite. Then I make manuscript transcripts of matters Russian that have been written on the tables of my memory during the day, on infinitesimal scraps of paper in a handwriting whose minuteness causes me not to despair of being able to earn my living some day by writing the decalogue within the circumference of a shilling. These, being desperately afraid—perhaps needlessly—of spies and duplicate-key possessors, I hide furtively in the lining of my hat, wondering whether—as usually happens to me—I shall manage to lose my hat in some steamboat-cabin or railway-carriage before I land in England, and be compelled to purchase in Dover or Brighton (I will except Southampton, whose hats are excellent) the hardest, heaviest, shiniest of English country-made Paris velvet-naps. My last hat was a Dover one, and impressed such a bright crimson fillet on my forehead that I must have looked, uncovered, like the portrait of one of those Jesuit missionaries you see in the Propaganda, who have gone to China, and have been martyred. There is amalgamated with this low art and furtive note-making, a strong suspicion of a Turkish chibouk somewhere in the room—a real Turkish one, with a cherry-stick tube —no mouthpiece (amber is a delusion, save for show,—kiss the pure wooden orifice with your own lips and let the latakia ascend into your soul to soften and enliven it) and a deep red clay bowl, inscribed with fantastic characters in thready-gold and as fragile as the tender porcelain—the egg shell china—our great grandmothers really delighted in, and our contemporaries say they delight in, and don't. Also, between this and the Gulf of Bothnia, there is, perhaps, on a table in the family vault, a largish tumbler filled with a steaming liquid of a golden colour, in which floats a thin slice of lemon. It is TEA: the most delicious, the most soothing, the most thirst-allaying drink you can smoke withal in summer time, and in Russia. But it is not to be imagined that, because this tumbler of tea is exquisite, I have foresworn cakes—or ale.

I have grown to love the family vault; it is gloomy, but cool and clean; it is so large that I am continually finding out new walks about it, and continually exercising myself in its outlying districts. There is a fair quantity of furniture dispersed about its roomy suburbs, but this is so thoroughly inadequate, when its size is taken into consideration, that were Heyde (represented by Barnabay) to furnish it thoroughly, so as to give it an air of being decently crowded with movables, I doubt not but that those enterprising brothers would be ruined hip and thigh.

My vault has many windows; but from every one of them I have a (to me) pleasant view. There is the kitchen aspect. The kitchen is not on the basement, but on a first floor, on a level with my vault—which, in its mortuary character, should properly be on the basement also; but, in this astonishing land they even have their churches one above the other in floors: the summer church in the parlour, the winter church in the garret. The kitchen's contiguity to me is not near enough to be olfactorily disagreeable, but near enough for me (with the aid of an opera-glass, for I am wellnigh as blind as a mole) to descry from my windows interiors that would have driven Ostade crazy; bits of still life whose portrayal would have made the fortune of Gerard Dow; green-stuffs and salads whose every leaf Mieris would have doted on; effects of firelight and daylight combined, from stewpan-laden furnaces, that Schalken would have loved to paint, but would have failed in reproducing.

The cook—rosy, corpulent, and clad in gravy-stained white from tasselled nightcap to flapping slippers—is a German, a free German—a Hamburg man, who but he. He fears nor knout, nor pleiti, nor rod, nor stick, nor Siberian pleasure jaunt. He is a Canterbury Tale cook to look upon: portly, jovial, with a rich, husky, real-turtle-soup-bred voice, which he ladles from a tureen rather than from his throat, and which I hear rolling in rich oily waves through the kitchen as he lectures his subordinates in bad Russian. He has many subordinates. One lank, cadaverous young Teuton, his nephew, who came from Cassel, and is always whining to go back to Cassel, and who, from the distaste he gives me, seeing him putting his fingers into the sauces so often, I unequivocatingly wish would go back to Cassel immediately. Two or three bearded acolytes, in the usual pink shirts and etceteras, who spill more than they cook, and break more than they spill, and are not kicked and cuffed for clumsiness, I think, much more than they deserve. And, finally, this field marshal of cooks has a flying cohort of culinary Amazons, nimble-fingered, quick-witted girls, with coloured kerchiefs on their heads, who fly about from point to point, baste, stir, stew, fry, dish up, and it strikes me, do the major part of the cooking at the Hôtel Heyde. Of course our chief cook's directing genius and superintending eye are everything, as to flavour. I may here mention a curious example of that laziness and desire for an easy, abundant pumpkin leading life inherent (through slavery, but to be eradicated by freedom) which you find in Ivan the moujik and Quashie the nigger. A peasant once told me, or rather the gentleman who was interpreting for me, that of all professions in life he should prefer that of head-cook in the house of a seigneur; for, argued he, what have you to do? just dip your finger in the sauce and lick it, and the babas (the women) do all the rest. He had no idea of there being any skill in the world save that purely manual. Sometimes Heyde's chief cook condescends to hold one end of a napkin for straining asparagus-soup purposes. Sometimes it will please his cookship to go through a light-hearted bit of legerdemain with two stewpans; but his ordinary position is with his broad back against the dresser, and his broad face turned towards the chief furnace, a paper cigarette between his pulpy lips (he smokes in the kitchen, this bold cook) and a tall tankard of real Bavarian beer (they have it real at Heyde's) by his side. Who expects field-marshals to head armies as well as direct their movements? Our Wellington, to be sure, was fond of exposing his life, and William of Orange was only tolerable and in good humour when he was in immediate personal danger. But Napoleon sat in a chair in the rear of Waterloo's carnage till he mounted that famous pale horse to fly from it. Edward the Third witnessed the battle of Crecy from a windmill, and Louis the Fifteenth had his wig dressed while his household troops were charging the English guards. Our cook looks on, directs, but does not fight. Who can carry the bâton of marshal and Brown Bess at the same time?

There is always a prodigious laughing and screaming, and, if truth must be told—romping—going on in this kitchen. The chief cook himself is a gay man, and flings his handkerchief to one of the kerchiefed damsels; the girls generally keep up a shrill clamour of tongues, to which the noise of a well-stocked poultry-yard, where Cochin-Chinas in good health and voice are not wanting, may serve as a comparison. I am of opinion that the Cassel-sick German (who is evidently a misanthrope) hits them occasionally with saucepans, or otherwise abuses them, for the prattle and laughter frequently change to sounds unmistakably those of invective and anger; and there is one young lady, very ugly she is, (I have her now under the lens of my opera-glass,) who discourses so loudly on some real or fancied grievance, with such vehement gesticulation and such frenzied utterance, that I am apprehensive, every moment, she will fall down in a fit. But she does not—thinking, perhaps, that were she to do so, she would be brought to her senses by the outward application of melted butter or hot gravy.

This cook, I learn, when I am not in the solitude of the family vault, is an excellent artist. If you make him a present of a blue bill—say five roubles

—and order a dinner—say for self and friends—he will cook you a repast succulent enough to make a bear leave off honey; which expression may be taken as equivalent to our "good enough to make a cat speak." He has one little fault: this. After any extra exertion in the culinary line, he departs in a droschky to the house of a friend of his, likewise a German and a tailor, who resides in a remote Pereoulok in the neigbourhood of the Alexander-Nevskoï convent, and there for three or more days and nights inebriates himself with Brantwein or corn brandy, specially imported from Germany by his sartorial friend: blowing a trumpet from time to time as a relaxation. Meanwhile, the culinary arrangements are under the control of the misanthrope who wants to go back to Cassel, and the dinners are very bad.

Another view I have, of a huge court-yard, surrounded by staring walls—all belonging to Heyde—round which run pent-houses or sheds, and beneath which are harboured droschkies, whose gaberdined drivers snore on box and bench till a pink-shirted messenger comes to pummel them into action, and tell them that a fare is waiting for them. The roofs of these pent-houses are leaded, and on them (how keeping their perpendicular I know not) more kerchiefed women are beating carpets; they beat carpets at Heyde's—tell it again to the nations—with willow rods; and more pink-shirted men are thrashing the dust out of fur pelisses, or peacefully slumbering on their diaphragms in the sunshine. Another view I have, through a window, and round a corner, of a strip of thoroughfare between two blocks of houses, which from the droschkies, the gray-coated soldiers, and the clouds of dust, must be either the Cadetten-Linie, or the Line (or street) parallel to it. And last of all, I can peep into a little private court-yard—I suspect the one appertaining to Barnabay's own separate and special apartments—where two little children, a boy and a girl, are gravely exercising themselves on stilts. Stilts in Russia!

Stilts in Russia; and why not more than these? for as, dazed with the blinding sunlight, I come into the gloomy interior of the family vault, and cast myself into an easy old arm-chair, (it would hold two with comfort,) I hear from a wandering band that have just entered the Balschoï-dvor, or great court-yard, first the hacknied but always delightful strains of the Trovatore, and then—but I must be dreaming—no; they are actually playing it, She wore a Wreath of Roses.

I see it all now. I have only been a few miles away from town to write this journey. Due North is but the North Kent Railway: this is Dumbledowndeary, not Wassily-Ostrow: the Shoulder of Mutton Inn and not Heyde's Hotel. Be it as it may, it is extremely hot; and if there be any law in Russia or in Kent against taking a siesta in the middle of the day, I have violated it. I go fast asleep, and live a life I never shall live fifteen hundred miles away; then wake to hear the cook's bad Russian, and to find the sun a trifle lower in the heaven.

This is the time for a gondola on the Neva; so I leave the family vault to the ghosts, and Heyde's to its devices.

XV.

I BEGIN TO SEE LIFE.

THEY do, certainly, see a great deal of Life at Heyde's. There is a convivial phrase, called, "keeping it up," which the Heydians seem perfectly well acquainted with, and act upon to a tremendous extent. If I come home from a ball very late,—or rather very early—say four o'clock in the morning, I find the jovial men who dwell at Heyde's just sitting down to supper, and ordering tankards of strong beer, (they have the genuine Baerisch here, and it costs thirty copecks—a shilling a pint,*) as a

* There is a very excellent beer (*Piva*) brewed at Moscow, which is (being Russian) of course abandoned to the moujiks. *Nous Autres* are very fond of Dublin bottled stout. At Dominique's café, on the Nevoskoï, feeling one night athirst for beer, I asked for and obtained a pint bottle of the brown and frothy beverage that has made the name of Guinness famous all over the world. For this same pint bottle of beer I was charged the small sum of one rouble—three and twopence. An English gentleman, long resident in Russia, and intimately conversant with things Muscovite, has since told me that I had been swindled, and that I ought not to have been mulcted in more than half a rouble. However, I know that I paid it; and the consciousness of having

preparative for subsequent sound and steady drinking. If I emerge from the family vault, to dine, to smoke, to "coffecate" myself, or to read the newspapers, still find I the Heydians keeping it up with unabated and unwearied joviality. All night long too,—at least whenever I wake during that season when deep sleep *should* fall upon men, but falleth not, alas, upon me!—I hear the clicking of the balls in the billiard-room, the shouts of the conquerors, the "Gleich, gleich!" or "Sitchasse! sitchasse!" (Coming! coming!) of the waiters. In the morning, going into the café to breakfast I find the brothers Barnabay with pale faces and encrimsoned eyelids, telling dreadful tales of long keeping it up; and as for Zacharaï, he has kept it up, I imagine, so long that he is now kept down—in bed—and does not appear at all. Finding this widely-spread determination to keep things up; and being rather tired of loneliness and keeping my room—or vault—it occurs to me to keep it up too; so I go into the public world of Heyde's, and see what it is made of.

In that rapid, scurrying journey I took when the two Ischvostchiks brought me here, I spoke of the spacious apartments I had traversed. In these the Heydians keep it up, by night and by day, and in this wise.

There is the Buffet or café, call it what you will —the Bar I call it. It is not unlike a railway re-

been cheated out of fifty copecks did not give me much more satisfaction than, I imagine, the worthy Justice Shallow experienced when Sir John Falstaff was good enough to inform him that he owed him a thousand pounds.

freshment-room ; for, traversing it longitudinally, there is a bar or counter, laden with comestibles. No soup, no scalding water discoloured and miscalled tea, no pork pies or sausage rolls, however, here recall memories of Wolverton and Swindon. The counter stores at Heyde's consist of that by me abhorred, by others adored, condiment, caviare: caviare simple, in little yellow hooped kegs: caviare spread on bread and butter: caviare artfully introduced between layers of pastry. Then there are all the dried, and smoked, and pickled fishes, on little crusts of bread, like what we call tops and bottoms; all the condiments in the way of spiced and marinaded meats, highly-peppered sausages, and Russian substitutes for our brawn and collared viands; of which I have already spoken, as being purchasable in the refreshment-room of the Cronstadt pyroscaphe. There are crabs, too, and craw-fish, and some mysterious molluscs floating in an oleaginous pickle, and which, shell for shell, and saucer for saucer, bear a curious family likeness to those immortal WHELKS that, displayed on stalls, supported by kidney puddings and hot eel-soup, were once the greatest glories of the pillars of Clement's Inn.

Now, all these condiments are simply incentives to appetite. You, who have travelled in Denmark and Sweden, know that in private as well as public houses, such buffets or counters are set out, and that dinner is invariably prefaced by a mouthful of caviare or salted fish, and a dram of raw spirits. We have but a very faint reflex of this epigastrium-spurring custom in Western Europe:—in France, in the oysters and chablis (or Sauterne) by which a dinner *bien monté* is preceded; in England, in the glass of sherry and bitters, in which gastronomes will sometimes indulge before dinner. In Russia, dram-drinking and condiment-eating preparatory to the prandial meal are customs very widely disseminated. In every restaurant you find such a counter —in every wealthy merchant's house. In old Russian families too—noble families, I mean—there are the buffet, the caviare, and the drams; it is only among the tip-top specimens of *Nous Autres*—the great counts and princes, in whose magnificent saloons you forget (for a moment) that you are among savages, and believe yourself to be in the Faubourg St. Germain, that you find a disdain of this homely, Sclavonic, tippling custom. The dram and fish buffet is abolished, the dinner is served according to the most approved models set forth by Ude and Carêsne; but even under these circumstances a slight innovation upon the Median and Persian discipline of a Parisian *cuisine* takes place. The apparently exiled drams and condiments are handed round to the guests by stealthy lacqueys. This is a mean, furtive, underhanded way, I take it, of drinking one's "morning," or rather "evening." We can excuse him who takes his grog honestly, manfully, openly; but what shall we say of the surreptitious toper who creeps home to bed, hides the gin-bottle under the pillow, and gets up to drink drams while honest men are sound asleep. In the United States of America, I have heard that pickled oysters and small cubes of salted cod are frequently to be met with on the marble bars of the palatial hotels; but I am given to understand, that they are regarded less as incentives to eating, than as provocatives to drinking. It is well known that it is impossible for our Transatlantic cousins to annex the Universe, rig the market for the millennium, and chaw up, whip, and burst up creation generally, without a given number of "drinks" (some authorities say fifty, some seventy-five) per diem. It happens sometimes that the Democratic stomach grows palled, the Locofoco digestive organs shaky, the Hard Shell nerves in an unsatisfactory condition. It is then that the pickled oysters and salted cod whets come into requisition. I wonder that some of the enterprising *aides-de-camp* to Bacchus—the ginshop and tavern keepers of London—do not take a leaf from the Russo-American book! Dried sprats might cause the "superior cream gin" to go off gayly, and little slabs of kippered-salmon might cause an immense augmentation in the demand for the "Gatherings of Long John," or the "Real Glenlivat," or the "Genuine L. L." As it is, broiled bones, cayenned kidneys, and devilled biscuits, are luxuries confined to the rich. Why should the middle and lower classes be deprived of the same facilities for the descent of that Avernus which leads to the devil, as are enjoyed by their more fortunate brethren?

As, in a "Journey Due North," it is competent for me, I hope, to notice the peculiarities of the countries one may traverse before reaching the Ultima Thule, I may mention that, in the taverns and beer-houses of Belgium and Holland, although no condiments are sold at the bar, women and boys are continually circulating round the tables with baskets, in which are hard-boiled eggs, crawfish, and sometimes periwinkles, which they offer for sale to the beer-drinkers.

Although Heyde's is a German hotel, and the younger Barnabay tells me that he is a Lutheran, there is in the buffet the ordinary inevitable joss, or saint's image. He is a very seedy saint, very tarnished and smoke-blackened, and they have hung him up very high indeed, in one corner. He is so little thought of, that Heyde's is the only public room I yet know in Petersburg, in which the guests sit, habitually, with their hats on. Nowhere else, in shop, lavka, Angliski or Ruski Magazin, would such a thing be tolerated. The hat goes off as soon as one goes into any place sanctified by the presence of the joss. When I go to buy a pair of gloves, or a book, or a quire of paper, I take off my hat reverentially; for is not Saint Nicholas, or Saint Waldemar, glowering at me from among bales of goods or cardboard boxes, blushing with the brightest paint, and winking with all his jewels, real or sham! The shopkeeper I know expects it. I hope he appreciates the respect which I, a heretic and pig, pay to his harmless superstitions. The joss at Heyde's is hung there, not because Heyde or any of its foregathering belong to the Greek Church, but because the place is frequented indifferently by Germans and Russians, and the latter might take offence at the absence of the religious symbol.

The same deference to the dominant party may be observed in numbers of the shops kept by foreigners in St. Petersburg. Perfumers from Lyons, tailors from Vienna, linendrapers from London, milliners from Paris, statuette-sellers from Milan, bow and are silent in the presence of the stick. In the fashionable modistes on the Nevskoï and in the Balschoï Morskaïa it is by no means uncommon to see a really magnificent saint's image, blazing with gilding and tinsel, and enshrined in costly lace. There is nothing like burning a candle to St. Nicholas—old St. Nicholas, I mean.

Mentioning what I supposed in my first crude notions of Russian manners to be a custom generally prevalent in Russia, that of taking off the hat, and remaining uncovered, while in any room or shop in which there was a saint's image, I have now, however, to confess that before I left Russia my ideas on the subject underwent a considerable change. I had a great deal of shopping to get through before leaving St. Petersburg, principally with a view to the purchase of curiosities for anxious friends at home; and as foreigners always have about three times more to pay for what they purchase than Russians have, I always took care to secure the services of a Russian acquaintance, to whom I confided my pocket-book and shopping commissions. It was a source of much chuckling to me to see my Muscovite agent beat down, higgle, haggle, and barter, with some merchant in the Gostinnoï-dvor,—say for a writing-case, an embroidered sash, or a model samovar, of which I wished to become the possessor, and when he had ultimately come to terms and secured the article at perhaps a tenth of the price originally demanded for it, to watch the rage of the merchant when my Russian friend laughingly informed him that the sash or the portmanteau was for an Angliski. I noticed in these shopping excursions that my Russian acquaintances, whether they were wearers of the cloak, of the tchinovnik, or the gray capote of the guardsman, never removed their caps when they entered a shop, however prominent the saintly image might be. I asked one of *Nous Autres* one day, as gently and discreetly as I could, why he departed from what I had conceived to be an inviolable custom? "*Parbleu!*" he answered, "who is to tell us to uncover ourselves? The Gassudar? Bon! but the Tchorni-Narod—the black people—the fellows who sell soap and leather. *Allons donc!*" This gentleman was right in his generation. Who indeed, in a country where WE are every thing, is to bid US to be uncovered? Fancy a lizard telling a crocodile that he opened his mouth too wide.

Touching upon hats—though still at Heyde's: I think this is not the worst of places to observe that the Russians are the greatest hat-lifters in the world. They need build their hats, as they do, of a species of brown paper covered with a silk or beaver nap; for were the brims of any hard material, they would inevitably be worn out after one day's course of salutations. Everybody takes off his hat, cap, helmet, or shako, to everybody. The Emperor takes his off to begin with, when he bids his hundred thousand "children" good morning at a review. The humblest moujik, meeting another as humble as he, takes off his hat and bows low. If very drunk, he not only takes off his hat and bows lower, but positively refuses to be covered till the interview be terminated, and continues bowing and bowing like the Chinese Tombolas we used to see on mantel pieces. The hat, indeed, is much more off the head than on.

And what manner of men are the midday, and the midnight, and-not-going-home-till-morning, revellers at Heyde's? There are portly German merchants from Leipsic and Stettin, come to buy or see; there are keen, dressy, dandified Hamburgers—no thumb-ringed, slow-going, sauerkraut-eating Germans these—but men who combine business with pleasure, and, speculating feverishly in corn and hides and tallow all day, drink and smoke and dance and play dominoes and billiards, and otherwise dissipate themselves, all night. What lives! Wondrous travellers are these Hamburg men. They know all the best hotels and best tables d'hôte all over the continent. They talk familiarly of Glasgow and Dublin, Wolverhampton and Cheltenham. Their Paris they know by heart; and there is another country they are strangely acquainted with—Italy; not artistic Italy, musical Italy, religious Italy, but commercial Italy. One Hamburger tells me about Venice. He touches not on St. Mark's square, the Bridge of Sighs, or the Bucentaur. He confines his travelling reminiscences to the custom-house regulations, and the navigation dues exacted by the Lombardo Venetian government. He has had ventures to Leghorn, and has done a pretty stroke of business at Naples, and has an agent at Palermo. I would call him a Goth, but that it is much better to call him a Hamburger. Then there are German ship-brokers, German sharebrokers, and a few of the wealthier German tradesmen of St. Petersburg, who come here to quaff their nightly bumpers, and play their nightly games at dominoes. The Russian element consists of students from the University of St. Petersburg, and pupils from the Ecole de Droit, (equivalent to our English law students,) and these alumni wear cocked hats and swords. Some of these days I am certain the Russian government in its rage for making every thing military will insist upon the clergy wearing cocked hats and swords; we shall have the Archbishop of Novgorod in a shako, and the patriarch Nikon in a cocked hat. Finally, there are a few Russian officers, but not guardsmen. Heyde's is not aristocratic enough for them; and the Russian officers of the line, though all noble *ex officio*, are as poor as Job.

It is among these motley people that I begin to see life, and smoke paper cigars, and play billiards (badly), and talk indifferent French and worse German, and a few words of Russian, at which my acquaintances laugh. For I have made acquaintances already, athough no friends.

An acquaintance with whom I have already adjourned once or twice to the condiment-counter, and whom I am now even attempting to initiate into the mysteries of the recondite game of cribbage, (our cribbage-board is a sheet of paper in which we stick pins,) is a gentleman whose name, inasmuch as he holds, I presume, to this day, an official appointment under the imperial government, I will veil with the classical pseudonym of Cato the Censor. Cato is a gross fat man, an amalgam of puddings, a mountain of flesh; when I meet him abroad, as I do sometimes, having twenty-five copecks-worth of droschky, I pity the Ischvostchik, and the horse, and the droschky springs, (had they sense to be pitiable,) and (prospectively) Cato the Censor himself, were he to fall off that ominously-oscillating vehicle. For, who could pick him up again—a shattered fat man? A crane might do it, or Archimedes' lever, or a pair of dock-yard shears, but not mortal Boutotsnik or Police-soldier. When Cato laughs, his fat sides wag; when he sits on one of Heyde's chairs, I tremble for that chair; when he walks on Heyde's floor, the boards creak with the agony of this oppression of fat; and I expect every moment to see Cato sink through the basement as through a trap-door.

Cato the Censor is a Tchinovnik, and wears a civilian's uniform, (that seems a paradox, but it is not one in a land where everybody wears a uniform,) to wit, dark green with double-eagle buttons, gilt. When abroad he wears a long cloak with a cape, and a cap with a green band, and a curious white-and-blue disk in front, half button, half cockade, but wholly Chinese. I believe it to be competent for the Tchinovniks to wear, if they choose, a tunic; but Cato, with the usual fatuity of fat men, wears a tail-coat with the slimest and scantiest of tails, the shortest of sleeves, and the tightest of waists. Fat men, properly, should wear togas; and yet you find them almost always inveterately addicted to zephyr jackets. Cato has a round, sleek, bullet head, very small feet in the tightest of patent boots—so small that they continually disturb my notions of the centre of gravity, and make me fear that, Cato's balance not being right, he must needs topple over—and very large, fat, soft, beefy hands, whose principal use and employment we shall presently discover.

For, why Cato the Censor? Thus much: that this fat Russian is one of the *employés* in the Imperial "Bureau de Censure," (I do not know, and it would be no use telling you its Russian name,) and it is his duty to read through every morning, every line of every foreign newspaper that now lies on Heyde's table, and to blot out every subversive article, every democratic paragraph, every liberal word, every comma or semicolon displeasing to the autocratic *régime* of the Czar of Stickland. For instance, Heyde's takes in the Illustrated London News, the Illustrated Times, (that other Times, which is not illustrated, is rigorously tabooed,) the Constitutionnel, the Journal des Débats, the Brussels Nord, the German Illustrieter Zeitung, and that quaint little Berlinese oposcule the Kladderadatch. These, with a Hamburg commercial sheet, and a grim little cohort of St. Petersburg gazettes and journals, which, for the political news they contain, might just as well be sheets of blank paper, are the only intellectual food we are allowed to consume at Heyde's. Cato of course knows all languages; and he goes through these papers patiently and laboriously, at his own private bureau in the censor's office. When the journals have been properly purified, he and an under-clerk, a sort of *garçon de bureau*, bearing the mental food, come down to Heyde's; the under-clerk deposits the newspapers on the reading-table, liquors at the condiment counter, and, I am inclined to think, receives, from time to time, some small gratuities in the way of copecks, from Barnabay. He departs, and Cato the Censor, forgetting, or at least sinking for the time his official capacity, sinks at once into Cato the convivialist, and keeps it up till the small hours, as gayly and persistently as the most jovial of the Heydians.

Formerly, the censorship of foreign journals was performed by means of simple excision. The pruning-knife, or rather the axe, as Mr. Puff would say, was employed; and the objectionable passages were ruthlessly cut out; the excised journal presenting, in its mutilated condition, a lamentable appearance of raggedness, "windowed," if not looped. You had to grin through the bars of such a newspaper, and, knowing that you were in prison, long for the freedom outside and over the window. In time, however, some beneficent minister of police (the censure falls naturally within his attribute) discovered that the bodily cutting out of part of a column, involved not only the loss of the reverse side to the reader—which might very likely be only a harmless narrative of "extraordinary longevity in a cat," but also possibly destroyed some matter favourable directly or indirectly to the interests of Holy Russia—thus cutting off the Czar's own nose, as well as the baneful branches from the tree of liberty. So, a new plan was adopted. The heretical matter was "blacked" or blocked out, by a succession of close stampings with black ink upwards, downwards, backwards, forwards and diagonally,—exactly as the grain of a steel plate for mezzotinto is raised by a "rocking-tool"—till every offending cross to a t or dot to an i was obliterated. The appearance of a newspaper thus blocked out is very wonderful. Sometimes a whole column becomes as dark as Erebus; sometimes one paragraph in an article of foreign intelligence will disappear; sometimes two lines and a half in a critical article on a purely literary subject, perhaps three columns in length, will assume an Ethiopian hue; sometimes one line in an advertisement will be numbered with the wonders of typography that were. The immediate why and wherefore of all this, lies with Cato the Censor. He is "Sir Oracle," and no literary dog dare bark at him. Sometimes a few of the old Heydians [but not Russians you may be sure] banter him playfully as to his morning's corrections; ask him if he took too much "ponche" over night, and, waking up in a bad humour that morning, had gone to work savagely with the blacking stamp—I had nearly said bottle—or whether he had been sent for by the Minister of Police and told that he had been far too lenient lately, and must stamp out several degrees more rigorously in future? When bantered too severely the fat man loses his temper, throws over his dominoes, casts grim official glances at his tormentors as though he would very much like to be Cato the Censor of men as well as words, and stamp out a few of the Heydians for their insolence.

A remarkable and very puzzling peculiarity in this absurd and useless system of censorship, is the fact that paragraphs positively rampant in their democratic and throne-subversive tendency are very frequently left untouched, and are visible to the naked eye. Whether this occurs through mere carelessness and oversight on the fat man's part, or through some deep and subtle design of the fat man's superiors to let certain things be known, while others are to be enveloped in obscurity, I am perfectly unable to state; but such is the fact. Just before I left Russia the affairs of Naples were beginning to attract attention. The probability of a rupture between the Western powers and the "Padrone assoluto" of the Lazzaroni was being freely discussed. The papers talked of the imminent arrival of an allied squadron in the Neapolitan waters; of the wrongs of Poerio; of the ripeness of the people for revolt; of the atrocities of the wretched Ferdinand, and his sobriquet of "King Bomba;" of the barbarities of the bastinade and the dungeons of Caserta and Ischia. All this was left untouched. I think, myself, that the Russian Government, in its dealings with newspapers, is much more afraid of ideas than of facts. It assumes it to be impossible for its reading subjects to be ignorant of the moon's rotation; but it does not wish them to know why it rotates, or, at least, to speculate on this or any other subject. Speculation might lead to inquiries as to the why and the wherefore of the Stick, the Police, Slavery, the Passport system, non-representation, an irresponsible government—nay, ultimately, to impertinent queries as to the cause and effect of the high and mighty and omnipotent Czar himself.

XVI.

HIGH JINKS AT CHRISTOFFSKY.

Perhaps Xhristovskoi—perhaps Cristofski; but, that it is an island in the Neva, and that there are high jinks there, I know. When the lexicological and harmonic value of the thirty-six letters in the Russian alphabet shall find a compensating equivalent, and shall be adequately represented by the poverty stricken twenty-six we Western barbarians possess, I shall be able, I hope, to get on better with my Sclavonic orthography; and philologists will cease to gird at me for not spelling correctly words for which there is no definite rule correctly to spell—will cease to denounce me for violating the law, when that law is yet a *Lex non scripta.*

This is the twenty-first of June—old, or Russian style; and Saint John's Day—Midsummer, in fact. Even as the little boys in England have by this time come home for the holidays; so have the big and little boys who wear the spiked helmets, and swords, and cocked hats, before their time in St. Petersburg, come home for their Midsummer holidays. From the first, and second, and third cadet corps; from the school of imperial pages, and the corps des Porte-Enseignes de la Garde; from the School of Mines, and the School of Forests, and the School of Roads and Bridges, and the School of Artillery, and the School of Fireworks and Blue Blazes, (which last educational establishment I have been led impatiently to surmise, so numerous are the military schools in Russia,) from all these gymnasia, teeming with future heroes burning to be thrashed at future Inkermanns, have come the keen-eyed, multi-faced, multi-langued (which is heraldic, though scarcely Johnsonian, as an epithet) Russians. I have scratched the Russ thoroughly to-night, and have found an immense quantity of Tartar beneath his epidermis. Alexis Hardshellovitch is here, home for the holidays, his head bigger than ever, and as few brains as ever inside it. Genghis Khan is here, with his white-kid gloves, his Parisian accent, and his confounded mare's milk and black sheepskin tent countenance. There is, to be brief, a mob of lads in uniform to tea this Midsummer night; the antechamber is full of helmets and cocked-hats, undress caps and swords, belts and sashes, and marine cadets' dirks; while the outer atrium or vestibule is a perfect grove of cloaks with red collars, and gray capotes with double-eagle buttons.

For, the kindest lady in the world is samovarising, otherwise, entertaining us at tea to-night in her mansion in the Mala Millionnaïa—otherwise *La petite Millionne*—why million, why little—for it is a much broader street than Portland Place—I know not. The windows are all open; and as there are a good many apartments *en suite*, and a good many windows to each, no man has as yet been suffocated; though the heat of the day last past was full of promise that the desirable asphyxiating consummation in question would occur somewhere or to somebody before midnight. We have made a famous tea; and one marine cadet has consumed, to my knowledge, twelve tumblers-full of that cheering, but not inebriating beverage. Alexis Hardshellovitch has overeaten himself as usual, on raspberries and cream,* and a professor of natural history in the University of Moscow—a tremendous savant, but strangely hail fellow well met with these school lads—has been cutting thin bread and butter since ten P. M. The samovar has grown so hot that it scorches those who approach it, and blights them like an upas tree; so the guests give it a wide berth, and form a circle round it; though the heroic lady

* The Russian raspberries are delicious, full-sized, juicy, and luscious, and devoid of that curious furry dryness, that to me make western raspberries as deceptive and annoying to the palate as the apples of the Dead Sea. In England, a raspberry, to my mind, is only to be tolerated—like the midshipman, who was hated by the purser—in a pie; but in Russia it is a bulb of thirst-allaying delight. The Russian strawberries, on the other hand, are execrable—little niminy-piminy, shrunken, weazened atomies, like Number-six shot run to seed, and blushing at their own decrepitude. I have seen hot-house strawberries, not in the fruit-markets, but in the great Dutch fruiterers' shops in the Nevskoï. Three roubles, sixteen shillings, was the moderate price asked for a basket containing half-a-dozen moderately-sized strawberries.

of the house still continues to do battle with it, at arm's length, and keeps up filling tumblers of tea and slicing lemons thereinto, regardless of trouble or expense. There are so many guests, and they are distributed in such an eccentric manner, that the two servants in waiting have long since abandoned —as a thing impossible of accomplishment—the practice of handing each visitor his own particular cup of tea. They come round with the tray and the tumblers; and the noble Russians make Cossack forays upon them. It is every man for himself, and tea for us all.

Start not, reader, nor, deeming our spirits fled, think that we are all men-folk in the suite of apartments in the Mala Millionnaïa, samovarizing on the bounty of the kindest lady in the world. Besides that good soul, who has lived for others all the days of her life, and shall assuredly continue to live for others when this turbid phantasm is over—but those others shall be angels for whom she shall live to be loved by them, and who will keep time to her cloud-pressing footsteps with harps of gold—besides the good woman, we are sanctified, this Midsummer night, by the presence of wise, and good, and beautiful women. We have the Queen of Sheba, radiant in the majesty of her haughty comeliness, proud, defiant, outwardly, but, ah! so tender, so loving within—a warrior's cuirass filled with custard (this is the same Queen of Sheba you heard about in connection with the Nevskoï perspective, a late interview, and a certain gent in a white-top coat); we have this fair woman, to whom Minerva stood godmother, but whom Venus stole away in her infancy, like a gipsy as she is, to adopt her, practising the trill at an Erard's grand pianoforte, under the guidance of the famous St. Peterburgian Italian music-master Fripanelli (this is not the etiolated old Fripanelli you wot of in Tattyboy's Rents, but his prosperous brother Benedetto Fripanelli, who emigrated from the Lombardo-Veneto kingdom soon after some Carbonari troubles in eighteen hundred and twenty-two—ostensibly because he was politically compromised, actually because he could not gain bread, olives, or rosolio—nay, not in Milan—nay, not in Bergamo—nay, not in Venice; and makes his six thousand roubles per annum in Petersburg now by persuading princesses that they can sing.)

The Principle of Evil, if we are to believe the old legends, suffers, among other deprivations, under the curse of banishment from HARMONY. The devil has no ear. He cannot sing second. Counterpoint is a dead letter to him. Base as he may be, thorough bass is a sealed book to him. He is never more to hear the music of the spheres. Goethe has wonderfully implied this in the discordant jangling of the sound of Mephistopheles' speeches. After the Spirit of Negation has spoken one of his devilish diatribes, the accents of Faust fall upon the ear like honey. *Humanum est errare* in the case of Faust; but the devil cannot err, because he cannot, in any case, be right. He who commences nothing, cannot be tardy in finishing his work. It seems a certain curse upon the Russian aristocracy that they, too, have no ear. They cannot sing in tune; the only melody they are capable of accomplishing is the tune the cow died of. I happened to mix much, while in Russia, in musical and operatic circles—of which, specially, I shall have to say something in the course of this wayward journey. The Russian ladies insist upon learning the most difficult morceaux from the most difficult operas. Where an angel would fear to tread in the regions of Wapping Old Stairs, the Princess Piccoliminikoff will rush in with Casta Diva. They (the ladies) are admirable, nay, scientific musicians. They are wonderful pianistes—but always in a hard, ringy, metallic manner, without one particle of soul; they are marvellous executantes vocally, and can do as much, perhaps, in the way of roulades and fioriture, as the most unapproachable Italian singer; but sing in time, or tune (especially,) they cannot. "*Tout ça chante faux.*" ("They all sing false,") a music-master told me at Count Strogonoff's, pointing to the whole cohort of musical ladies gathered round a pianoforte. On the other hand the brutish, enslaved, unmusic-mastered people are essentially melodious. I have heard in villages Russian airs sung to the strumming of the Balalaïka, or Russian lute, with a purity of intonation and truth of expression, that would make many of our most admired ballad-singers blush.

To the Queen of Sheba is joined a timid little fluttering fawn of a thing—one Mademoiselle Nadiejda. Nadiejda what? Well, I will say Dash. Mademoiselle Dash (the Christian name is a pretty and tender one, and signifies, in the English language Hope (is one, well, not of those *raræ aves*, but certainly of those pearls beyond price, Russian pretty girls. She is not beautiful; the Russian beauties are either of Circassian, Georgian, or Mingrelian origin—dark-eyed, dark skinned, full bee-stung lipped, and generally Houri-looking; or they are the rounded German-Frauleins—from Esthonia, Livonia, and Courland: North German beauties, in fact, and you must have travelled with me, unavailingly, all this way Due North, if you do not know, by this time, what a handsome young German lady is like. Nadiejda is a pretty girl—a white one. She was not printed in fast colours, and has been washed out. Do you know what simply colourless hair is?—she has it. Do you know the eye, that although you may be as innocent as the babe unborn, looks upon you mournfully, reproachfully, till you begin to have an uneasy fancy of the possibility of the metempsychosis, and wonder whether you ever saw that eye before—thousands of years since—or did its possessor some grievous wrong? Nadiejda's lips are not red—the colour seems all kissed out of them. Her cheeks are deadly pale, as though she were so timid that she had blushed, and blushed till she could blush no more, and so turned to Parian marble.

Then we have some ladies who certainly might be a little younger than they look (the atrocious climate, fatal to every complexion, being considered,) but who are decidedly much older than they wish to look. Then we have some old ladies (very few—old ladies are not plentiful in St. Petersburg; if you wish to see venerable age you must go into the provinces,) and we have a few little girls of the bread-and-butter-eating school-girl genus, who sit silent and demure in corners, and only speak when they are spoken to: which is very seldom indeed.

I have had occasion, speaking of the "Baba" in the pictures of Russian village life, to remark upon the general hideousness of the purely Russian peasant woman. A girl of "sweet sixteen" is a loutish wench, a woman of thirty is a horrible harridan. The only comely exception is to be found in villages partially femini-colonized by Turkish women. In the Russo-Turkish campaign of eighteen hundred and twenty-nine, very large numbers of Turkish ladies became, on a truly Sabine or nolens-volens willy-nilly principle, the spouses of Russian soldiers; they were brought to the native villages of their impromptu husbands, and there reared progeny, which, in the female line at least, reminds the traveller of the agreeable fable of Mahomet's Paradise. It is not very conclusive evidence in favour of the innate fanaticism of the followers of Islam, that these Turkish women consented with scarcely an exception to be baptized, and received into the Greek church, and subsequently cheerfully performed all the religious duties required by that exigent communion.

Grown-up young ladies, with no doughtier cavaliers than cadets and imperial pages—beardless, albeit brave, in spiked helmets and gold lace—would form but an insipid and juvenile-party-sort-of gathering round the social samovar; but the fact is, that the great majority of the boys in uniform have brought their big brothers with them, who now, in all the glories of their hussar, and cuirassier, and Cossack of the Guard uniforms, lounge upon ottomans and hang over pianofortes, and peg at the polished flooring with their spurs, and twirl their moustaches, and pervade the salons of the kindest lady in the world with a guard-room and mess-room flavour, generally. The bond of union between all these dissimilar elements—ladies, schoolboys, and dragoons—is the gentle Turki-krepi-Tabak, or Turkish tobacco, which, rolled into little paper cigarettes (called papiros) by the fair hands of ladies, is being complacently exhaled by nearly every one present. The little schoolgirls, it is true, refrained from the weed; but the officers and cadets, and—I blush to write it—the majority of the grown-up young ladies—yea even the Queen of Sheba—are all puffing away, consistently and complacently, at their papiros. As to the old ladies, there is no exaggeration in saying they are smoking like lime-kilns; and tobacco-ash is abundant on the furniture, and the floor, and the keys of the pianoforte. I am not great at the papiros myself, ordinarily regarding it as a weak figment—a tiny kickshaw or side-dish, unworthy the attention of a steady and serious smoker, and am, besides, afraid that I shall some day swallow the flimsy roll by a too vigorous inhalation. For this reason perhaps it is, or may be because I am naturally modest, not to say awkward, clumsy, and born with two left hands and two left feet, I do not mingle much with the gay throng, but retire within myself and a powerful Havana cigar behind the window-curtain. I miss nothing, however, either of the conversation or of the music; I have my full and proper allowance of tumblers of tea; nay, the kindest lady in the world is good enough, from time to time, to convey me almond cakes in the smoky seclusion I have chosen for myself.

We go on chatting, pianoforte-tinkling, French romance-telling, smoking, and samovarizing, till past one in the morning. There is an apology for illumination in the shape of a moderator lamp on a guéd-iron in one corner; but nobody minds it: nobody has need of it. The night-daylight in the sky is quite sufficient for us to smoke and chat—and shall I say it?—make love by.

It is quite time I think that I should explain to you why there should be high jinks at Christoffsky to night (the height of those jinks, is the cause of our samovarizing, this twenty-first of June, so late or early,) where Christoffsky itself is, and what the jinks I have entitled high are like.

Christoffsky is one of the many beautiful islands that jewel the bosom of the Neva; and every year, on the Eve of St. John, the whole German population of St. Petersburg, rich and poor, men, women, and children, emigrate in steamers and gondolas, and cockboats to Christoffsky, and there picnic, or bivouac, for three days and nights. They snatch odd instalments of forty winks during this time, but the vast majority of it is devoted to the congenial task of "keeping it up," and this they do with a vigour of conviviality approaching the ferocious.

To tell the honest truth, the German bivouac at Christoffsky is an unmitigated saturnalia, and my pen will require a great amount of reining up and toning down while I attempt to describe its Teutonic eccentricities.

The noble Russians, who despise the German nation and hate the German language, (whose acquirement to perfect fluency is compulsory to all candidates for military service, even to *Nous Autres*,) and loathe the Russo-German nobility, condescend on this twenty-first of June to cross in gondolas to Christoffsky, and there to watch the bacchanalian orgies of the Germans, with the same sort of sneering contempt that might have moved an educated Lacedemonian of the old time at the sight of a drunken Helot; but with the same half-pleased, half-scornful interest that flickers on Mephistopheles' visage when he sees the piggish revelries of the students in Auerbach's cellar.

We have made up a party (of gentlemen, be it understood) to go see the high jinks at Christoffsky; we are about eight for one gondola load; among them there are but two civilians: myself—if a member of the press militant can be called a civilian—and a distinguished young and closely-shaven Tchinovnik, who has a startling resemblance to the mind-picture I had formed of what Ignatius Loyola, formerly a soldier, and afterwards a Jesuit, was like in his youth. This Tchinovnik—I will call him Fedor Escobarovitch—though barely twenty-three, is high up in the department of foreign affairs; in the secret department, where the archives are, and the pretty little notes are concocted, and the fat is extracted from the otherwise dry bones of diplomacy, which afterwards falls into the political fire, and sets all Europe in a blaze.

We bid the ladies good night, and setting forth, well wrapped up in coats and capotes, you may be sure, gain the Troïtza-most, or Great Timber Bridge of the Trinity. I ought to have mentioned that cadets have been rigorously—with but one exception—excluded from our party, on the motion of an exceedingly impertinent cornet of light cavalry, with a cherry-coloured cap, a braided surtout—like that of M. Perrot in the Varsoviana—a very sunburnt face and a very white forehead (he has been down to his terres or estates lately.) This young Tartar, who has not possessed a commission three months yet, says that it will compromise his uniform to be seen, publicly, in company with a cadet. To samovarize, or play cards with him—*bon!* but to be seen with him in a gondola, or at the High Christoffian Jinks—that would never do. The exception at last in favour of a very mild, inoffensive, blue-eyed pupil of the engineer corps is made; ostensibly on the ground of the cherry-coloured cornet waiving his objections on the score of not wishing to disturb the harmony of the evening—which was the morning of the next day. Nobody makes any objection to me, though I am in plain black, am not a Tchinovnik—nay, not even a cadet in the engineer corps; but I am simply an Angliski who can talk and smoke with, and be asked questions by them. So we go away gayly in a gondola, (for which we have to pay an enormous fare,) and in due time land at Christoffsky, I sitting among these jovial young nobles, as Gubetta sat among the Orsinis and Gazellas in the play—they little wotting that Donna Lucrezia Borgia was waiting for me, in the shape of a printing-press at home. They would have thrown me out of the boat had they known that, I think.

The high jinks fully answer our expectations: they are exceedingly high. The immense expanse of green sward is covered with an encampment of gipsy-like tents—some white, some black, some red, some striped in white and blue. There are other tents, or rather wigwams, constructed of branches covered in with green leaves, beneath whose verdant covering some fat German children in the wood are smoking and drinking and snoring. There are some more fortunate members of the class the Russians so contemptuously designate as "Ganz Deutsch," who display a degree of luxury almost amounting to ostentation in the temporary edifices they have erected to have their orgies and their Midsummer madness in. These are quite pavilions, the canvas of gay colours, looped and fringed, and banners waving from the apex of the conical roof. There are many simple bivouacs, belonging probably to artizans too poor to have tents, and who squat in a circle—always smoking, drinking, and occasionally howling, round a tremendous bonfire of green wood, which crackles and blazes and fumes in approved gipsy fashion. But, in place of the time-honoured pot containing the surreptitiously-obtained supper of the Zingari—the stolen fowls, the purloined turkeys, the snared pheasants, and the ill-gotten rabbits, with other dishonestly-annexed addenda in the way of vegetables, which go towards furnishing forth the hot supper of a British Bohemian,—instead of the pot, suspended by a triangle and a hook over the blaze, we have here in every case the samovar: big, brazen, and battered. As to its serving for purposes of tea-making at this German carousal, I strenuously and determinedly disbelieve it. It is punch, sir—hot punch—punch, made not of cognac, made not of Jamaica rum or Irish whiskey—though both are to be obtained (at an enormous price) in Russia—made not even from the native Vodki; but, brewed from the hot, potent, dark-coloured Brantwein of Deutschland the beloved; especially imported, or smuggled, through the custom-house, which comes in the main to the same thing, for the festivities, otherwise high jinks, of Christoffsky.

To give you a notion of the crowds of persons of both sexes, of all ages, and apparently of all conditions, who are sprawling or tumbling, or leaping or dancing about this "green isle," would be difficult, if not impossible. To give you a notion of the great circles, formed, I thought at first, for kiss-in-the-ring, but, I soon discovered, for waltzes and quadrilles; of the debauched Germans lying about dead drunk, or rushing about mad drunk; of hunchbacks, with bottles of liquor, capering up to you, with strange mouthings and writhings; of the roaring choruses, the discordant music, the Punch's shows—Punch's shows in Russia!—the acrobats, the dancing dogs and monkeys, the conjurers, the gambling tables, the Russian moujiks, not mingling among the revellers to revel with them, but to sell quass, tea, meat pies, hard eggs, and salted cucumbers; to see all this made you dizzy, almost drunk. And the swings, and the round-abouts, and the gray-coated *Polizeis*, ever watchful, ever ruthless, making savage forays on the revellers, and conveying them to prison, there to learn that their evening's amusement would not bear the morning's reflection.

We did not return from Christoffsky by water, but on several droschkies—there is a bridge uniting the scene of the high jinks to Wassaily Ostrow—and for which droschkies, in their severality, we had to pay several roubles. Going to bed at about six o'clock, very tired and worn out, I fell into a weary sleep, and dreamt that I had been to Greenwich Fair at night, having been at the Derby all day, and having seen the masque of Comus the night before. Which is about the best notion I can give of the high jinks at Christoffsky.

XVII.

THE GREAT RUSSIAN BOGUEY (THE POLICE).

Droschkying one day along the Gorokhovaïa, or Street of the Peas, there passed me, darting in and out of the usual mounted escort of dust, one of the neatest turn-outs in the way of a private droschky that I had seen since my arrival in St. Petersburg. The horse was a magnificent Alézan, worth from eight hundred to a thousand roubles probably—an arch-necked, small, proud, wicked-headed brute. The Ischvostchik was a picture—stalwart, well-proportioned, full-bearded, and white-teethed; his caftan well-fitting, his sash resplendent, his neck-cloth so snowy in its hue, so irreproachable in its uncreasiness, that it might have shone to advantage at a Sunday-school revival—nay, might have been thought not unworthy to gleam with a sanctified shimmer on the platform of Exeter Hall the Great, itself. He held his reins delicately, and dallied with them digitally, more as though he were playing on the harpsichord than guiding a vicious horse. Behind this grand-ducal-droschky-looking charioteer, there sat a stout man with a stouter, flabbier, and very pale and unwholesome-looking visage. It was the reverse of good to see those pendant cheeks of his, gelatinizing over the choking collar of his uniform. Moreover, he wore gold-rimmed spectacles; moreover, his shiny black hair was cropped close to his head, much more in a recently-discharged English ticket-of-leave than in a Russian and military fashion; mostover, he had not a vestige of moustache about him; and this last circumstance, combined with a tiny equilateral triangle of turn-down collar that asserted itself over each side of his stock below where his cheeks were wagging, puzzled me mightily, mingling as both together did a dash of the civil with the military element in him. For, as to the rest of his attire he was all martial—coat buttoned up to here, spiked and doubled-eagled helmet, gray capote, buckskin gloves, and patent-leather boots. Could this be the Czar himself? I asked myself. I had heard of the studiously unostentatious manner in which the autocrat perambulates the streets of his capital; but then I know also, from the columns of that morning's Journal de St. Petersbourg, that the Gossudar was at Revel, indulging in the innocent delights of sea-bathing with his wife and family. Who could this be—the governor of St. Petersburg? Count Nesselrode? Say.

Let me here remark that the Russians, who are the cutest sophists, if not the closest reasoners, to be found in a long life's march, frequently allude with exulting complacency to the quiet, modest, and on-his-people-confiding manner in which the emperor goes about. "We have no walking on jealously-guarded slopes in Russia," they say; "our emperor takes his morning walk from nine to ten on the Quay de la Cour, in front of the Winter Palace, where the poorest moujik or gondola boatman can salute him. We have no barouches-and-four, no glass coaches with cuirassiers riding with cocked pistols at the windows, or escorts of Cent Gardes, or hussars, or lancers following behind. We have not even outriders or equerries—nay, not a single footman nor groom. The Czar is driven about in a one-horse chay, an Ischvostchik to drive him, just as you may have one, only a little dirtier, for your five-

and-twenty copecks; and that is all. Our Czar's escort is in the people he loves so well; his greatest safeguard is in their unalterable veneration and affection for him." Unto such Russians I have ordinarily answered, True, O king! but what needs your master with an escort when St. Petersburg is one huge barrack, or rather one huge police station? What need of Cent Gardes when there are thousands of police guards walking within the Czar's droschky-sight on the Nevskoï? What need has a keeper to be afraid of a fierce bear, when the beast is muzzled, and chained, and shackled to the floor of his den, and barred in besides?

I had with me on this occasion a companion of the Russian ilk, and made bold to ask that Muscovite who this gray-capoted unmoustachioed apparition in the handsome droschky might be. I must explain that I was very young to Russia at this time—a month's longer residence would have made me wondrously uniform wise; for being necessarily and constantly in contact with persons wearing some uniform garb or other, a man must needs grow learned in buttons, and facings, and coat-cuts, and sword-hilts, and can nose a guardsman or a linesman on the Nevskoï by what is nautically—and perhaps naughtily—expressed as the cut of his jib, as easily as Polonius was said to be susceptible of nasal detection by the Danish gentleman who saw the ghost, and used bad language to his mother.

The Russian to whom I addressed this query responded, first by the usual shrug, next by the usual smile, and lastly by the inevitable Russian counter-query:

"Do you mean to say you don't know?"

"I have not the slightest notion. A field-marshal? Prince Gortschakoff? General Todleben?"

"My dear fellow, that is a major of police."

"His pay must be something enormous then, or his private fortune must be very handsome," I ventured to remark; "he being able to drive so elegant an equipage as the one we have just seen."

"That dog's son," the Russian answered leisurely, "has not a penny of his own in the world, and his full pay and allowances may amount, at the very outside, to about two hundred and fifty roubles a year," (forty pounds.)

"But whence the private droschky, the Alézan horse, the silver-mounted harness, the luxury of the whole turn-out?" I asked.

"*Il prend*," (he takes,) the Russian answered very coolly; whereupon, as by this time we had arrived at the corner of the Great Moorskaïa, he deigned to descend from the vehicle, and, leaving me to pay the Ischvostchik, he went on his way, and I saw him no more till dinner-time.

Which is so much of the apologue I have to tell concerning my first definite notions of the Russian police.

The Russian Boguey, like the police system of most despotic countries, is divided into two great sections—the judicial or public, and the political or secret. As I purpose to tell all I know anent both these peculiarly infamous bodies, but as I have made a vow (among a great many vows, one of a charmingly Asdrubalic, Hannibalic nature, which has revenge for its object) against digression, I will be as succinct as I can, and, treating of the judicial police first, take you at once to the nearest police-station.

This is called a SIEGE or Seat, synonymous with the police Præsidium of German towns. The head of the judicial or municipal police of St. Petersburg (under the great Panjandrum and Archimandrite of all the Russian bobbies—the chief of the gendarmerie who has that house on the Fontanka) is called the Grand Master of Police. He has his acolytes, and his offices, and chancellerie, and attributions. He is Commissioner Sir Richard Mayne, in fact, subject to the beneficent control of a police home secretary. Under this Grand Master, the capital is divided into districts and arrondissements, each having a central station, bureau, barrack, prison, hospital, torture-yard, fire-engine house, and watch-tower. The amalgamated entity is the Siège.

Take a Siège and place it in one of the score of linies that run in grim parallels across Wassily Ostrow.*

* I have frequently been on the point of giving way to a pleonasm, and speaking of the island of Wassily Ostrow—Ostrow, Ostrov, or Ostroff, meaning itself an island—which would render me amenable to as much ridicule, I opine, as that Parisian café proprietor who advertised in his window that Eau de Soda Water was always to be had on the premises. As regards the etymology of Wassily Ostrow it is written that in Peter the Great's time it was but a swampy islet in the Neva (it is now nearly entirely built upon) with but one small fort, which was under the

You have a vast stone packing-case—a sepulchre of justice carefully whited without. Above the door there must be of course the usual lengthy inscription in Russ which is to be found on every public building in Russia, about Heaven, the Czar, and the imperial something or other. Every thing is imperial Due North. The packing-case, understand, is not the whole of the building. It might be said, with more justice perhaps, to resemble a very squat, unornamented copy of the New Houses of Parliament; for, from one corner rises the Victoria Tower of the Siège, in the shape of that celebrated watch-tower you have already heard about—in the Nevskoï, close to the Gostinnoï-dvor and the town-hall, as also at Volnoï-Volostchok. The watchtower may, and frequently does rise to the height of one hundred feet; this one appertaining to a police Siège that has been but recently erected, is of solid stone. Wooden buildings of every description are common throughout Russia; but, it is an inflexible and laudable principle with the government never to allow any building of wood in a town once de-

government of one Basil, pronounced by the Russians Vacil. When Peter, from his wooden house in the Island of Petersburg, had occasion to send despatches to his isolated lieutenant, he was accustomed to address his letters thus:—"Vacil na Ostrow"—To Vacil at the island. Contraction and ellipsis soon take place; and no man wots of Governor Basil now. Wassily Ostrow is full of houses: the Byrsa or Exchange, the Custom-house, the School of Mines, the Academies of Arts and Sciences, the Great Cadet School—all these magnificent edifices are there; and the swampy islet, the wooden fort, and Peter Veliké's lieutenant are forgotten.

stroyed to be built up again of the same combustible material. Stone or brick must be the only wear, or the house itself never rise again from its foundations. Within the balcony on the summit of the tower, and round about the iron apparatus of rods and uprights on which the different coloured balls and flags denoting the phases of a fire are displayed [a yellow flag flies during the whole time a conflagration is actually raging], walk round around, in moody contemplation of the vast marble panorama spread out at their feet, two gray-coated sentinels, searching with impassible gaze into the secrets of the city, and signalling with equal indifference a fire at the monstrously magnificent Winter Palace, or a fire at the log-built cabin of some miserable lighterman who dwells in the slums of Petersburg far down among the ooze below the arsenal and the tallow warehouse. What matters it to them or to the master they are compelled to serve—the Sultan Kebir—the Czar of Fire? For, is not fire like DEATH, and does it not

. . . . æquo pulsat pede
Pauperum tabernas, regumque turres?

At the base of the watchtower there stretches out, in a line with the packing-case, a long stone wall, with a door painted bright green in the centre; when that door is open you may, peeping through it, descry the yard of the fire-engine establishment, and see, ranged under sheds, the fire-engines and water-carts. The former are clumsy-looking machines enough; the latter are simply barrels upon wheels, like the old Parisian water-carrier's carts;

but, all are painted bright green picked out with scarlet. I am not digressing in speaking of the Petersburgian fire-brigade while my topic is the Petersburgian police, for the fire-engines and the men who serve them are under the immediate control of Boguey. The Russian fire-engineers do not appear to take that pride and pleasure in the smart, trim, dandified appearance of their engines, hose, buckets, fittings, and general plant, which so eminently distinguish the bold Braidwood brigadiers of London, and the grisette-adored, brass-helmeted sapeur-pompiers of Paris. They seem dull, listless, ponderous fellows—afflicted with the general police malady, in fact—and look upon the engines as though they had taken them in charge, and were afraid of their running away. You would imagine that in Russia, where the equine race is remarkable for strength, swiftness, and endurance, the fire-engine horses would be the very best in the world. It is not so. By a strange perversity of martinet desire to keep up appearances, the authorities instead of harnessing to a fire-engine a team of fighting, kicking droschky horses, unapproachable for tearing over the stones and stopping at nothing, provide huge, showy, clumsy brutes, whose breed appears to hover between that of an overfed mourning-coach horse, and a Suffolk Punch grown out of all stable knowledge. The Russians brag—as they do, indeed, about most things—of the tremendous pace these horses are up to; but I have seen them out, over and over again, when the cry of "Agôn!" (fire) has arisen, and there has been a conflagration somewhere. Where wheels and hoofs have assuredly the best chance, on the smooth wooden pavement of the Nevskoï, they go at a tolerable rate; but elsewhere their performances are, in my humble opinion, contemptible. Much clattering, much flint and steel pyrotechnics between horseshoes and pavement, much smacking of serpentine whips, much rattling of wheels, much yelling from mounted police-soldiers to moujiks and Ischvostchiks to get out of the way, much knocking down of those unhappy souls if they are tardy in doing so: but, of real speed—of that lightning flashing of locomotion which we, in London, are dazed with when the scarlet fire-annihilator with its brave band of life-savers is seen for a moment in the eye's field—there is positively none. The Russian firemen are very brave; that is, they will stand on a roof till it tumbles into the flames, calmly holding the hose in their hands, unless they are ordered to come down; that is, they will walk gravely up a blazing staircase, at the word of command, into a blazing drawing-room to seek for a bird-cage or a lady's fan. They are especially great in standing to be burnt, because they have been posted at certain spots; and scarcely a fire occurs in St. Petersburg without one or more lives being sacrificed through this stolid, stupid, inert bravery of the firemen.

Loitering listlessly on the threshold of the grim Police Siège, (and a man may do worse than loiter and look before he leaps into the Cave of Trophonius,) I fell into a strange reverie, gazing up at those two impassible gray-coated sentinels in the watchtower's balcony. I am no longer Due North in Russia: I am North, among the mountains of Cumberland, and somebody has sent me a letter. It is full of news about Jones, Brown, and Robinson, at a place I love. It tells me how Miss Myrtle, who has been going to be married so long, is married at last; how Tom Daffy has taken orders, and Jack Edwards has taken to drinking; how my old Schoolmaster has gone to Australia, and my old sweetheart has gone dead. But, there is a remarkable paragraph that interests me, above all things, and, I know not why, fills me with a strange feeling of envy. I have asked for news of two friends, and I am told they are leading bachelor lives, enjoying themselves upon hot roast goose and whiskey punch! Heavens! what a life! Is it not the summum bonum of human felicity? What could a man desire more? To live on hot roast goose—hot, mind!—with whiskey punch (hot also, I will be bound) *à discretion.* Mahomet's paradise, Gulchenrouz's abode that we read of in Vathek, the Elysian Fields, Fiddler's Green, all the 'baccy in the world and more 'baccy, an opium eater's most transcendant trance—none of these states of beatitude surely could compare with the goose and the punch condition of happiness. And, with this silly theorem still running in my mind, I find myself still gazing, gazing moonwards, and to where the sentinels are watching, and still find myself repeating, What a life! what a life! till a vagrant shaft of thought from the hot goose and punch quiver, flies straight to one of those gray-coated targets of watchers, and hits him in the bull's-eye or the button-hole; and, still repeating What a life! I run off at a tangent of reverie when I think what a life *his* must be!

If they were to put a musket and bayonet into your hands, and bid you walk up and down before a door for two hours; if they were to clap me a-top of the Monument, and bid me look out, and note if between Shooter's Hill and Hampstead Heath there happened to be a house on fire; would not you and I go mad? I am sure I should. Suppose yonder gray-coat, or this slow-pacing grenadier to be a man god-gifted with imagination, with impulses; suppose him to have any human passion or scintillation of human thought in him; and reconcile this, if you can, with his watching or keeping guard, without casting himself from the tower, without attempting to swallow the contents of his cartouche-box, or balancing his musket and bayonet on the tip of his nose, or howling forth comic songs, or essaying the Frog hornpipe! You will say that it is habit, that is that use which is our second nature that makes him go through this weary pilgrimage quietly and uncomplainingly. Are there not lighthouse guardians, omnibus time-keepers, men who watch furnace fires? It may be so: we are as glib, I opine, in talking of habit in men, as we are in talking of instinct in animals; but, I say again, What a life! what a life! And suddenly remembering that I promised, in the outset of this paper, not to digress, nay vowed—rashly, I am afraid, like Jephtha—and have already broken my vow, I hurry away from the octagonal watchtower, its silent watchers remaining as mysterious to me as the Sphinx.

Two more gray-coated men, but with helmets (the watchers on the tower wear flat caps like exaggerated muffins,) who are cracking nuts lazily at the ever-yawning doorway of the Siège, point out the entrance to that abode of misery. Straight from the door, and perforating the centre of the stone packing-case, there runs a vaulted corridor of stone and of immense length, ending at last in a back-yard with very high walls, of which I shall have to tell presently.

Opens into this corridor, a bureau or counting-house, or writing-room—call it by what name you will. From a great deal table with inkstands resting in holes cut in the wood, and from a multitude of clerks scribbling furiously thereat, you might imagine yourself in the reporters' room of the office of a daily newspaper in the old days, before the comfortable cushioned-seated writing-rooms were attached to the reporters' gallery of the Houses of Parliament; you might imagine these scribblers to be gentlemen of the press, transferring their short-hand notes of a day's sitting in the Commons into long hand. But they are not: these are Tchinovniks—police and government *employés*—of the very lowest grade, for no person of noble birth would, under any circumstances, consent to serve in the police. The lowest grade in the Tchinn confers nobility *per se;* but, that nobility is not transmissible; and though a police-office clerk belongs to the eighteenth grade, and has the right to the title of Your Honour, his son after him is no more than a free moujik, and is subject to the stick as well as Ivan the moujik and slave. The *employés* of the police are mostly recruited from that mysterious and impalpable body who in Russia do duty as a bourgeosie or middle-class, but do not at all answer to our ideas of what a middle-class should be, and utterly fail, as Curtii, in filling up that yawning gulf that separates the Russian noble from the Russian serf. They are sons of military cantonists, who have shown some aptitude; they are orphans adopted by the government, and educated in one of the government schools; they are priests' sons, who have declined, contrary to the almost invariable rule, to embrace their fathers' profession; they are waifs and strays of foreigners naturalized in Russia, of Germans trade-fallen, (many of the higher police *employés* are Prussians,) of Fins under a cloud, of recreant Poles, of progeny of byegone Turkish and French prisoners of war. An abominably bad lot they are. See them in their shabby uniforms, with their pale, degraded faces, and their hideous blue cotton pocket-handkerchiefs with white spots: mark their reeking odour of stale tobacco-smoke, onions, cucumbers, and vodki: watch them scrawling over their detestable printed forms—forms printed on paper that Mr. Catnach of Seven Dials, London, would be ashamed to send forth a last dying speech upon—but all duly stamped with the Imperial stamp, and branded with that Imperial bat, which is nailed on every Imperial barn-door in Russia, the double eagle. Let all this pass. They may not be able to help their shabbiness, their evil odour, or their evil looks; but, their evil doings are open and manifest, and infamous. A police-office *employé* is known to be—with the single exception of an *employé* in the custom-house at Cronstadt, who may be said to whop all creation for villany—the most dishonest, rapacious, avaricious, impudent, and mendacious specimen to be found of the Tchinovnik. And that is saying a great deal.

Lead from this bureau, but not from the corridor, sundry chambers and cabinets, where, at smaller tables covered with shabby green baize, sit chiefs of departments of the great Boguey line of business; but, all filling up the same forms, spilling the same ink, nibbing or splitting up the same pens, raining the same Sahara showers of pounce, and signing the same documents with elaborate signatures in which there is but a halfpenny-worth of name to an intolerable quantity of paraphe or flourishing. Heaven and Boguey himself only know what all these forms are about; why, if it be true, as the Russians boast, that there is less criminality in St. Petersburg than in any other capital in Europe, there should be two score clerks continually scribbling in the office of one police-station. It is true that the Russian police have a finger in every pie; that they meddle not only with criminals, not only with passports, but with hotels, boarding and lodging houses, theatres, houses not to be mentioned except as houses, balls, soirées, shops, boats, births, deaths, and marriages. The police take a Russian from his cradle, and never lose sight of him till he is snugly deposited in a parti-coloured coffin in the great cemetery of Wassily Ostrow. Surely, to be an orphan must be a less terrible bereavement in Russia than in any other country; for the police are father and mother to everybody,—uncles, aunts, and cousins, too!

The major of police is a mighty man, and dwells in a handsomely-furnished cabinet of his own,—lofty and spacious, and opening also from the vaulted corridor. Here he sits and examines reports, and, not filling up those eternal forms, deigns to tick off his approval of their contents, and to affix his initials to them. Here he sits and interrogates criminals who are brought before him chained. Here he decides on the number of blows with stick, or rod, or whip, to be administered to Ischvostchiks who have been drunk over night, or to cooks who have been sent to the police-station to be flogged for burning the soup, or serving the broccoli with the wrong sauce. Here he sits, and here he Takes.

Taking, on the part of the police, is done in this wise. As the recommendation and even license of the police is necessary to every one, foreigner or native, who wishes to establish an hotel, an eating-house, a café, or a dram-shop, in St. Petersburg, it is very easily to be understood that the expectant Boniface hastens to square the police by bribing them. It is not at all incomprehensible either, that the proprietors of houses—public or private—which are the resort of loose or disorderly characters,—of houses where thieves are notoriously harboured, or where dissipation is rampant, should exhibit a laudable celerity in keeping up the most friendly financial relations with the police. And they must not only bribe the major, but they must bribe the *employés*, and even the gray-coated police-soldiers. It is a continual and refreshing rain, of gray fifty-rouble notes to the major, and of blue and green fives and threes to the *employés*, and of twenty-five copeck pieces to the gray-coats. Then the major has his immediate subordinates, his polizei-capitan, his lieutenants, his secretaries, his orderlies, who must all be feed—and feed frequently; woe-betide the hotel, grog-shop or lodging-housekeeper who forgets that the police are of their nature hungry, and that the stomachs of their purses must be filled! Any stick is good enough, they say, (though I don't believe it,) to beat a dog with; but, it is certain that any accusation trumped up against a financially recalcitrant licensed victualler in St. Peterburg, is sufficient to stir the official wrath of the grand-master of police, who will, unless feed to a tremendous extent himself, shut up that unbribing man's house incontinent.

This is why I have called the Russian police Boguey. I am not speaking of it now, under its aspects of espionage, and slander, and midnight outrage. I am speaking of it, simply as a body organized to protect the interests of citizens, to watch over public order and morals, to pursue and detect, and take charge of criminals. It does not do this. It simply harasses, frightens, cheats, and plunders honest folks. It is as terrible to the ignorant as the Cock Lane Ghost, and is as shameful an imposture.

In the course of one month's residence in St. Petersburg—from May to June—I was robbed four times; of a cigar-case, of a porte-monnaie,—luckily with no gold and very little silver in it,—of an over-coat, which was coolly and calmly stolen—goodness knows by whom—from the vestibule of a house where I went to pay a visit; and lastly, of an entire drawerful of articles,—shirts, neckerchiefs, papers, (not notes on things Russian,—I always took care of those about me,) cigars, and an opera glass. The drawer I had left securely locked on leaving home in the morning. On returning, I found it broken open, and the contents rifled as I have described. Of course, nobody knew any thing about it; of course, the servants were ready to take their Russian affidavits that no one had entered my apartment during my absence,—by the door at least; some one might, they delicately hinted, have come in by the window: and, indeed, I found that my casement had been ingeniously left wide open, with a view of favouring the out-door theory. I was inclined, however, most shrewdly to suspect a certain stunted chambermaid, with a yellow handkerchief tied round her head, and an evil eye, which eye I had frequently detected casting covetous glances at the drawer where my effects lay *perdu*. I was in a great rage. It is true I had lost no jewellery. My diamond solitaire was in safe keeping; and my gold repeater (by Webster) was in England, four pounds ten slow. But I was exasperated on account of the loss of my papers, (might there not have been a sonnet addressed to Her with a large H among them!)

and on the first flush of this exasperation I determined to lay before the police authorities, at least a declaration of the robbery of which I had been the victim. In the nick of time there came and arrested me in my mad career a certain sage. He was not a Russian,—being, in truth, of the French nation, and a commercial traveller for a Champagne house at Rheims; but he had travelled backwards and forwards in Russia for years, and had spied out the nakedness of that land thoroughly from Riazan to Revel. He was a high-dried coffee-coloured man, who wore a wig and a black satin stock, and carried a golden snuff-box with a portrait of Charles the Tenth on the lid. Said this sage to me:

"At how much does Monsieur estimate his loss?"

"Well," I replied, "at a rough guess, one might say thirty roubles."

"Then," resumed the sage, "unless Monsieur wishes to spend, in addition to his already disbursed thirty, another fifty roubles, but very probably more, and over and above, to be very nearly *tracassé* to death, I should advise Monsieur to put up quietly with his loss, and to say nothing about it,—especially to Messieurs de la Police."

The oracle thus delivered with much Delphic solemnity, made me much more inquisitive to know why in this strange land a man should not only be robbed, but made to pay besides, for having been plundered. In the pursuit of knowledge, it appears to me, if I remember the circumstance with correctness, that the sage and I adjourned to the refreshment buffet of the Hotel Heyde, and that there, after the consumption of several malinka riunkas, or petit verres of curaçoa, and the incineration of sundry papiros or cigarettes, I became strangely enlightened as to what an expensive luxury being robbed is in Russia.

If ever you journey for your sins, my dear friend, Due North, and happen to have any thing stolen from you,—be that any thing your watch, your fur pelisse, or your pocket-book full of bank-notes,—never apply to the police. Grin and bear it. Put up with the loss. Keep it dark. Buy new articles to replace the old ones you have lost; but, never complain. Complaints will lead to your being replundered fourfold. They will end in your being hunted like a fox, and torn up at last piecemeal by the great fox-hunter Boguey and his hounds.

I will put a case: I have a handsome gold watch (which I haven't), and I am in St. Peterburg (where I am not). I go for an evening's amusement to the Eaux Minerales, where the chalybeate springs are the pretext, and Herr Isler's gardens, with their military bands and fireworks and suspicious company, the real attraction. My watch is quietly subtracted from my fob by some dexterous pickpocket in the gardens; and I deserve no sympathy for my mishap, for Isler's is famous for its *filous*. The next day I go like a fool, and according to my folly, and lodge my complaint at the police Siège of my arrondissement. I have the number of my watch. I give the maker's name. I describe it minutely, and narrate accurately the circumstances under which it was taken from me. I do not see the major of police, but one of his aids. The aid tells me in German (the judicial police, as a rule, do not speak French; the secret police speak every language under the sun,—Chinese, I am sure, included) that justice is on the alert, that the thief will certainly be caught and brought to condign punishment, and that of the ultimate recovery of my watch there cannot be any reasonable doubt. Clerks have got through a prodigious quantity of manuscript all about me and my watch, by this time; and a number of the everlasting forms are pushed towards me to sign. I have been told beforehand what I must do, and that there is no help for it, so I slip a red note for ten roubles, en sandwich, between two of the forms, and hand the triplet to the aid, who with a greasy smile bids me good morning.

Henceforth I belong no more to myself, but to Boguey. I am hunted up in the morning while I am shaving, and at night as I am retiring to rest. I am peremptorily summoned to the police office five minutes before dinner, and five minutes before I have concluded that repast. With infernal ingenuity Boguey fixes on the exact hours when I have a social engagement abroad, to summon me to his cave of Trophonius, and submit me to vexatious interrogatories. Boguey catches sham thieves for me—worsted stocking knaves with hearts in their bellies no bigger than pins' heads—mere toasts and butter, who would as lieve steal the Czar's crown as a gold watch, and whose boldest feat of larceny would probably be the purloining of a pickled cucumber from a stall. I am confronted with these scurvy companions, and asked whether I can identify them. Boguey's outlying myrmidons bring me vile pinchbeck saucepan lids, infamous tinpot sconces, which they call watches; and would much like to know if I can recognize them as my property. All this time I am paying rouble after rouble for perquisitions, and inquiries, and gratifications, and messengers' expenses, and stamps, and an infinity of other engines of extortion. At last (under advice) I rush to the major of police, and ask him plainly (but privately,) for how much he will let me off. He smiles and refers me to his aid, saying that justice cannot have her course impeded. I go to the aid, and he smiles too, and tells me that he does not think the disbursement of twenty roubles will do my Excellency any harm; and that if I choose to place that sum in his hand to be administered in charity, he thinks he can guarantee my not being again troubled about the robbery. So, I give him the money, (which I don't,) and, thank Heaven, I I am rid of Boguey, as Andrew Miller thanked Heaven he was rid of Doctor Johnson.

Now do you understand why every sensible man in Russia, who is unfortunate enough to be robbed, leaves Boguey alone?

It would be easy to multiply instances illustrative of the taking propensities of the Russian police, among whom, in St. Petersburg and Moscow—as well as in other government towns of the empire—there is really not one pin to choose. Bogueyism is synonymous with police management throughout all the Russias. I shall confine myself to one or two salient traits of character to be found in those terrifiers of well-doers who ought to terrify evil-doers, but who are the worthy successors, and have in Muscovy continued the glorious traditions of that most illustrious of all takers—Jonathan Wild the Great.

The Sire de Brantome generally commences his chivalrous tittle-tattle with the exordium: *Une grande dame, forte honeste, que j'ay bien cognu* (a great lady, and a mighty honest one, whom I know extremely well;) and I find myself as constantly giving an anecdote on the authority of some Russian acquaintance far nobler than honest. In this present instance, however, my informant was a French hairdresser and perfumer, who had settled at Moscow, with the stern and inflexible determination to stay there five years, acquire a fortune of fifty thousand francs, and then quitting that beastly hole, (by which abusive epithet he qualified the holy empire of Russia,) to return to Arcissur-Aube; which much whitewashed French town was his native place, and there to *planter ses choux*,—or cabbages,—defeat the curé of St. Symphorien at his favourite game of tric-trac; become, in course of time, mayor of some adjacent village, and eventually, perhaps, reassume his ancestral title of Monsieur de la Bandoline (now lying perdu, like the Spanish Hidalgo's rapier, under the modest *nom de circonstance* of Hyacinthe, coiffeur et peruquier de Paris,) and become sub-prefect of his department.

A friend of M. Hyacinthe's—say M. Mélasse—likewise a sprightly Gaul, kept a magazine for the sale of those articles called by the Americans notions, in the Tverskaïa Oulitza, or great street of Tver, in Moscow. But here I must digress with a word or two on shops: it is only in old world cities, where the civilization is old—very old—that you find actual shops—special establishments for the sale of special articles. As in the rude and remote country village, you have Jerry Nutt's Everything Shop, where you can procure almost every article—from a birch broom to a Byron-tie, from a stick of barley-sugar to a lady's chemisette; so, in newly-settled or newly-civilized lands you have not shops but Stores, where edibles are mixed up with potables, and textile fabrics with both, and books with beeswax, and carpeting with candles. Our American cousins have repudiated the Everything element, and have Shops that can vie with, if they do not surpass the counter-jumping palaces of Regent Street, London, and the Rue de la Paix, Paris. Yet they still retain the name of a Store, for an establishment, say a shawl-shop, more magnificent than Swan and Edgar's, corruscating with glass and gilding, and mural paintings, and variegated marbles; and the Russians, for all the bigness of their cities, have not yet, as a rule, progressed beyond stores—in their streets. In the bazaars there are, certainly, special standings for special articles; but, these are more properly stalls than shops. In the two great shops of St. Petersburg—the Angliski Magazin, in the little Millionne, and the Ruski Magazin, on the Nevskoï—the incongruous nature of the articles sold is astonishing, and, in the smaller shops, there is a distracting confusion in the classification of the articles purchased. The hairdressers sell almost everything. You have to go to the grocers for picture-frames. The tobacconists sell tea; the glove-makers sell porte-monnaies. The best cigars to be had in Petersburg are purchased at an apotheka or druggist's shop, in the little Morskaïa, (the druggists sell camera-obscuras, too.) You may buy French painted fans of the confectioners, and there is scarcely a fashionable *modiste* who does not sell flesh and blood. Altogether, our respected friend Mother Hubbard would have enormous trouble in Russia in attempting to purvey for that insatiable dog of hers, who (like a minister's mother-in-law) was always wanting something. She would have had to go to the bishop's to buy him ale, or to the Winter Palace to buy him a bone.

M. Mélasse sold groceries and a little millinery, and a considerable quantity of coloured prints, and some Bordeaux, and much Champagne. But, M. Mélasse happened, though doing a good business, to have a temper of his own. Why should M. Mélasse's temper interfere with the success of M. Mélasse's business? So far, that the black dog which occasionally sat on the worthy burgess's shoulder, could not abide that other and Blacker Dog, Boguey, the Police of Moscow, and barked at him continually. *Ches Chiens*, (these dogs,) the impudent Mélasse called the guardians of public order. One afternoon two gentlemen in gray called on M. Mélasse, (he spoke Russ tolerably, which in a Frenchman is something marvellous,) and saluting him cordially, produced from a remarkably dirty envelope of sacking two fine sugar-loaves—the apex of one of them considerably damaged. These, they told him, had been found in the open street opposite his house on the previous night; were evidently the produce of a robbery committed on his premises; and were now brought to him, not to be restored, but to be identified, in order that justice might inform itself, and perquisitions be made respecting the thief. Now, the seller of notions happened to be entirely out of sugar in loaves, had broken up his last a fortnight before, was rapidly exhausting his stock of lump sugar, and was anxiously expecting a fresh consignment. He therefore energetically protested that the robbery could not have taken place in his house; because, imprimis he had securely fastened doors and windows, and kept a fierce watchdog; secondly, because he had no sugar-loaves to be robbed of. The men in gray smiled grimly, and showed the astonished grocer his own private trademark on both the loaves. He could not even surmise them to be forged; they were evidently his. The men in gray therefore proceeded to commence their perquisitions, which they effected by ransacking the house and shop from garret to basement—spoiling every article of merchandise they could conveniently spoil—avowedly for the purpose of seeking traces of the burglarious entrance of the thieves. Ultimately they left a man in possession, to watch, in case the robbers renewed their nefarious attempt. This assistant Boguey turned out to be a gray-coated skeleton in every closet in the house. He smoked the vilest

Mahorka; he drank vodki like a vampire; his taking snuff was as the sound of a trumpet; he demanded victuals like a roaring lion; he devoured them like a ghoule; he awoke the family in the dead of night with false alarms of fire and thieves; he drove M. Mélasse to frenzy, Madame M. to passionate indignation; Mademoiselle M. to tears and hysterics; the younger M.'s nearly into fits of terror; and he stayed a fortnight. The thieves didn't come, and he didn't go. In the mean time the wretched grocer lived the life of a hunted cur. The police put the sugar-loaves (metaphorically) into a tin kettle, and attaching them to his dorsal vertebræ, hunted him perpetually. The same process of summoning, resummoning, interrogating, and cross-interrogating, which I have already described in my own (suppositious) case, was gone through with him. The police found out that he was in the habit of going daily on 'change, (for the good man speculated a little in Volga Steamboat and Russ-American Iron-work shares.) Of course he had to attend the police office daily, for a week, exactly at 'change time, and was released by his tormentors exactly as the Exchange gates closed. The police captured two poor devils of moujiks, who, setting aside the fact that they had been previously convicted of robbery, were as honest men as the Governor of Moscow, and had no more to do with the robbery (which had never been committed) than I had. These unfortunate rogues they kept chained for some time, and living on bread and water in an infamous den at the Police Siège, averring that there was the strongest presumption of their guilt. They suddenly discovered that they were as free from blame as the driven snow; setting them at liberty, they sent in a peremptory demand to M. Mélasse for a corpulent sum of roubles, to defray the expenses of their board and lodging during their imprisonment, and to compensate them for the injury they had suffered. He at first refused to pay, but ultimately disbursed the sum demanded, in despair. He was beginning to entertain the notion of a plunge, for good and all, into the Moskva River, when he received a communication from the mayor of police, informing him in the most polite terms that it had been considered expedient to refer his case, which was considered to be a very intricate one, to the Ouprava Blagotschinia, or Bureau de Bon Ordre, presided over by the Grand Master of Police in St. Petersburg, and begging him to take the necessary steps to present a petition to the Governor-General of Moscow, in order that he might procure a passport, and proceed to head police quarters at St. Petersburg, there to be interrogated concerning the most remarkable robbery that had for a long time baffled the sagacity of justice;—the more remarkable, I may myself remark, for its never having taken place. Mélasse, the unhappy, rushed on the wings of the wind, and the polished runners of a sledge (it was in winter) to the police office. He thrust five roubles into the first gray-coat's hand he met, and promised him ten, if he would procure him immediate speech with the Mayor of Police. Ushered into the presence of that functionary he conjured him, without halting for breath, to tell him how much, in the name of Heaven, he would take to release him from this intolerable persecution. The polizei-mayor laughed, poked him in the ribs, and offered him to snuff.

"I am glad to see you returning to better sentiments, my dear M. Mélasse," he said quite cordially. "What is the good of fighting against us? Why omit doing what must be done? You are in Russia, you must be content to have things managed *à la Russe*. When you live with wolves you must needs howl, M. Mélasse."

"How much?" the victim palpitated.

"There, there, brat," (brother,) continued the warm-hearted police-mayor. "You shall be absolved easily. I think if you were to place a hundred and fifty silver roubles in that blotting-book, I should know how to relieve many destitute families. We see so MUCH misery, my dear friend," he added with a sigh.

M. Mélasse set his teeth very closely together; drew the hundred and fifty silver roubles in paper-money from his pocket-book, shut his eyes, that he might not see his substance departing from him, and crammed the money into the blotting-book.

"And I tell you what, uncle of mine," the mayor resumed, jauntily fluttering the blotting-book leaves, and twirling (quite accidentally, of course) the greasy little packet of wealth into his ravenous palm, "you shall not say that the Russian police never return any of the goods they have recovered; for, this very afternoon, I will send down two of my men, and YOU SHALL HAVE YOUR SUGAR-LOAVES BACK AGAIN."

With a suppressed shriek, the emancipated-loaf captive entreated the mayor never to let him hear or see more of that accursed sweet-stuff. The mayor was a placable man, and open to suasion. He promised to allow the sugar-question to drop forever; and dignifying the unroubled grocer with the affectionate cognomen of Batiouschka—little father—bade him an airy good morning, and retired into his sanctum sanctorum: there, doubtless to lock up his honestly-earned roubles in his cassette, and, perhaps, to laugh somewhat in that official sleeve of his, at the rare sport of swindling a Fransoutz. The moral of the story is, that Mélasse did not quit Moscow at once, and in disgust. He stopped, for he also was possessed of that fixed idea common to most foreign traders in Russia, of acquiring a given number of thousand silver roubles, and retiring, in the end, to an Arcissur-Aube of his own, where he could enjoy his *otium cum dignitate*, and abuse the land where he had made his money. He stopped; and there was great joy among the police-population of Moscow the holy, that there was no Inostranez, or stranger, in Moscow who kept on better terms with Boguey, or was prompter and more liberal in his felicitations (silver rouble felicitations) on New Year's Day than M. Mélasse of the Tvershala.

Now, New Year's Day is the Russian (as it is the French) Boxing Day. Apart from the genteel cadeaux of bon-bons, gloves, and jewellery, which you are expected (under pain of banishment from soirées and ostracism from morning calls) to make to genteel acquaintances, you have your servants to tip;

your dvnornik to tip; and, especially, your police to tip. If you are fortunate enough to be a private individual, you get off with a visit from the Nadziratelle of the Quartal, or quartier (a sub-division of the arrondissement), who, with many bows, offers you his felicitations, and to whom you give ten roubles. But, if you are a nobleman or an hotel-keeper, your lot is far harder. By a compliment of fifty (many give a hundred) roubles you may purchase impunity during the ensuing year for almost every act or deed, legal or illegal, over which the police exercise any amount of control. The hotel-keepers give and tremble; the nobles give and despise. That same newly-fledged cornet I told you of, who had the big house to himself, assured me that he never allowed an officer of the judicial police to cross the threshold of his apartment. The secret police come in without being asked, and leave their marks behind them. "When New Year's Day arrives," my young friend would say, "and the pigs come with their salutations, I send them out the money, but, as to entering my house—never!" Horror, hatred, and contempt for Boguey are, I believe, the only definite and sincere feelings of which *Nous Autres* are capable.

I wish that I could leave M. Hyacinthe, the perfumer, without telling you about somebody I met there one Sunday, (I used frequently to dine with that genial barber,) somebody whose face and voice, and gestures and miserable story, came with me adown the Gulf of Finland, and through the Baltic Sea; came with me through the Little Belt up

Flensburg Fjord; came with me throughout the timber-town of Rendsburg, and by the iron way to Hamburg, and so to Brussels in Brabant, and at last to where I now write this. You shall hear.

There is, perchance, no family circle so difficult of access as a French one. A man may live twenty years in France, without once enjoying even the spectre of a chance of being admitted into a French interior. You, boastful Paris men who pay your first-class fare at London Bridge at half-past eight, P. M., and are in Paris by half-past nine the next morning—who live in Paris for months, and fancy you know Paris life thoroughly—to what extent are you cognizant of the real ways and means, of the real manners and customs of the inscrutable Lutetia? You walk about the Boulevards or the Palais Royal; you stay at Meurice's or the Hôtel Bedford; you dine at the Trois Frères or at Phillipe's; you even, if you be of Bohemia, and determined to see life, live in the Rue St. Jacques, or that of the Ecole de Médécin, frequent the Prado and the Closerie des Lilas, and mistake some milliner's girl for Béranger's Lisette. Have you ever seen the French at home? Do you know what manner of people they be? When you do know, we shall have fewer foolish books written about foreign countries. But what am I saying about foreign countries? Have I not been to a foreign country myself, and am I not (it may be) writing an excessively foolish book about it? Are we not living in the days of embassies, and of literary secretaries of embassy who seem determined to verify the maxim of Sir Henry Wotton:—

that "an ambassador is one sent abroad to lie for the good of his country;" adding, by way of rider to his dictum, the axiom of La Rochefoucault, that "great names dishonour rather than elevate those who do not know how to bear them with propriety."

Without enlarging at all upon any opportunities I might or might not have had of seeing French people at home, in their own country, I hope I may be allowed to allude to the very pleasant Sundays I spent with my friend the French barber. It was a model French interior. There was the grand old French lady with snow-white ringlets, tight, long, and cylindrical, like frozen sausages. There was the imbecile grandfather, with a black silk skull-cap on his poor old pate, and his shrunken limbs wrapped in a gray duffell dressing-gown; an old man past every thing, except forbearance—weak, helpless, useless—a baby come back to the primeval baldness, but uncommonly good at his meals—loved and tended, and cared for, however, as though he had been grandfather Weguelin, and could ask his grandchildren to tea in the bank parlour of the Bank of England every evening, and hand round to them boiled bullion, and sycee silver Sally Lunns. The picture would not be even artistically complete without a *jeune personne*—a blushing young maiden of sixteen—swathed up to the chin in white muslin, who is told that she must always keep her eyes cast down; who will be married shortly, to somebody she does not like; and who will eventually run away, or otherwise misbehave herself, with somebody she does like. The middle distance would be wanting to the picture were I to omit a peculiarly sharp boy in a black velvet jacket and sugar-loaf buttons, and a pair of cream-coloured trousers, much resembling—as regards their degree of inflation—balloons. A youth who is continually (and I am afraid with detriment to the progress of his studies) practising inquiries into the laws of gravitation, with a cup and ball, and who assuredly must do a considerable amount of damage to his father's stock of pomatum, if we are to take into consideration the prodigious accumulation of fatty substances patent on his hair. There would be something out of keeping, too, were the painter to omit the inevitable accessory to all French families at home or abroad, from Caen to Kamschatka, in the shape of an aunt, a cousin, a niece, a dependent of some sort, in fact—ordinarily a subdued female with a bulbous nose, and clad in very scanty, snuffy habiliments, who sits and works, and tends children, and is the friend of the family; and whose only amusement, when she is left quite alone, seems to be to sit and cry her eyes out, with the assistance of a very sparse square of pocket-handkerchief. Her name is usually Mademoiselle Hortense. Last of all, there must perforce be put on the canvas a minute point of detail answering to the name of a poodle or a mongrel, as the case may be—a dog who does exactly as he likes, is addressed by affectionate nicknames by the simple French folk, and is generally made much of.

Not last of all, at least in the barber's household. There was the old lady, the *jeune personne*, the velvet and sugar-loafed boy, the dubious aunt or niece, the dog; and there was Somebody.

A perfectly white, haggard, worn-out, spectral girl. A girl robbed from her coffin. An awful sight, with restless, travelling eyes, with a horrible head rocking backwards and forwards, with hands continually clasping and unclasping, with knees that (you could see beneath her drapery) continually sought each other, and then gave time to her feet, which beat the devil's tattoo incessantly. She had rich glossy hair, massed on each side of her head; her eyes were dark and lustrous; her teeth were gates of ivory; her form was slender and graceful; yet, had she been as hideous as the witch Sycorax, as terrible as Medusa, she could not with all her beauty, have impressed you with a greater sense of horror and back-shrinking. The girl was mad, of course. She was quite harmless, only rocking herself backwards and forwards, and rolling those wild eyes of hers, and (when she was unobserved) muttering something about her mother. She used to dine with us, and ply her knife and fork, and drink her weak wine and water with the best of the sane people present; but, she always relapsed into the rocking, and the rolling, and the muttering about her mother, as we were sitting down to dominoes or lasquenet. Nobody took much notice of her. She sat by the fire-place, with her haggard face, and a tight-fitting black velvet dress; and, when she was spoken of, was alluded to as Cette pauvre Josephine.

That poor Josephine's story was a very simple and a very sad one. She was the daughter of a

French dancing-master, long settled in Russia, and a Russian subject. Her mother had been some French ballet-dancer, who had waltzed away from her obligations, and had pirouetted into an utter abnegation of her social ties. Such things happen. She was Madame Somebody at Palermo, while her husband was Monsieur Somebody-else at Moscow. He had gained enough money by his profession to send his daughter to France for her education, whence she returned (to her misfortune) young, beautiful, and accomplished. Her father pleased himself with the notion that his Josephine must indubitably become the wife of some puissant seigneur; but, unfortunately, in the midst of this dream he died. He, it is to be remembered, had been naturalized a Russian subject, and his child was one after him.

The girl, left alone and unfriended in this Gehenna of a country, fell. The dancing-master had dissipated all his economies of roubles, and she had no money. She went to St. Petersburg, having no money, in a calèche with eight horses (it was before the railway time,) with a government Padaroshna,*

* A padaroshna is an official permission to travel with post-horses, without which you might draw your carriage yourself, for no post-horses would you obtain. Government couriers have special padaroshnas, which entitle them to take horses before any other traveller; and it is by no means uncommon at a post-house in the interior to see a serjeant of infantry, who happens to be a bearer of despatches, quietly order the horses just harnessed to a carriage containing a whole family, to be taken out, and attached to his own telega or kibitka.

and a courier riding twenty versts a-head to secure relays of horses. M. de Sardanapalasoff, of the Empress's regiment of cuirassiers of the guard, took a magnificent apartment for her in the Italianskaïa Oulitza; she had a calèche, a brougham, a country-house—the very model of a Swiss châlet in the islands—saddle horses, a gondola with a velvet awning, white satin cushions, and a Persian carpet; a box at the Balschoi theatre, and one at the French house; a lady's maid, a chasseur, a maître d'hotel, a Danish dog nearly as large as a donkey,—every luxury, in fact. M. de Sardanapalasoff gave some magnificent champagne banquets at her apartments. La Bérésina, as the Muscovite-Parisienne was called, was the reigning beauty of the demi-monde of St. Petersburg. A prince of the imperial blood positively came to one of the Bérésina's petit soupers, and deigned to express his opinion that she was charming.

M. de Sardanapalasoff's mamma was the Princess Zenobiaschkin, and he was the most dutiful of sons; so, when she signified to him her maternal commands that he should obtain the imperial permission to travel for two years, and escort her to Paris, Italy, and the baths of Hombourg, he hastened to comply with her mandates in the most filial manner. Some unjust constructions were of course put on this alacrity. Some envious persons declared that the emperor himself had, through the medium of the Princess Zenobiaschkin offered the alternative of foreign travel or the Caucasus to the young guardsman; an of course unfounded report having got abroad that M. de Sardanapalasoff while on duty at the palace of Tsarski-Selo, had been kicked in full uniform by a vindictive major of dragoons: the cause of the humiliating correction being alleged to be the detection of the Bérésina's noble friend in the act of cheating at écarté. Be it as it may, M. de Sardanapalasoff was desolated to part with the Bérésina, but he did it; it must have affected him greatly to be obliged to sell off the whole of his (or her) splendid furniture—nay, as much of her own private jewellery as he could, by fraud or force, lay his hands upon. So much did it affect him in fact, that he went off with the whole of the proceeds of the sale in his pocket, and left the Bérésina without a friend in the world, and with scarcely a hundred roubles in her pocket.

Josephine (she had done with the name of the Bérésina now) did not flow down that golden tide that runs over the sands of Shame in that great, salt, fathomless sea of tears, on which you shall descry no land on lee-bow, or weather-bow, save the headlands of Death. With a stern and strong determination to sin no more, she went to Moscow, where she had some acquaintances, if not friends. She was clever with her needle. She could embroider; she could make bonnets; she had both taste and talent. It was not long before she obtained employment in the shop of one of the most famous French milliners in Moscow.

For her misery, she was still very beautiful. I have said that the fashionable milliners of Moscow are dealers in other wares than millinery. The buyers of those goods are the dissolute young nobles of the guard. Josephine might very soon have had another splendid suite of apartments, another chasseur, another lady's maid, had she so pleased; but the poor girl was sick of it, and was determined to be a milliner's workwoman all her life, rather than be a golden toy to be tossed aside when its attraction had worn out. She refused solicitation after solicitation, offer after offer from the snuffy old French hag, (there is nothing so bad as a bad French woman,) into whose employ she had entered. This unprotected, outraged girl declared that she would no longer remain in her service. She would go, she said, that very instant, and rose to leave the work-room. The woman put out her arm to prevent her passing the threshold, and Josephine naturally pushed it away. This was all the milliner wanted.

"Very well, very well!" she said, "bear witness, mesdemoiselles all, this person, my servant—my SERVANT, mind—has been guilty of insubordination and rebellion towards me, her mistress. We shall see, we shall see!"

She went that day and lodged a complaint against her workwoman at the police-office. The girl was a Russian subject, and the daughter of a Russian subject, and there was no help for her on this side Heaven. She was arrested that afternoon, and carried to the Siège, her mistress accompanying her. There, in the bureau, she was asked certain questions, the milliner signed a paper and paid certain moneys to the aide-major of police, and Josephine was led away by two of the gray-coats.

That same night, very late, a French hairdresser settled in Moscow, who was crossing the Smith's Bridge on his way home, was fortunate enough to rescue a woman, who, without bonnet or shawl, was standing on the parapet of the bridge, and was just about to cast herself into the Moskva. There was, luckily, no Boutotsnik, or watchman, near, or it would have fared ill with both preserver and preserved. The kindly barber took this miserable creature, who could do nothing but sob and wail, and ejaculate, " O Mother, Mother!"—he took her to his home, and delivering her to his womankind, enjoined them to treat her with every care and solicitude. They told him, the next morning, that when they came to undress her, they had found her from the shoulder to the waist one mass of bloody wheals. The police had simply done their infamous duty. The milliner, her mistress, had a perfect right to order her to be flogged; she had paid for the flogging; and the police had nothing further to do, save to inflict. The unhappy creature had been beaten with rods, (willow canes split each into three,) and in the frenzy of her agony and shame had immediately after her liberation from the police-den of torture, rushed to the river with the intention of committing suicide.

The hairdresser, than whom a kinder-hearted seizer of ringlets never existed, would not allow this poor waif and stray to depart out of his house. Learning by degrees her unhappy story, he offered her an asylum, and treated her as one of his own children. She went on improving for a time; but by degrees she fell into a sable melancholy. When I saw her, she had been mad for eighteen months.

I have done, now, for very sickness, with the judicial police. I have heard some curious tales, in my time, about the Austrian police, and about the Neapolitan police, which all plain men know to be intolerably abominable. The *employés* of the Rue de Jerusalem are not wholly immaculate, I believe; nay, under our honest, hard-working, plain-sailing, Scotland Yard *régime*, we have had policemen who have stolen geese, and others who have broken into houses. But, as grand masters of the art and mystery of villany; as proficients in lying, stealing, cruelty, rapacity, and impudence; I will back the Russian police against the whole world of knavery.

XVIII.

MUSIC AND THE DRAMA.

I HAVE in my possession a square piece of yellow paper, highly varnished, and with one corner torn off, on which there is the ordinary amount of typographical Abracadabra, or Russian word-spinning, inevitably to be found in all Russian documents; namely, as much as can possibly be squeezed into the space available, and headed (it is almost superfluous to remark) by a portrait *en pied* of that monster Bird, that Roc of Russia, and yet decided opposite to a Rara Avis, the double-headed Eagle. This document is as large as one of those French schedules of insolvency, a Reconnaissance of the Mont de Piété, and is considerably bigger than an English excise permit. It is, in reality, no such formidable affair; but simply a pass check (something billiet in Russ) to the orchestra stalls of the Gossudaria-Tchirk-Teatr,' or Imperial Circus Theatre of St. Petersburg.

There never was, under Jove—with the exception of the Mandarinized inhabitants of the Flowery Land, who, in a thousand respects, might run or be driven in couples with the Muscovites—such a nation of filling up formalists as are the Russians. In Russia, indeed, can you appreciate in its highest degree the inestimable benefits of a lot of forms. The Russian five-copeck (twopenny-halfpenny) postage-stamp is as important-looking, as far as fierceness and circumference go, as that foul mass of decayed rosin and wax, symbolizing rottenness and corruption somewhere, whilom attached, in a species of shallow pill-box, at the end of a string to a patent, and called the Great Seal of England. If, in St. Petersburg or Moscow, you wish to post a letter for foreign parts, and send your servant with it to the Gossudaria-Pochta, or Imperial post, he brings you back an immense pancake, like a Surrey Garden's posting bill, with your name, and your correspondent's name, and columns of figures, denoting the amount of copecks charged for postage, and the date, and signatures, and countersignatures, and a big double eagle, in black, at the top, and a smaller one in blue at the bottom, and a great sprawling white one in the water-mark, besides the usual didactic essay upon things in general in incomprehensible Russ; all which cautious, minute, and business-like formalities do not prevent the frequent failure to reach its destination of your letter, and its as frequent seal-breaking and spying-into by officials in its transit through the post-office.

Petropolis, considering its enormous size, has by no means a profusion of theatres. There is the superb Balschoï-Teatr'; the Grand Opera, where Grisi and Mario sing, and Cerito and Bagdanoff dance. The Great Theatre was originally erected by Semiramis-Catherine; then reconstructed in eighteen hundred and three, and in the reign of the first Alexander, by the architect Thomon. It was burnt down, according to the rule of the Three Fates, in all theatrical cases made and provided, in eighteen hundred and eleven; when another French architect, M. Mauduit, was intrusted with the task of acting as a vicarious phœnix, and raising the theatre from its ashes. Some acoustic defects having been found, nevertheless, to exist in the new edifice, the Czar Nicholas caused M. Cavos, again a Frenchman, to turn it as completely inside out, as our old Covent Garden was turned by Mr. Albano. It is now, with the exception of the Grand Theatre at Moscow, the most magnificent and the most convenient of all the theatres in Europe, and (I believe) as large a theatre as any. The Scala may surpass it, slightly, in size but in splendour of appointment it is, so the cosmopolite operatics say, a mere penny gaff to the Balschoï. At the Grand Theatre, take place, during the carnival, the famous Bal Masqués of St. Petersburg.

Next, the northern capital possesses the Alexandra Theatre, situated in the place, or square, as the gallicized Russians call it, which bears the same name, and opens on the Nevskoï Perspective. The Alexandra Theatre is the home of the Russian drama; that is, purely Russian plays (on purely Russian subjects) are there performed. Thirdly, there is the Théâtre Michel, in the Place Michel, also on the Nevskoï, built in eighteen hundred and thirty-three, under the direction of M. Bruloff; which elegant and aristocratic dramatic temple may be called the St. James's Theatre of St. Petersburg, being devoted to the alternate performances of French and German troupes, and—being closed a good many months in the year. There is a fourth and very pretty theatre, built of wood, in the island of Kammenoï-Ostrow, or Stone Island, (so called from a huge mass of stone on its banks in the Little Nevka,) a Swiss cottage kind of affair embosomed among trees, and which stands in front of the bridge leading to the island of Yelaguine. In this theatrical châlet, the French vaudeville company give representations during the summer; the islands at that season being crammed with the élite of the aristocratic Petersburgian society—at least of that numerous section thereof who can't afford, or who can't obtain the government permission to travel. There was another and extensive theatre, likewise built of timber, on Wassily-Ostrow; but, it was burnt down some years since, and being a simply German theatre was allowed, contemptuously, to sink into oblivion, and was never rebuilt. There is but one, and the fifth theatre, that remains to be noticed, and that is the Tchirk, or Circus Theatre, and thither, if you please, we will pay a visit this night.

This is not by any means the first theatre I have visited since I have been biting the dust of Petersburg. I have been to the German house, at the pressing recommendation of Barnabay, backed by Zacharaï, and have seen a German farce, of which I have understood very little, if any thing; but from which I have come away screaming with laughter. It was called *Der Todte Neffe*, (the Dead Nephew,) and was from the pen of that dramatic writer who has made me have recourse to my knuckles (I was ashamed to use my pocket-handkerchief) many and many a time in that stupid, delightful, unnatural, life-like, tedious, enthralling, ridiculous, sublime, worthless, and priceless drama of the Stranger—I mean Herr von Kotzebue. Why is it, I wonder, that so many men who know this play to be one of the worst that ever was written, that it is as much an insult to art as to common sense, yet in a secret, furtive manner, love to see it, and had they the privilege of a bespeak—as the mayor and the regimental-colonel have in a garrison town—would command it for that night only! I do not care one doit for the sorrows of Miss Clarissa Harlowe: shamefully as Mr. Lovelace behaved to her. I have not the slightest sympathy with Miss Pamela Andrews's virtue or its reward, and declare that on my conscience I believe her to have been an artful and designing jade, who had her eye on Squire B—— from the commencement, and caught him at last with a hook. I think that Mademoiselle Virginie lost her life through a ridiculous piece of mock modesty, and that she would have bored Paul awfully had she been married to him. I am of opinion that six months with hard labour in the House of Correction would have done Manon Lescaut all the good in the world. For me, Werter may go on blowing out his batter-pudding brains, and Charlotte may continue cutting butter-brods, and wiping the little noses of her little brothers and sisters, to infinity. I have no tears for any of these sentimentalities; but, for that bad English version of a worse German Play—the Stranger—I have always an abashed love and a shy reverence, and an unwearied patience. I can always bear with Peter, and his papa with the cane, and the countess who comes off a journey in a hat and feathers and a green velvet pelisse, and Miss Adelaide Haller the housekeeper, and that melancholy dingy man in black who has fixed upon Cassel for his abode. I don't tell people that I am going to see the Stranger; but I go, and come home quite placid, and for the time moral, and full of good thoughts and quiet emotions. For who amongst us has not done a wrong, but repents in secret places where vanity is of no avail, and where there are none to tell him that he is in the right, and that he "oughtn't to stand it, my boy?" And who has not been wronged, that but seeks solace in sowing forgiveness broadcast, because he thinks the tares in that one place where forgiveness is most needed are too thick for any good seed to bear fruit there? And who has lost a lamb, and wandering about seeking it, can refrain from pleasant thinkings when he comes upon a flock, though his firstling be not among them, and can stay himself from interest and cheerful imaginings in the joys and sorrows of little children? That Italian songstress who sings so magnificently, in which is she greater: in the "*Qual cor tradisti*," where she pours out the vials of a woman's resentment and vindictiveness upon that contemptible cur in the helmet, Pollio; or in the duet with Adalgisa, where the children are? I saw the other night, in the pit of the Haymarket Theatre, during the performance of a pantomime, for which Mr. Buckstone had provided the fun, and Mr. William Calcott had painted the pictures—the "Babes in the Wood"—I saw a great, burly, red-faced man in a shaggy great-coat and a wide-awake hat, who looked very much like a commercial traveller for a Bradford cloth-house, blubbering—that is simply the word—at a superbly ridiculous part of the entertainment, where the Robins (represented by half-a-dozen stalwart "supers" in bird masks and red waistcoats, like parish beadles) come capering in, and after an absurd jig to the scraping of some fiddles, cover up the babes who have been abandoned by their cruel uncle, with green leaves. And the Stranger will be popular to the end of time—as popular as the Norfolk tragedy—because it is about forgiveness, and love, and mercy, and children; and here is the health of Herr von Kotzebue, though he was a poor writer, and (I have heard it whispered) a government spy.

The week I arrived in Petersburg was the last of the season of the Grand Opera; and I had the pleasure of enjoying some toe-pointed stanzas of the poetry of motion as rendered by the agile limbs of the renowned Russian dancer, Mademoiselle Bagdanoff. The Russians are deliriously proud of this favoured child of Terpsichore. The government will not allow her to dance, even out of the Grand Opera season, on any stage in the empire, save those of the two great theatres in Petersburg and Moscow, where the prices are high, the audience aristocratically cold, aristocratically *blasé* and *ennuyé*, and aristocratically broken-in to the laws of Western aristocratic etiquette. For, were the Bagdanoff to dance at a native Russian theatre, the audience would infallibly encore her at least eight times after every *pas;* and the poor child would be danced off her legs. The Russians affect to sneer at Cerito and Rosati, and Fanny Ellsler; they only condescend to admit Taglioni to have been incomparable because she has retired from the stage, and has married a Russian prince. Plunket, Fleury, Fusco, Guy-Stephan, they will not have at any price. The Bagdanoff is their Alpha and Omega as a dancer. Last spring she was more the rage than ever. Her portrait, lithographed, was in all the printsellers' windows, with a sprawling autograph at the base, and a German epigraph at the summit:—"*In lebe immer die selbe,*" "In love always the same." I don't know why; but this motto always gave me an idea of an implied defiance or implied guarantee. It seems to say: "Advance, ye Crimean field-marshals, ye Caucasian generals, ye aids-de-camp of the Emperor, ye members of the directing senate, ye attachés of foreign legations. Don't be afraid! Approach and place your diamond bracelets, your bouquets with a bank-note for a thousand roubles twisted round the stem, your elegant coupés with coal-black horses, your five-hundred-rouble sable pelisses, at the feet of Nadiejda Bagdanoff. Walk up. There is no deception. In love she is always the same." I saw Mademoiselle Bagdanoff, and didn't like her. Have I not seen Her (with a large H) dance? She flung her limbs about a great deal; and in dancing, as in love, she was *immer die selbe* —always the same. It afterwards fell out that from the fumes of that great witch's caldron of Russian gossip, the Samovar, I distilled a somewhat curious reason for the immense popularity of the Bagdanoff.

The imperial government granted her a ticket of leave, or passport for foreign travel, just before the war with the allied powers broke out. Nadiejda went abroad, remained two years, and came back at last, radiant, as Mademoiselle Bagdanoff, of the Académie Impériale de Musique at Paris. She had stormed the Rue Lepelletier; she had subdued the Parisians; she had vanquished the stubborn hearts and claque-compelling white-gloved palms of those formidable three first rows of fauteuils d'orchestre, courted and dreaded by all cantatrice, by all ballerine. In a word she had triumphed; but it was never exactly ascertained in what ballet she made her début. It was certain, however, that she had been engaged at the Académie, and that her engagement had been rescinded during the war time; the manager having, with fiendish ingenuity, endeavoured to seduce her into dancing in a ballet whose plot was inimical to Russian interests. But, the fair Nadiejda, patriotic as fearless, indignantly refused to betray her country and her Czar. She tore her engagement into pieces; she stamped upon it; she gave the directors of the Académie Impériale a piece of her mind: she demanded her passports, and danced back to St. Petersburg—there to be fêted, and caressed, and braceleted, and ear-ringed, and bouqueted, and reëngaged at the Balschoï Teatr' at a higher salary; and, by Jupiter! were she not lucky enough to be a crown serf, instead of a slave at obrok, to be sent back to her proprietor's village whenever he was so minded, there to be made to dance her best *pas seuls* for her noble proprietor's amusement, when he and his guests were drunk with wine; there, if she offended him, to be sent to hew wood and draw water, to go clad in gray sacking, instead of gauze and silk, and spangles; to have those tresses shorn away, whereon the diamond sprays glittered so bravely now; to be beaten with rods when her master was in a bad temper, and compelled unmurmuringly to pick up the handkerchief he designed to throw her when amiably disposed.

If the Bagdanoff deserved the gold medal, which I believe was awarded to her by the government for the Spartan fortitude with which she had withstood the insidious promptings of the malevolent Fransoutz, she was certainly entitled to the medal of St. Anne of the first class, set in brilliants of the finest water, for the heroism she displayed in coming back to Russia at all. The return of Regulus to Carthage was nothing to it. Shiningly, indeed, does her self-denying conduct contrast with that of the other (vocal) operatic star, M. IVANHOFF, who, being a slave, and a pupil of the Imperial Vocal Academy, and possessing a remarkably fine voice, was commanded by the Czar to repair to Italy, there to perfect himself in the art of singing, and then to return to Petersburg, to delight the *habitués* of the Balschoï Teatr' with his dulcet strains. The faithless Ivanhoff went, and saw, and conquered all the difficulties of his art; BUT HE NEVER CAME BACK AGAIN: withstanding, with an inflexible pertinacity, the instances of ambassadors and the commands of ministers. "Well out of it," thought M. Ivanhoff; and betook himself to making money for himself with admirable sprightliness and energy. He made a fortune; retired from the stage; bought an estate; and was ungrateful enough to live and enjoy himself thereupon, utterly unmindful of his kind friends in Russia, who were anxious that he should return, and to assure him that the past should be forgotten, that his wishes should be fully met, and that the warmest of receptions awaited him.

I cannot tell the title of the ballet whose subject the Bagdanoff considered inimical to Russian interests; but there are very many dramatic and operatic performances that lie under the ban of the Muscovite Boguey, on the inimical plea. M. Scribe's vaudeville of the Verre d'Eau is proscribed in Russia. Rossini's William Tell, has, of course, never been heard there in public. The Etoile du Nord achieved an immense success; but as there were some inconvenient little matters in the libretto about Peter the Great's madness and drunkenness, the title was quietly metamorphosed into Charles the Twelfth. So with numerous dramas and operas with inconvenient titles or inconvenient incidents. Have any of my readers ever heard of an opera, usually considered to be the *chef d'œuvre* of Auber, in which there is a market chorus, and a tumult, and a dumb girl, and an insurgent fisherman riding on a horse from the circus? That dear old round-nosed, meek-eyed white horse, that seems to be the only operatic horse in the world, for he is himself alone his parallel, and nought else could be it, in any country I have visited:—a patient horse, bearing burly baritones, or timid tenors, or prima donnas, inclined to *embonpoint*, with equal resignation; a safe horse, never shying at the noise of the big drum, never kicking out at the supers, and, above all, never, as I am always afraid he will, inclining his body from his centre of gravity at an angle of sixty degrees, and setting off in a circular canter round the stage with his mane and tail streaming in the opposite direction, till brought to a sense of his not being at Franconi's or Astley's by a deficiency of whip, and an absence of saw-dust, and a sudden conviction that there must be something wrong, as his rider is sitting on his back, instead of standing thereupon on the saddle with the red velvet table-cloth, and is uttering shrieks of terror, instead of encouraging cries of "Houp la!" There is a general blow-up and eruption of volcanoes at the end of this opera, and it is known, unless I am very much mistaken, by the name of Masaniello. They play it in Russia; but, by some means or other, the tumult, the market scene, and the insurgent fisherman, have all disappeared; there is nothing left but the dumb girl, and the beautiful music, and the blow-up; and the opera is called Fenella. The other elements (to say nothing of the name of that bold rebel: oh, scour me the Chiaja and turn up the sleepers at Naples' street-corners, for another MASANIELLO; for we live in evil days, and the paralytic remnants of the Holy Alliance are crying out to be knocked down and jumped upon, and thrown out of window, and put out of their pain as soon as possible)—those revolutionary elements would suggest allusions, and those allusions might be inimical to Russian interests.

There was a little bird in Petersburg, in these latter days of mine, who went about whispering (very cautiously and low, for if that big bird, the Double Eagle, had been aware of him, he would have stopped his whispering for good) that there was another reason for the Bagdanoff's secession from the Académie at Paris. The French, this little bird said, quite confidently, though quietly—the French wouldn't have her! She had rehearsed, and the minister of state had shaken his head. The Jockey Club had presented a petition against her. The *abonnés* had drawn up a memorial against her. They considered her to be inimical to French interests. Two feuilletonistes of the highest celebrity and social position had declared publicly that they would decline and return the retaining fee, sent by débutantes and accepted by feuilletonistes, as a matter of course, in such cases. In fact, the Bagdanoff was *crêveé* before she ever saw the French foot-lights twinkle, and if she had not pirouetted away Due North as fast as her ten toes would permit her, she would in another week have been caricatured in the Journal pour Rire—figuration in which formidable journal is equivalent to civil death on the Continent.

All of which minor gossip on things theatrical and operatic you may imagine, if you like, to have been useful to wile away the time this hot afternoon. Signor Fripanelli and I have been dining at Madame Aubin's French table d'hôte at the corner of the Cannouschnïa or Great Stable Street; and have agreed to visit the Circus Theatre in the evening to see Lucrezia Borgia, the opera: music by the usual Donizetti, but words translated into Russ. I anticipated a most awful evening of maxillary-bones-breaking sounds. Fancy "*Di pescatore ignobile*" in Slavonic!

Fripanelli and yours truly have proceeded, dinner being over, to Dominique's café on the Nevskoï, there to do the usual coffee and chasse; and at the door of that dreary and expensive imitation of Bignon's or Richards's stands the Signor's droschky, (for Frip is a prosperous gentleman; gives you, at his own rooms, as good Lafitte as you can obtain on this side Tilsit; and has a private droschky to himself, neat, shining lamps, tall horse, and coachman in a full suit of India-rubber.) "One mast 'ave, oun po di louxe," a little luxury, the Signor tells me, as if to apologize for his turn out. "If I vas drive op ze Princesse Kapoustikoff vith Ischvostchik, sapete, fifty copeck, zay would take too rouble from my next lesson. *Ah! quel pays! quel pays!*"

"Imagine yourself," (to translate his polyglot into something approximating to English,) he tells me as we sip the refreshing Mocha and puff at the papiros. —"Imagine yourself, I go to the Countess Panckschka. She receive me how? As the maestro di canto? Of none. I sit at the piano-forte, and open the book and wait to hear that woman sing false as water, that which always she do. Is it that she sing? Of none. She sits and makes little plaits in her robe, and spins little gold toys, and says, Signor Fripanelli, what is there of news en ville. Tell me, I pray you, all the cancans you heard last night at the Princess Kapoustikoff's. What, devil! I go to-morrow to the Kapoustikoffs, and she says, Tell me, Signor of mine, what is there of new en ville, and who are the imbecile whom that old woman, ugly, the Countess Panckschka, can now persuade to enter her faded saloons. Deity of mine, this they call taking lessons of the song! And if you do not talk cancans; if you say that you are a master of music, and not a merchant of news; they will write to you a billet with but this sole line in it, *Monsieur, je ne vous connais plus*, Sir, I know you no longer; and no longer will they know you, or the two, five, eight hundred roubles they owe you, besides their bad tongues, ruining your fame and honour in salons with histories of lies that you know not your art; that you are of the Jew, and have been *galerian*, *là bas*, down there with letters marked on your back for theft of watches from mantelpiece, and have wife without bread in Bergamo, whom in the time you bastinadoed because she would not dance on the cord," (the tight-rope, I presume.)

The recital of Fripanelli's woes carries us well out of Dominique's, and his droschky takes us at an enlivening rate towards the theatre. Frip has been years in Petersburg, yet I question whether he has ever walked ten miles in it since his arrival. "What to do?" he asks, lifting up his hands, and shrugging up his shoulders. "To walk, where? Among these wild men savage, these barbarous? Of not." He knows the Nevskoï, the Italianskaïa, the English and Palace Quays, the two Morskaïa's and the Litennaïa, because in those streets his aristocratic patrons reside. He has heard of Wassily-Ostrow, and has been (in a gondola) to Kammenoï-Ostrow, the Princess or the Countess Panckschka having a châlet there in the summer; also to Tsarski-Selo, and even as far as Pavlowsk by railway, for he gives lessons to one of the Grand-Duchesses. He has seen the outside of the Gostinnoï-dvor; but he is quite ignorant of what manner of markets exist behind that stately edifice. He knows not the Gorokhovaïa from Adam; and if you were to tell him that the Nevskoï started from the shores of the Neva, at right-angles to it, and ended three miles off, still on the shores of the Neva, and still at right-angles thereto, he would stare with astonishment.* I could show you full a score of foreign residents in Petersburg who are brethren in ignorance to Fripanelli, and have been as long in Russia, and know as little of it as he.

This good-natured little music-master is madly in love with the Queen of Sheba. He is most respectful and quite hopeless in his attachment, never telling his love to its object, but allowing concealment to prey on his olive cheek. Watching him, however, at his music lessons, while the Queen is singing (and she sings divinely), I catch him furtively wiping his right eyelid with the extreme end of a very fine cambric handkerchief. He composes romances and cavatinas for the Queen to sing, which, when she sings, makes him urticate his eyelid more than ever. He weeps frequently to me over coffee on the subject. *Elle n'a pas de l'âme.* "She has not of the soul," he says. "If she knew how to shed the tears as well as how to beam the smiles, she would be *la Donna* of the world. But she cannot. *Elle n'a pas de l'âme.*" And so we go to the Circus.

* Here the Neva forms an arc in its myriad windings, and the Nevskoï is the chord of the arc. The difficulty of orienting one's self without a compass in Petersburg, or finding out whether you are steering topographically, is positively distracting. Owing to the twistings and twinings of the river, the innumerable back waters, branches, canals, and bridges, you may walk five miles and still find yourself over against where you started from.

Which, beyond being externally circular in form, (with the ordinary quadrangular excrescences inseparable from round buildings,) and having been, it may be, originally built with a vague view towards equestrian performances at some future period, has nothing whatever to do with horses. For, as you already know, it is the home of operas sung in Russ.

We heard Lucrezia Borgia, and I confess that I was most agreeably disappointed. I became convinced that the epithet "soft-flowing Russ" is one eminently due to the mother-tongue of our late enemies. It is, indeed, for vocal purposes a most mellifluous and harmonious language, and, for softness and euphony, is about five hundred per cent. more suited to musical requirements than the French language. As to its superiority over our own (for singing) I at once and candidly admit it. I don't think that from my due northern antecedents, I shall be accused of entertaining any very violent Russian sympathies, or that I shall be denounced as an emissary of the Czar in disguise, when I appeal to all linguists to bear me out in the assertion, that our own English tongue is the very worst language in the world for singing. There is an incessant hiss in the pronunciation which is as annoying as it is productive of cacophony; and I would sooner hear Lucrezia half-a-dozen times over in Russ than in English. As to the opera itself, it was, as I dare say it is all the world over—at the Scala, the Pergola, and the Fenice; at the St. Charles at New Orleans, at the opera in Pera, at the Tacon theatre in Havana, at our own great houses, or in country theatres, occupied for the nonce by some peripatetic opera company—always beautiful, glorious, fresh, and one which shall endure for aye, like the grand old marbles of those who have gone before, though legions of Goths and Vandals, though myriads of Keemo Kimos and My Mary Anns shall have desecrated its altars and profaned its hearth.

XIX.

TCHORNI NAROD: (THE BLACK PEOPLE.)

THE Black People I am going to tell about are not of the unhappy race of Ham, though they are intimately connected with, and are, indeed, the bone, and basis, and marrow of, the Domestic Institution of the Russian empire. The Russians (I feel a glow of pleasure come over me when I have any thing positively favourable to say of them) are entirely free from any prejudice against negroes. I think, on the whole, they would rather have Uncle Tom made Governor of Woronesch, than find an individual of German extraction appointed to a clerkship in the Ministry of Foreign Affairs. The people's—the Tchorni-Narods'—notion concerning negroes is peculiar and preposterous, but harmless. They call them Obeziania monkeys; and, perhaps, imagine them to be bipeds of the genus Simia, who have compromised themselves by speaking, and who, as a natural consequence of their indiscretion, have been made to work, like any other inferior human beings. The poet, whom his countrymen delight to call the Byron of Russia, was the lineal descendant of a negro slave, purchased by Peter the Great when very young; he was sent to Paris to be educated, and afterwards rose to high command in his service. Yet he never suffered any discredit through the sable complexion of his great-grandfather. He was M. de Pouschkin; and held lands and serfs, and fell in a duel with a Russian noble. Had he been born in a, say, less despotic country, that damning evidence in his finger-nails would have been sufficient to banish him from every table-d'hôte, from every railway car, and from every place of worship, save the black one; and to place him in danger of a cowhiding if he presumed to walk on a public promenade with a white woman. Yet the Russians are as white as I am—or as you are.

The Tchorni Narod is briefly the generic name familiarly given to the great popular element in Russia; the Black People are the equivalents for our great unwashed, or enlightened public, or raffish mob, or free and independent citizens, or swinish multitude, or the masses, or the lower orders, or whatsoever else you choose to call the English people, according to your high and mighty taste. The Tchorni Narod is the people that enlists, digs, delves, cheers, throws brickbats, takes the horses of His Serene Excrescence the Grand Duke from his carriage, and draws him in triumph to the palace; tears his S. E. into small pieces sometimes, and carries his head about on a pole; is drunken, mad, vicious; prudishly moral, indignant, indulgent, enthusiastic, icy cold, by turns, and, for a short time; that surges about like a sea and has its ebb and flow, its tempests and calms, as capriciously as that monster; that brings forth pale children, and is not washed nor taught, but works, and is beaten, and soddens, and starves.

How many weeks have these journey-notes been cast on the waters of publicity, and how little have I told of the real people I came all these leagues to observe, and study, and paint in words, and strive to understand and distil the truth from! The Ischvostchik; the Starosta and his belongings down at that gray Russian Dumbledowndeary of mine yonder; the bearded man in the red shirt at Heyde's; and a moujik I have caught up here and there, staring in at a shop window; these are all the popular Russian types I have as yet given. Yet, what should I myself think of an American, or a French, or a German—or to speak prospectively—of a New Zealand traveller, who came among us, English people, to depict our national manners and customs, and who confined himself chiefly to sketches of eccentric foreigners he had met at table-d'hôtes in Leicester Square or Soho, to the description of a Spanish boarding-house in Finsbury, a German sugar-baker's in Whitechapel, a Chinese crimp's in Rotherhithe, a Lascar beggar's den in Referden Street, an Italian organ-grinder and image haunt off

Leather Lane, a French café in the Haymarket, the Portuguese walk on 'Change, or a Parisian ballet at Her Majesty's theatre;—leaving out all the real true-born British characteristics of London; the cabmen, prize-fighters, oyster-women, coster-mongers, jockeys, crossing-sweepers, policemen, beggars, Quakers, garotters, Barclay and Perkins's draymen, Argyle gents, compositors, barristers, apple-women, authors, and ticket-of-leave men?

I know that my intentions, in the first instance, were conscientious. "Be it mine," I said, the very first night I lay down in my bed in the family vault at Heyde's, "to take this Russian people, and spread it out between sheets of paper like caviare in a sandwich for the million at home to digest as best they may. But, dear and forbearing reader, *I couldn't find the people.* Over sixty millions of souls does this empire contain; yet types of character are not to be picked up at the rate of more than one a day, on the average.

A Russian crowd is as rare a thing to be met with, as Johannisberg at a second-rate hotel, or a fine day in Fleet Street. Moscow coronations do not happen every day, notwithstanding that stock story told of Peter, Alexander I., Nicholas, and the present sovereign, as well of, if I mistake not, our George the Fourth, and the French Charles the Tenth, of the enthusiastic but inconsequent young lady, who was so delighted with the Kremlin solemnities, that she begged the Czar to let his subjects have another coronation as soon as possible. Popular gatherings are studiously discouraged by the government. The moujiks cry Gossudar, Gossudar! (the Lord, the Lord!) when the Czar comes flying along in his droschky; if they must needs be near him, they crouch down bareheaded, and bite the dust. Islers, the Sommer-Garten, the Wauxhall, at Pavlowsk, and the gardens of Tsarski-Selo,—which, in St. Petersburg, like the Sparrow-hills and the Hermitage Gardens, at Moscow, are very nearly all the places of out-door public reunion in the two capitals;—are tabooed to the moujik; dancing al fresco is forbidden; street shows are forbidden; street bands are forbidden. I have not the slightest wish to be suspected of pretending to polyglot attainments; yet such a suspicion may perhaps arise from the names drawn from different languages I have given to different buildings and things in St. Petersburg. The Russian name for the Sommer-Garten is (I believe) the Dvorsovaïa Sad, yet it is very rarely translated into French as the Jardin d'Eté, but is almost invariably spoken of by the Russians (when speaking Russ) by the German appellation of Sommer-Garten. Perhaps it was laid out by a German Gardener. Again the Police-Bridge is scarcely ever called by its Russian name (save when directing an Ischvostchik) of the Polineisky Most, but is accepted and Gallicised as Le Pont de Police. Again, I never heard the English Quay (Angliskaia Nabirejenaia in Russ) so spoken of by a Russian, even when speaking English,—it is always Le Quay Anglais; and, lastly, Basil's Island, or L'ile de Basile, is peremptorily restricted, this time, to its Russian name of Wassily Ostrow. At fires, the soldiers, the firemen, and the thieves (a fire is quite a government affair in Russia, and a member of the imperial family, if not the Czar himself, is almost always present,) form a crowd of themselves; and the moujiks run away for fear of being pressed to pump, and beaten if they do not pump hard enough. When there is a crowd, you may be certain that it is on the occasion of a national holiday, or a national tumult,—for this tightly reined-in country enjoys both occasionally. There are, you know, the Montagnes Russes, the Ice Mountains of the New Year, the Blessing of the Neva's Waters; the Katchelis and Shows of the Blinni Week, the eggs and kissings in all sorts of rings at Easter. At other times there are not even groups to stud the pavement of the enormous Perspectives and Ploschads; and though you know St. Petersburg to have a population of three-quarters of a million inhabitants, you might everywhere, save in the Gostinnoï-dvors, (where there is no crowd, but a continuous stream of human beings of all classes,) fancy yourself in a howling desert. I had a balcony once on the Nevskoï, and could, with my blind man's holiday eyes, see from the Anitchkoff Bridge to the Admiralty clock spire, (of course with the aid of a good opera-glass,) which is at least a third of the length of that unrivalled street. I have seen it, between three and four o'clock in the afternoon, what one might call—vehicles, horses, and a few regiments of cavalry and infantry marching past, being taken into consideration—thronged; sable-spotted as a turnpike road in England might be by half-a-dozen anthills slowly disgorging themselves thereon, (this was exactly the position, so high was my balcony, so vast and far extended the sweep of vista:) but I never saw a crowd collected on roadway or foot-pavement, that could equal in a tithe of numerical denseness, the gathering one sees every day on a Paris boulevard round a captured pickpocket, or the man in the helmet who sells the lead-pencils to the music of a barrel-organ fixed on to the top of his carriage, or the industrial in a blouse, who cuts (on his knees) a pane of glass into fragments with a diamond of dubious water, the original (of course) of which he afterwards sells you for the small sum of one sou; or that can come up to the assemblage to be brought together twelve hundred times every day in Fleet Street or the Strand, by PUNCH, or a horse falling down.

So rare are crowds in this teeming city, that even the public infliction of the KNOUT (which, to the honour of the Russians, is rarer still of occurrence) fails to bring the Tchorni-Narod together; and, when a murderer or a brigand is knouted, the attendance of a certain number of the Black people is made compulsory. I am not going to describe the knout or the process of its infliction; and I don't think I have mentioned it, as yet, by name, half-a-dozen times in the course of these papers. I never saw it, or the knout-masters, or the miserable wretch who had had it. I wish to say here, however, that this knout is really another Great Russian Boguey, —not to the Russians, who know all about it, but to us Western Europeans. There is scarcely a book, of travels you can open—English, French, or German, without a chapter bearing this special heading, the Knout, and in nine cases out of ten the description of the punishment is taken from the old wonderful magazine account of Madame Lapoukhin, who suffered in the reign of the Empress Anne Elizabeth; or from some of the Faubourg St. Denis travels of the vivacious author of the Mystères de la Russie. The Russians use the stick, the whip, and the rod, freely enough, Heaven knows; but the extreme agony of the knout, they are exceedingly chary in having recourse to. There was not one criminal knouted during my stay—at least, in the capitals, (for the imminence of the ultimo ratio is always made public a week before hand, in all the newspapers,) though I daresay some dozens, males and females, were daily beaten, cruelly but not dangerously, in the police-yards. The infliction of the knout in cases of murder (brigands and female criminals, who, the latter, only receive from five to twenty strokes, are allowed to survive,) amounting to one hundred and fifty lashes of that terrible instrument, is almost always fatal; indeed I have often heard Russians, whose humane dispositions I have had no reason to doubt, say that the police-surgeons had, generally, instructions not to attempt to cure the criminals after their torture. It is not the actual knout that kills, but the gangrene that supervenes in the neglected wounds. The old traveller's assertion that a skilful executioner can kill his patient with three strokes of the knout, is, if surgical authority be of any value, a pure fable. In any case, I am enabled to state my conviction that the Russian knout kills fewer criminals for capital offences in two years than we hang in one.

Crowds at such executions are, therefore, rare. Even the gathering together of two or three in no name save that of tyranny is an infrequent occurrence: though the Czar, in the summer, can have his crowd, and does have it, to the amount of some hundred and fifteen thousand men to be reviewed on the Czarinski Loug, or Champ de Mars,—a square, compact crowd of men, good enough to fill a pit, who shout from their one hundred and fifteen thousand throstles, "We thank you, Father," as one man, or rather one machine, when the Czar graciously says: "Good morning, my children;" and shout again: "We hope to do better next time!" when, if the evolutions have been satisfactory, his majesty says, "Well done, my children!" who, in cavalry charge in one pulk, to use Cossack parlance, —in one plump of spears, to use chivalric phraseology, to the number of fifty thousand, and sweep, pricking fast as a Simoon from the Sommer-Garten to the grim marble palace where the "frank, open-hearted sailor," the Grand Duke Constantine lives. So notable a thing is a mob, that the few there have been, have become historical, and are remembered like battles, or pestilences, or famines, or comets. Old men whisper low, now, of the great silent crowd of Black People that gathered round the old Winter Palace one morning at the commencement of the present century; when it began to be not noised—not bruited, but sinuously trailed about in movements of fingers, by glanceless eyes, by voiceless opening and shutting of telegraphic lips—that a dreadful deed had been done during the night by the great Boyards; that the mad Czar was dead, and that Alexander Pavlovitch reigned in his stead.

Most reverend seigneurs—potent and grave likewise—you have entertained at your boards, you have sat at council with, you, most beauteous ladies, you have waltzed and flirted with, and have had your slender waists encircled by the kid-gloved hands of, and have accepted bouquets and ices from—not the sons or the grandsons of, but the very men who were guests among those bloody sixty who supped at a house in the Pourschlatskaia Oulitza on the twenty-third of March, eighteen hundred and one, who formed part of the band of murderers who, under the guidance of Platon Zouboff and Pahlen and Benningsen, maddened with hatred and drunk with champagne, rushed after the orgies were over to the Winter Palace on the canal, and took the Czar, naked and a-bed, and slew him. They say that Alexander the First never recovered from the first fit of (I hope not guilty) horror into which he was thrown by the deed he profited so largely by; that the triumphs of the Borodino and the Bérésina, the splendours of Erfurt and Tilsit, the witticisms of Madame de Staël, the patronage of the first gentleman (and we hope the last gentleman of that pattern) in Europe, including as that patronage did a Guildhall banquet, the pencil of Sir Thomas Lawrence, the Temple of Concord on the Serpentine, and Sir William Congreve's fireworks—nay, not these nor the invocations of Madame Krudener could ever efface from his mind the memory of that night of abominations. They say that on his doubtful bed of death at Taganrog he writhed with more than pain, and continually moaned: "*Oh! c'est épouvantable! c'est épouvantable!*" and then, after a lapse, "*Empereur!*" The gentlewoman was not by as in the tragedy, but the physician was; and he knew his patient was suffering from ills that physic could not cure. The lord of sixty million souls was haunted by the remembrance of that night. He saw in imagination the bed-room; the conspirators reeling in; the Czar in his shirt, hiding behind a screen; the incoherent torrent of adjurations and menaces in French and Russ; and then the dreadful knocking at the outer door; the fear of rescue (though, indeed, it was but another band of conspirators arriving); the overturn of the lamp, and the end of that monarch. I say, seigneurs and ladies, you have walked and talked with some of those who supped and killed afterwards. They are very old, white-headed men now, high in office, decorated from the nave to the chaps, great diplomatists, adepts in statecraft; but there was a time when they were dashing young officers in the guards, and they saw in reality that which Alexander saw only in imagination. They could tell you whether it was Platon Zouboff or Count Pahlen who smashed Paul's skull in, with the hilt of his sword; they could tell you whether it was Pahlen or Benningsen who knelt on the Czar's breast, and put him out of his misery by strangling him with an embroidered scarf. I wonder whether the survivors of that scene ever think of the matter at all! Whether at congress table, or court ball, or civic banquet, in opera-box, or silk-lined carriage, or actresses' boudoir, they ever think of the overturned lamp, the sword-hilt, and the scarf. Does the Avenger of Blood pursue them? does Atra Cura, the black horseman, ride behind them? Or do they look at the twenty-third of March, eighteen hundred and one, as a mere boyish freak—a peck of wild oats which they have sown profitably, and reaped abundant crops of protocols and paraphes, stars, crosses, and titles from?

Haud obliviscendum, indeed! Life would be impossible without a shower-bath of the waters of Lethe every quarter of a century or so; without the sponge being applied when the slate is too full, and the tub of whitewash being brought in when the schedule has swelled too grossly. This man, I know, forged when he was twenty—rector's church-warden now. This, stole a goose, and was whipped for the theft, somewhere in the West Indies—high up in the Wooden-Spoon Referendaries Office now. This, robbed his father, deserted his children, broke his own wife's heart, and ran away with another man's —knighted last week. This, was the most covetous hunks, the hardest-hearted usurer, the unjustest steward that money-bags have been clutched by since Harpagon or Hopkins—he is dead. The Reverend Hango Head, M. A., is writing a Latin epitaph for him, and his disconsolate widow has ordered a memorial window, setting forth his virtues (in pre-Raphaelitically painted glass) in the chancel of

Saint Jonathan and Saint Gyves Great Wilderton Church.

Once again the Black People met, silently and timorously to learn that they had changed masters, when, in eighteen hundred and twenty-six the news arrived of Alexander's death, and the cruel Constantine abdicated, and the Czar who was to do so much and so little for good and evil, for the glory and the shame of Russia, had to sieze his diadem, perforce with ensanguined hands, and wrap a gory shroud round his imperial purple. As before, the Black People had neither act nor part in the events of which they were frightened spectators. Constantine or Nicholas, it was not one salted cucumber, one copeck's worth of black bread, one keaker of quass, the more to them. The boyards alone were to change masters; and they were to be the slaves of slaves for ever and ever. The real crowd was one of soldiery, who fought regiment against regiment, some for Nicholas, some for Constantine; some for a cloudy myth of a constitution and a republic their leaders had got, heaven knows how, into their muddled heads—perhaps while in garrison in some German town among moon-struck illuminati in eighteen hundred and thirteen; some for they knew not what,—for a fancied millennium, perhaps, of more vodki, and the stick being broken and cast into the pit for a thousand years. They fought in the Great Admiralty Square till the crisp snow was patched with crimson pools, and the cavalry horses, dabbling in them, pimpled the expanse with their hoof-nails for hundreds of yards around. So, as all men know, General Miloradovitch was slain; the cannon began to thunder; the Czar Nicholas came to his own; Pestel and the others were hanged; princes and counts and generals went in chains to Siberia; and the Tchorni-Narod, having stripped the corses of the slain lying on the now russet snow on the Admiralteskaïa Ploschad, went to sell the old clothes and trinkets in the Tolkoutchji-Rinok (Great Elbow Market), and then to their several avocations of droschky driving and quass selling, and hewing the wood, and drawing the water.

There was to come a time though, when, for once in their oppressed lives, the Black People were to make a public appearance as a Mob, tumultuous, ferocious, and dangerous. The crowd of the moujiks in the Sinnaïa or Haymarket of St. Petersburg, is the one historical crowd in which the people were actors and not looking on. This was in the first year of Asiatic cholera declaring itself *en permanence* at St. Petersburg. It is now domiciled there *en permanence*, and the Tchorni-Narod are as accustomed to it as to dirt, or to vermin, or to the stick. The Government had very praiseworthily taken the best sanitary precautions for the prevention of, and had adopted the most accredited remedies for the cure of, this awful malady. It seemed like a stern measure of retribution meted out to the wicked rulers of an oppressed people, that where they were really endeavouring to do good the Tchorni-Narod rebelled against it. They could swallow the camel of tyranny—they strained at the gnat of benevolence. The Government had sown in ignorance; they reaped in revolt. The great hospitals of Oubouk-hoff and Kalinkine had both been placed under the superintendence of German physicians, who exerted themselves to the utmost to treat successfully the almost innumerable cases of cholera that were daily brought in.

The average number of cholera cases in St. Petersburg alone, in the summer last past, was, according to the Gazette de l'Académie, (as reliable a Russian document as, I believe, can well be found,) three hundred and ten per diem. Of the average in Moscow I have no information. The vast majority of these cases were among the Tchorni-Narod, and were fatal. This can easily be understood, if we remember the diet and positively Nomad habits of the masses in Holy Russia. The Ichvostchiks frequently sleep on their droschky benches, in the open air, exposed to every fluctuation of the always fluctuating weather. The dvorniks or yard men always sleep *al fresco*, wrapped in their sheepskin touloupes or pelisses. The mechanics and labourers who come into St. Petersburg, for the summer months, from the outlying provinces of Carella and Ingria, sleep also *à la belle étoile*, wherever the most convenient scaffolding or mortar-heap can be found; and there are thousands of the Black People who sleep wheresoever, and under whatever circumstances, they can. The Russians, who are so studiously looked after by the police, to the minutest shade of passports and police, are perhaps the people in Christendom who habitually, and to the greatest extent, possess the key of the street. When, in addition to this, it is borne in mind that the Russian moujik scarcely ever tastes meat, and that his ordinary food is salted cucumber, black bread, and quass, the prevalence of cholera in St. Petersburg will be easily accounted for.

The people, in their miserable ignorance of right and wrong, caught hold of an idea. This idea was no doubt industriously disseminated among them in the first instance by agents of that secret democratic and socialist party which—Siberia, the mines, Count Orloff's cabinet and its scourgings, exile, confiscation, fortress-dungeons and espionage notwithstanding—existed occult, indomitable, and active as Balzac's Treize has always continued to exist in Russia from the time of the first French Revolution. The idea was that the moujiks, their brethren, were being systematically poisoned by the German doctors, and by express direction of the Government. For once Ivan Ivanovitch forgot that the Czar was his father, his pastor and master, his guide, philosopher, and friend, and Heaven's vicegerent upon earth. An analogous report of the wells having been poisoned was, it will be remembered, current among the populace in Paris in the first year of the cholera's visitation, and several *êmeutes* took place; nor in England, in eighteen thirty-two, were there wanting alarmists of the Mrs. Grundy school, to ascribe the pestilence—on the one side to the machinations of the disappointed boroughmongers; on the other to the malevolence of Levellers, Radicals, and Trades-union men. Ivan forgot the power of the police and his own helplessness. He and his comrades in thousands stormed the hospitals, massacred the doctors and their assistants under circumstances of the most shocking brutality, threw the beds and bedding out of the windows, carried off the patients, (to die, poor wretches, in carts and cellars, and under vegetable-stalls and horse-troughs;) and then, like a mob of schoolboys who have screwed up their courage to pelt an unpopular usher, and who afterwards with outward words of boasting and rebellion, but with an inward sinking of their hearts into their high-lows, bar themselves into the school-room, defying the masters, but knowing full well that authority will get the best of it, and that Birnam Wood will be brought to Dunsinane, for brooms to thrash them with;—the Ivan did his barring out. All cowering and wondering that he could have been so bold in the Sennaïa; entrenching himself behind trusses of hay and piles of fruit and vegetables—beneath the bulks of butchers' stalls and among crates of crockery, (for they sell all things in the Haymarket;) armed with such rude instruments of defence as hatchets, and straightened scythes attached to poles, and the great three-pronged forks with which the bread is drawn from the peetch, or stove; he awaited the coming of the troops.

I have no doubt, that had the soldiery really arrived and set to work, the moujiks would have suffered the most violent cannonade and musket practice, without attempting to move until they were routed out by the bayonet. Their energy was over; their rebellion was, thenceforth, inert and passive. But the Czar Nicholas knew too well the temperament of his children to send against them or horse, or foot, or artillery. To cowhide your slave: good; but to destroy valuable property by taking your slave's life, none but a foolish slaveholder would do that. It is an old story, but worth the telling again, that Nicholas, unattended by escort, or aide-de-camp, or groom, was driven in his single droschky, with the one single Ischvostchik before him to drive him to the place of the revolt. That, arrived on the Sennaïa, he quickly alighted, and, wrapped in his gray coat, and helmed and plumed, stalked through the masses of rebellious thousands, (who made an astonished vaccillating lane for him to pass,) towards the church with the four copolas, and the dome with the silver stars, that stands in the right hand upper extremity of the Haymarket. That, ascending the marble stairs of that fane, he prostrated himself before the image of the saint that stood in the porch; and then suddenly turned round to the gazing masses, and, extending his right hand, cried out, with the full strength of his magnificent voice, "People, on your knees!" That the thousands, as one, knelt down and bowed their foreheads to the dust; that the Czar then pronounced a short allocution to them, bidding them ask pardon for their sins, telling them how wicked they were; how good he was; that, while he was speaking, some cat-like police agents glided in among the people and took, without a shadow of resistance, some hundreds of prisoners, who were noiselessly removed to suffer the Pleidi, or the Battogues, and to be afterwards sent to Siberia;—and that the trick was done. Yet I have heard, in Russia, Russians say that the Czar Nicholas, like Sir Robert Peel—THE Sir Robert Peel, I mean—was so constitutionally timorous, that a spaniel yapping about his heels, or a monkey leaping on to his shoulder, was sufficient to thow him into an agony of terror. To my mind, the artilleryman, who, meeting the Bengal tiger, stooped down and looked at that beast from between his legs, so that the terrible tiger, not knowing what on earth the strange animal gazing at him could be, howled in affright, took to his paws, and enjungled himself in the rattle of a snake's tail, was the only compeer I have ever heard of, worthy to rank, for real courage and presence of mind, with him who bade the people who had massacred the doctors fall on their knees; and was obeyed.

The Tchorni-Narod can assert their individuality sometimes, therefore; but, it is only transiently and spasmodically; and the fit is followed by pitiable reaction. It has been before observed, that an enraged sheep is for the moment nearly as troublesome a customer to deal with as a roaring lion. Almost always the Russian peasant takes his thrashing, and general ill-treatment, quietly: nay, will thank his corrector, and kiss the rod. He will not cry out: "How long, O Lord! How long?" but will bear (as a rule) his to us intolerable miseries, as long as that miserable life of his endures. But times will come when the sheep goes furious. He has the gids—to speak as a shepherd. Then he rages; then he storms; then he whirls round; then he butts forward in a momentarily potent frenzy; and then woe betide Bourmister and Starosta—commander of punishment and executant of punishment: woe betide even the noble Boyard; for Ivan Ivanovitch will rend him asunder, and spare not his noble wife nor his noble daughters, nor the very children that are unborn: and after this come speedily, reaction, and repentance, and a dreadful retribution on the part of outraged authority.

As I have pointed out, a riotous crowd—a crowd, indeed, at all in St. Petersburg or Moscow, is a novelty and an event to be remembered, and made a thing historical of—will my reader ask any Russian acquaintance to relate a few anecdotes of the peasant crowds, who, from time to time, gather themselves together down south—towards the east, or in the far west of the gigantic empire—in governments you never heard of, in provinces you never dreamed of? You shall hear how some delicate countess who has been the belle, not only of the salons of the northern capital, but of Paris, and London, and Vienna; who has retired, after some love-pique against a *chargé-d'-affaires*, or some scandal with her husband, to her vast estates, hundreds of versts beyond Moscow, and has there devoted herself to the task of torturing her slaves; has invented and practised such unheard-of cruelties upon her bower-maidens and her wretchedest dependents, down to her cooks and scullions, that some direful evening there has been a crowd; that the crowd have poured boiling oil on her, and have hung her up by the hair of her head, while they have scarified her by drawing infuriated cats over her; that they have plucked out her nails and her eyes, and singed her before a slow fire, and finally have hacked her to pieces with hatchets, and eaten her brains.* That after the frightful retaliation had been committed came a reaction, and terror, and abject cringing. The general commanding the provincial government came down; there was a reign of terror; many were beaten to death: more had their nostrils torn out, and were sent to Siberia, there to work in the mines and in chains, as slaves, for life.

You don't see these narratives in the Journal de St. Petersbourg, or in the Abeille du Nord, or in the Invalide Russ, among the catalogue of recent promotion in the illustrious orders of St. Anne, St. Wladimir, and St. Alexander Nevskoï, or among the official despatches announcing new victories over the Circassians. They do occur though, from time to time. The government keep them dark: and you hear them after dark and subtle whispers, as "*cette chose terrible qui est arrivé dernièrement*"—that terrible event in the government of Orel, or Kharkoff, or Tamboff, which has happened lately, and which is so very regretable;—but which will happen again and again, I opine, as long as the Tchorni-Narod, the Black People of Russia, are ground down and oppressed, as they are in this present era of grace.

* At Bagatoi, in the government of Kowrsk, in eighteen hundred and fifty-four.

XX.

THE IKS.

THE title of this paper may seem excedingly absurd. But there are many Iks and Chiks and Niks in Russland, whom it behoves to have information about.

In the Nevskoï—the great avenue of the Tents of Kedar I am so strangely constrained to dwell amongst and in its immediate ducts, the Great and Little Morskaïas—you will see panorama-passing during the day, all the Iks worth noticing. In these streets only will you be able to view any thing approaching to the Johnsonian or Fleet Street aspect of City Life. Away from the Nevskoï and the Morskaïas, the vast streets of Petersburg are, at all seasons, little better than deserts. Solitary figures of slaves and soldiers glide by occasionally, ghostlike; but, on Quay or Esplanade, in Oulitza, Perspective, Ploschad, or Pereoulok, there is (as I have hinted in the Tchornï-Narod) nor throng nor pressure—and I have seen, at high-noon, standing in the centre of the Admiralty Square, one dog; a mangy cur with a ridiculous tail—who, in the insolence of undisputed possession, set his four paws all wide apart, and wagging that truncated handle of his, barked shrilly and scornfully at the high palaces, as though they had been the walls of Balclutha, and he was delighted that they were desolate.

Very slowly, but with crustaceous tenacity, has

the Nevskoï in its ways, its inns and outs, and its Iks, fixed itself upon me. It was shy and coy at first. Let me, as briefly as I may, essay to go round the clock with you on the Nevskoï, and trot out the Iks, in their morning as well as evening aspects. Remember, this is summer-time; the beginning of July; (for I know nothing of Acris Hyems in Russia;) and take note, if you please, that the time is four o'clock in the morning.

I am not at all ashamed to say that I have been out all night—at least all the time usually set apart in civilized countries for that appalling season of existence—at a ball, and that I am rattling home behind an Ischvostchik from the seventeenth line at Wassily-Ostrow; and, though wrapped in a thick overcoat, shivering with cold. The sun is manifest enough and bright enough in all conscience, and the smiling morn (smiling a polite, heartless, soulless, Sheffield plate, thoroughly Muscovite smile) is busily employed in tipping the gaudy domes with a brighter lustre than their gold leaf gives them. Not a shop, above ground, is open as yet—the aristocratic Boutiquiers of the Nevskoï are as late risers as their customers—but, in the basement, there are plenty of small "Lavkas"—grocery, chandlery, and bakery shops open; to say nought of the vodki-dens with the great bunches of grapes in gold leaf suspended over their portals, to show, I presume, that wine is not sold there—which dram establishments never seem to be closed at all. The water-carts go heavily lumbering past; then I hear a clanking as of many tin-pots, or of marrowbone and cleaver music, in which the metal unduly preponderates; and see advancing towards me a gaunt, bony, ill-favoured woman in a striped petticoat held up by the usual braces, the usual full-sleeved innermost garments, a crimson handkerchief tied over her freckled face, and streaming behind, like a Bedouin's burnouse when the capuchin is thrown suddenly back from the head. Over each shoulder she carries a heavy arc of wood, like a fully bent bow, but hollowed out in the centre so as to fit her shoulder, and serve as a yoke; to either end of which are suspended fasciculi of the before-mentioned tin-pots, much battered, and with brazen lids and spouts. This is a milk-woman. She does not deliver the caseous beverage from house to house, as with us, but takes her stand at some patented spot—generally at the "Auge" or feeding-trough of a droschky-stand. There are no such things as nosebags in the cabbicular hierarchy in this country; and, by a most humane provision, the animals are rendered independent of the caprice, or cruelty, or stinginess of their drivers, and are fed under police superintendence at the public auges or troughs, to whose support all the Ischvostchiks contribute their quota at stated times and in abundance. She either stands at one of these or close to the cabane or wooden hut of a Boutotsnik. Hither come either the dvorniks (yardmen), or the slough (man-servants), or the sloujanka (maid-servants), to lay in a stock of milk for the day. What the Petersburgers, who are not Tartars (for these live almost entirely upon milk) can want with milk, I am puzzled to discover. They almost uniformly drink black coffee after dinner, and seldom indulge in that beverage for breakfast (the rich prefer champagne and Lafitte; the poor, quass or vodki); they drink their tea without milk in ninety-nine cases out of a hundred; I never saw any remarkable profusion or custards or ice-creams at Russian dinner-tables; and it is my firm impression that there are no children in St. Petersburg to drink it. There are little men and women, little cadets, little grand-dukes, small Tchinovniks, miniature policemen, Lilliputian admirals, infinitesimal Archimandrites and Protopopes, minified countesses, minute coquettes; diamond, ruby, and pearl editions of that Book which will be Reviewed some day; but, of bouncing, bawling, buoyant, bothering, delightful children, there are none to be found here. It makes one shudder here to see the small tots of humanity, who only knew your ankles yesterday, and are scarcely tall enough to be on speaking terms with your kneecaps even now, conversing gravely in two or three languages, and bowing, and scraping, and lifting their caps, and unbuckling their sword-belts, as though, good Lord! as though they had been bandied about, and worn, and punched, and bitten, as often as a George the Third sixpence, instead of being silver pennies, bright, sharp, fresh, new from Nature's mint. The babies here, too—the very babies in arms—frown sternly on you as they pass by, or solve mathematical problems on their nurses arms, with their limp tiny fingers, biting their lips thoughtfully the while.* These precocious civil and

* Whenever I go into a strange country I set myself sedulously

military functionaries, incipient diplomatists, sprouting philosophers, conquerors—what need have they of a milk diet? Babies though they be, they require strong meat. Give them their bird, let them crack their bottle, light their pipes, lace them the tightest of corsets, hand them the daintiest of fans, for they are grown up, before they are grown at all.

to work to discover (and this you may perhaps have already inferred) something like a national and picturesque costume. Generally I am disappointed, and find nothing but prosaic hats and coats, bonnets and shawls, black cotton stockings, and linsey woolsey petticoats. I experienced great delight, however, and thought I had at last found a land of handsome dresses, when, walking the streets during my nonage in Petersburg, I lighted upon divers females, generally ruddy, comely often, and clad in the same description of gala costume I have attempted to describe in the holiday dress of the "Baba." The most plainly attired had sarafannes or tunics of crimson silk edged with broad gold lace, embroidered shoes, petticoats of rich stuff, necklaces, massive gold earings, and kakoschniks glistening with sham jewels and seed-pearls. They invariably had small Russians with them, either in arms or toddling by their sides; and I conjectured them to be wives of wealthy native merchants; but I was very soon afterwards, and to my extreme disappointment, informed that they were WET-NURSES; and that this masquerade costume was worn by them as a matter of course, and with as little picturesque truth as John Thomas wears the maroon plush and chrome yellow aiguillettes of the Countess of Squllpington. These wet-nurses are usually from Southern Russia. (They say no babies can live that are nursed by women from the marshy government of St. Petersburg.) Not one in five hundred of them is married. They have a child, and cast it into the Foundling Hospital, get a certificate of health from a doctor, and become wet-nurses in noble families. It is a profession. It is a paying one. A discontented Sloujanka (if she be not a serf) will say, "This does not suit me; I cannot support the Barynia. I shall go and be a wet-nurse."

Whoever drinks the milk, there are plenty of *Laitières* and *Cremières* in the capital. They have a quarter to themselves too, not exactly in St. Petersburg, but on the other side of the water, in the village of Okhta, where they dwell among their pots and keep their cows. The Petersburg milk-women are, I believe, mainly the property of that colossal slave proprietor (he has a hundred thousand they say) Count Tcherémétieff. SUCH cows, too, the milk-women have! You may frequently see them being led about the streets, gaunt, bony, woebegone little brutes, and I declare not one whit bigger than Shetland ponies; or perhaps, indeed, Shetland cows, if the cattle of the Ultima Thule are as diminutive as their horses. It is only very early in the morning that cattle or sheep are seen about the streets; they are then mostly on their way to Wassily-Ostrow, where are the slaughter-houses and the majority of the summer butcher's shops. I see, still rattling along in this early-late droschky of mine, (the Ischvostchik has not, probably, been to bed for a week, but is considerably fresher than I am,) multitudes of horned beasts and sheep, yet for all their numbers, only speckling the vastness of the Open, coming adown the great street from the Smolnoï road, along the quays, across the Pont-Neuf or Novi-Most, and so on to their doom to be made meat of. The sheep, albeit somewhat longer-woolled, are much like ours; they are not ruddled, but appear to be branded with a curious cross within a circle, and a distinguishing letter, on the left flank. I wonder they don't stamp them with the double eagle! The pigs are truculent, evil-eyed animals enough, with gashed snouts and switch tails. Observing the remarkable bright russet hue of some of these porcine Russians, I can for once acknowledge as a truth that legend of the "Red Pig," which in my skepticism I had hitherto been led to rank, as fabulous, with Guy Earl of Warwick's Dun Cow, and More of More Hall's Wantley Dragon. The sheep (in Russia) are driven by moujiks, clothed in toulopes or loose leathern coats, which, with an utter disregard of delicacy and consideration for the feelings of the animals themselves, are evidently made of sheepskin. Their legs—the moujiks', I mean—are swathed in criss-cross bandages of leather or bark, much resembling the cruciform-leggings worn by Mr. James Wallack in the melo-drama of the brigand. These Corydons wield the instrument we so often read about, and so seldom see, the real shepherd's crook—not the long pole with a squeezed-up hook, which the Sussex pastors carry, but exactly resembling a bishop's crozier. The shepherds have no collies—no dogs to worry the sheep, or keep them together; their crook serves them for all in all; and they possess a peculiar agility in intertwining the hook with the woolly locks of the sheep's fleece, and then, dexterously reversing the instrument, driving the end of the staff (sharpened and shod with iron) into his ribs in a manner calculated to cause great agony to the mutton, but highly conducive to discipline and good order. The pig-drivers have Cossack whips, with thongs about six times as large as the staff, with a little perforated ball of lead, strung, which runs up and down the lash, so that the pig is sure to have it somewhere. This whip makes, when cracked, a tremendous noise; and from the expression I have observed on the baconian physiognomy, I don't think that animal likes it. Finally, the cattle drivers, clad (also in seeming insult to their victims) in loose capes of pie-bald calf-skin, as if they had been foraging in the Pantechnicon, London, and had robbed some hair-trunks of their coverings. They blow veritable cow-horns, which make an unearthly wailing noise, and sound so discordantly that I very much marvel that the cows don't die of that tune.

Over the glassy Neva, blue as the sky that roofs it, with ships from all parts of the world mirroring their cobweb rigging in its depths, over the Neva by the new bridge on to the Quai Anglais, and I am not half home yet. See, here are the Iks all at once, and in great force all over the new bridge without crowding it, and stationary, though there is no show to see, no orator to hear, no time to laze away; for they are all bound for a weary day's work.

That man with a short, stunted, scrubby, but thick beard, with the leathern cap and blue cloth band in lieu of the ordinary Ischvostchik's hat; with the blue-striped shirt, pink-striped breeches, and immutable boots, and fluttering over all like the toga of an ancient Roman in difficulties, or the time-worn, and by stern-creditor-not-renewed mantle of Don Cæsar de Bazan—a tattered, patched, greasy, stained, villanous, but voluminous leathern apron—

is a Batchmatchnik, a shoemaker. He beside him, with the cunning fox-face, the unwholesome complexion, the bloodshot eyes, the slight stoop in the back, the large hands with lissom fingers crooked somewhat at the tips, the general weary, done-up, hunted-dog look, telling of late hours, and later vodki; he who has a square bonnet of stiff blue paper something like a lancer's cap on his head, a black calico apron over his caftan, and black calico sleeves reaching half-way up his arms, must be a Typograpschtchik—a journeyman printer, who has just knocked off work at the bureaux of the Journal de St. Pétersbourg in the Pochta-Oulitza, or General Post-Office-street hard by; or else he has been setting all night in type, positive or superlative lies in some imperial oukase, or edict, or prikaz. Yonder fellow, with the herculean frame, the fair-haired, blue-eyed, full-bearded, Richard-Cœur-de-Lion head, and the eye like Mars to threaten or command, (he was whipped yesterday,) is—it needs not his bared arm, his coarse canvas suit, but always with boots, the rope tied round his waist, and the tape round his forehead, and the film of fine drab powder with which he is covered from hair of crown to ball of toe—to tell you, a Kammenstchik, or stone-mason. Beside him is his brother in building—not an Ik this time, but an Ar; but he may be allowed, I hope, to press in with the ruck—a ruddy fellow in a pink shirt and the usual etceteras, with a hatchet stuck in his girdle; a merry-faced varlet, with white teeth, who, if he had but an ass to lead, might be Ali Baba; but who is his own beast of burden, wots of no caverns, and is simply Axinti Ivanoff the Stoliar, or carpenter. He can do more feats of carpentry, joinery, ay, and cabinet-making and upholstery, with that single clumsily-made, blunt-looking toula hatchet of his, than many a skilled operative in London who earns his three pounds per week. Axinti, of course, is a slave; and, being very clever at his trade, is at high obrok, and is very profitable to his master. The facility and dexterity with which the Russian mechanics handle the hatchet, and make it serve in lieu of other tools, are marvellous and almost incredible, are certainly unequalled, save by the analogous skill of the peasants of the Black Forest, who are reported to be able to cut down trees, square timber for houses, carve comic nutcrackers and ugly-mugged toys, shave themselves, and cut their meat, all with the aid of one single penknife. The hatchet of the Russian carpenter seems to serve him in lieu of plane, saw, chisel, and mallet, and (it would almost seem) gimlet and screwdriver. I knew a Russian who declared "*qu'il avait un paysan*," ("*J'avais un paysan*"—I had a peasant—is as common a commencement to a Russian conversation as "once upon a time" to a fairy tale, or "it is now some eighteen years since" to the speech of a virtuous venerable in a melo-drama at home) who could glue boards together with his hatchet. No men (I except the Batmen) who have traversed Moscow or Petersburg streets, and have watched carpenters at work, either in their open shops or at the ligneus pavement, can have failed to remark the wonderful dexterity with which they convert a rough, shapeless piece of wood, into a plank, a panel, an hexagonal paving-block, a staff, a batten, a fagot, a quoin, a board, or a shelf. The process seems instantaneous. The carpenters have other tools besides the hatchet, doubtless; though I never saw a Russian Stoliar with a complete basket of tools beside him. But the hatchet is emphatically an implement germane and to the Russian manner born, as the cloth-yard shaft was to the English bowmen of yore, before the long-bow came to be used in England in a manner that our stout ancestors of Crecy and Agincourt never dreamt of. With the hatchet, the Russian moujik hews at the black pine-forests of Olonetz and Wiborg, for logs for his houses, for timber for the Czar's ships; with the hatchet he defends himself against the grisly bear and ravenous wolf; with the hatchet he cuts a way for his sledge in winter through the frozen snow; with the hatchet he joints frozen meat, and cuts up frozen fish, and chops frozen vegetables. The hatchet is his principal aid in building his house, and in constructing his furniture, and in cutting his fuel; all of which he does himself. If your Kibitk, or Tarantasse, or Telega break down on the road, you holloa out at the full strength of your lungs for assistance; whereupon a group of peasants presently appear, crying "*Stichasse!*" (directly!) who mend your broken trace, or spring, or axle, or reshoe your near-wheeler, or heal your drunken yemstschik's broken head, with a hatchet!—charging you many roubles for the accommodation. With a hatchet Peter the Great commenced the massacre of the Strelitzas; with a hatchet some say he murdered his own son; with a hatchet sometimes, even in these days of grace, the Russian moujik, maddened by drink and despair, rushes on the lord who has oppressed him, and with that murderous tool dashes out his brains. It puzzles me that the government should allow the slaves to carry these ugly-looking weapons constantly in their girdles. I shouldn't like to offer my serf fifty blows with a stick when he had an axe in his belt. I wouldn't have minded trusting Uncle Tom with a bowie-knife; but I should have kept my hatchets under lock and key if I had Sambo, or Quimbo, or Three-fingered Jack about my property.

It is not only in the use of the hatchet that the Russian peasant displays extraordinary dexterity, and power of achieving great things, with apparently the most contemptible and inadequate means. There is a well-known anecdote, which I may be excused for repeating here, of a Russian peasant, named Telouchkine, who, some thirty years since, contracted, for the sum of eighty silver roubles, (the materials of course being found him,) to regild the spire, the cross, and the angel surmounting it, of the cathedral of St. Peter and St. Paul (the burial-place of the Czars, from Peter to Nicholas) in the fortress of Petersburg. He accomplished this gigantic task without the aid of any scaffolding or platform work whatsoever, simply sitting astride on a little saddle suspended by cords. The spire, from its base to the summit of the cross is sixty-five *sagènes*, or four hundred and fifty-five English feet in height (455): the cross alone being eight *sagènes* or fifty-six feet high. I never heard the authenticity of this feat disputed. I have never heard what reward, beyond the eighty roubles contracted for, was bestowed on Telouchkine. Perhaps his proprietor, as a compliment to his talents, increased his yearly obrok; but I am afraid that when he died, he did not leave his secret to any one. When I left St. Petersburg, the angel and cross in the church in the fortress had fallen, as to gilding, into a woful state of second-hand-looking dinginess. It had become again a question of regilding these ornaments; but, this time, no Telouchkine came forward with an eighty-rouble offer. A most elaborate scaffolding, whose symmetry of proportions seemed to me quite astonishing, had been erected round the spire for the use of the workmen. It had cost, I was told, a good many thousand roubles, and was to cost a good many thousand more, before even a book of gold-leaf could be applied to cross, or angel, or spire.

No man who knows these poor Russian people with their rude tools, and hands seldom disciplined by regular apprenticeship, can doubt that it is faith that helps them along in such works as Telouchkine accomplished. That strong and blind belief in the Czar and in the saints, in a material reward from St. Peter and St. Paul, St. Sergius or St. George, St. Wladimir or St. Nicholas, in the shape of heaven-sent roubles, or a dupe sent by the saints in their way to swindle, or a cash-box for them to steal, (without the possibility of detection,) or a miraculous softening of their masters' hearts, and their exemption from the stick for years; together with a certain hope and trust that for this good deed done to the saints and the Czar, they will be rewarded with a real golden crown, a real white robe, a real harp, a real cloud to sit upon, to all eternity, while the Barynn, the Starosta, and the Bourmister, go to the devil, to be beaten to pieces by Gospodin Schrapschin, (Lord Beelzebub,) and burnt to cinders by Gospodin Tchort (Lord Lucifer: the Russians are very polite to their devils, and give them titles of honour.) This strong belief leads men like Telouchkine to swing four hundred feet high on six inches of wood hung to a hempen cord; it led the moujiks who built up the Winter Palace in eleven months, and perished by thousands building it, to work cheerfully, patiently, enthusiastically, in the broiling sun and the icy blast, because it was the Gossudar, the Czar's house, and because the government had caused it to be given out, that the works had been blessed by an angel; it led the gaunt gray-coated men in the flat caps to fight, and stand and march, and charge, and starve and die, uncomplainingly, unyieldingly, heroically, on the heights of Alma and in the valley of Inkermann, in casemates full of blood and smoke; in hospitals, where the wounded could not lie for the dead that were a-top of them; on bone-covered steppes, in pestilential marshes; on muddy tongues of ooze, and weed, and treacherous sand, that skirt the Putrid Sea.

Are not these all Iks?—for what is the Soldatt, the soldier, but a shaven moujik?—and have I been digressing? I know, though, these Iks are not those I left on the bridge. There is another Ik. Big beard, red face, but all the rest as white and floury, as the mason is gray. This is a boulotchnik, or baker—a journeyman baker, mind; for were he a master, he would not be a Russian or a serf at all, but a free German. For a wonder, he is not booted, but wears a pair of coarse canvas trousers, and drab list slippers. You must not confound him with that bow-legged industrial, clad also from head to foot in white, but not floury, who is circulating restlessly among the Iks, and bears before him a flat tray, or shallow basket, full of bread of the multiform shapes the Russians delight in—bread in long twisted rolls; bread in double semicircles, hollow, like a pair of handcuffs; bread in round balls, and bricks, and tablets, and big flat discs, and lumps of no particular shape. Some of this seems white and light enough, almost cake or puff-paste in appearance; but the great mass is of the approved Rye or Pumpernickel pattern; and though appetisingly light in its rich brownness without, is, when cut, as dark as the skin of a mulatto. This Ik is a Xhlaïbchik literally Bread-man—if indeed Ik or Chik or Nik may be understood to mean man. Perhaps the Ik is only synonymous with our "er" in Costermonger, Fishmonger, Fruiterer, Poulterer. The Xhlaïbchik is doing a smart trade on the bridge among the Iks; (whom I hope you have by this time discovered form part of the Tchornï-Narod, the Black people;) for from four to five in the morning is breakfast time with them. Some other peripatetic tradesmen min ister to the co-epicurean wants of the Iks. There is the Tchaïchik—the tea-man—who carries a glowing samovar beneath his arm wrapped in a thick cloth, from whose centre protrudes a long horizontal spout and tap. He also carries, by a strap over his shoulder, a flat tray, covered with a fair linen cloth, on which is his array of tumblers, and earthen mugs, pewter spoons, lumps of sugar, (seldom called for,) and slices of lemon, much in demand. He serves his tea, all hot, as the merchant in the cab-rank centre of the Haymarket, London, does his potatoes. The tea is of the very coarsest, bitterest, and vilest of flavour. I tasted it, and it costs two copecks a tumbler. It is full of strange ingredients that float about in it, herbaceous, stony, gritty, and earthy; but it is not adulterated in Russia, being made from the cheap brick tea mixed with sheep's blood, as coffee with chicory—so called from the bricks or ingots into which the leaf is compressed—brought by caravans out of China, by way of Kiatki. It is written that you must eat a peck of dirt before you die; and I think that about four tumblers of hot Petersburg street tea would go a long way towards making up the allowance. There is another Tchaïchik—the cold-tea-man. He with a prodigious vase of glass, with a pewter top, and through whose pellucid sides (the vase's) you can see the brown liquid frothing with much oscillation, and with much sliced lemon bobbing up and down in it, leans moodily against the parapet of the Novi-Most; for the morning air is a nipping and an eager one, and the cry is, as yet, almost entirely for warm tea. Not so with the Kolbasnik, or dealer in characuterie:—there is positively no strictly English word for it, but seller of "pork fixings" will explain what I mean. He is a blithe fellow with a good face and a shirt so bright that he looks like a Russian robin red-breast, and goes hopping about among the Iks, vaunting his wares, and rattling his copecks, till a most encouraging diminution begins to be apparent in his stock of sausages, pig's and neat's feet, dried tongue, hung beef, salted pork fat, (a great Kolbasnik delicacy, in lumps, and supplying the place of bacon, of whose existence the Russians seem unaware,) and balls of pork mincemeat, resembling the curious viands known in cheap pork butchery in England, I believe, as Faggots.

There are, as yet, few women or children crossing the bridge; and of those few the former are counterparts of the Okhta milk-woman, without her yoke and bundle of tin cans. There pass, occasionally, silent files of soldiers, clad either in vile canvas blouses, or else in gray capotes gone to rags, whose military character is only to be divined by their shaven chins, and closely-cropped heads, and long moustaches. These are men drafted off from the different regiments not on actual duty, to work in the docks, at unloading ships at the custom-house; or warehousing goods; or at the private trades or occupations at which they may be skilled. They receive wages, which are said facetiously to go towards the formation of a regimental reserve fund; but which in reality go to augment the modest emoluments of his excellency the general, or his high-born honour the major, or his distinguished origin the captain.

The background of these groups is made up by the great Iks of all Iks, the Moujiks, the Rabotniks, (the generic term for workmen, as a Moujik and Christian are for slaves,) the indefinable creatures in the caftans, who are the verb active of the living Russ condemned for their lifetime to be, to do, and to suffer. This is why they tarry on the bridge on their way to work—those multifarious Iks. There is a shrine-chapel at its foot towards Wassily-Ostrow:—a gilded place, with pictures, filagree railings, silver lamps suspended from chains, huge waxen candles continually burning, and steps of black marble. Every Ik, every woman and child, every soldier, every Ischvostchik as he passes this shrine, removes his hat or cap, crosses himself, and bows low before it. Many bow down and worship it—literally grovelling in the dust; touching the earth repeatedly with their foreheads, kissing the marble steps and the feet of the saint's image, and looking devoutly upwards as though they longed to hug the great, tall, greasy wax candles. Not the poorest Ik but fumbles in his ragged caftan to see if he can find a copeck for the saint's money-boxes, which, nailed to the wall, guards the staircase like sphinxes.

Drive on thou droschky, (of which the Ischvostchik has reverently lifted his hat, crossing himself repeatedly as we passed the joss-house,) for I am very hungry and want my breakfast.

L'ENVOI.

It is the lot of every man who aspires to, who achieves publicity, or who—as very frequently happens—has publicity thrust upon him, to be favoured by the attention of that numerous, and apparently increasing class, the "people who go about saying things." I am afraid that I shall never attain sufficient celebrity for these small scandalmongers to take the trouble of reporting that I have gone raving mad, that I have sold myself to a publisher for a thousand guineas per annum, that I was tried at the Old Bailey in early life for the offence of piracy on the high seas, or that I have run away from my wife, and am residing at Hombourg with a Mingrelian princess. Yet, when I returned to England, in December, 1856, I found that the "people who go about saying things" had hung upon the the very slight peg of its being known in a few London "circles" that I was the author of a "Journey Due North," an amusing budget of scandal. I have to thank those industrious and well-informed gentlemen, the London correspondents of the minor provincial journals, for their sedulous circulation of a cheerful report that I had been sent to Siberia, that I had been expelled from the Russian territory by the secret police, and that I was dead. This last *échantillon* of journalistic waggery obtained considerable currency, and I receive to this day occasional communications from anonymous correspondents who are anxious to know whether I am yet in the land of the living. A bolder gazetteer hazarded the insinuation that I was in the pay of the Russian government, and that the somewhat extreme views I had adopted with regard to Russian institutions were but to be regarded as a proof of deep cunning and exceeding Jesuitry. It may afford the last-alluded-to journalist some satisfaction when I publish the confession that I have twice visited the Russian embassy in Chesham Place, once in the company of a lady who required Baron Brunnow's signature to her passport, and once to pay a visit to my esteemed friend, Mr. Pierce, who of course is a secret agent of the Autocrat, being the baron's accomplished *maître d'hôtel.* Secret agents, it will be observed, always go down the area-steps; and I only regret that I cannot favour my "London Correspondent" with an accurate report of my interview with the Secretary of Legation in the pantry. Perhaps, however, the most ingenious report to which these unpretending sketches gave rise was one that *I had never been to Russia at all*, and that, establishing a Patmos at Ostend or Ghent—some said Brussels, some went so far as Spa—I had provided myself with a good library of books of Russian travel, and so "fudged" my "Journey Due North" in the manner attributed (I believe with about equal justice) to M. Alexandre Dumas anent his *Impressions de Voyage.*

Curiously, now, sitting at home among English scenes and English faces, I am not altogether without grave doubts of my own as to whether I ever visited Russia in the flesh, and whether mine was after all but a spiritual journey Due North, a Pisgah view of the Muscovite Palestine. True; here is my passport scrawled and stamped all over by his Imperial Majesty's police agents; here is a penknife with the Toula mark on the haft; here is the rouble-note I brought away (against the law) as a *souvenir;* here are my Russian hotel bills, post letters, banker's *bordereauz;* here the Gazette de L'Académie, where I, the "well-born Lord von Sala," (save the mark,) am described by public advertisement as having the intention to quit St. Petersburg in a fortnight from the date affixed. Still do I doubt; still do those Russian experiences loom so dimly in the distance; still are they so unreal, so shadowy, that by times I am half convinced that my "London Correspondent" must be right, that I was labouring under hallucination the summer before last, and mistook the Montagne de la Cour for the Nevskoï Perspective, the Place d'Armes at Ghent for the Tsarinski Loug. It is only when from time to time I visit some dear Russian friends; when by the pleasant waters of the Avon we talk about old times, about Alexis Hardshellovitch, and the undarkened nights we spent so happily in gondolas on the Neva, in groups upon the Palace Quay, in the cool saloons of the Mala Morskaïa; when returning home the dear old samovar is lighted again, and the blue smoke of the papiros begins to curl from fair lips; when the tea gleams in the tumbler, and the delicate lemon floats on the surface, and when somebody's voice murmurs low the plaintive notes of *Vos na pouti celo balschoïa*—that I am once more in Russia, that the shadow becomes substance, and that we laughingly bid the London Correspondent go hang for a backbiter.

But they are gone too, now, the friends ; and things Russian become mistier than ever. Positively the only course that remains open to me in order to avoid falling into utter skepticism concerning matters "Due North," is to revisit Russia. I wonder whether the little old gentleman at Berlin will give me a *visâ* to my passport again, and tell me that it is *gut nach Russland?* Next time, however, if I am once more brought beneath the talons of the double eagle, you shall know what the Czar's strange land looks like in winter. Adieu.

THE END.

Boston, 135 Washington Street.
October, 1858.

NEW BOOKS AND NEW EDITIONS

PUBLISHED BY

TICKNOR AND FIELDS.

SIR WALTER SCOTT.

ILLUSTRATED HOUSEHOLD EDITION OF THE WAVERLEY NOVELS. Price 75 cents a volume.

THOMAS DE QUINCEY.

CONFESSIONS OF AN ENGLISH OPIUM-EATER, AND SUSPIRIA DE PROFUNDIS. With Portrait. Price 75 cents.
BIOGRAPHICAL ESSAYS. Price 75 cents.
MISCELLANEOUS ESSAYS. Price 75 cents.
THE CÆSARS. Price 75 cents.
LITERARY REMINISCENCES. 2 vols. Price $1.50.
NARRATIVE AND MISCELLANEOUS PAPERS. 2 vols. Price $1.50.
ESSAYS ON THE POETS, &c. 1 vol. 16mo. Price 75 cents.
HISTORICAL AND CRITICAL ESSAYS. 2 vols. $1.50.
AUTOBIOGRAPHIC SKETCHES. 1 vol. Price 75 cents.
ESSAYS ON PHILOSOPHICAL WRITERS, &c. 2 vols. 16mo. Price $1.50.
LETTERS TO A YOUNG MAN, and other Papers. 1 vol. Price 75 cents.
THEOLOGICAL ESSAYS AND OTHER PAPERS. 2 vols. Price $1.50.
THE NOTE BOOK. 1 vol. Price 75 cents.
MEMORIALS AND OTHER PAPERS. 2 vols. 16mo. $1.50.

CHARLES READE.

PEG WOFFINGTON. A Novel. Price 75 cents.
CHRISTIE JOHNSTONE. A Novel. Price 75 cents.
CLOUDS AND SUNSHINE. A Novel. Price 75 cents.
'NEVER TOO LATE TO MEND.' 2 vols. Price $1.50.
WHITE LIES. A Novel. 1 vol. Price $1.25.
PROPRIA QUÆ MARIBUS and THE BOX TUNNEL. Price 25 cents.

HENRY W. LONGFELLOW.

POCKET EDITION OF POETICAL WORKS. In two volumes. $1.75.

POCKET EDITION OF PROSE WORKS COMPLETE. In two volumes. $1.75.

THE SONG OF HIAWATHA. Price $1.00.

EVANGELINE: A TALE OF ACADIE. 75 cents.

THE GOLDEN LEGEND. A Poem. Price $1.00.

POETICAL WORKS. In two volumes. 16mo. Boards, $2.00.

HYPERION. A ROMANCE. Price $1.00

OUTRE-MER. A PILGRIMAGE. Price $1.00.

KAVANAGH. A TALE. Price 75 cents.

THE COURTSHIP OF MILES STANDISH. 1 vol. 16mo. 75 cents.

Illustrated editions of EVANGELINE, POEMS, HYPERION, and THE GOLDEN LEGEND.

ALFRED TENNYSON.

POETICAL WORKS. With Portrait. 2 vols. Cloth. $2.00.

THE PRINCESS. Cloth. Price 50 cents.

IN MEMORIAM. Cloth. Price 75 cents.

MAUD, AND OTHER POEMS. Cloth. Price 50 cents.

POCKET EDITION OF POEMS COMPLETE. Price 75 cents.

OLIVER WENDELL HOLMES.

POEMS. With fine Portrait. Boards. $1.00. Cloth. $1.12.

ASTRÆA. Fancy paper. Price 25 cents.

WILLIAM HOWITT.

LAND, LABOR, AND GOLD. 2 vols. Price $2.00.

A BOY'S ADVENTURES IN AUSTRALIA. Price 75 cents.

NATHANIEL HAWTHORNE.

TWICE-TOLD TALES. Two volumes. Price $1.50.

THE SCARLET LETTER. Price 75 cents.

THE HOUSE OF THE SEVEN GABLES. Price $1.00.

THE SNOW IMAGE, AND OTHER TWICE-TOLD TALES. Price 75 cents.

THE BLITHEDALE ROMANCE. Price 75 cents.

MOSSES FROM AN OLD MANSE. New Edition. 2 vols. Price $1.50.

TRUE STORIES FROM HISTORY AND BIOGRAPHY. With four fine Engravings. Price 75 cents.

A WONDER-BOOK FOR GIRLS AND BOYS. With seven fine Engravings. Price 75 cents.

TANGLEWOOD TALES. Another 'Wonder-Book.' With Engravings. Price 88 cents.

BARRY CORNWALL.

ENGLISH SONGS AND OTHER SMALL POEMS. Enlarged Edition. Price $1.00.

DRAMATIC POEMS. Just published. $1.00.

ESSAYS AND TALES IN PROSE. 2 vols. Price $1.50.

JAMES RUSSELL LOWELL.

COMPLETE POETICAL WORKS. In Blue and Gold. 2 vols. Price $1.50.

POETICAL WORKS. Revised, with Additions. Two volumes, 16mo. Cloth. Price $1.50.

SIR LAUNFAL. New Edition. Price 25 cents.

A FABLE FOR CRITICS. New Edition. Price 50 cents.

THE BIGLOW PAPERS. A New Edition. Price 63 cents.

COVENTRY PATMORE.

THE ANGEL IN THE HOUSE. BETROTHAL.

" " " " ESPOUSALS. Price 75 cents each.

CHARLES KINGSLEY.

TWO YEARS AGO. A New Novel. Price $1.25.
AMYAS LEIGH. A Novel. Price $1.25.
GLAUCUS; OR, THE WONDERS OF THE SHORE. 50 cents.
POETICAL WORKS. Price 75 cents.
THE HEROES; OR, GREEK FAIRY TALES. 75 cents.
ANDROMEDA AND OTHER POEMS. 50 cents.
LECTURES, ESSAYS, AND MISCELLANEOUS WRITINGS. (In Press.)

CHARLES SUMNER.

ORATIONS AND SPEECHES. 2 vols. $2.50.
RECENT SPEECHES AND ADDRESSES. $1.25.

JOHN G. WHITTIER.

POCKET EDITION OF POETICAL WORKS. 2 volumes. $1.50.
OLD PORTRAITS AND MODERN SKETCHES. 75 cents.
MARGARET SMITH'S JOURNAL. Price 75 cents.
SONGS OF LABOR, AND OTHER POEMS. Boards. 50 cents
THE CHAPEL OF THE HERMITS. Cloth. 50 cents.
LITERARY RECREATIONS AND MISCELLANIES. Cloth. $1
THE PANORAMA, AND OTHER POEMS. Cloth. 50 Cents.

ALEXANDER SMITH.

A LIFE DRAMA. 1 vol. 16mo. 50 cents.
CITY POEMS. 1 vol. 16mo. 63 cents.

EDWIN P. WHIPPLE.

ESSAYS AND REVIEWS. 2 vols. Price $2.00.
LECTURES ON SUBJECTS CONNECTED WITH LITERATURE AND LIFE. Price 63 cents.
WASHINGTON AND THE REVOLUTION. Price 20 cents.

GEORGE S. HILLARD.

SIX MONTHS IN ITALY. 1 vol. 16mo. Price $1.50.
DANGERS AND DUTIES OF THE MERCANTILE PROFESSION. Price 25 cents.
SELECTIONS FROM THE WRITINGS OF WALTER SAVAGE LANDOR. 1 vol. 16mo. Price 75 cents.

HENRY GILES.

LECTURES, ESSAYS, AND MISCELLANEOUS WRITINGS 2 vols. Price $1.50.

DISCOURSES ON LIFE. Price 75 cents.

ILLUSTRATIONS OF GENIUS. Cloth. $1.00.

BAYARD TAYLOR.

POEMS OF HOME AND TRAVEL. Cloth. Price 75 cents.

POEMS OF THE ORIENT. Cloth. 75 cents.

WILLIAM MOTHERWELL.

POEMS, NARRATIVE AND LYRICAL. New Ed. $1.25.

POSTHUMOUS POEMS. Boards. Price 50 cents.

MINSTRELSY, ANC. AND MOD. 2 vols. Boards. $1.50.

ROBERT BROWNING.

POETICAL WORKS. 2 vols. $2.00.

MEN AND WOMEN. 1 vol. Price $1.00.

CAPT. MAYNE REID'S JUVENILE BOOKS.

THE PLANT HUNTERS. 1 vol. 16mo. Price 75 cents.

THE DESERT HOME: OR, THE ADVENTURES OF A LOST FAMILY IN THE WILDERNESS. With fine Plates, $1.00.

THE BOY HUNTERS. With fine Plates. Just published. Price 75 cents.

THE YOUNG VOYAGEURS: OR, THE BOY HUNTERS IN THE NORTH. With Plates. Price 75 cents.

THE FOREST EXILES. With fine Plates. 75 cents.

THE BUSH BOYS. With fine Plates. 75 cents.

THE YOUNG YÄGERS. With fine Plates. 75 cents.

RAN AWAY TO SEA: AN AUTOBIOGRAPHY FOR BOYS. With fine Plates. 75 cents.

a *

GOETHE'S WRITINGS.

WILHELM MEISTER. Translated by THOMAS CARLYLE. **2 vols.** Price $2.50.

FAUST. Translated by HAYWARD. Price 75 cents.

FAUST. Translated by CHARLES T. BROOKS. Price **$1.00.**

R. H. STODDARD.

POEMS. Cloth. Price 63 cents.

ADVENTURES IN FAIRY LAND. Price 75 cents.

SONGS OF SUMMER. Price 75 cents.

REV. CHARLES LOWELL, D. D

PRACTICAL SERMONS. 1 vol. 12mo. $1.25.

OCCASIONAL SERMONS. With fine Portrait. $1.25.

GEORGE LUNT.

LYRIC POEMS, &c. Cloth. 63 cents.

JULIA. A Poem. 50 cents.

PHILIP JAMES BAILEY.

THE MYSTIC, AND OTHER POEMS. 50 cents.

THE ANGEL WORLD, &c. 50 cents.

THE AGE, A SATIRE. 75 cents.

ANNA MARY HOWITT.

AN ART STUDENT IN MUNICH. Price $1.25.

A SCHOOL OF LIFE. A Story. Price 75 cents.

MRS. JAMESON.

CHARACTERISTICS OF WOMEN.	Blue and gold.		75 cents.
LOVES OF THE POETS.	"	"	75 cents.
DIARY OF AN ENNUYÉE.	"	"	75 cents.
SKETCHES OF ART, &c.	"	"	75 cents

MARY RUSSELL MITFORD.

OUR VILLAGE. Illustrated. 2 vols. 16mo. Price $2.50.

ATHERTON, AND OTHER STORIES. 1 vol. 16mo. $1.25.

MRS. CROSLAND.

LYDIA: A WOMAN'S BOOK. Cloth. Price 75 cents.

ENGLISH TALES AND SKETCHES. Cloth. $1.00.

MEMORABLE WOMEN. Illustrated. $1.00.

GRACE GREENWOOD.

GREENWOOD LEAVES. 1st & 2d Series. $1.25 each.

POETICAL WORKS. With fine Portrait. Price 75 cents.

HISTORY OF MY PETS. With six fine Engravings. Scarlet cloth. Price 50 cents.

RECOLLECTIONS OF MY CHILDHOOD. With six fine Engravings. Scarlet cloth. Price 50 cents.

HAPS AND MISHAPS OF A TOUR IN EUROPE. Price $1.25.

MERRIE ENGLAND. A new Juvenile. Price 75 cents.

A FOREST TRAGEDY, AND OTHER TALES. $1.00.

STORIES AND LEGENDS. A new Juvenile. Price 75 cents.

MRS. MOWATT.

AUTOBIOGRAPHY OF AN ACTRESS. Price $1.25.

PLAYS. ARMAND AND FASHION. Price 50 cents.

MIMIC LIFE. 1 vol. Price $1.25.

THE TWIN ROSES. 1 vol. Price 75 cents.

MRS. HOWE.

PASSION FLOWERS. Price 75 cents.
WORDS FOR THE HOUR. Price 75 cents.
THE WORLD'S OWN. Price 50 cents.

JOSIAH PHILLIPS QUINCY.

LYTERIA: A DRAMATIC POEM. Price 50 cents.
CHARICLES: A DRAMATIC POEM. Price 50 cents.

ALICE CARY.

POEMS. 1 vol. 16mo. Price $1.00.
CLOVERNOOK CHILDREN. With Plates. 75 cents.

MRS. ELIZA B. LEE.

MEMOIR OF THE BUCKMINSTERS. $1.25.
FLORENCE, THE PARISH ORPHAN. 50 cents.
PARTHENIA. 1 vol. 16mo. Price $1.00.

MRS. JUDSON.

ALDERBROOK. BY FANNY FORRESTER. 2 vols. Price $1.75.
THE KATHAYAN SLAVE, AND OTHER PAPERS. 1 vol. Price 63 cents.
MY TWO SISTERS: A SKETCH FROM MEMORY. Price 50 cents.

POETRY.

LEIGH HUNT'S POEMS. Blue and gold. 2 vols. $1.50.
GERALD MASSEY'S POETICAL WORKS. Blue and gold. 75 cents.
W. M. THACKERAY. BALLADS. 1 vol. 16mo. 75 cents.
CHARLES MACKAY'S POEMS. 1 vol. Cloth. Price $1.00.
HENRY ALFORD'S POEMS. Just out. Price $1.25.
RICHARD MONCKTON MILNES. POEMS OF MANY YEARS. Boards. Price 75 cents.
GEORGE H. BOKER. PLAYS AND POEMS. 2 vols. Price $2.00.
CHARLES SPRAGUE. POETICAL AND PROSE WRITINGS. With fine Portrait. Boards. Price 75 cents.
GERMAN LYRICS. Translated by CHARLES T. BROOKS. 1 vol. 16mo. Cloth. Price $1.00.
MATTHEW ARNOLD'S POEMS. Price 75 cents.
W. EDMONSTOUNE AYTOUN. BOTHWELL. Price 75 cents.
MRS. ROSA V. JOHNSON'S POEMS. 1 vol. 16mo. $1.00.

THOMAS W. PARSONS. POEMS. Price $1.00.

JOHN G. SAXE. POEMS. With Portrait. Boards, 63 cents. Cloth, 75 cents.

HENRY T. TUCKERMAN. POEMS. Cloth. Price 75 cents.

BOWRING'S MATINS AND VESPERS. Price 50 cents.

YRIARTE'S FABLES. Translated by G. H. DEVEREUX. Price 63 cents.

MEMORY AND HOPE. A BOOK OF POEMS, REFERRING TO CHILDHOOD. Cloth. Price $2.00.

THALATTA: A BOOK FOR THE SEA-SIDE. 1 vol. 16mo. Cloth. Price 75 cents.

PHŒBE CARY. POEMS AND PARODIES. 75 cents.

PREMICES. By E. FOXTON. Price $1.00.

PAUL H. HAYNE. Poems. 1 vol. 16mo. 63 cents.

PERCIVAL'S POEMS. Blue and Gold. (In Press.)

MISCELLANEOUS.

G. H. LEWES. THE LIFE AND WORKS OF GOETHE. 2 vols. 16mo. $2.50.

OAKFIELD. A Novel. By LIEUT. ARNOLD. Price $1.00.

ESSAYS ON THE FORMATION OF OPINIONS AND THE PURSUIT OF TRUTH. 1 vol. 16mo. Price $1.00.

WALDEN: OR, LIFE IN THE WOODS. By HENRY D. THOREAU. 1 vol. 16mo. Price $1.00.

LIGHT ON THE DARK RIVER: OR, MEMOIRS OF MRS. HAMLIN. 1 vol. 16mo. Cloth. Price $1.00.

WASHINGTON ALLSTON. MONALDI, a Tale. 1 vol. 16mo. 75 cents.

PROFESSOR E. T. CHANNING. LECTURES ON ORATORY AND RHETORIC. Price 75 cents.

JOHN C. FREMONT. LIFE, EXPLORATIONS, &c. With Illustrations. Price 75 cents.

SEED-GRAIN FOR THOUGHT AND DISCUSSION. Compiled by MRS. A. C. LOWELL. 2 vols. $1.75.

A PHYSICIAN'S VACATION. By DR. WALTER CHANNING. Price $1.50.

MRS. HORACE MANN. A PHYSIOLOGICAL COOKERY BOOK. 63c

ROBERTSON'S SERMONS. 3 vols. 12mo. $3.00.

SCHOOL DAYS AT RUGBY. By AN OLD BOY. 1 vol. 16mo. Price $1.00.

WILLIAM MOUNTFORD. THORPE: A QUIET ENGLISH TOWN, AND HUMAN LIFE THEREIN. 16mo. Price $1.00.

NOTES FROM LIFE. BY HENRY TAYLOR, author of 'Philip Van Artevelde.' 1 vol. 16mo. Cloth. Price 63 cents.

REJECTED ADDRESSES. By HORACE and JAMES SMITH. Boards, Price 50 cents. Cloth, 63 cents.

WARRENIANA. A Companion to the 'Rejected Addresses.' Price 63 cents.

WILLIAM WORDSWORTH'S BIOGRAPHY. 2 vols. $2.50.

ART OF PROLONGING LIFE. By HUFELAND. Edited by ERASMUS WILSON, F. R. S. 1 vol. 16mo. Price 75 cents.

JOSEPH T. BUCKINGHAM'S PERSONAL MEMOIRS AND RECOLLECTIONS OF EDITORIAL LIFE. With Portrait. 2 vols. 16mo. Price $1.50.

VILLAGE LIFE IN EGYPT. By the Author of 'Purple Tints of Paris.' 2 vols. 16mo. Price $1.25.

DR. JOHN C. WARREN. THE PRESERVATION OF HEALTH, &c. 1 vol. Price 38 cents.

PRIOR'S LIFE OF EDMUND BURKE. 2 vols. $2.00.

NATURE IN DISEASE. BY DR. JACOB BIGELOW. 1 vol. 16mo. Price $1.25.

WENSLEY: A STORY WITHOUT A MORAL. Price 75 cents.

GOLDSMITH. THE VICAR OF WAKEFIELD. Illustrated Edition Price $3.00.

PALISSY THE POTTER. By the Author of 'How to make Home Unhealthy.' 2 vols. 16mo. Price $1.50.

DOUGLAS JERROLD'S WIT. 1 vol. 16mo. Price 75 cents.

LIFE AND TIMES OF SIR PHILIP SIDNEY. 1 vol. 16mo.

LIFE OF GEORGE STEPHENSON: RAILWAY ENGINEER. $1.25.

TRELAWNY'S RECOLLECTIONS OF SHELLEY AND BYRON. 75 cents.

BARTOL'S CHURCH AND CONGREGATION. $1.00.

THE BARCLAYS OF BOSTON. BY MRS. H. G. OTIS. 1 vol. 12mo. $1.25.

HORACE MANN. THOUGHTS FOR A YOUNG MAN. 25 cents.

F. W. P. GREENWOOD. SERMONS OF CONSOLATION. $1.00.

THE BOSTON BOOK. Price $1.25.

ANGEL-VOICES. Price 38 cents.

SIR ROGER DE COVERLEY. From the 'Spectator.' 75 cents.

S. T. WALLIS. SPAIN, HER INSTITUTIONS, POLITICS, AND PUBLIC MEN. Price $1.00.

MEMOIR OF ROBERT WHEATON. 1 vol. Price $1.00.

LABOR AND LOVE: A TALE OF ENGLISH LIFE. 50 cents.

MRS. PUTNAM'S RECEIPT BOOK; AN ASSISTANT TO HOUSEKEEPERS. 1 vol. 16mo. Price 50 cents.

MRS. A. C. LOWELL. EDUCATION OF GIRLS. Price 25 cents.

THE SOLITARY OF JUAN FERNANDEZ. By the Author of Picciola. Price 50 cents.

RUTH. A New Novel by the Author of 'MARY BARTON.' Cheap Edition. Price 38 cents.

EACH OF THE ABOVE POEMS AND PROSE WRITINGS, MAY BE HAD IN VARIOUS STYLES OF HANDSOME BINDING.

☞ Any book published by TICKNOR & FIELDS, will be sent by mail, postage free, on receipt of publication price.

Their stock of Miscellaneous Books is very complete, and they respectfully solicit orders from CITY AND COUNTRY LIBRARIES.

IN BLUE AND GOLD.

LONGFELLOW'S POETICAL WORKS. 2 vols. $1.75.
do. PROSE WORKS. 2 vols. $1.75.
TENNYSON'S POETICAL WORKS. 1 vol. 75 cents.
WHITTIER'S POETICAL WORKS. 2 vols. $1.50.
LEIGH HUNT'S POETICAL WORKS. 2 vols. $1.50.
GERALD MASSEY'S POETICAL WORKS. 1 vol. 75 cents.
MRS. JAMESON'S CHARACTERISTICS OF WOMEN. 1 vol. 75 cents.
do. DIARY OF AN ENNUYÉE. 1 vol. 75 cents.
do. LOVES OF THE POETS. 1 vol. 75 cents.
do. SKETCHES OF ART, &c. 1 vol. 75 cents.
BOWRING'S MATINS AND VESPERS. 1 vol. 75 cents.
LOWELL'S (J. RUSSELL) POETICAL WORKS. 2 vols. $1.50.

ILLUSTRATED JUVENILE BOOKS.

CURIOUS STORIES ABOUT FAIRIES. 75 cents.
KIT BAM'S ADVENTURES. 75 cents.
RAINBOWS FOR CHILDREN. 75 cents.
THE MAGICIAN'S SHOW BOX. 75 cents.
OUR GRANDMOTHER'S STORIES. 50 cents.
MEMOIRS OF A LONDON DOLL. 50 cents.
THE DOLL AND HER FRIENDS. 50 cents.
TALES FROM CATLAND. 50 cents.
AUNT EFFIE'S RHYMES FOR LITTLE CHILDREN. 75 cents.
THE STORY OF AN APPLE. 50 cents.
THE GOOD-NATURED BEAR. 75 cents.
PETER PARLEY'S SHORT STORIES FOR LONG NIGHTS. 50 cents.
THE HISTORY OF THE AMERICAN REVOLUTION. 38 cents
THE HISTORY OF THE NEW ENGLAND STATES. 38 cents.
THE HISTORY OF THE MIDDLE STATES. 38 cents.
THE HISTORY OF THE SOUTHERN STATES. 38 cents.
THE HISTORY OF THE WESTERN STATES. 38 cents.
THE SOLITARY OF JUAN FERNANDEZ. 50 cents.
JACK HALLIARD'S VOYAGES. 38 cents.
THE INDESTRUCTIBLE BOOKS FOR CHILDREN. Each 25 cents.

www.ingramcontent.com/pod-product-compliance
Lightning Source LLC
LaVergne TN
LVHW020929110826
845150LV00004B/809

* 9 7 8 1 4 2 5 5 5 3 6 4 7 *